# DEEP Scar

**Story and Art**
**Rossella Sergi**

D1157208

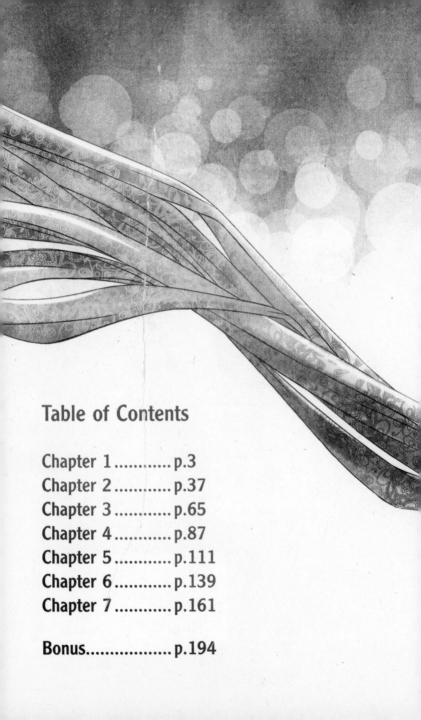

## Table of Contents

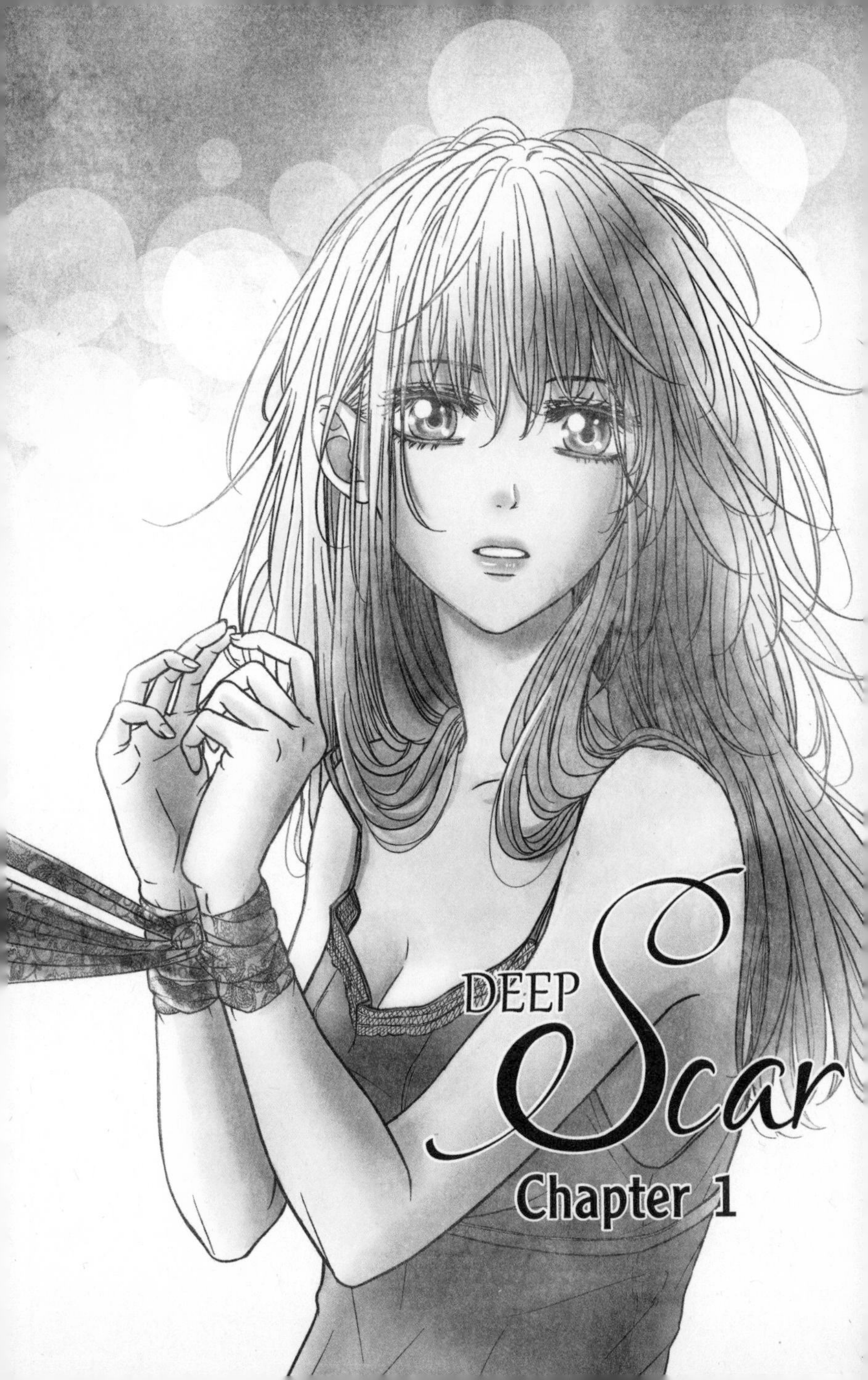
DEEP Scar
Chapter 1

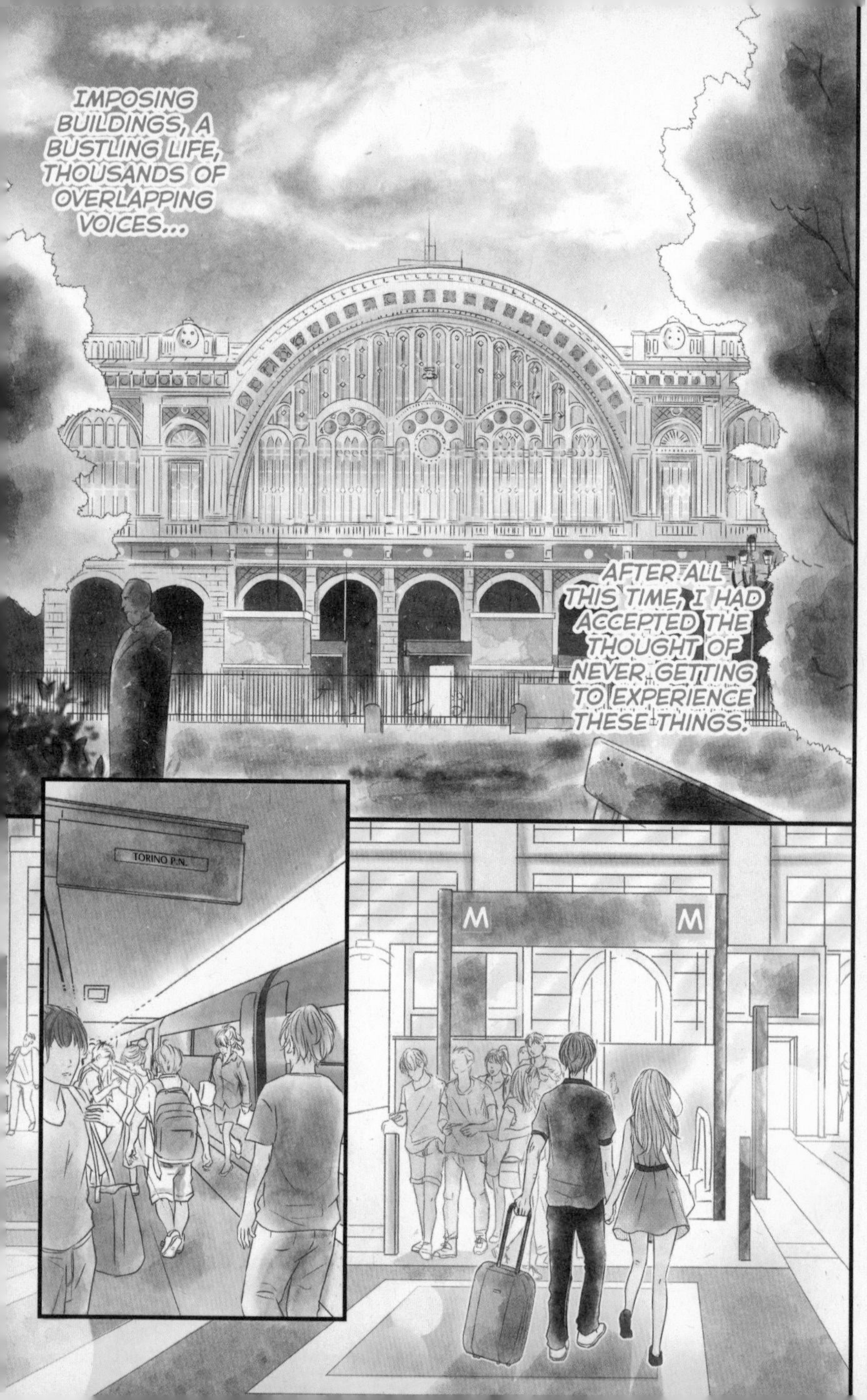
IMPOSING BUILDINGS, A BUSTLING LIFE, THOUSANDS OF OVERLAPPING VOICES...
AFTER ALL THIS TIME, I HAD ACCEPTED THE THOUGHT OF NEVER GETTING TO EXPERIENCE THESE THINGS.
M
M
TORINO P.N.

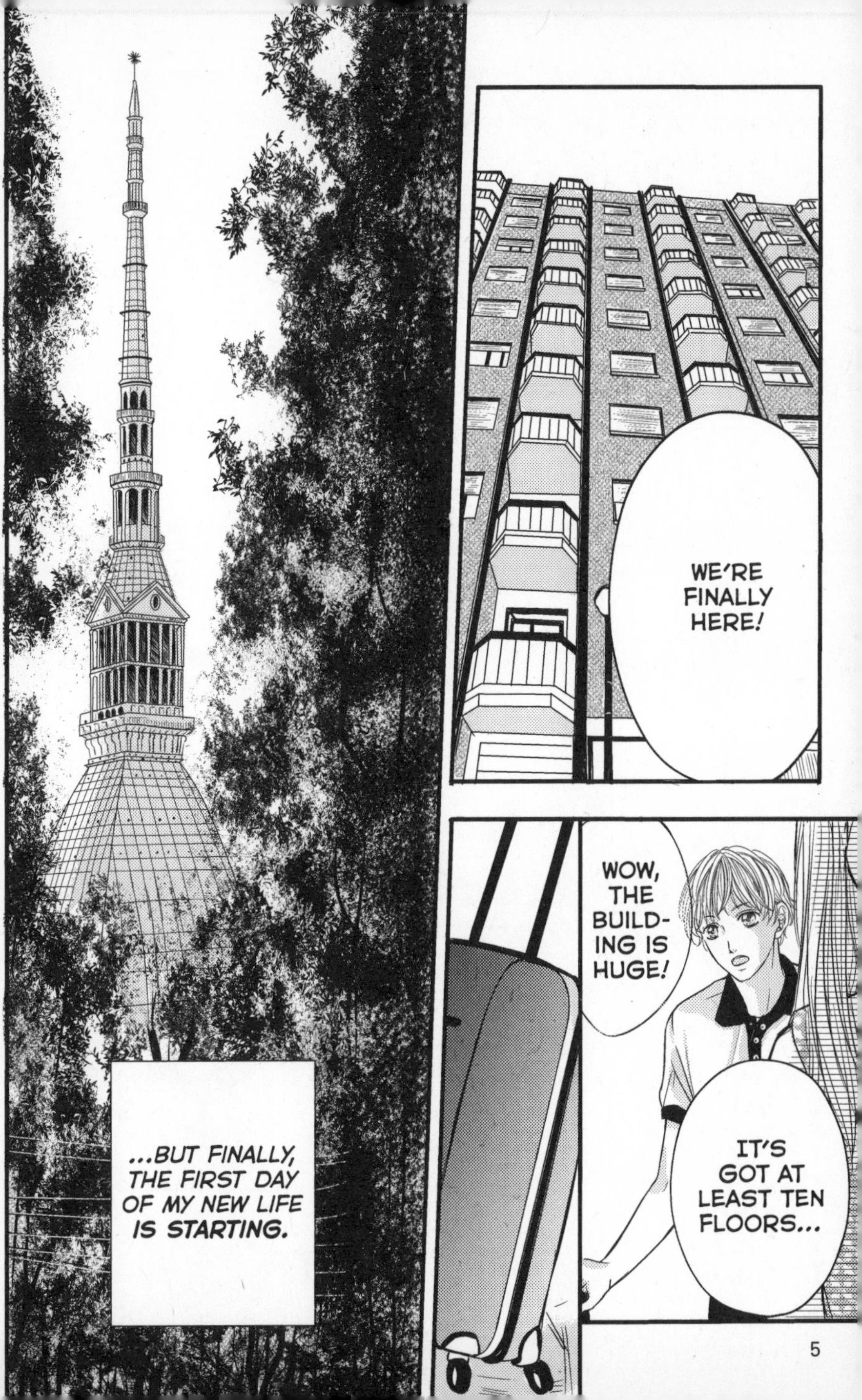
WE'RE FINALLY HERE!
WOW, THE BUILDING IS HUGE!
IT'S GOT AT LEAST TEN FLOORS...
...BUT FINALLY, THE FIRST DAY OF MY NEW LIFE IS STARTING.

COME ON, BABE, LET'S GO UPSTAIRS! I CAN'T WAIT TO MEET MY ROOMMATE!

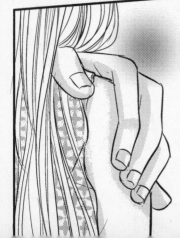

I'M HAPPY YOU GET TO EXPERIENCE THIS...

YOU DESERVE IT.

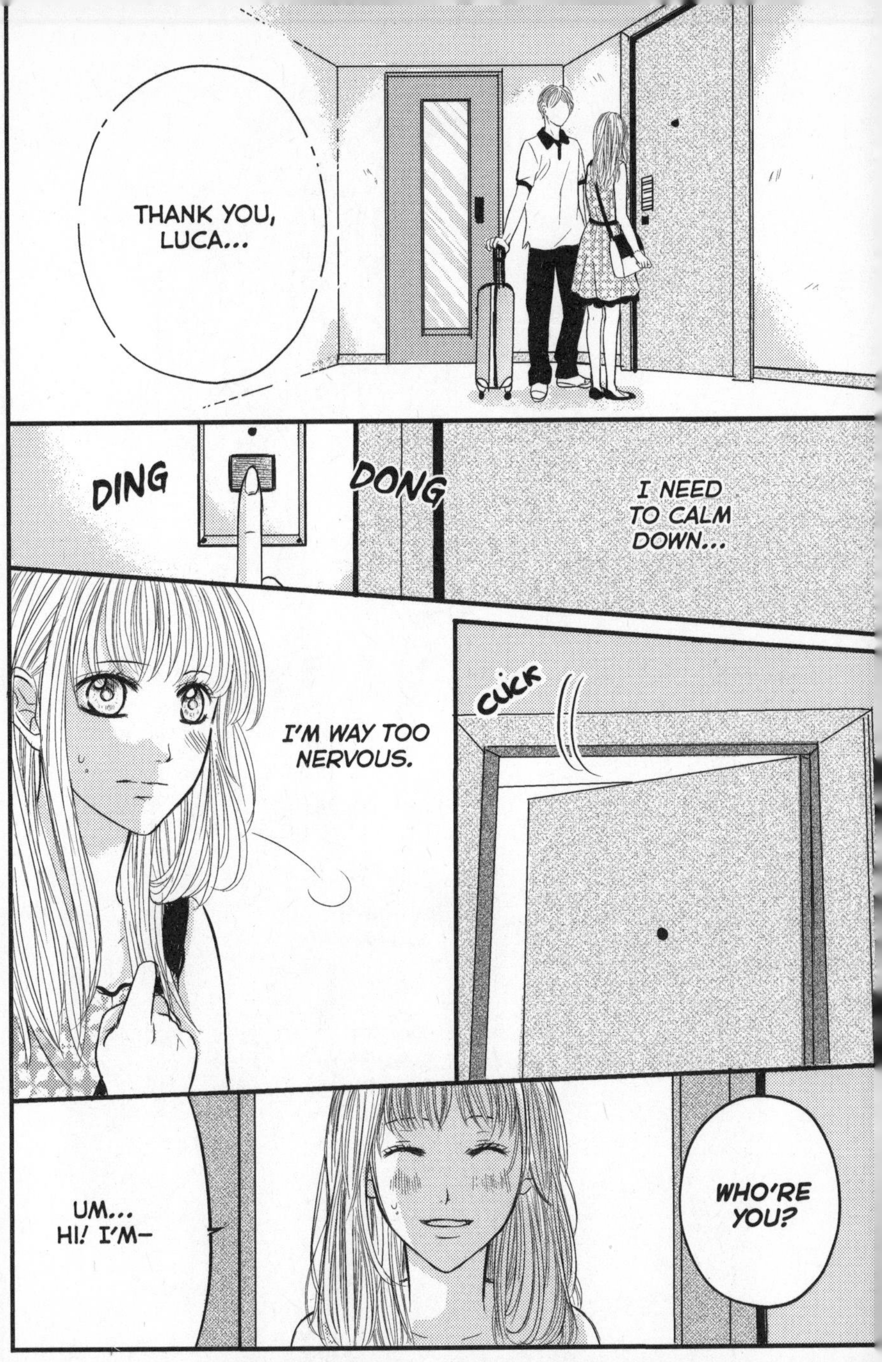
THANK YOU, LUCA...
I NEED TO CALM DOWN...
DONG
DING
CLICK
I'M WAY TOO NERVOUS.
WHO'RE YOU?
UM... HI! I'M–

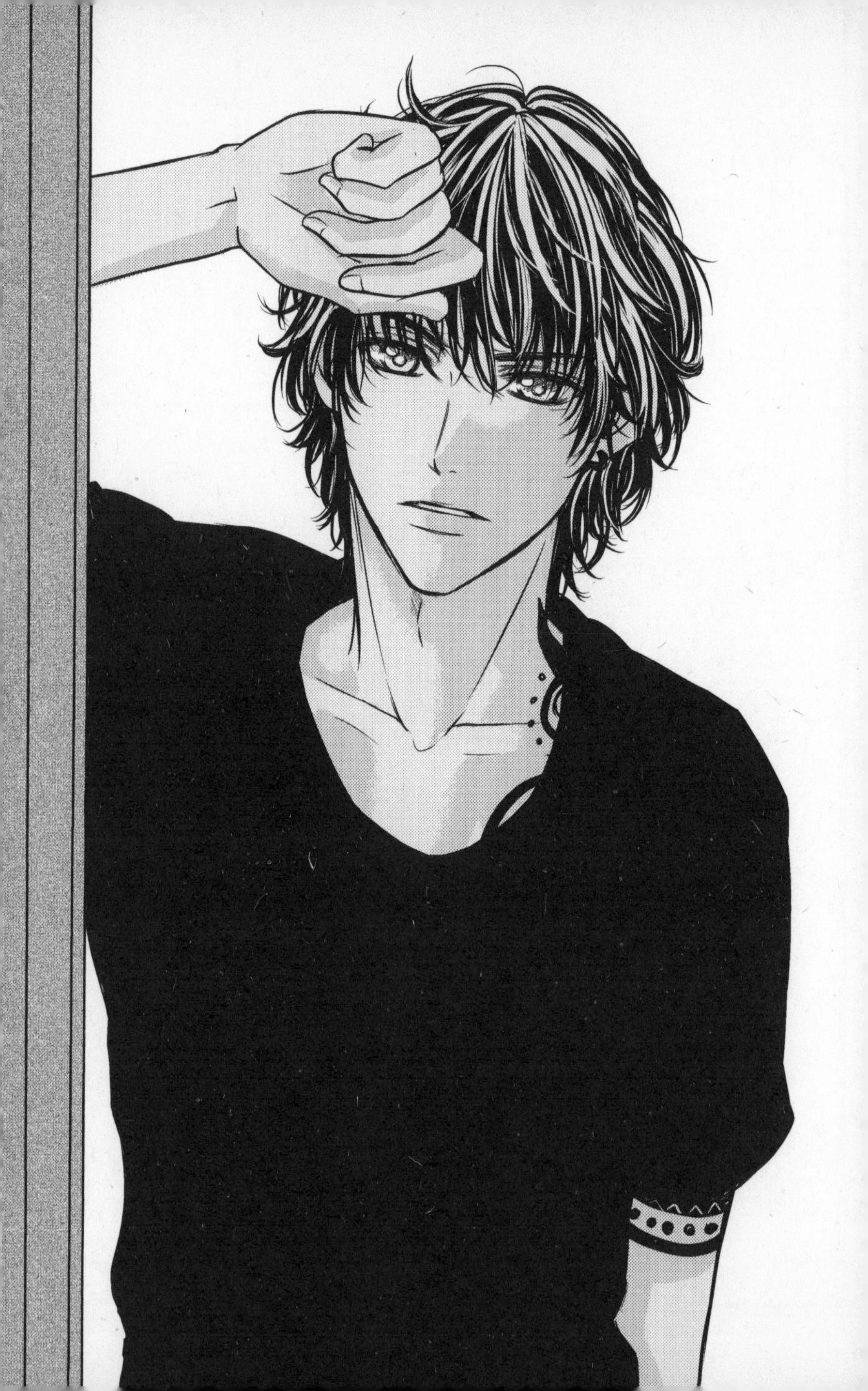

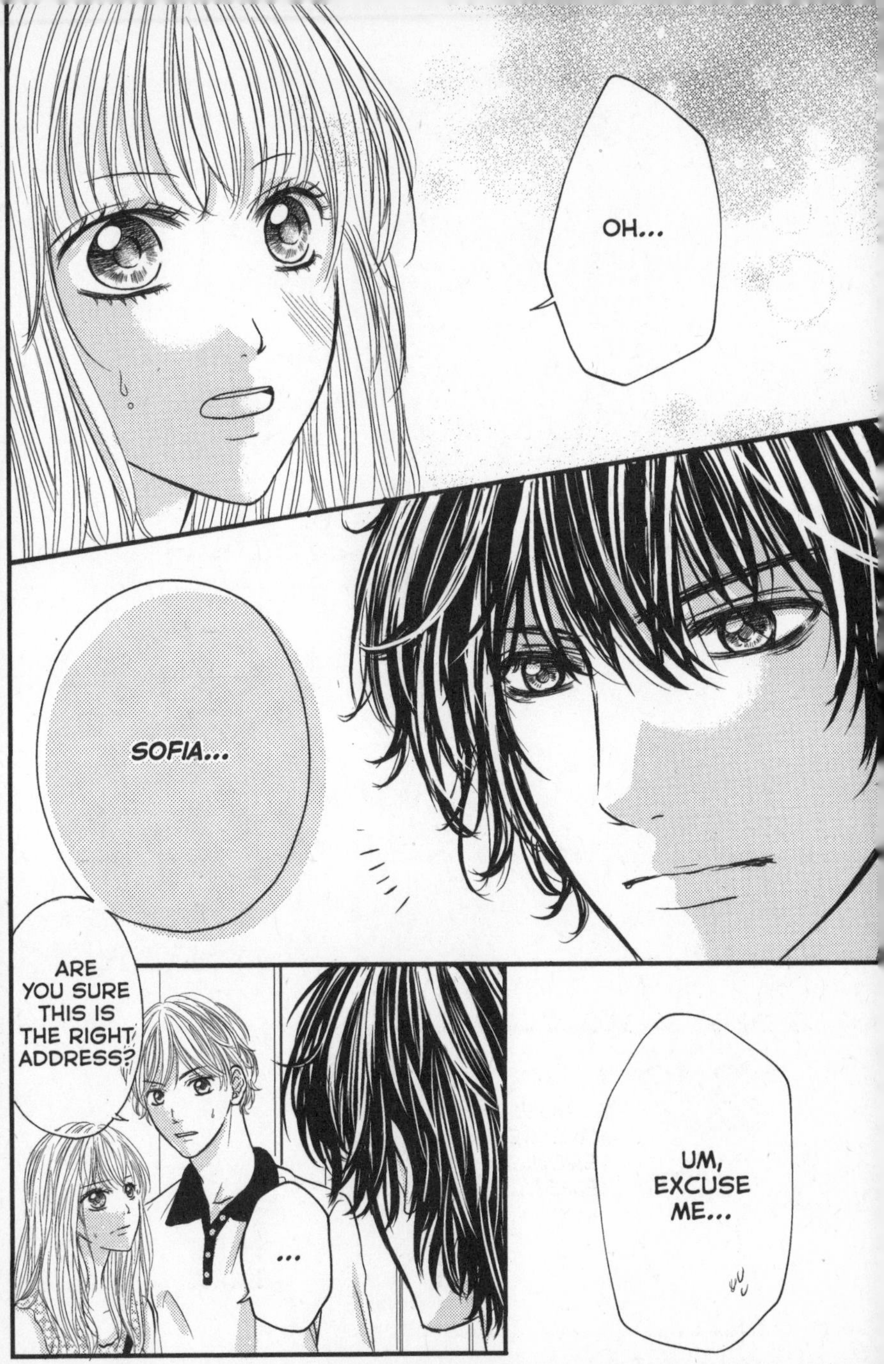
OH...
SOFIA...
UM, EXCUSE ME...
ARE YOU SURE THIS IS THE RIGHT ADDRESS?
...

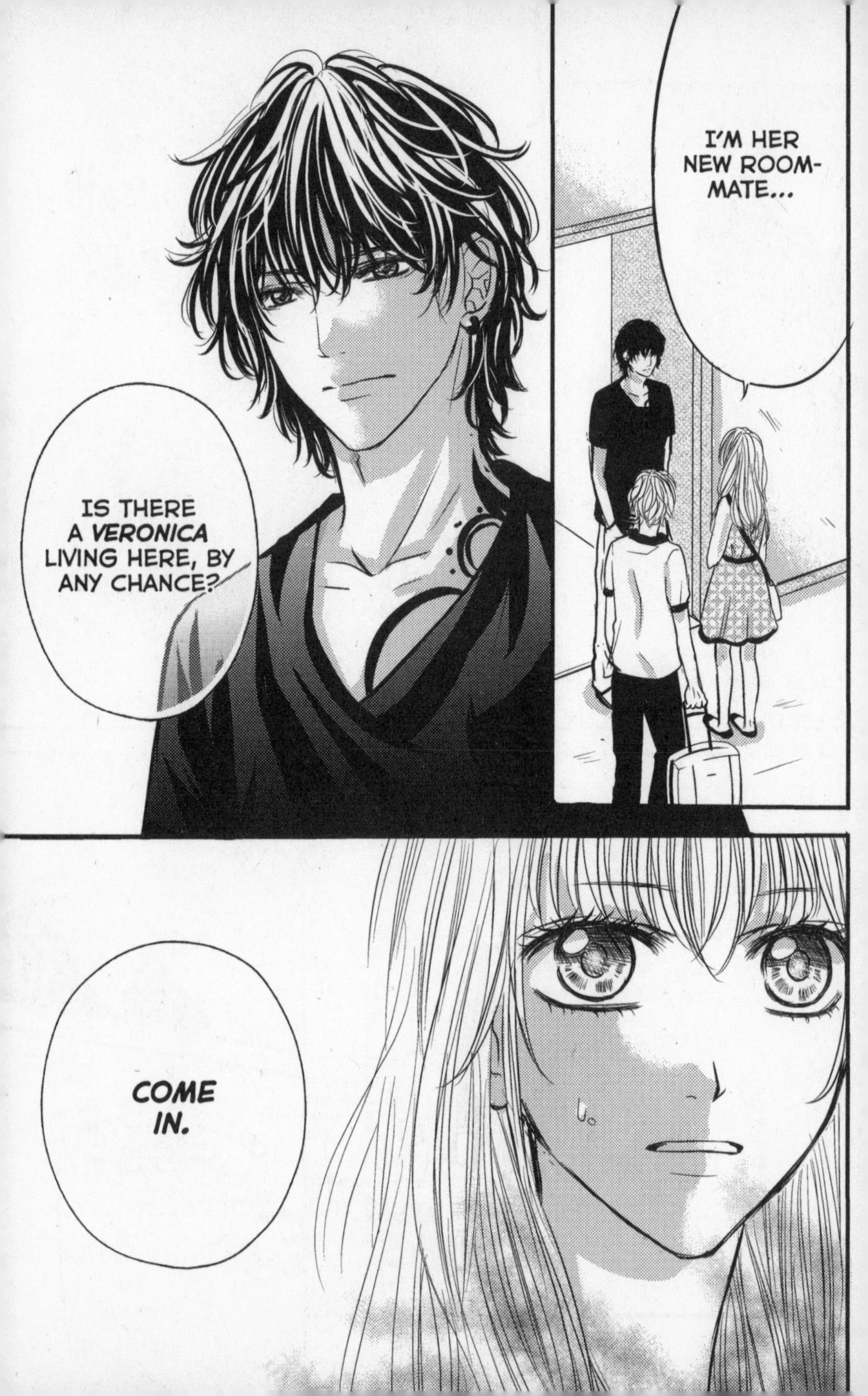
I'M HER NEW ROOM-MATE...
IS THERE A *VERONICA* LIVING HERE, BY ANY CHANCE?
*COME IN.*

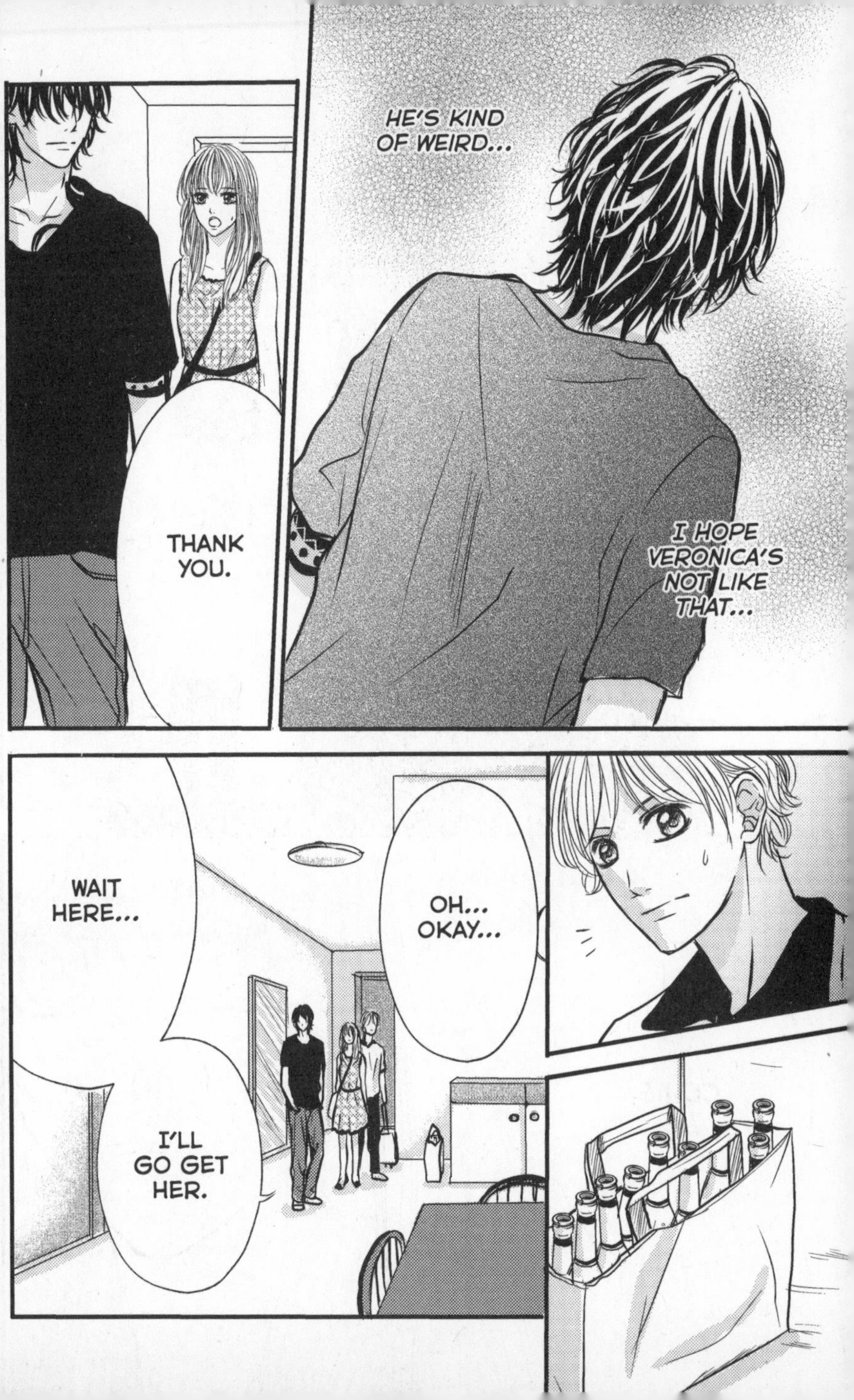
HE'S KIND OF WEIRD...
I HOPE VERONICA'S NOT LIKE THAT...
THANK YOU.
WAIT HERE...
I'LL GO GET HER.
OH... OKAY...

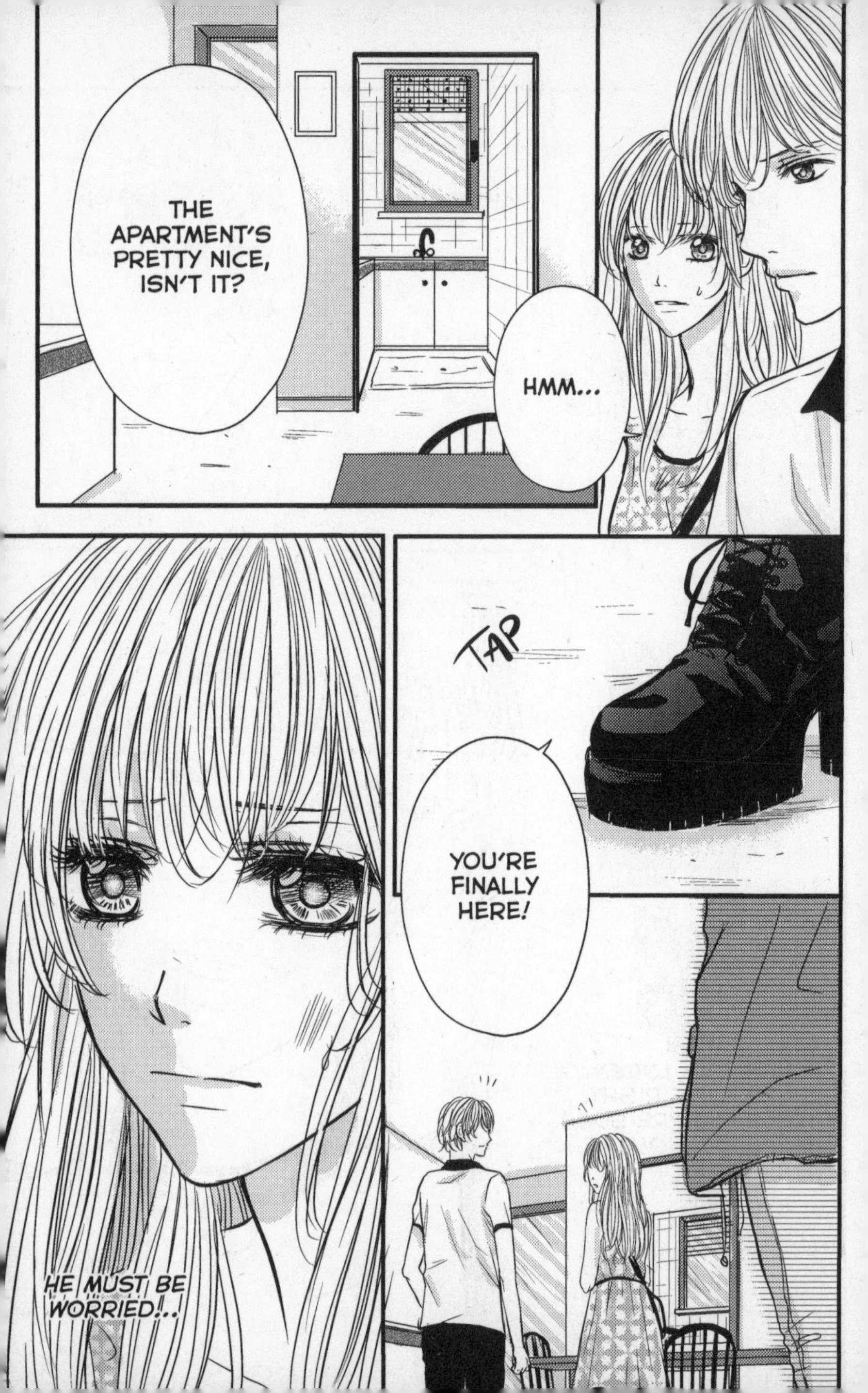
THE APARTMENT'S PRETTY NICE, ISN'T IT?
HMM...
TAP
YOU'RE FINALLY HERE!
HE MUST BE WORRIED!...

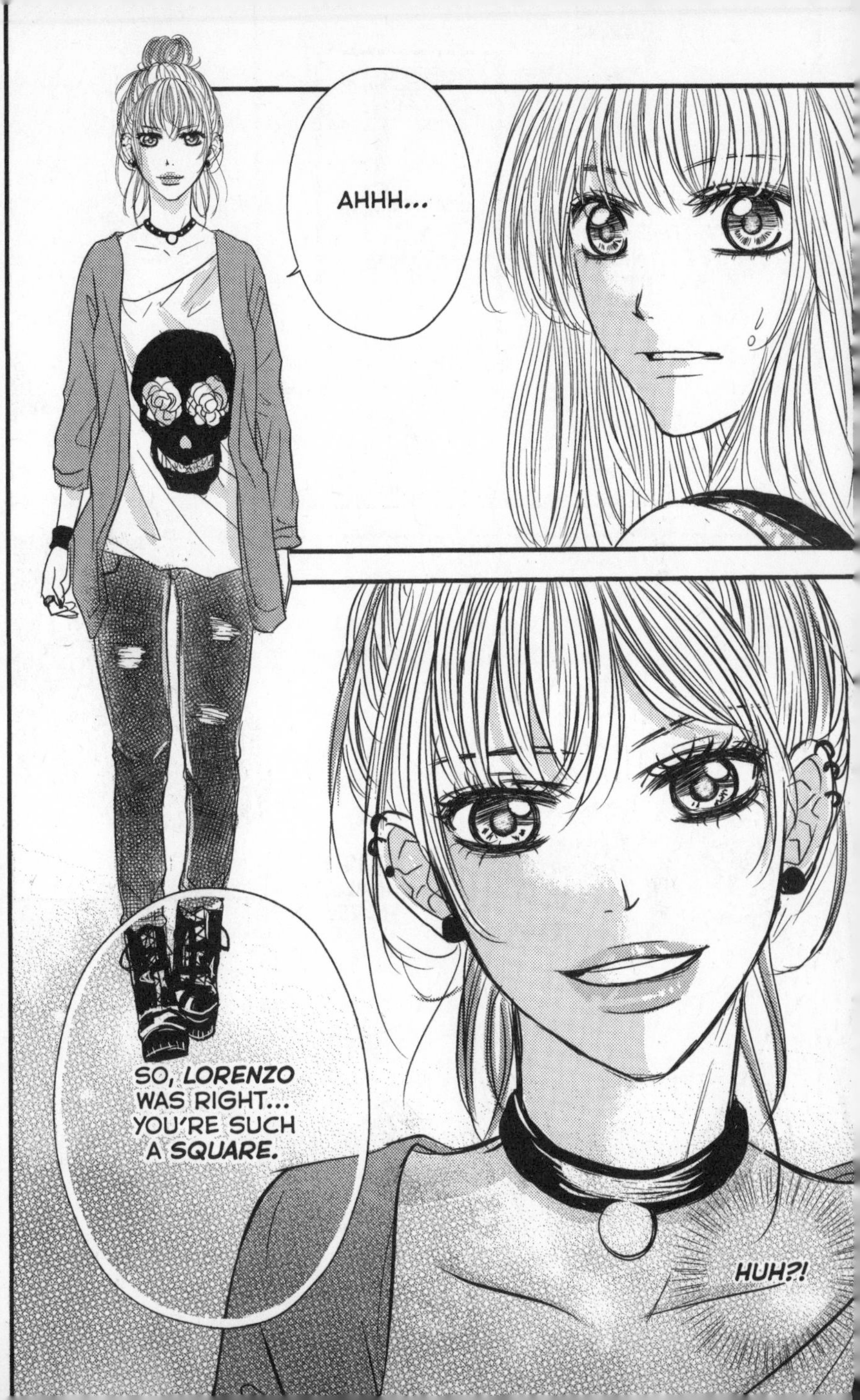
AHHH...
SO, LORENZO WAS RIGHT... YOU'RE SUCH A SQUARE.
HUH?!

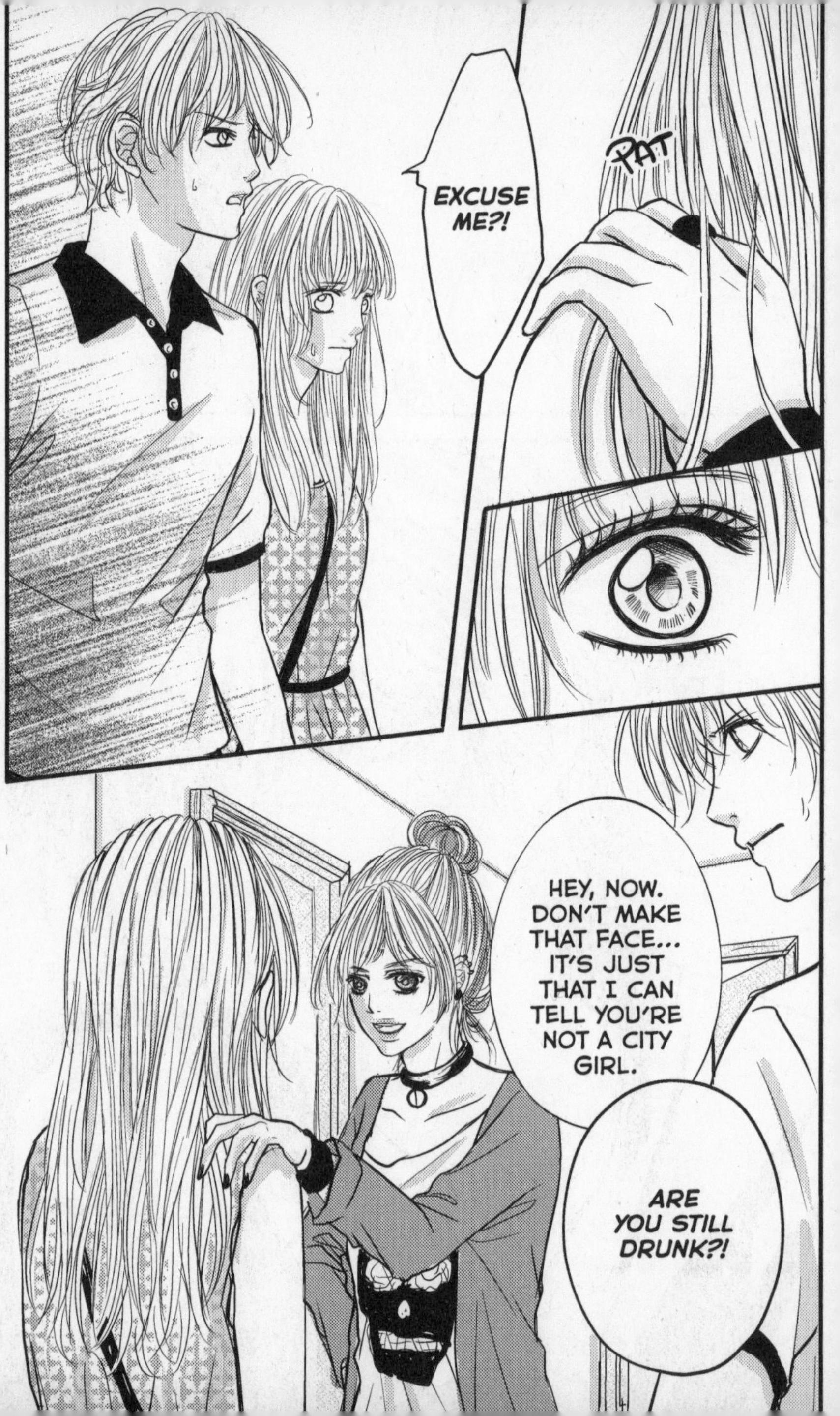
PAT
EXCUSE ME?!
HEY, NOW. DON'T MAKE THAT FACE... IT'S JUST THAT I CAN TELL YOU'RE NOT A CITY GIRL.
ARE YOU STILL DRUNK?!

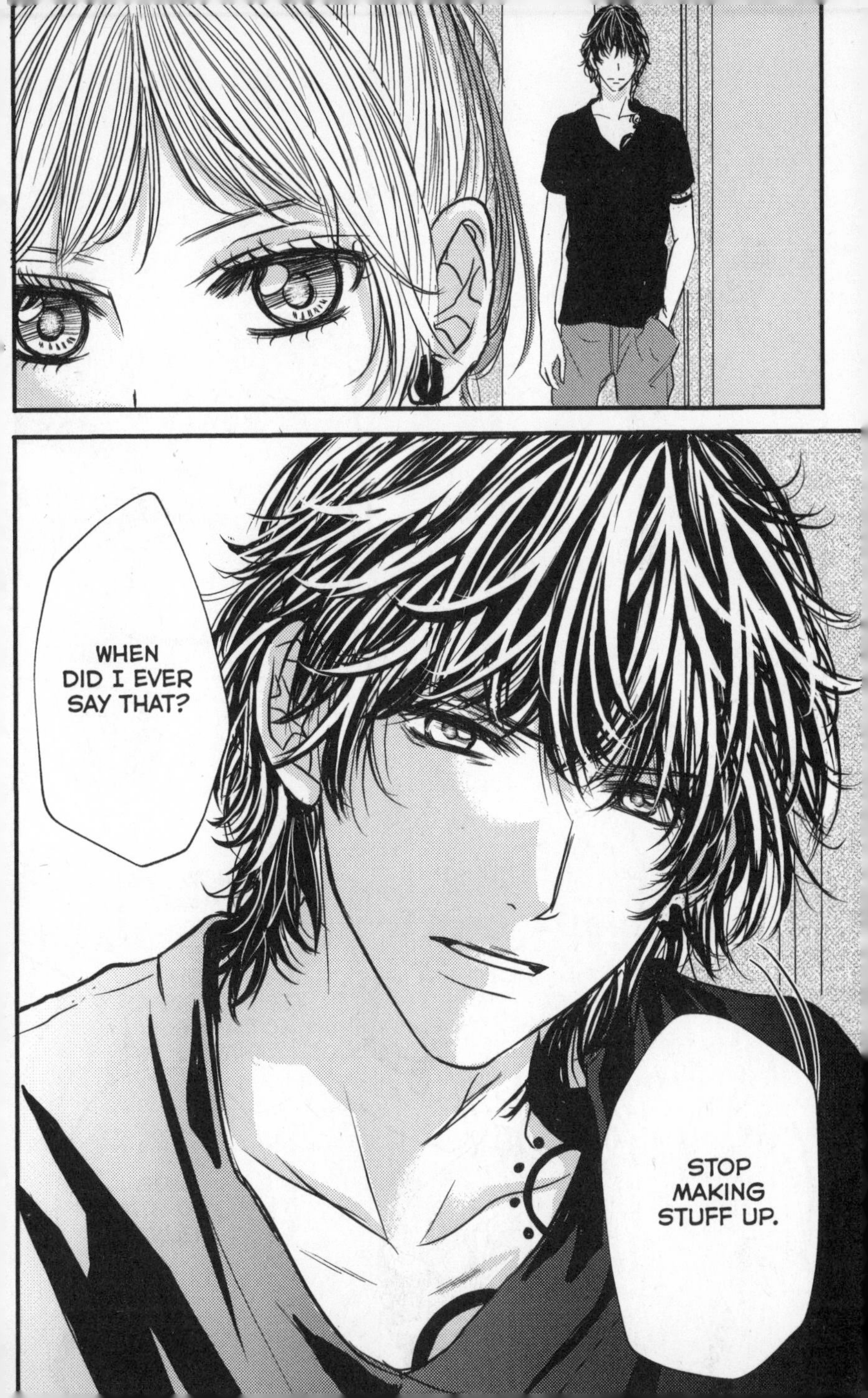
WHEN DID I EVER SAY THAT?
STOP MAKING STUFF UP.

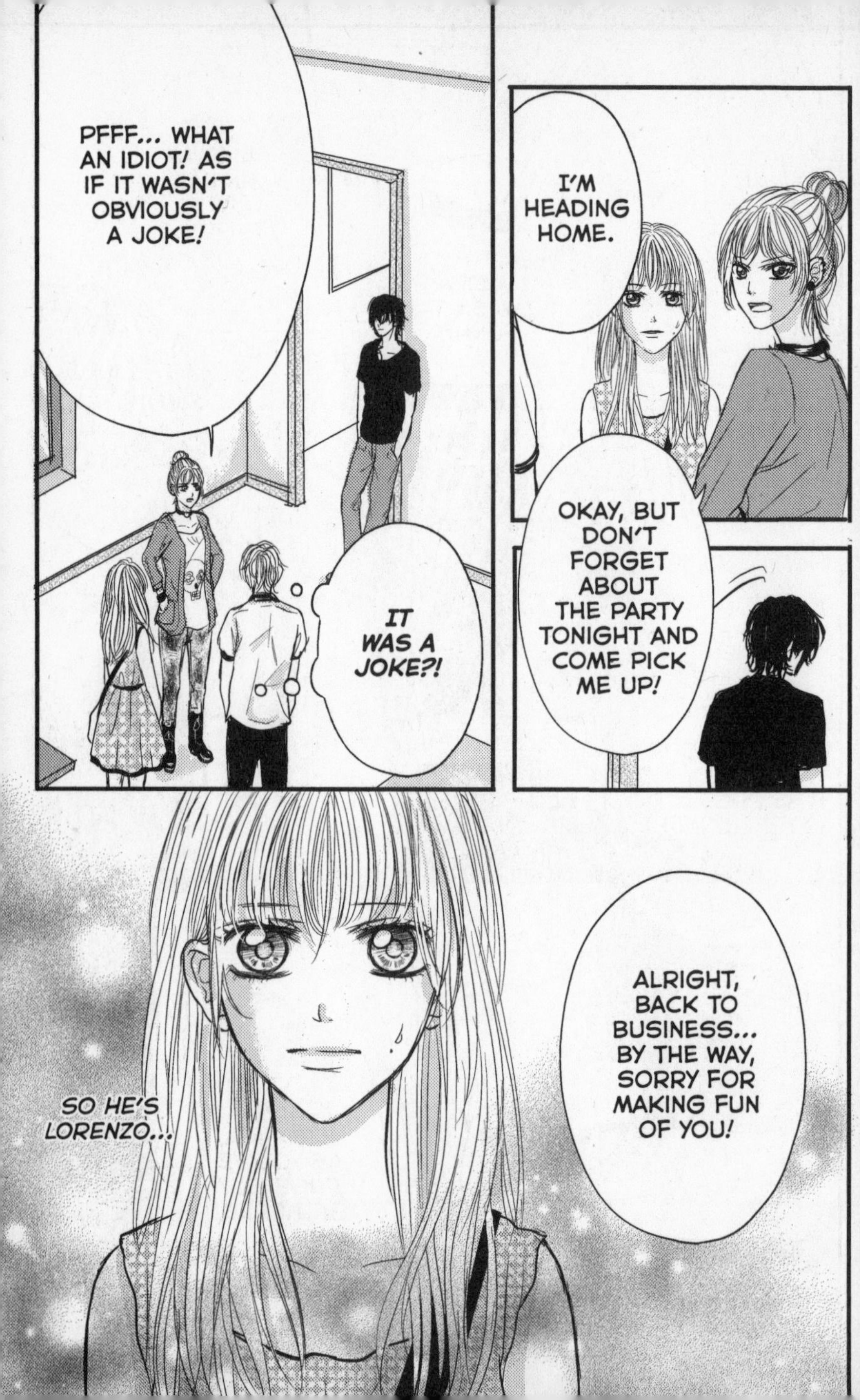
PFFF... WHAT AN IDIOT! AS IF IT WASN'T OBVIOUSLY A JOKE!
IT WAS A JOKE?!
I'M HEADING HOME.
OKAY, BUT DON'T FORGET ABOUT THE PARTY TONIGHT AND COME PICK ME UP!
ALRIGHT, BACK TO BUSINESS... BY THE WAY, SORRY FOR MAKING FUN OF YOU!
SO HE'S LORENZO...

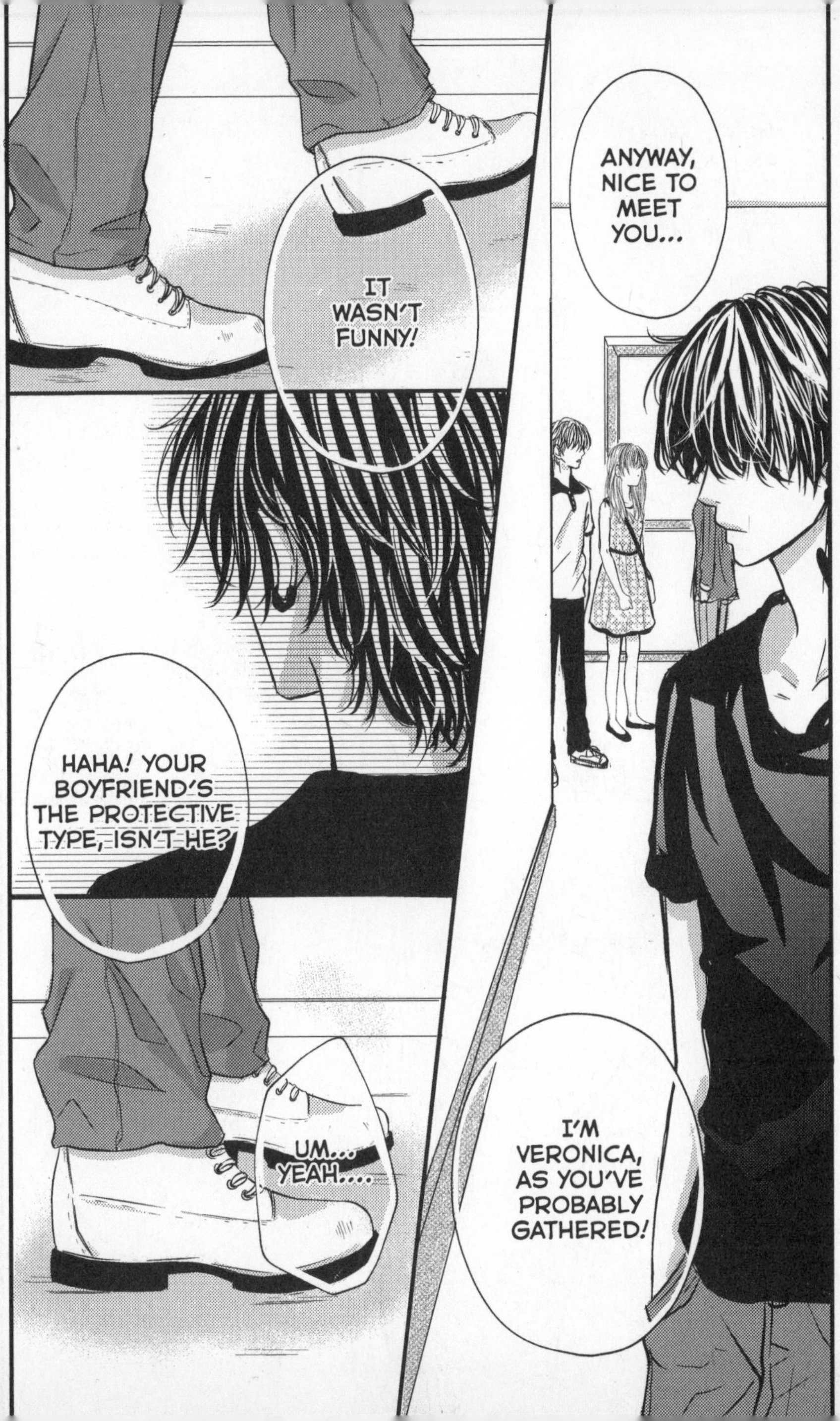
ANYWAY, NICE TO MEET YOU...
I'M VERONICA, AS YOU'VE PROBABLY GATHERED!
IT WASN'T FUNNY!
HAHA! YOUR BOYFRIEND'S THE PROTECTIVE TYPE, ISN'T HE?
UM... YEAH...

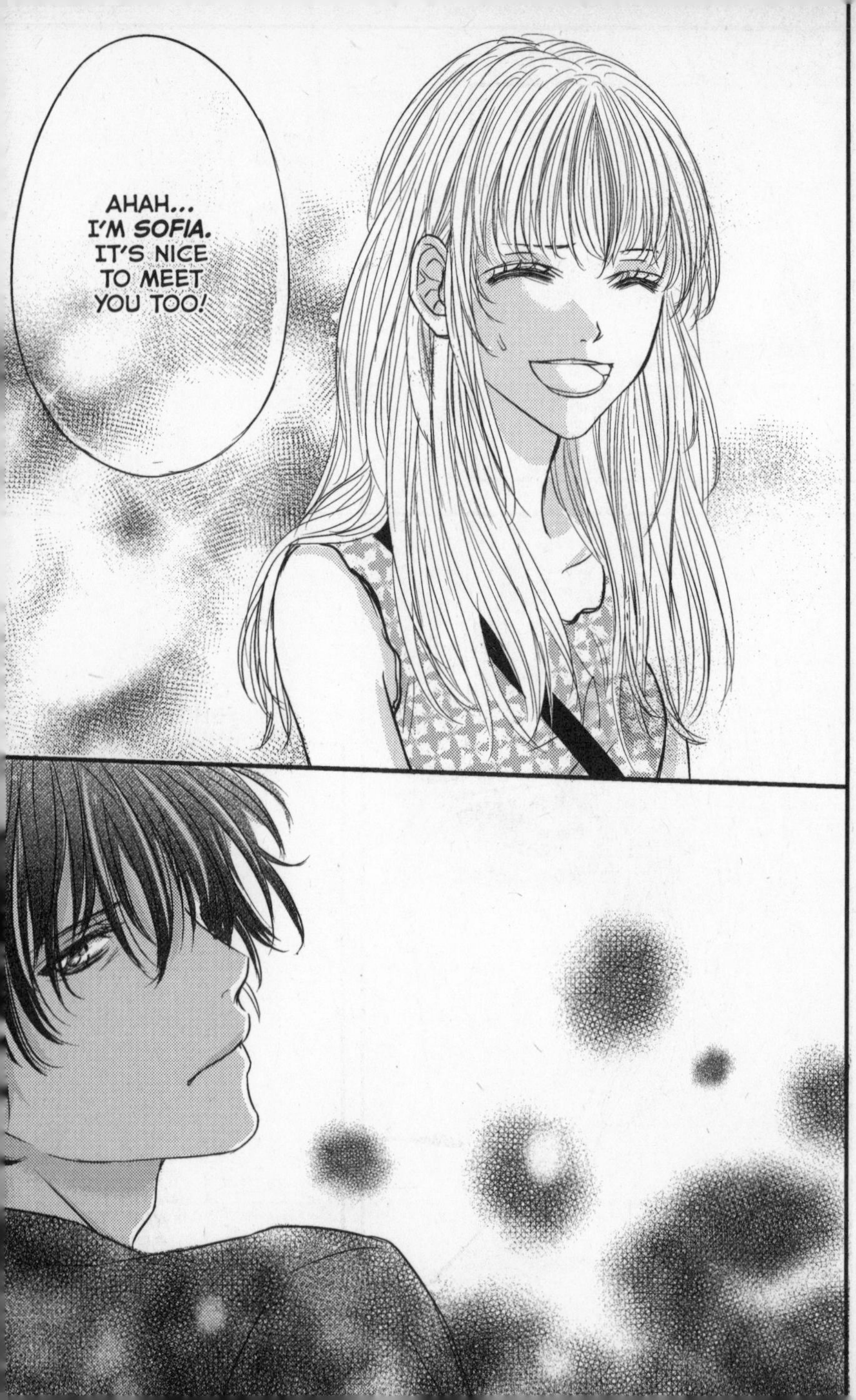
AHAH... I'M SOFIA. IT'S NICE TO MEET YOU TOO!

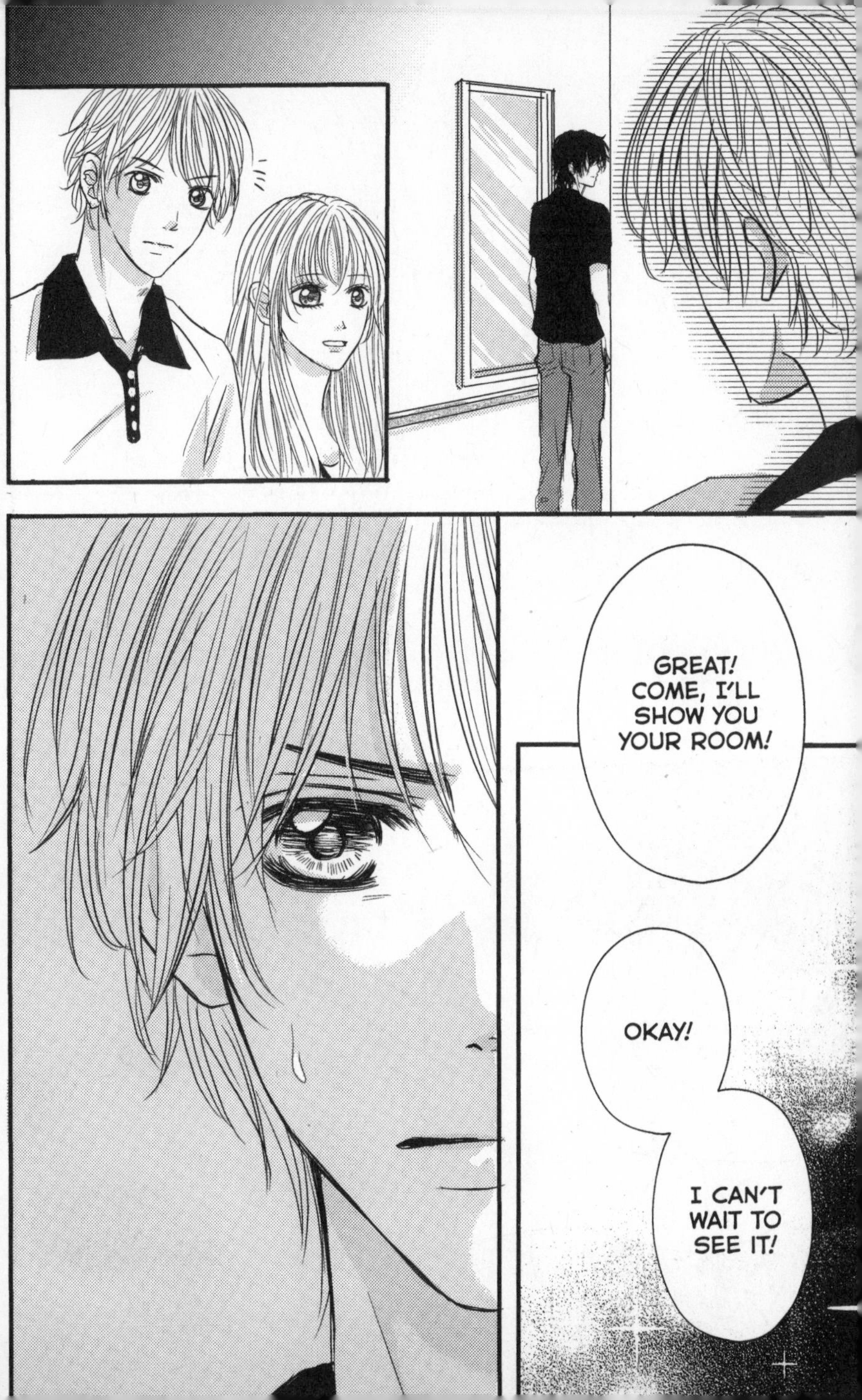
GREAT! COME, I'LL SHOW YOU YOUR ROOM!
OKAY!
I CAN'T WAIT TO SEE IT!

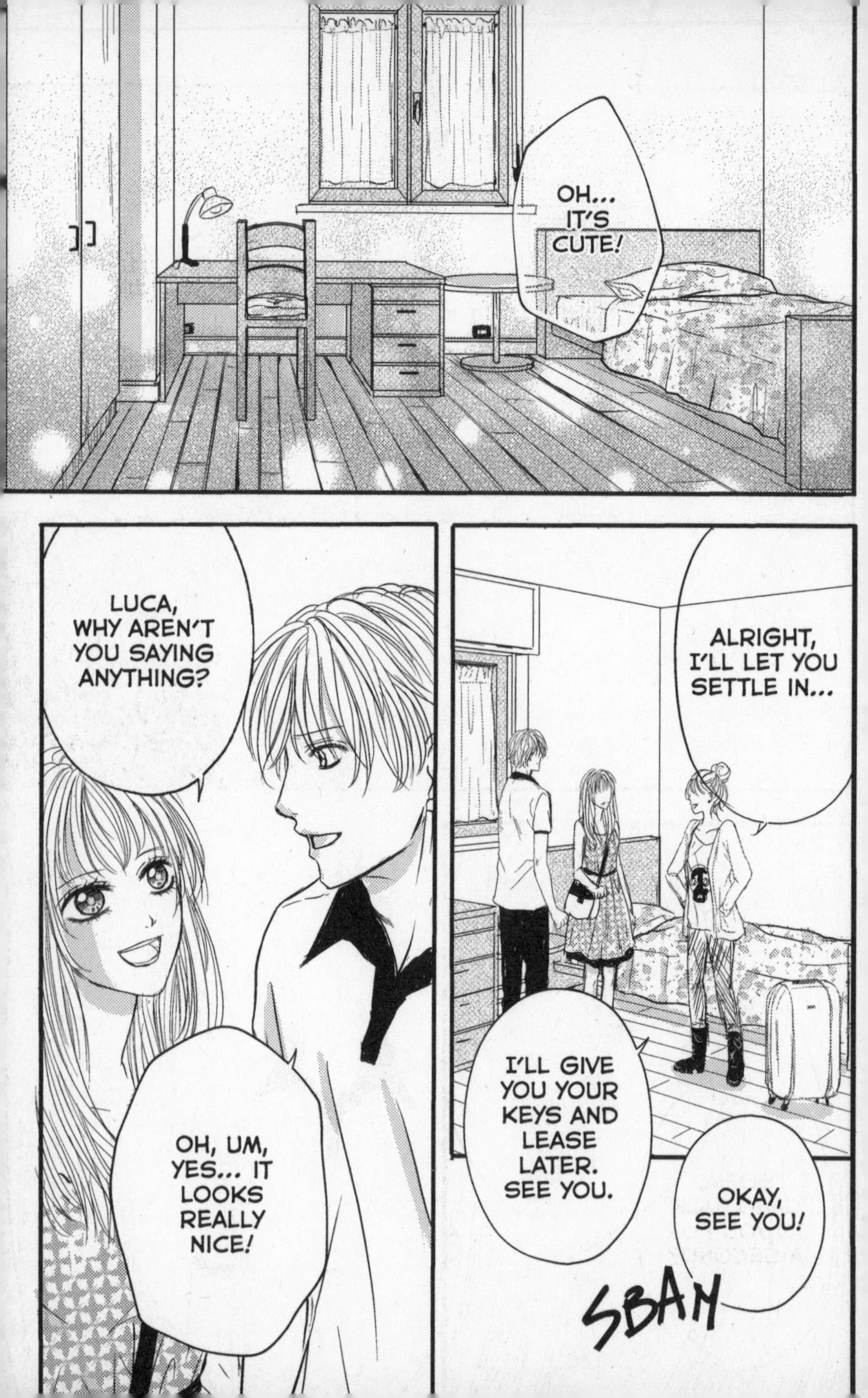
OH... IT'S CUTE!
LUCA, WHY AREN'T YOU SAYING ANYTHING?
OH, UM, YES... IT LOOKS REALLY NICE!
ALRIGHT, I'LL LET YOU SETTLE IN...
I'LL GIVE YOU YOUR KEYS AND LEASE LATER. SEE YOU.
OKAY, SEE YOU!
SBAM

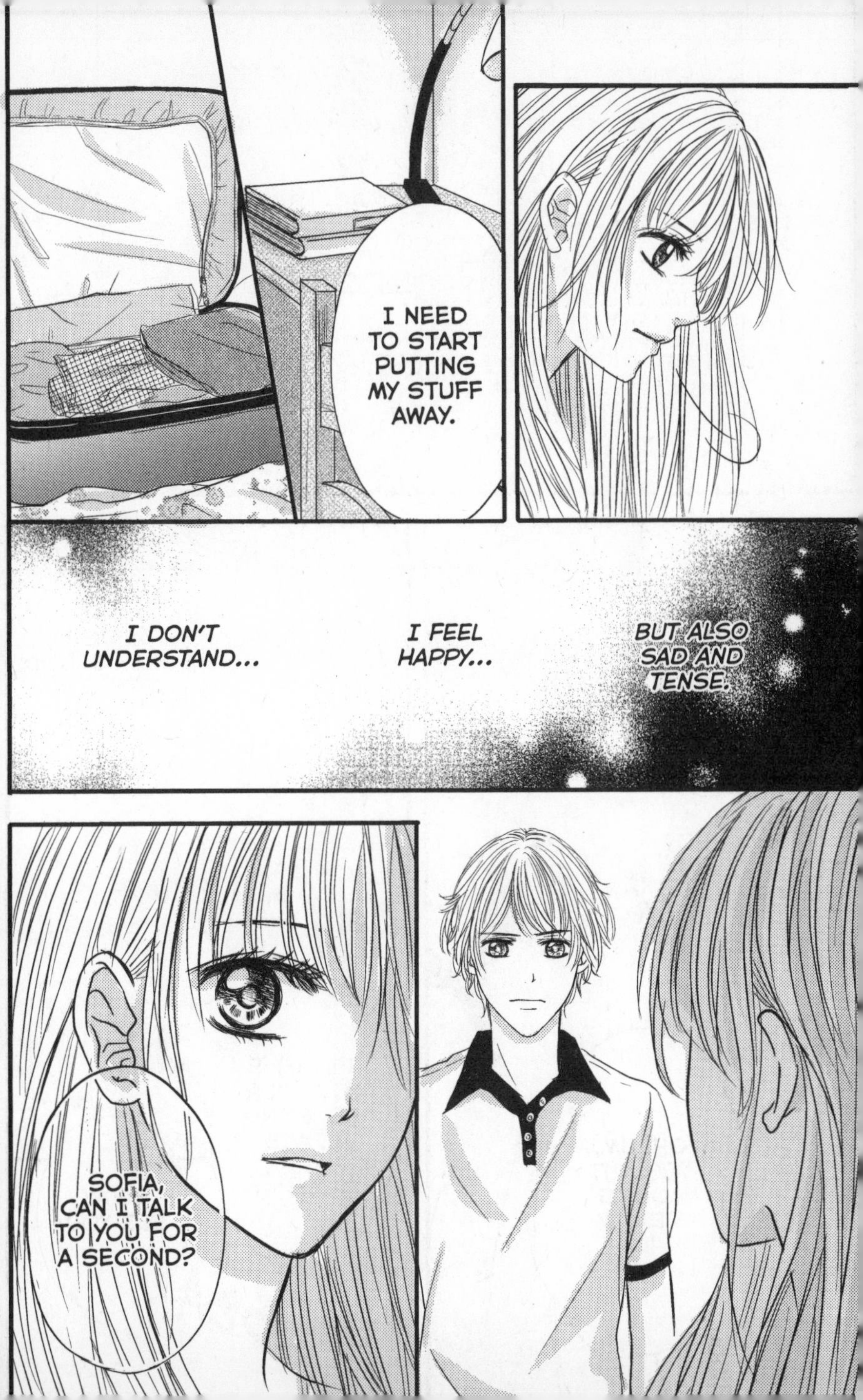
I NEED TO START PUTTING MY STUFF AWAY.
BUT ALSO SAD AND TENSE.
I FEEL HAPPY...
I DON'T UNDERSTAND...
SOFIA, CAN I TALK TO YOU FOR A SECOND?

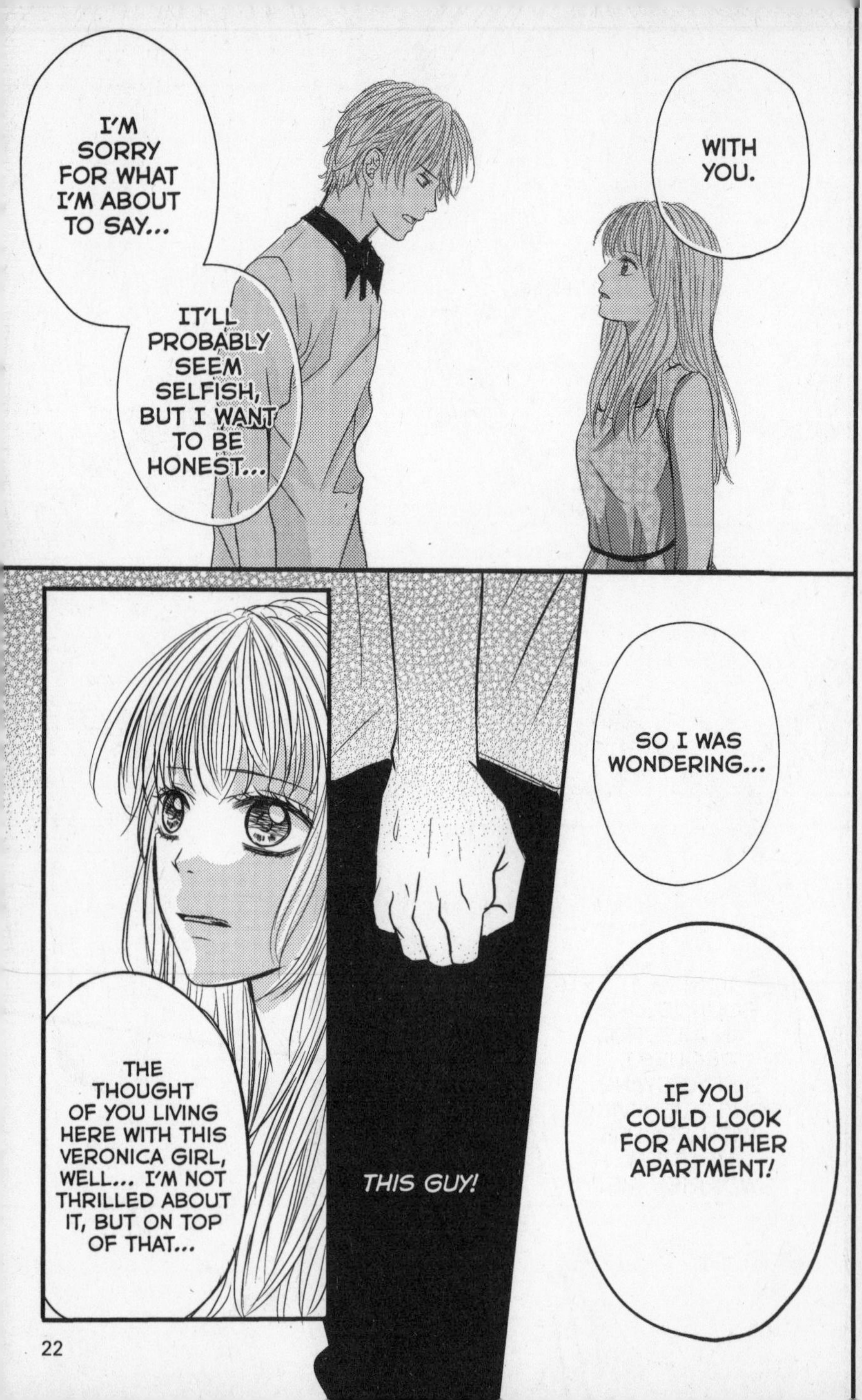
I'M SORRY FOR WHAT I'M ABOUT TO SAY...
IT'LL PROBABLY SEEM SELFISH, BUT I WANT TO BE HONEST...
WITH YOU.
THE THOUGHT OF YOU LIVING HERE WITH THIS VERONICA GIRL, WELL... I'M NOT THRILLED ABOUT IT, BUT ON TOP OF THAT...
THIS GUY!
SO I WAS WONDERING...
IF YOU COULD LOOK FOR ANOTHER APARTMENT!

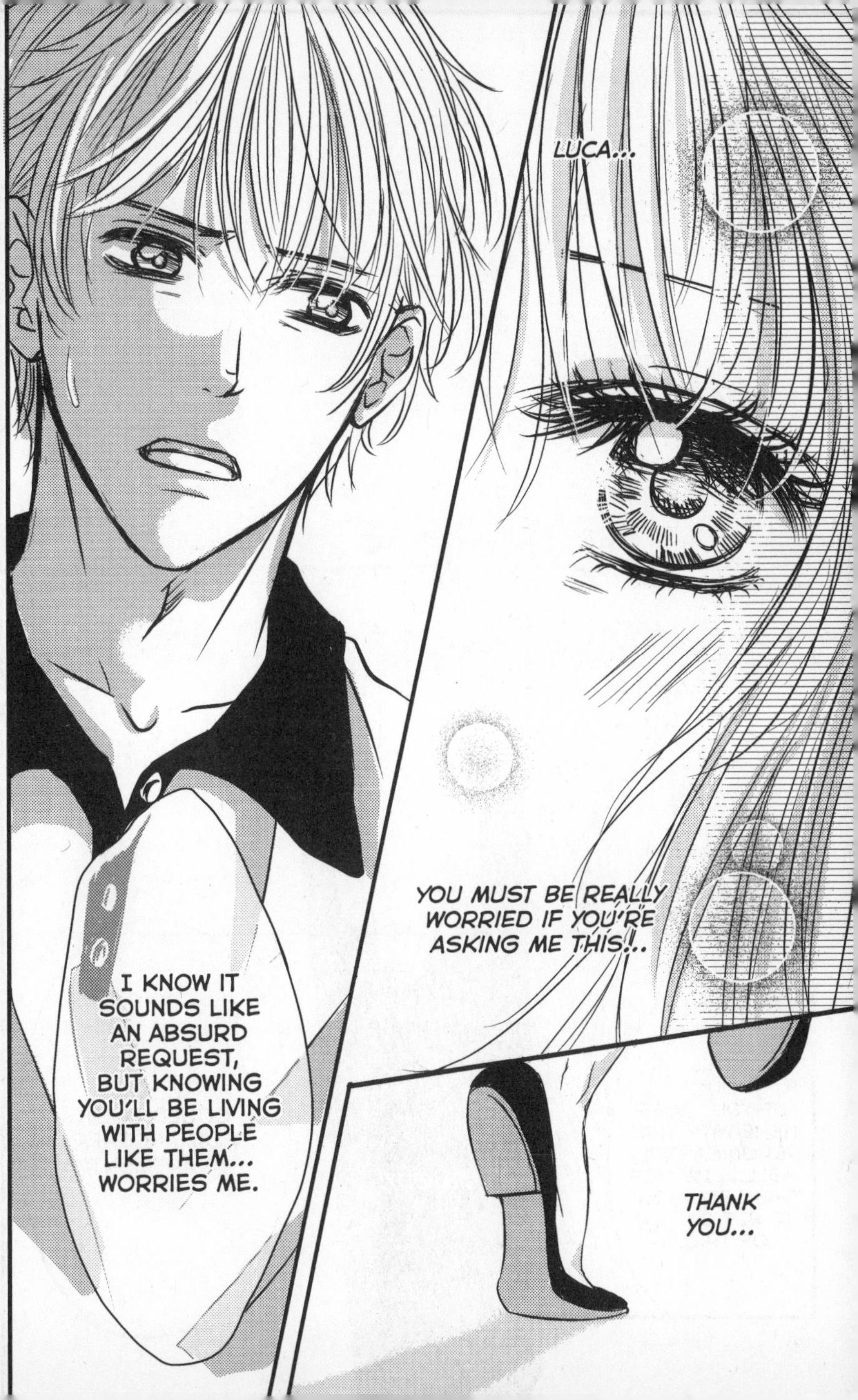
I KNOW IT SOUNDS LIKE AN ABSURD REQUEST, BUT KNOWING YOU'LL BE LIVING WITH PEOPLE LIKE THEM... WORRIES ME.
LUCA...
YOU MUST BE REALLY WORRIED IF YOU'RE ASKING ME THIS...
THANK YOU...

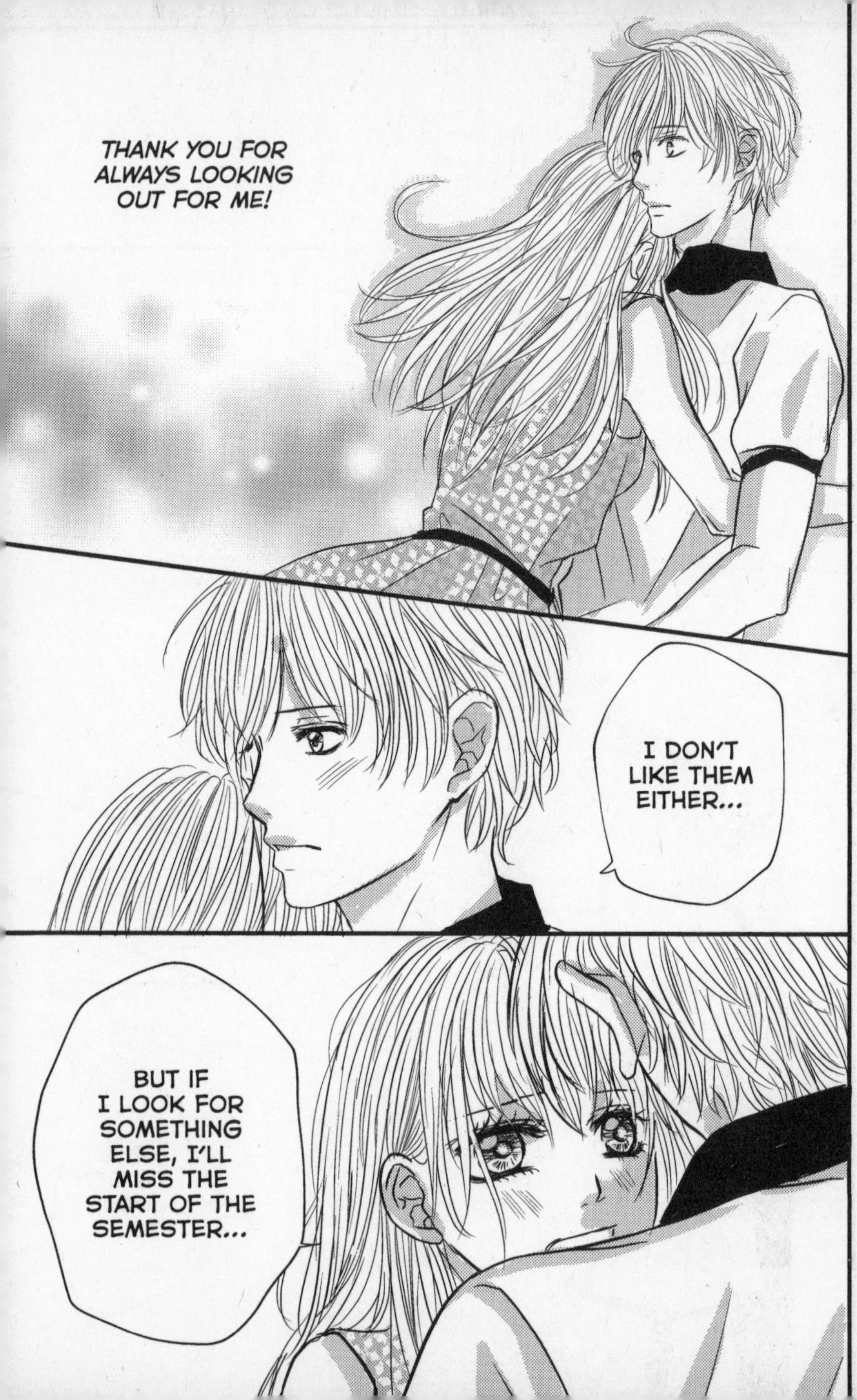
THANK YOU FOR ALWAYS LOOKING OUT FOR ME!
I DON'T LIKE THEM EITHER...
BUT IF I LOOK FOR SOMETHING ELSE, I'LL MISS THE START OF THE SEMESTER...

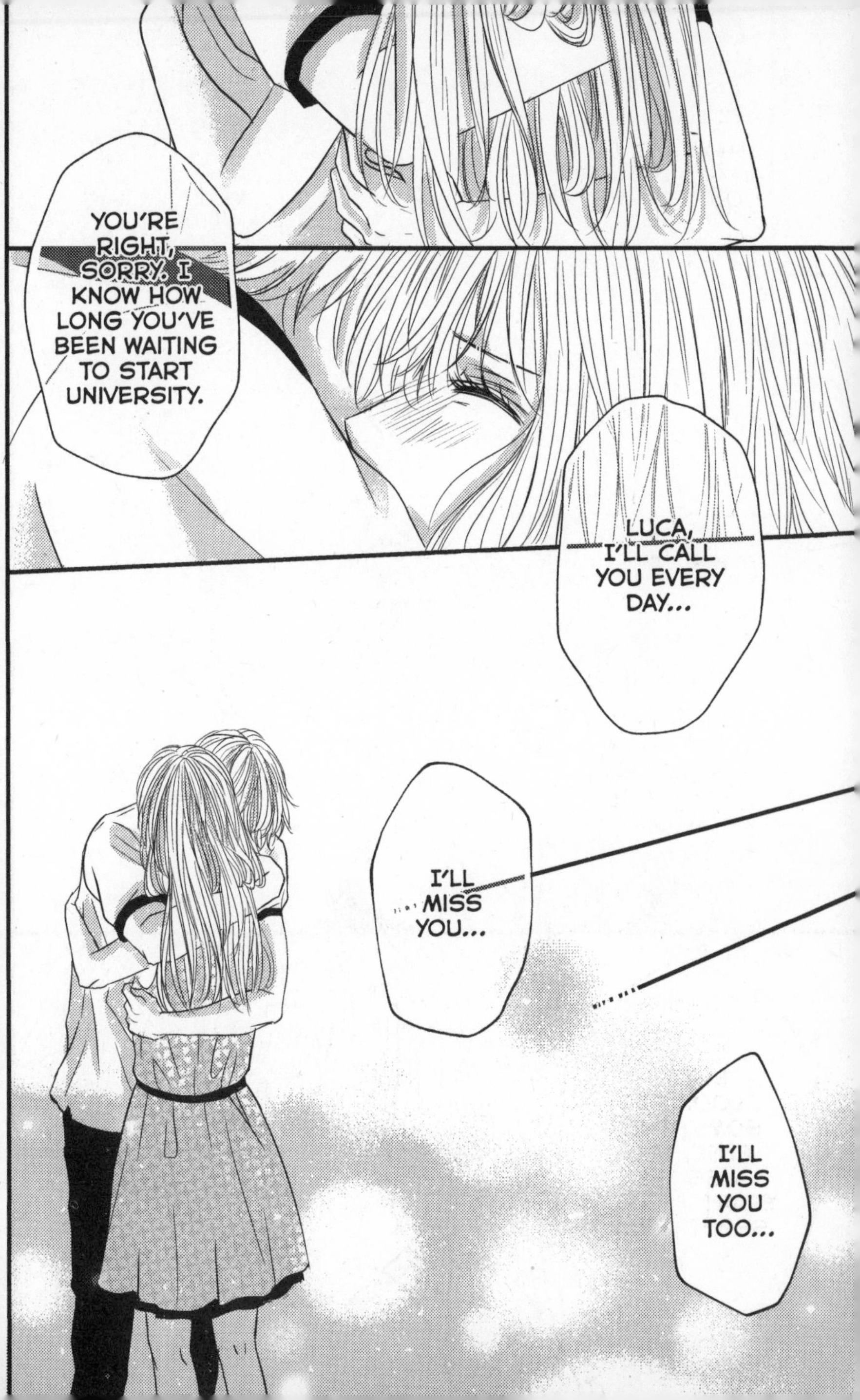

YOU'RE RIGHT, SORRY. I KNOW HOW LONG YOU'VE BEEN WAITING TO START UNIVERSITY.
LUCA, I'LL CALL YOU EVERY DAY...
I'LL MISS YOU...
I'LL MISS YOU TOO...

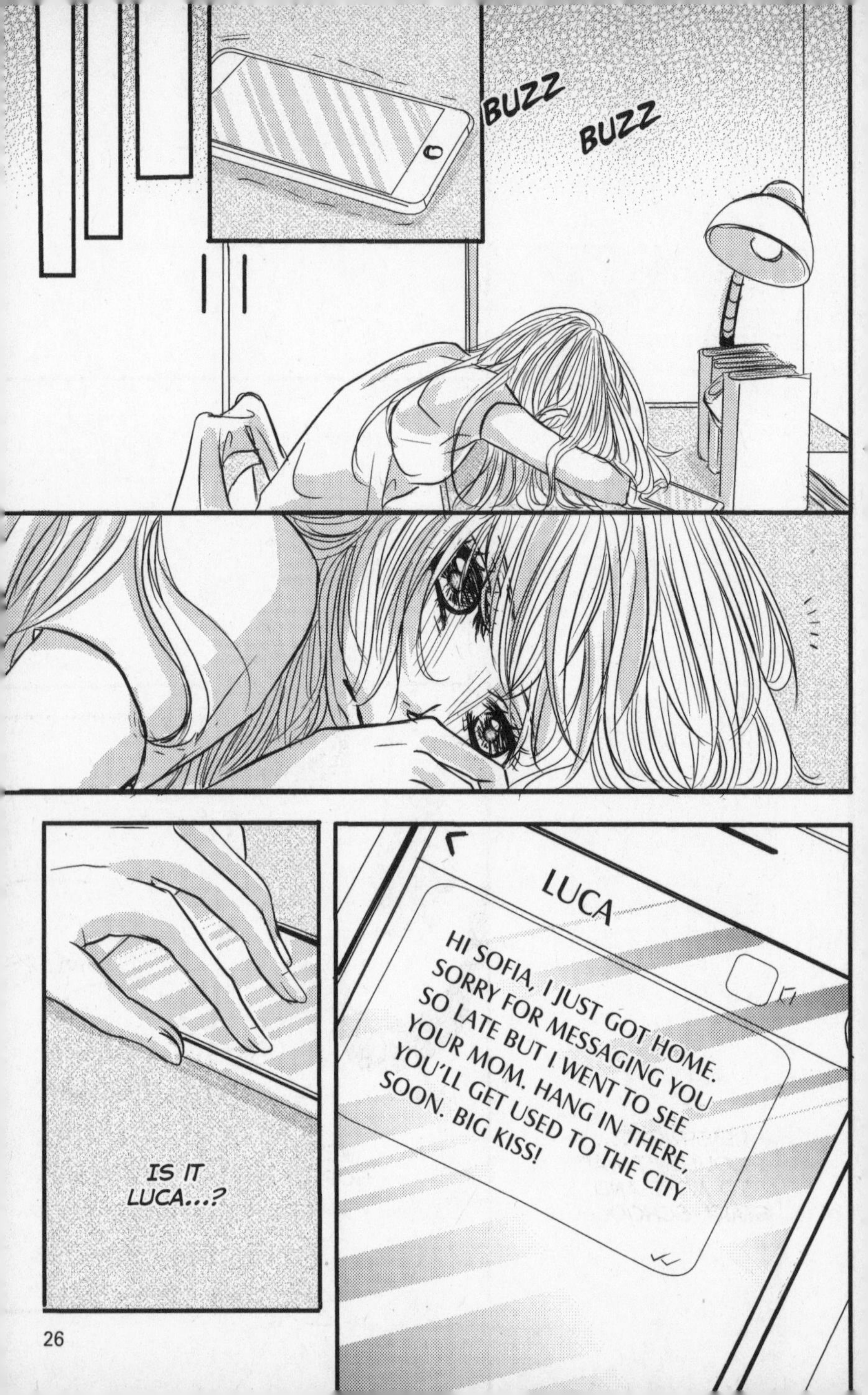
BUZZ
BUZZ
LUCA
HI SOFIA, I JUST GOT HOME. SORRY FOR MESSAGING YOU SO LATE BUT I WENT TO SEE YOUR MOM. HANG IN THERE, YOU'LL GET USED TO THE CITY SOON. BIG KISS!
IS IT LUCA...?

*HE'S RIGHT...
I COULDN'T WAIT
TO MOVE AND
START SCHOOL...*

*I NEED TO
BE STRONG.*

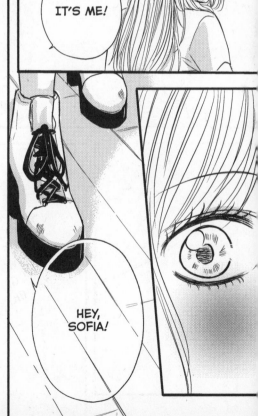

KNOCK
KNOCK

IT'S ME!

HEY,
SOFIA!

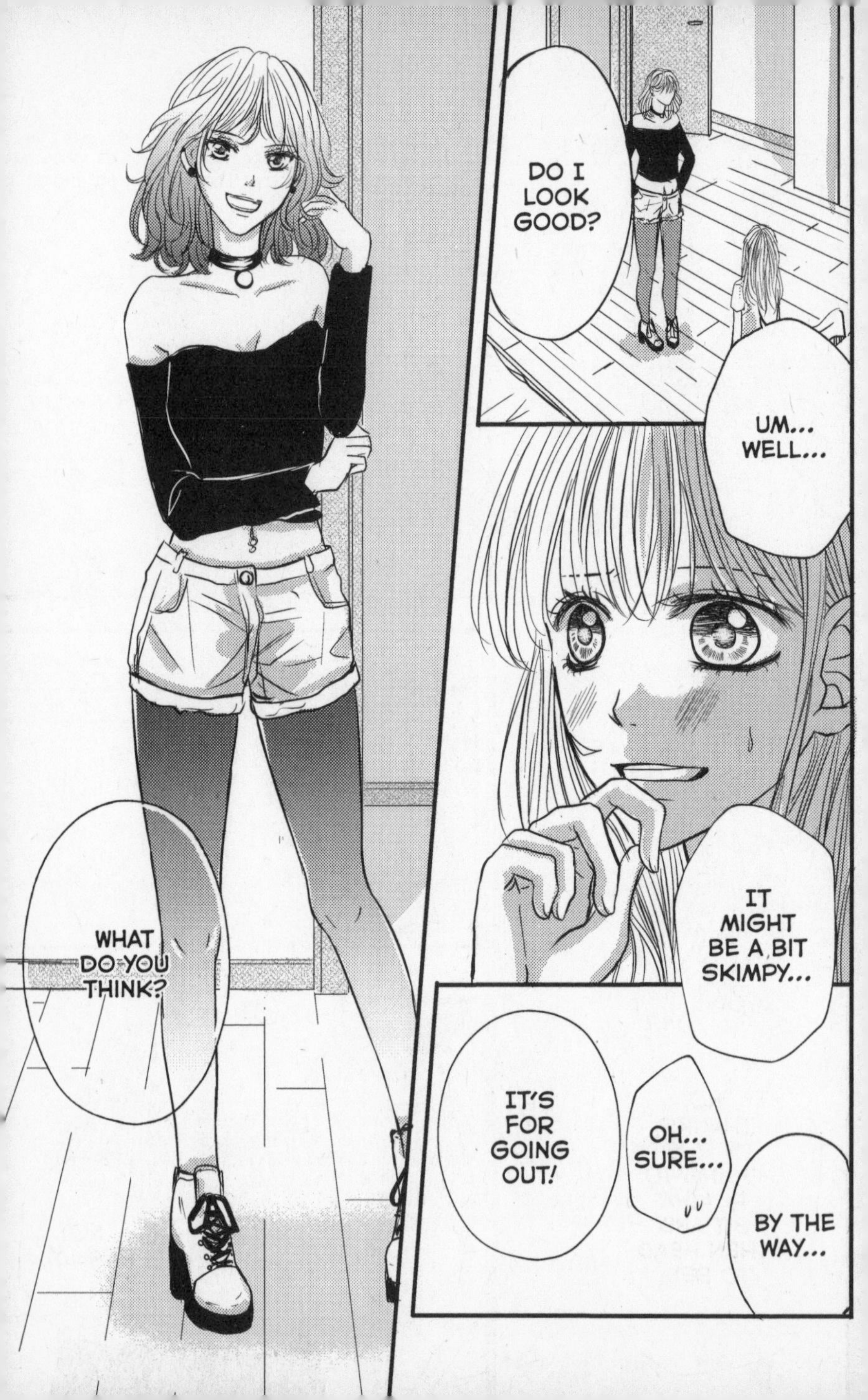
WHAT DO YOU THINK?
DO I LOOK GOOD?
UM... WELL...
IT MIGHT BE A BIT SKIMPY...
IT'S FOR GOING OUT!
OH... SURE...
BY THE WAY...

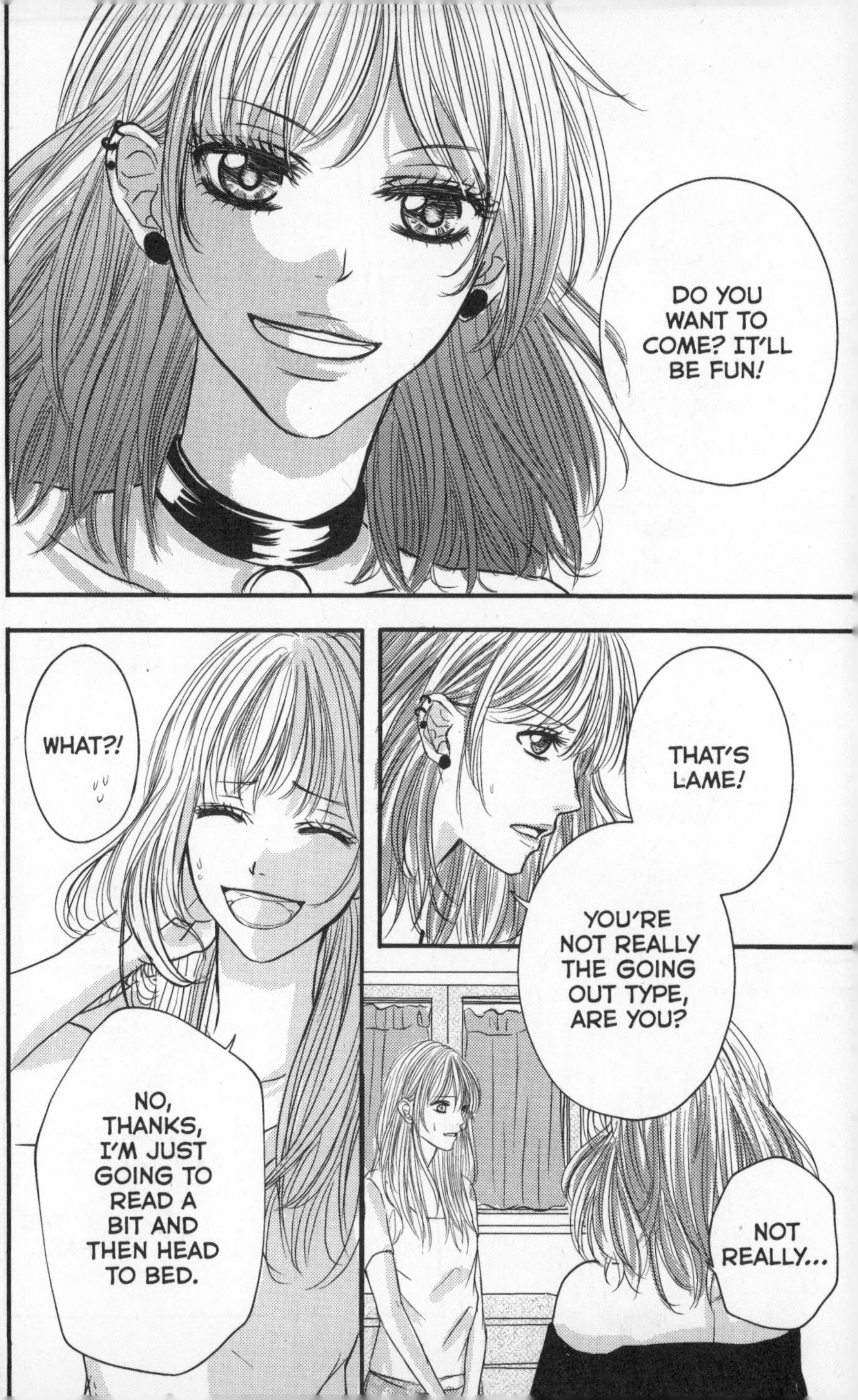
DO YOU WANT TO COME? IT'LL BE FUN!
NO, THANKS, I'M JUST GOING TO READ A BIT AND THEN HEAD TO BED.
WHAT?!
THAT'S LAME!
YOU'RE NOT REALLY THE GOING OUT TYPE, ARE YOU?
NOT REALLY...

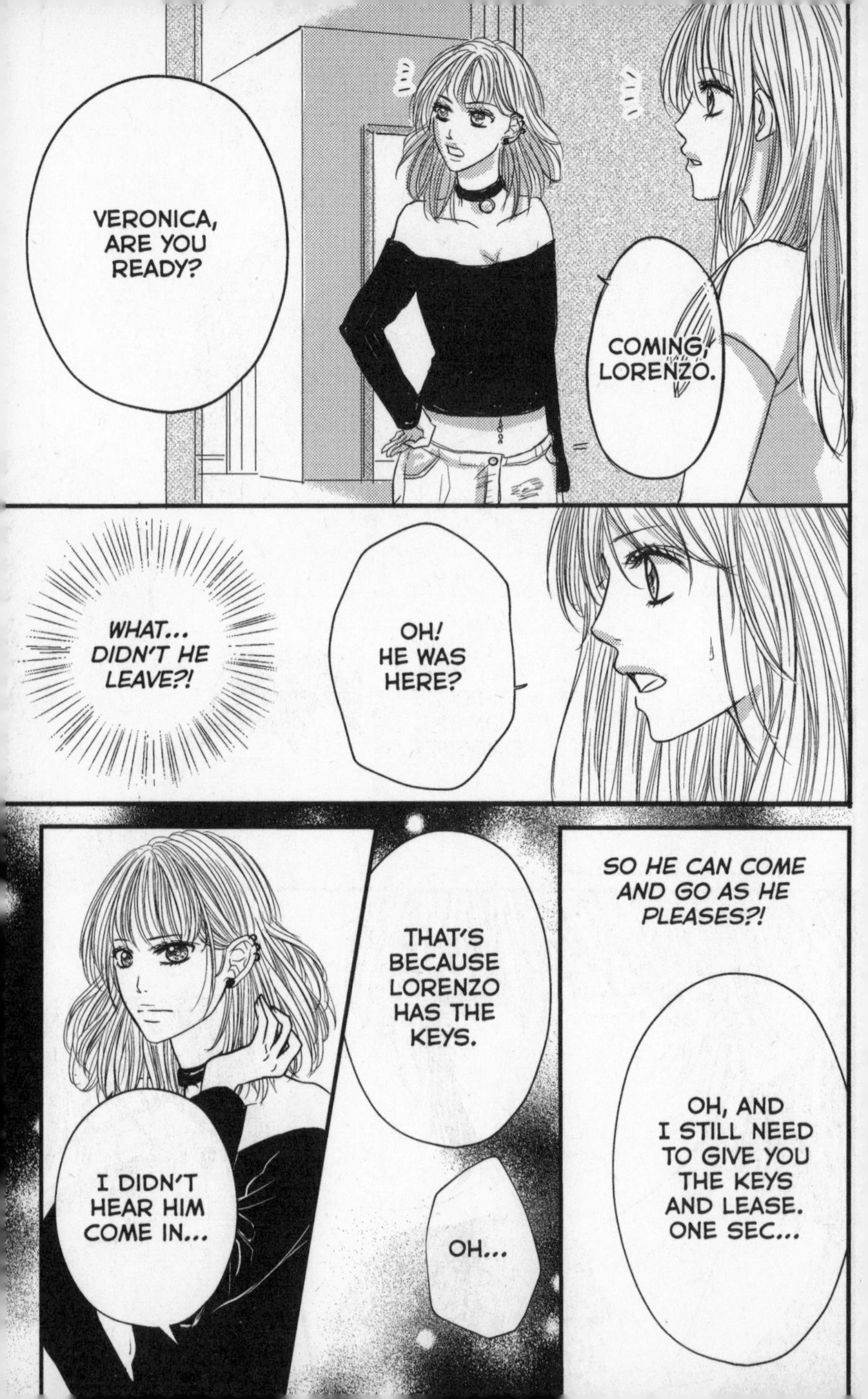
VERONICA, ARE YOU READY?
COMING, LORENZO.
OH! HE WAS HERE?
WHAT... DIDN'T HE LEAVE?!
I DIDN'T HEAR HIM COME IN...
THAT'S BECAUSE LORENZO HAS THE KEYS.
OH...
SO HE CAN COME AND GO AS HE PLEASES?!
OH, AND I STILL NEED TO GIVE YOU THE KEYS AND LEASE. ONE SEC...

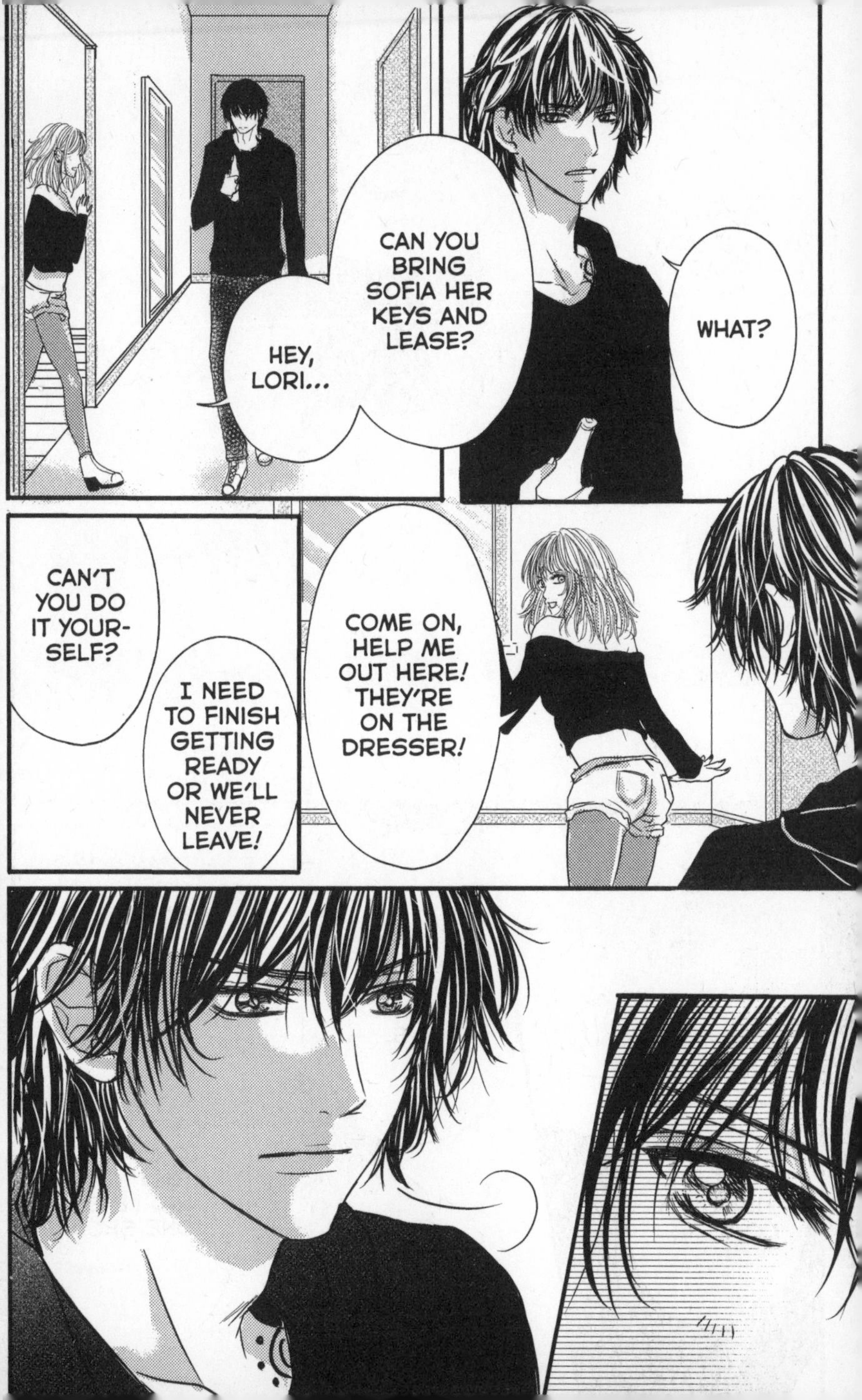
HEY, LORI...
CAN YOU BRING SOFIA HER KEYS AND LEASE?
WHAT?
CAN'T YOU DO IT YOUR-SELF?
I NEED TO FINISH GETTING READY OR WE'LL NEVER LEAVE!
COME ON, HELP ME OUT HERE! THEY'RE ON THE DRESSER!

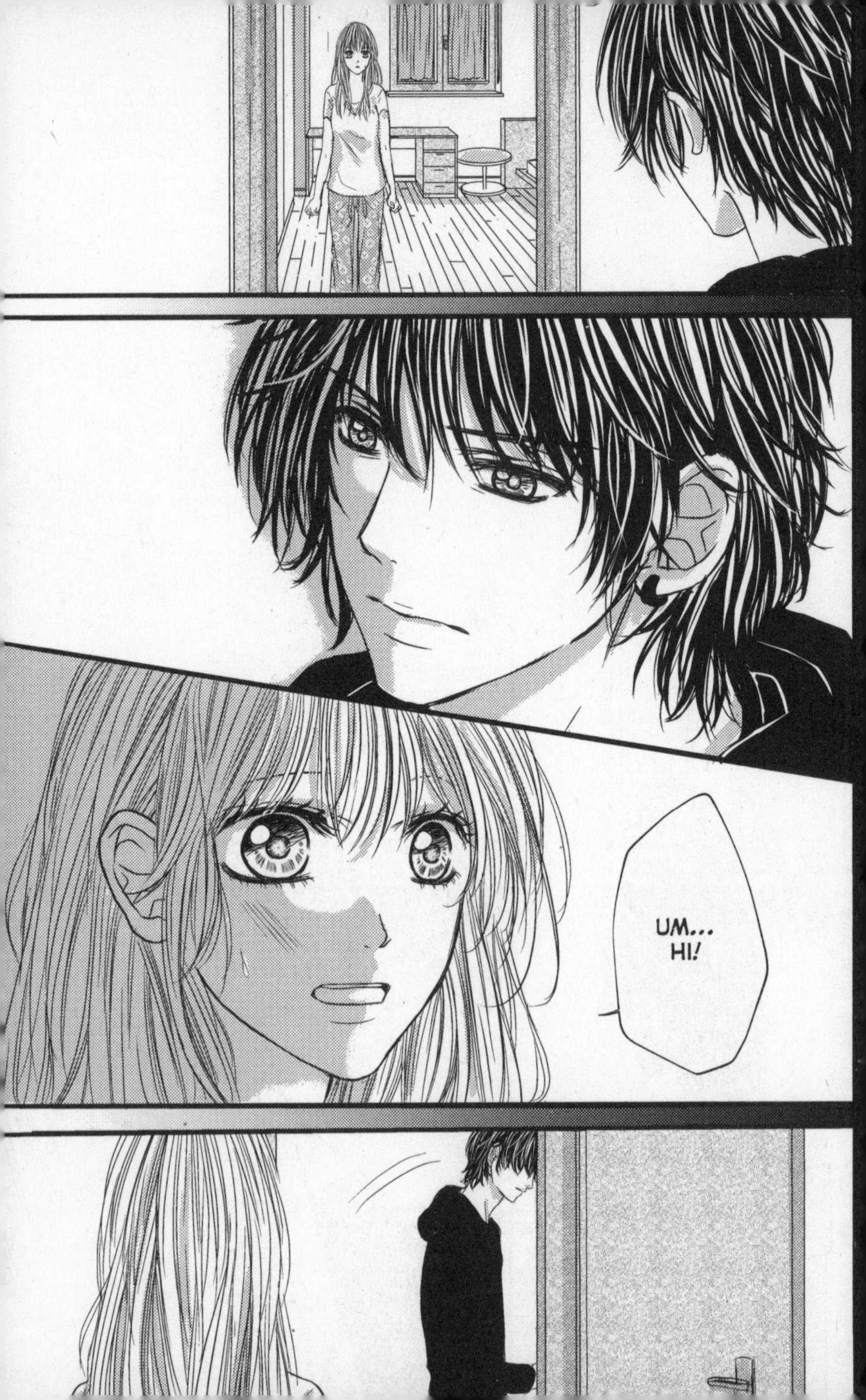
UM... HI!

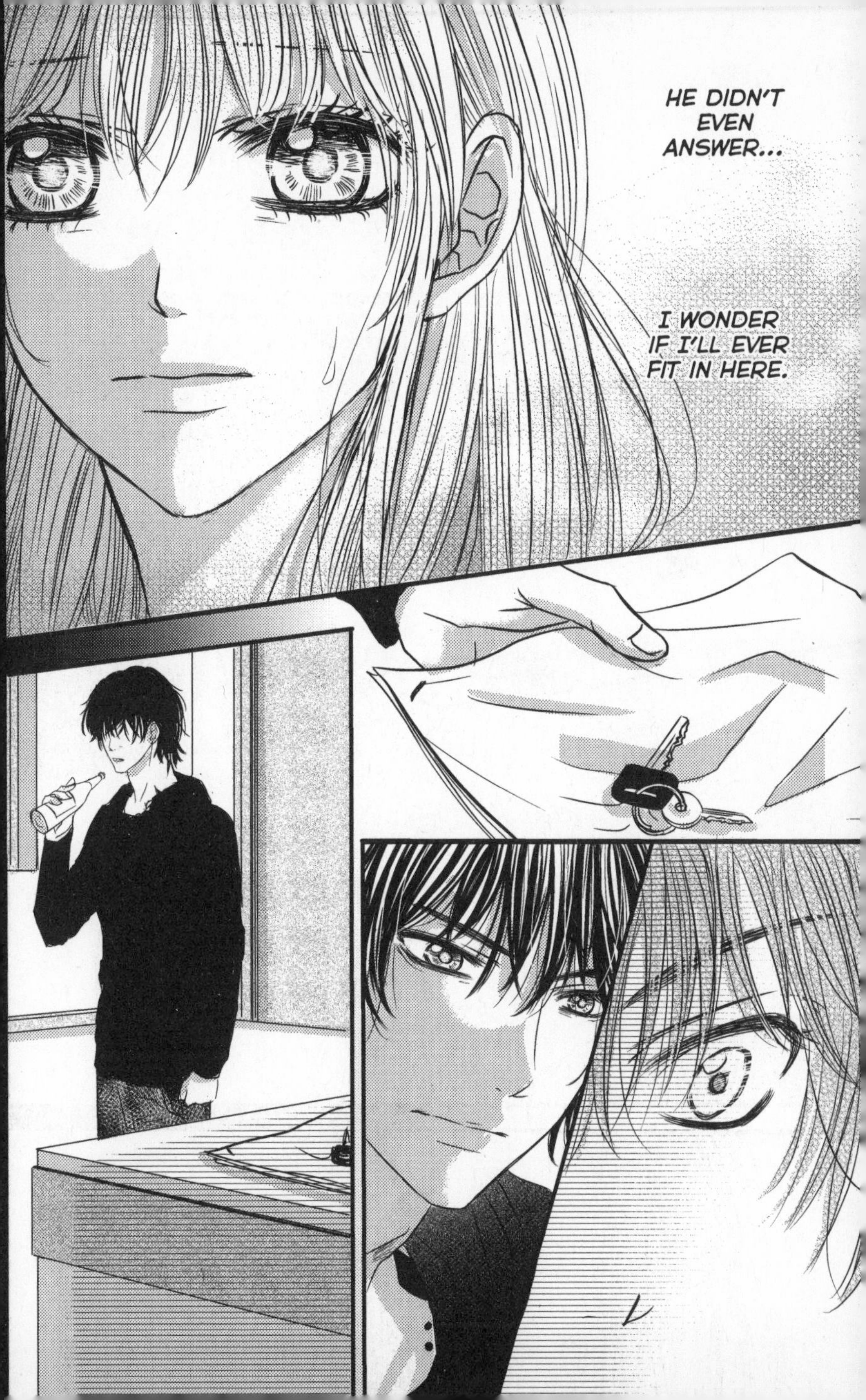
HE DIDN'T EVEN ANSWER...
I WONDER IF I'LL EVER FIT IN HERE.

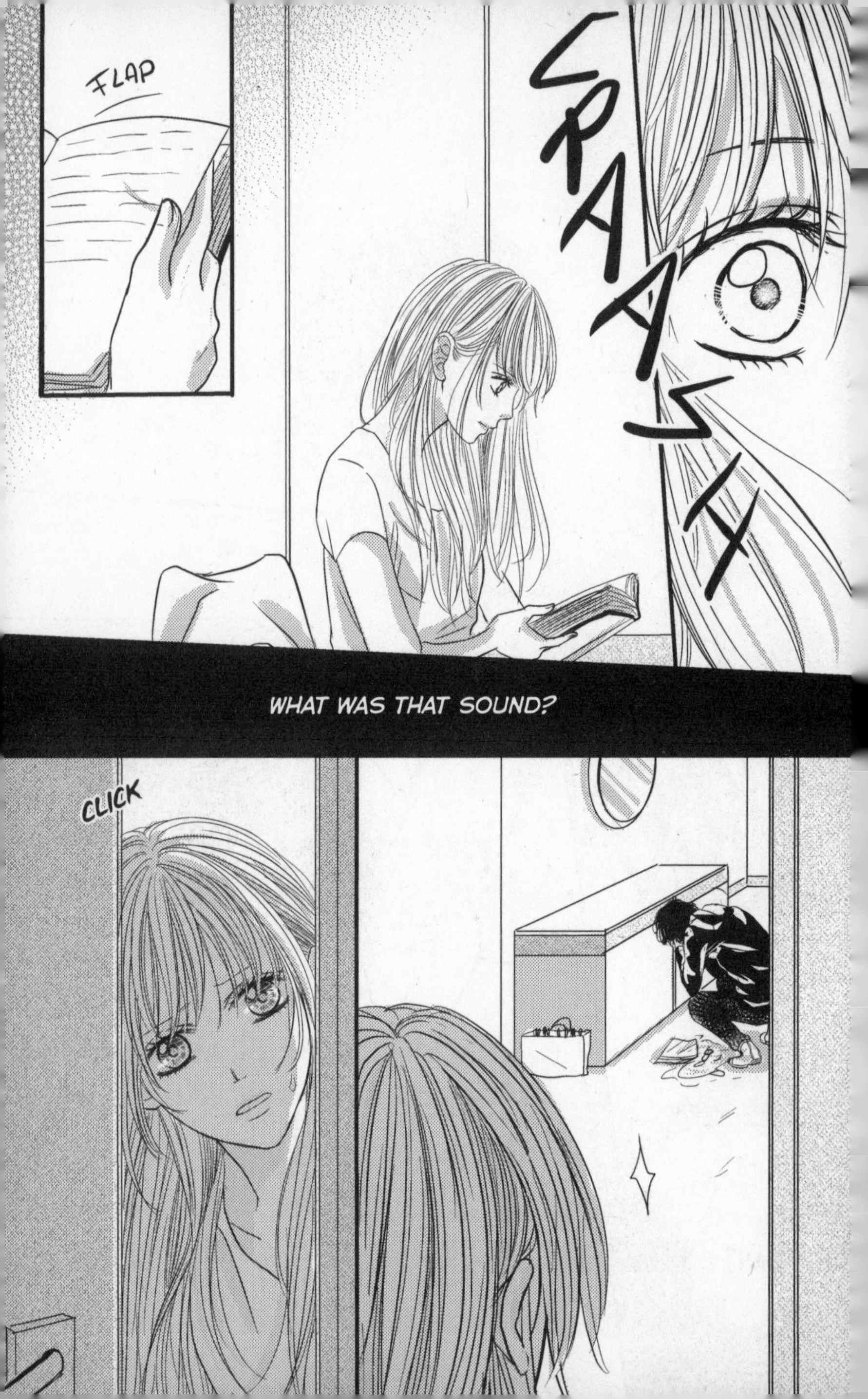
CRAASH
FLAP
WHAT WAS THAT SOUND?
CLICK

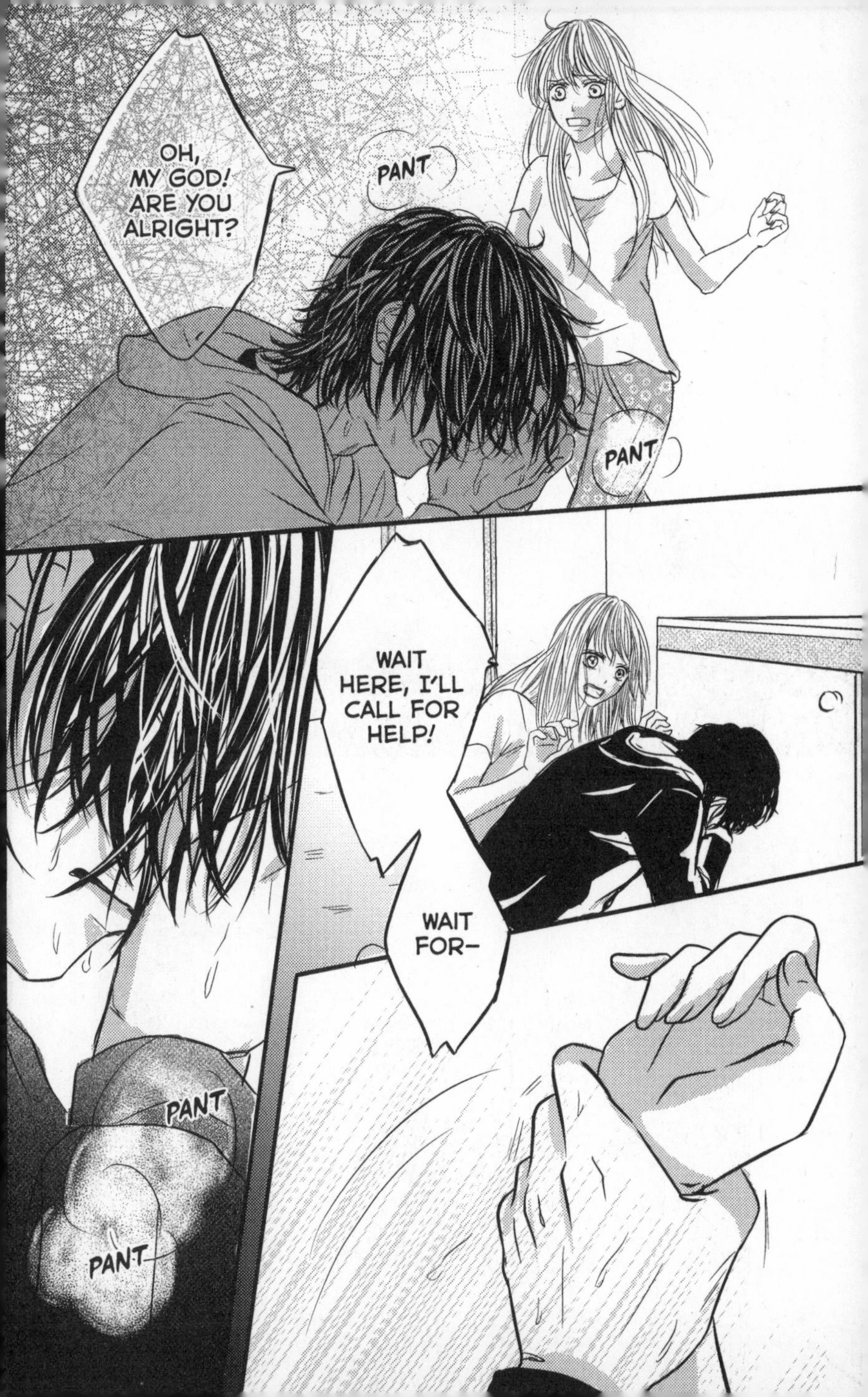
PANT
OH, MY GOD! ARE YOU ALRIGHT?
PANT
WAIT HERE, I'LL CALL FOR HELP!
WAIT FOR–
PANT
PANT

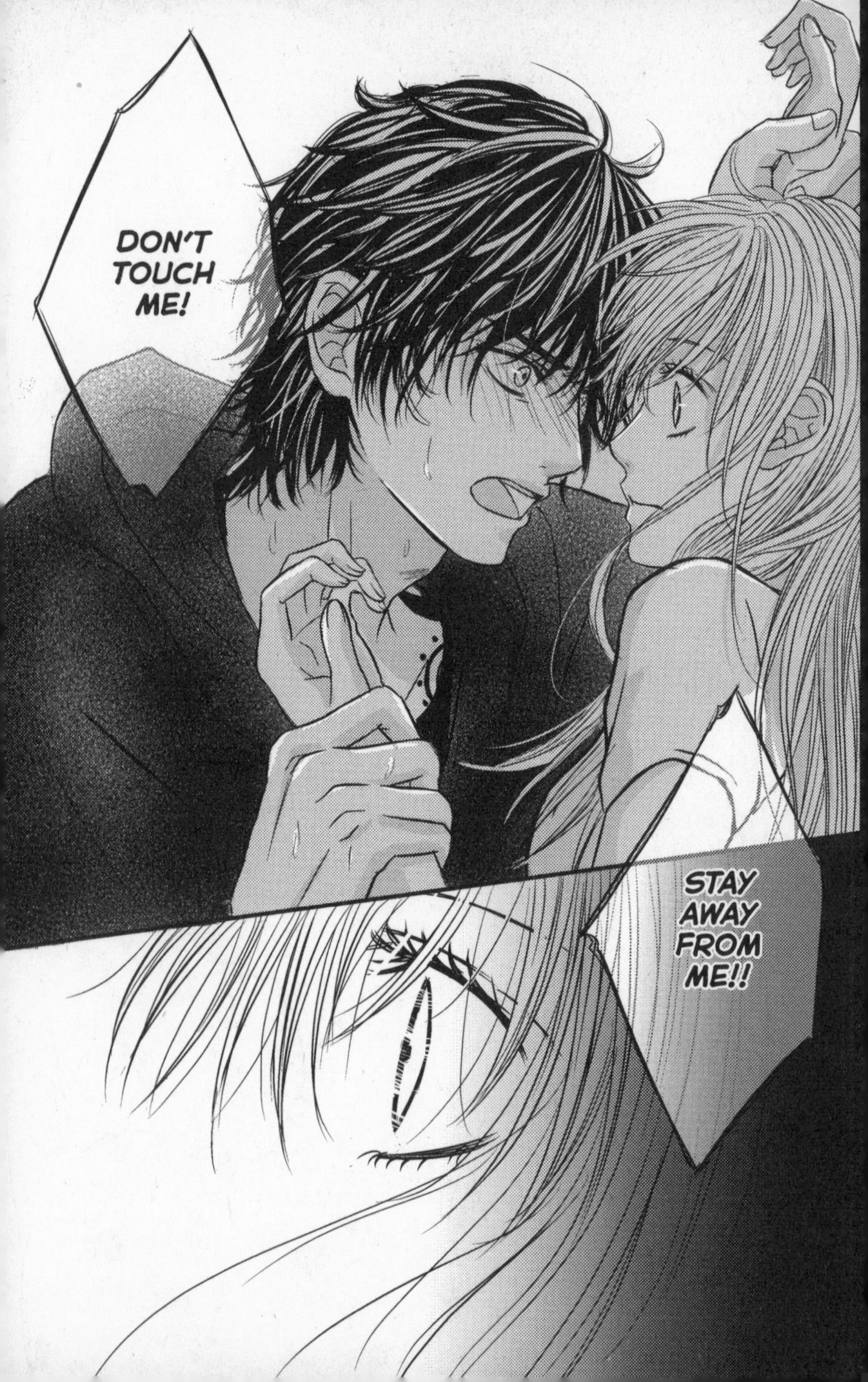
DON'T TOUCH ME!
STAY AWAY FROM ME!!

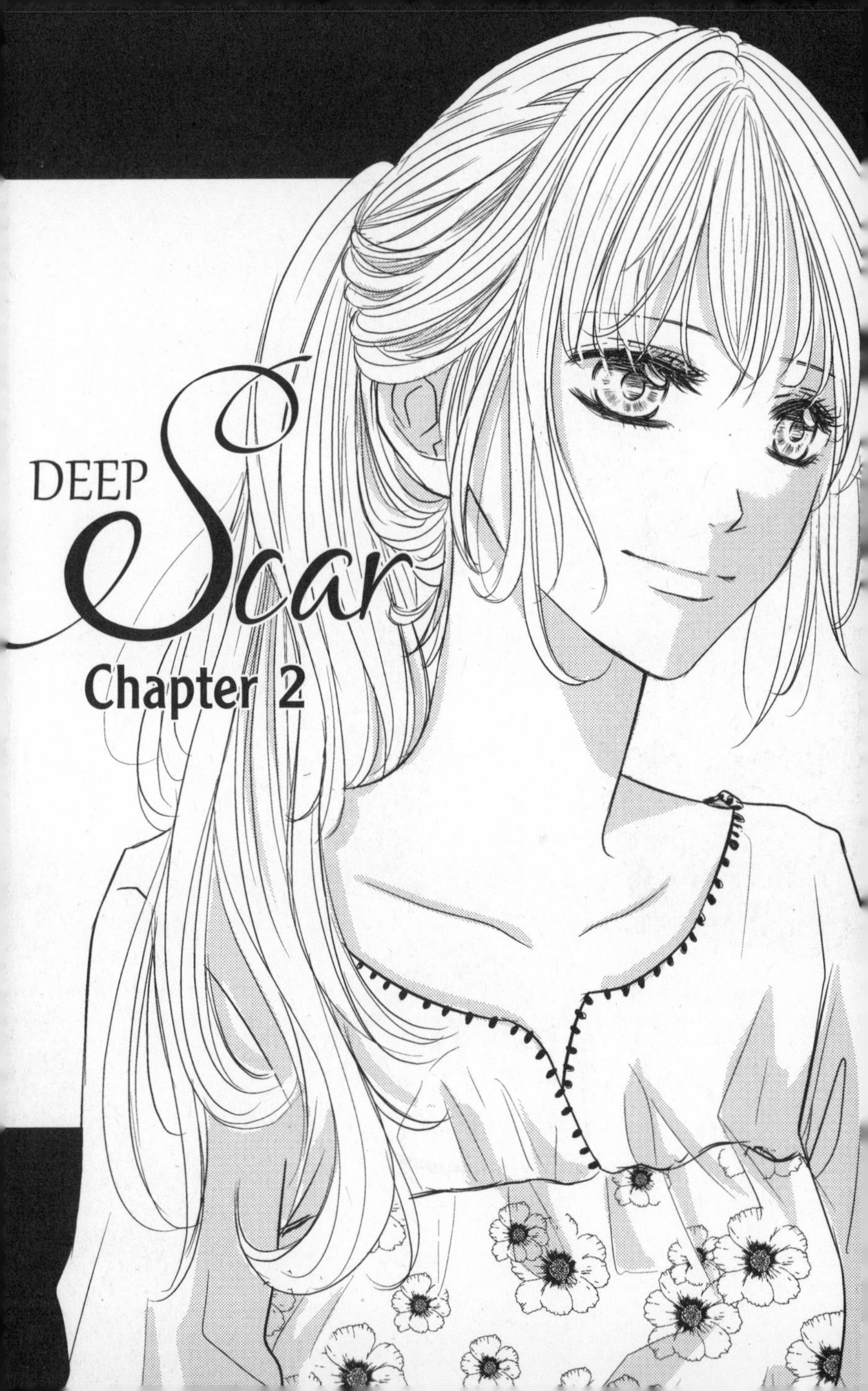
DEEP Scar
Chapter 2

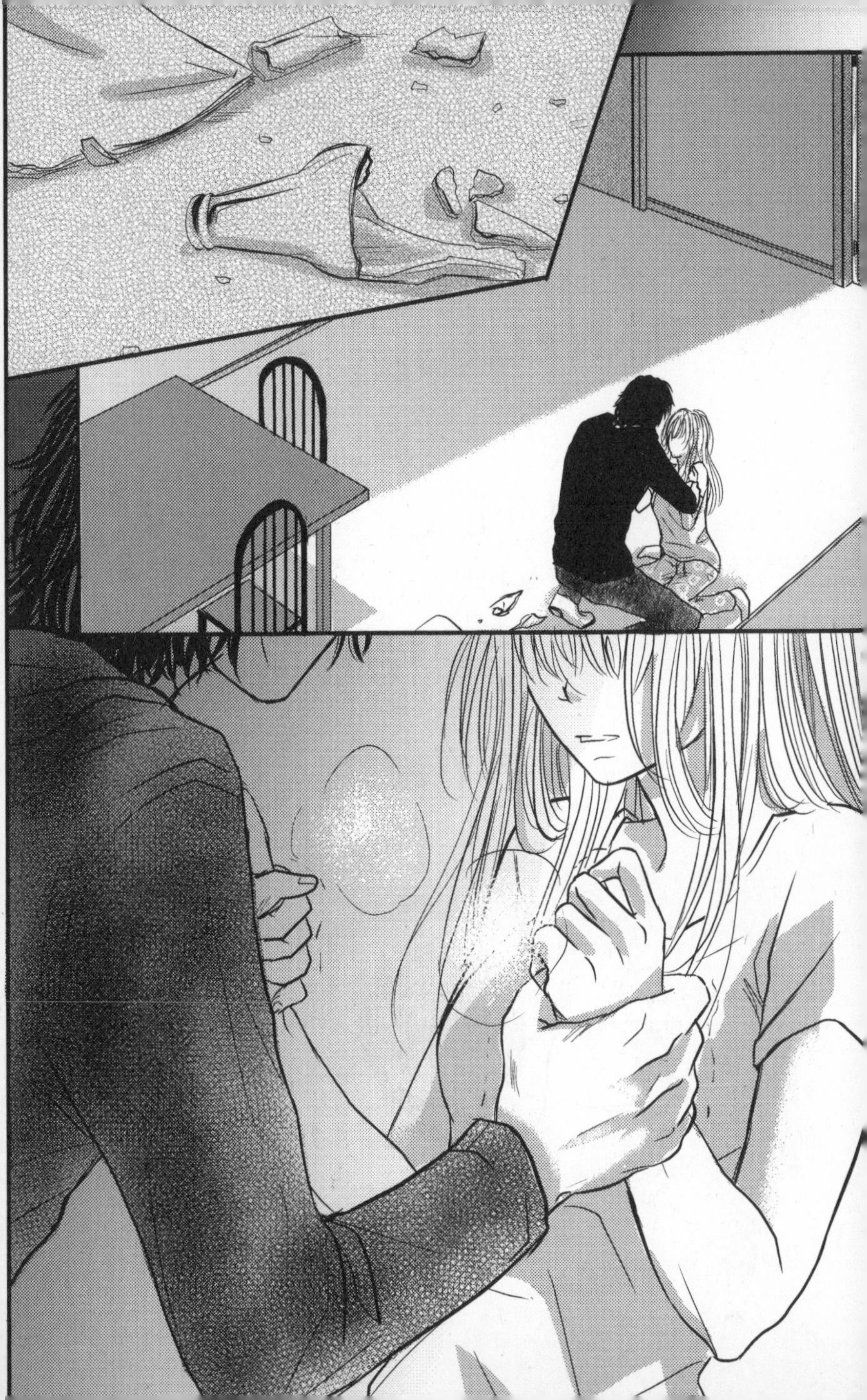

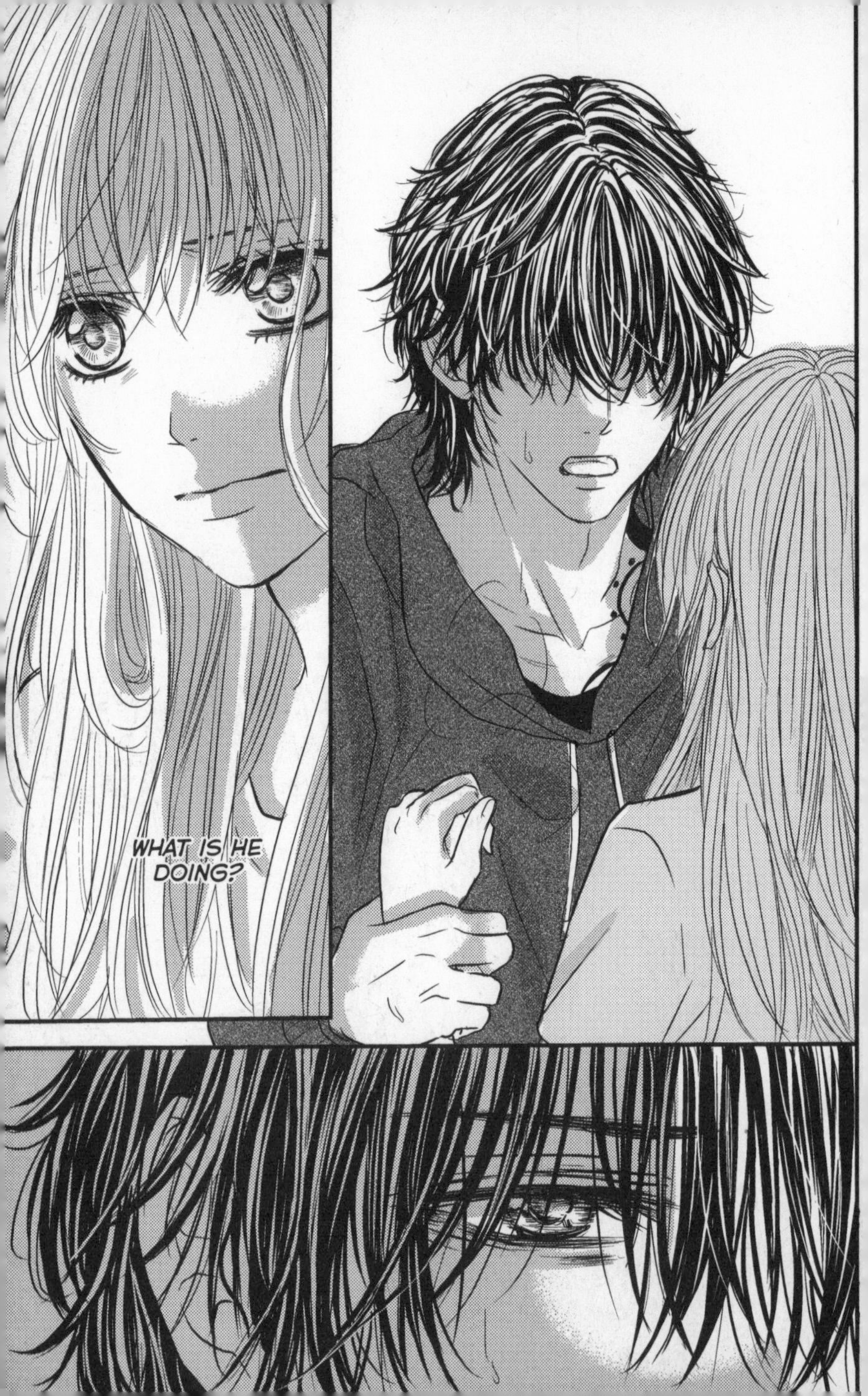
WHAT IS HE
DOING?

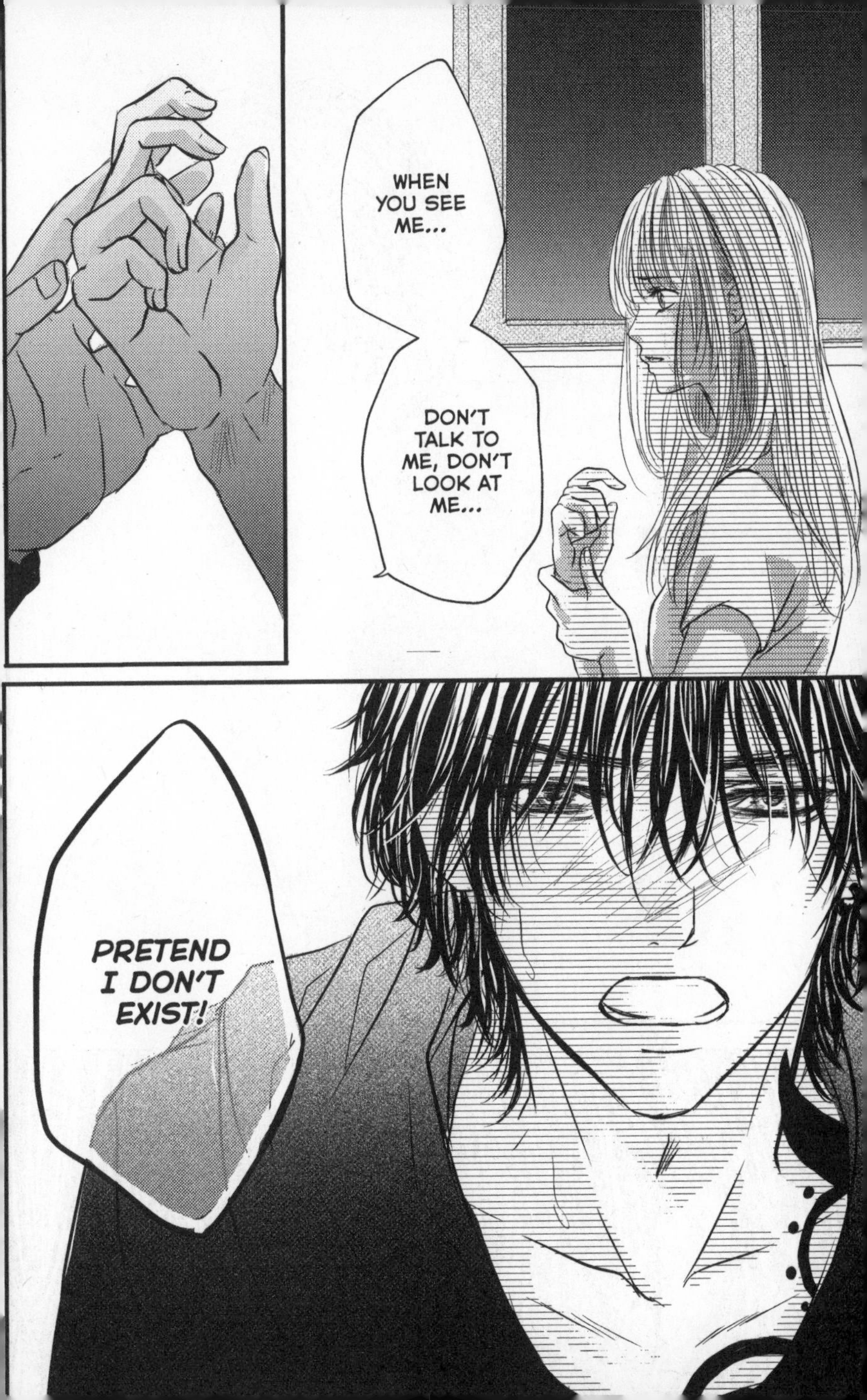
WHEN YOU SEE ME...
DON'T TALK TO ME, DON'T LOOK AT ME...
PRETEND I DON'T EXIST!

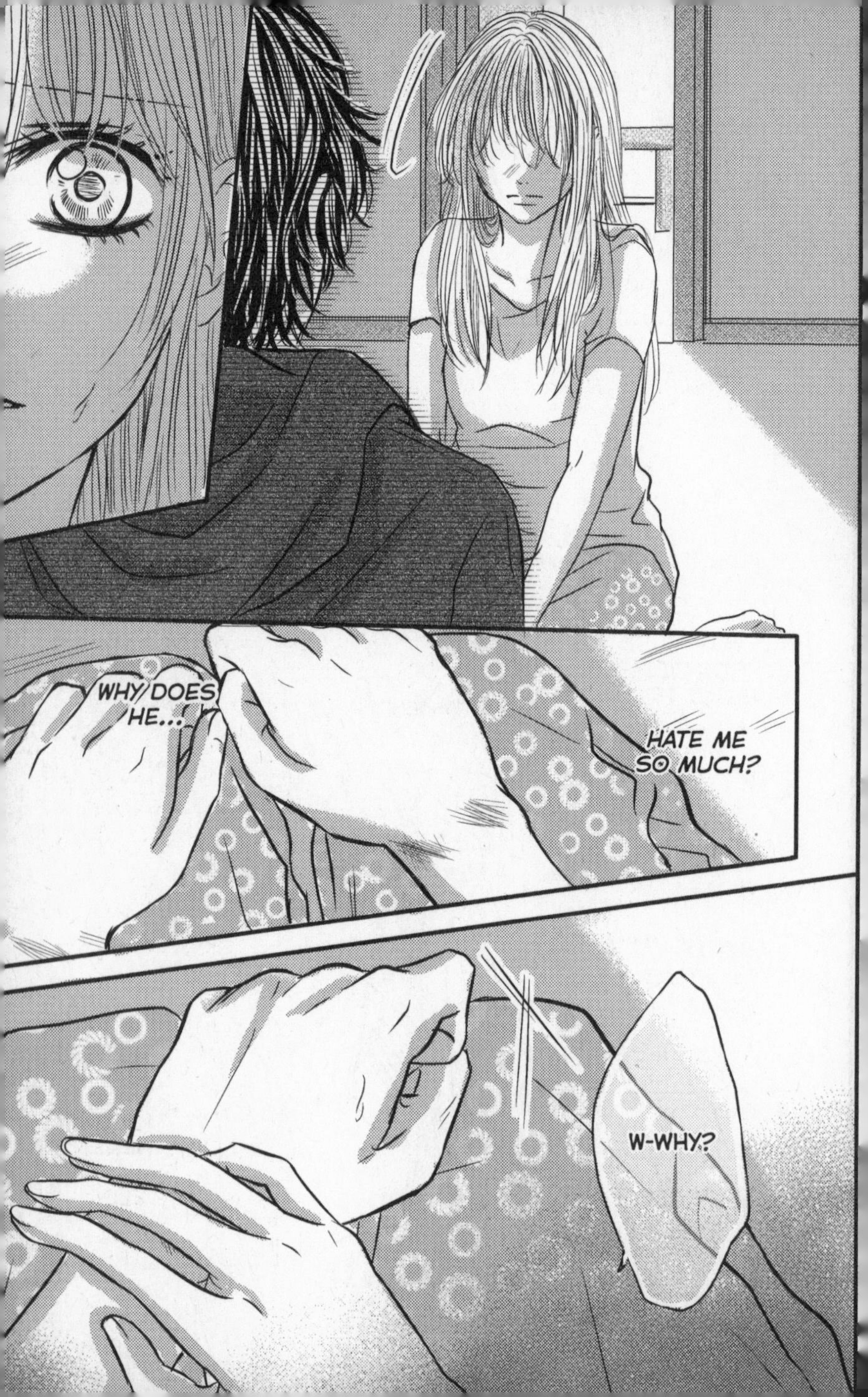
WHY DOES HE...
HATE ME SO MUCH?
W-WHY?

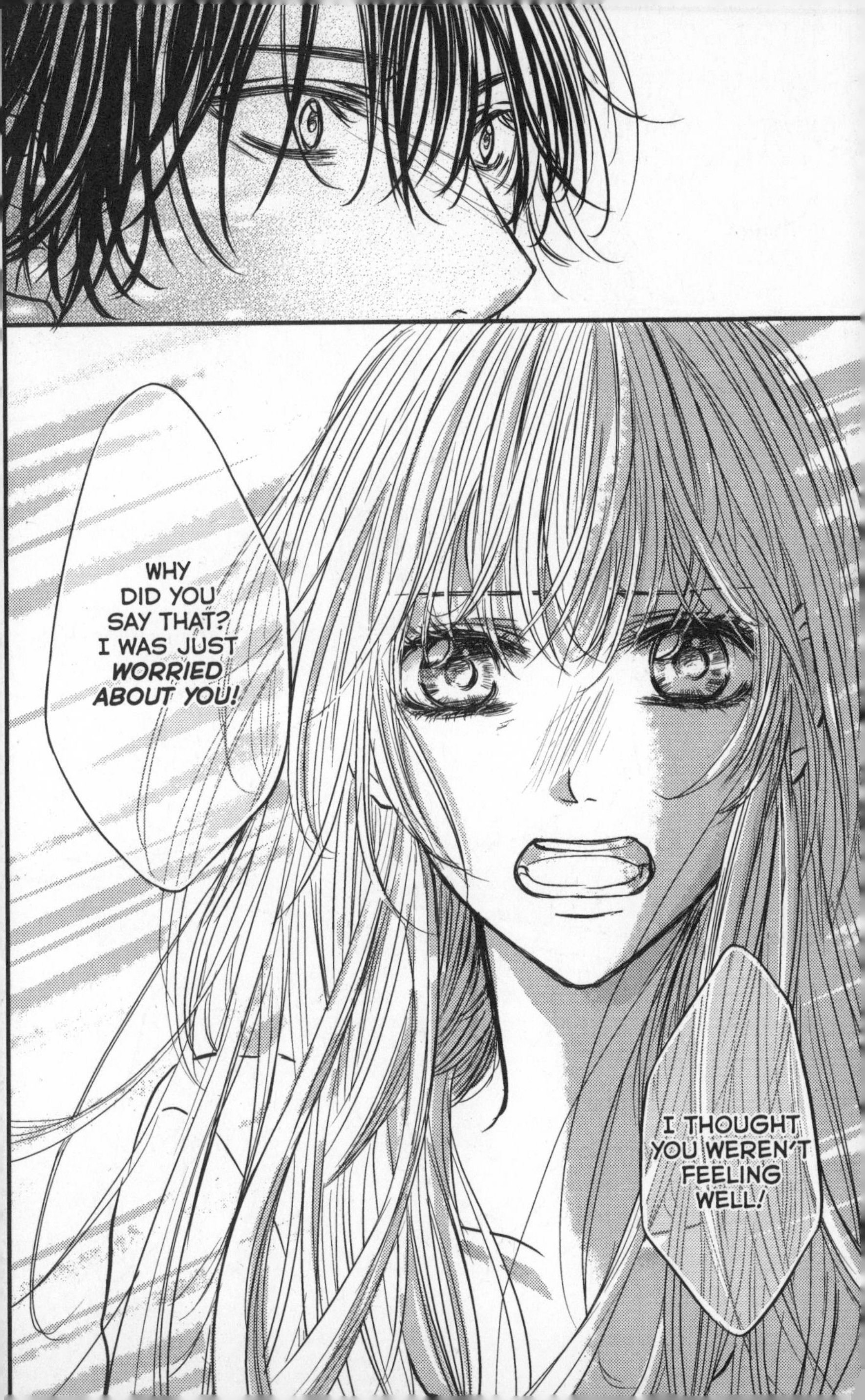
WHY DID YOU SAY THAT? I WAS JUST *WORRIED* ABOUT YOU!
I THOUGHT YOU WEREN'T FEELING WELL!

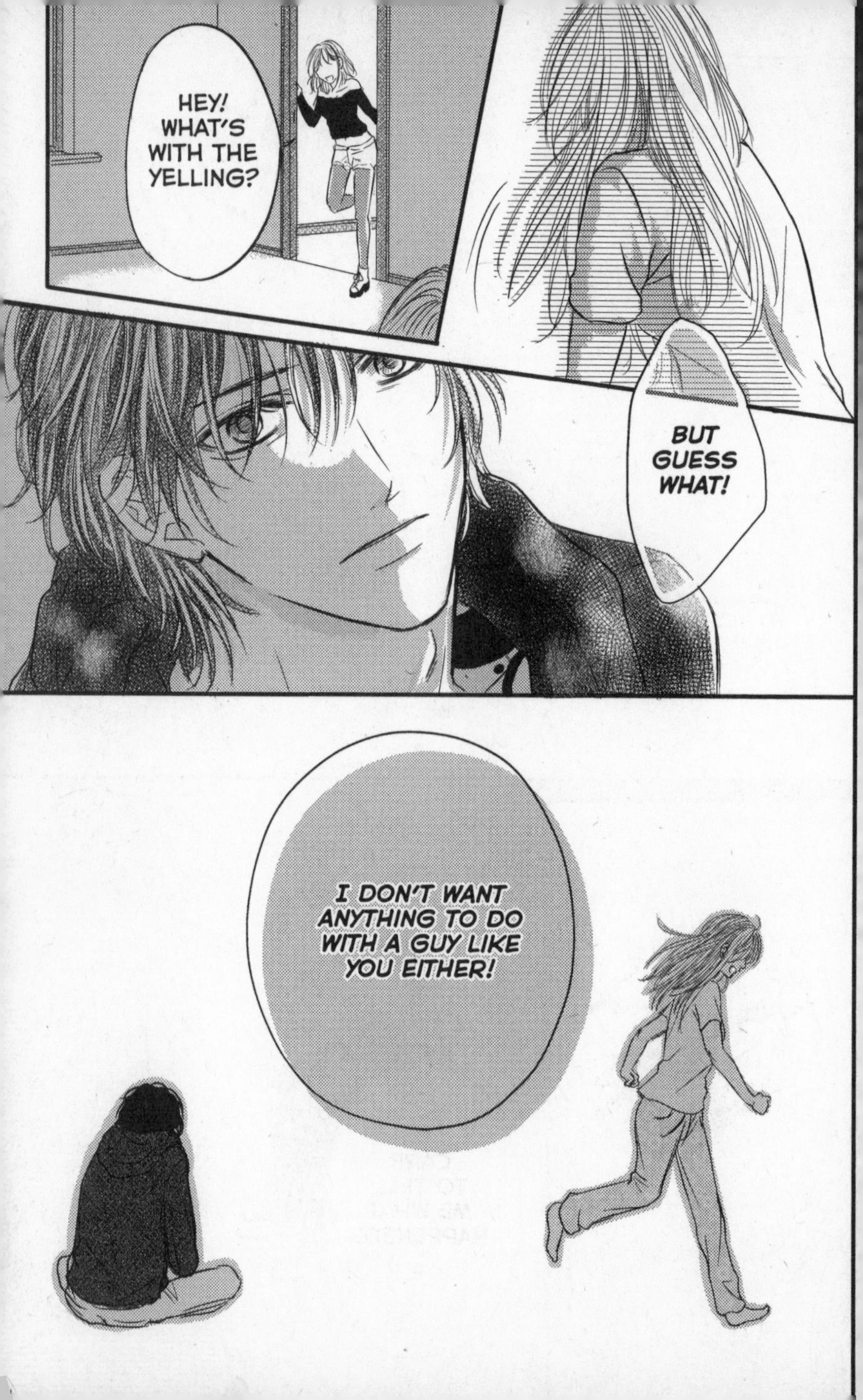
BUT GUESS WHAT!
HEY! WHAT'S WITH THE YELLING?
I DON'T WANT ANYTHING TO DO WITH A GUY LIKE YOU EITHER!

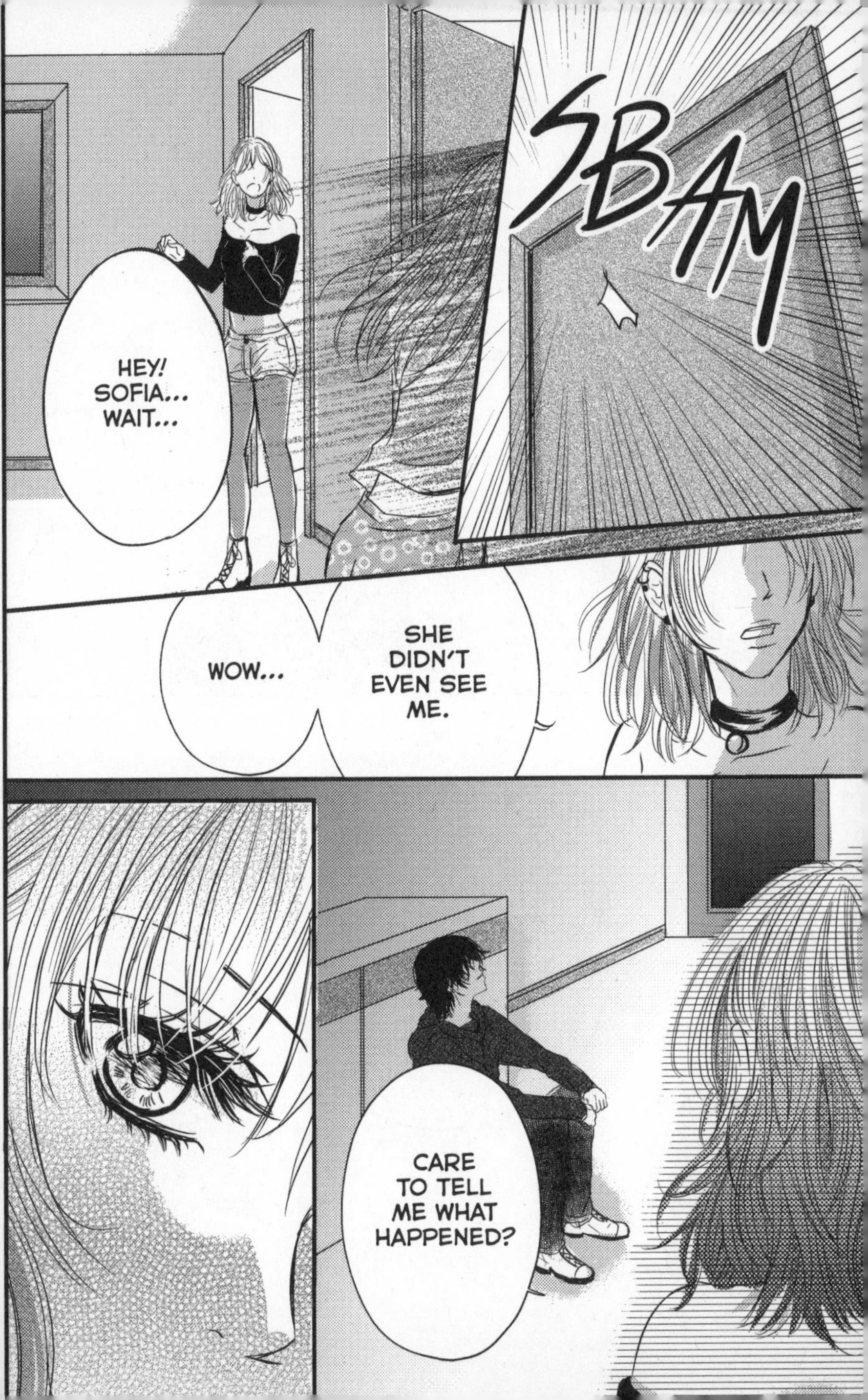
HEY! SOFIA... WAIT...
SBAM
WOW...
SHE DIDN'T EVEN SEE ME.
CARE TO TELL ME WHAT HAPPENED?

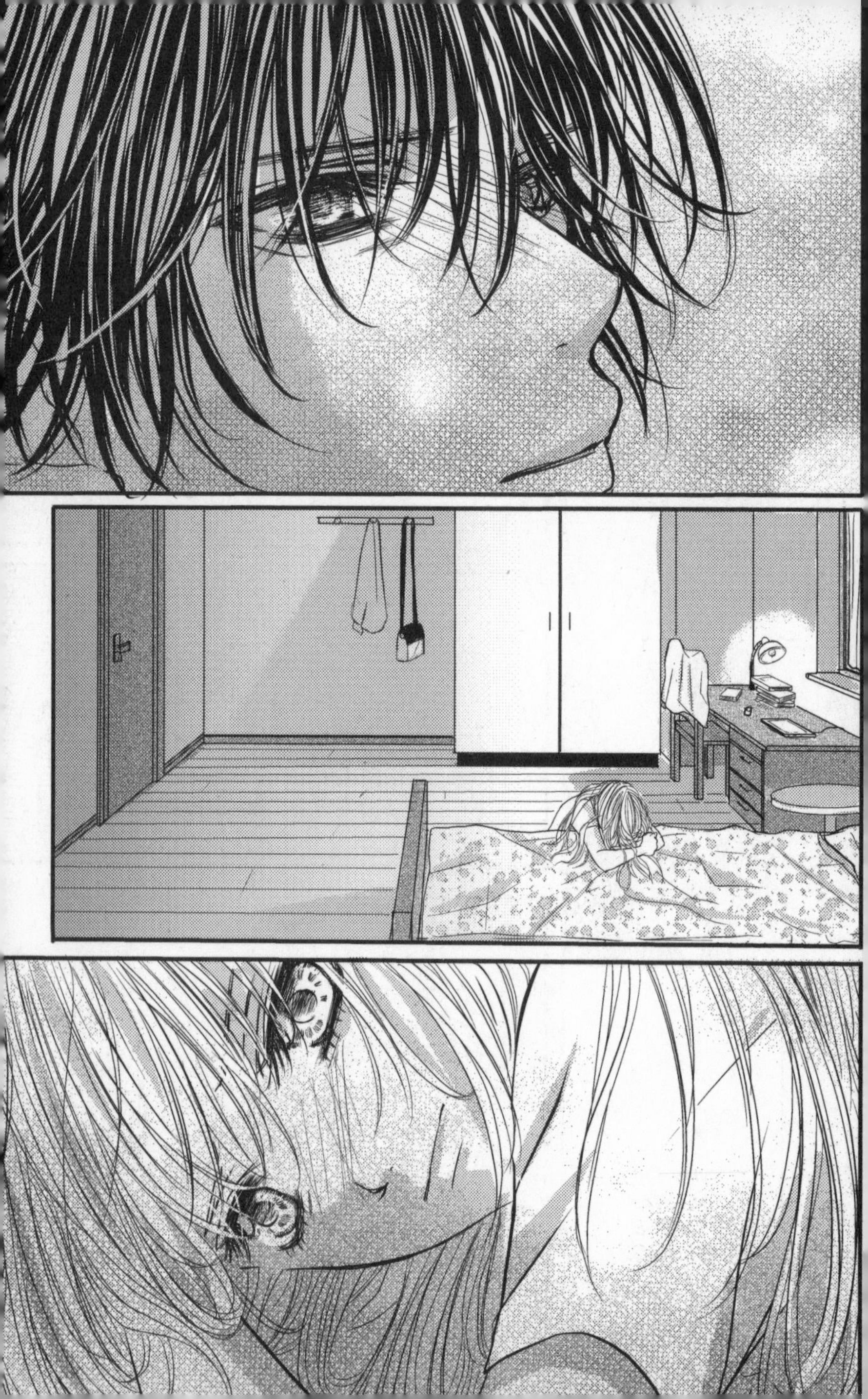

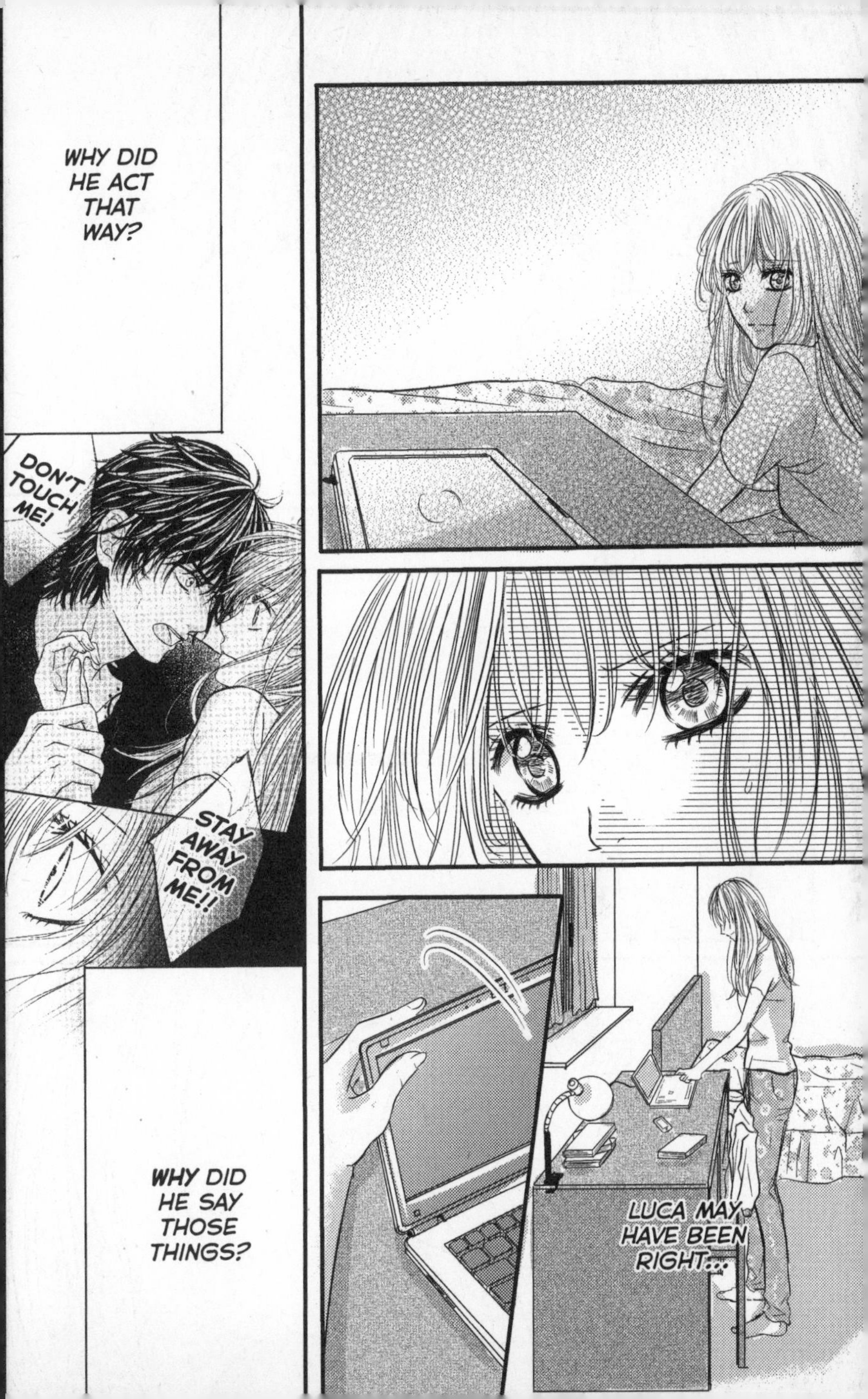
LUCA MAY HAVE BEEN RIGHT...
WHY DID HE ACT THAT WAY?
DON'T TOUCH ME!
STAY AWAY FROM ME!!
WHY DID HE SAY THOSE THINGS?

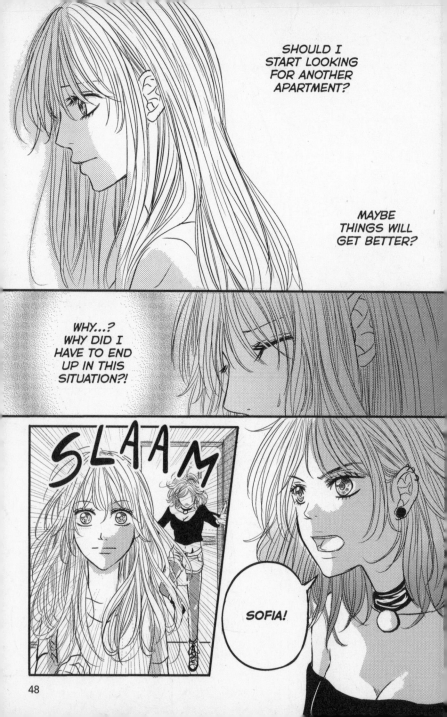

SHOULD I START LOOKING FOR ANOTHER APARTMENT?

MAYBE THINGS WILL GET BETTER?

WHY...? WHY DID I HAVE TO END UP IN THIS SITUATION?!

SLAAM

SOFIA!

48

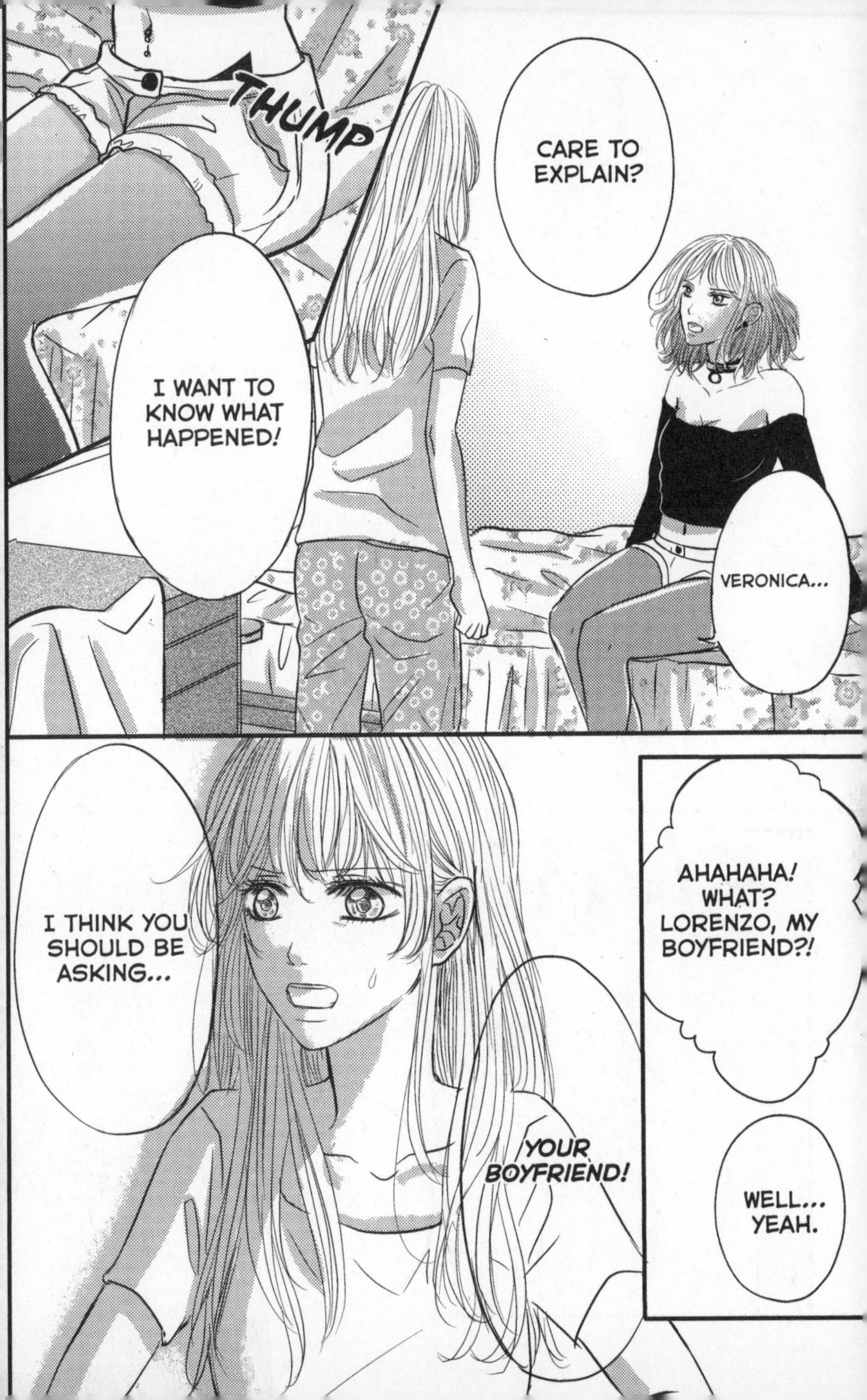
THUMP
I WANT TO KNOW WHAT HAPPENED!
CARE TO EXPLAIN?
VERONICA...
I THINK YOU SHOULD BE ASKING...
YOUR BOYFRIEND!
AHAHAHA! WHAT? LORENZO, MY BOYFRIEND?!
WELL... YEAH.

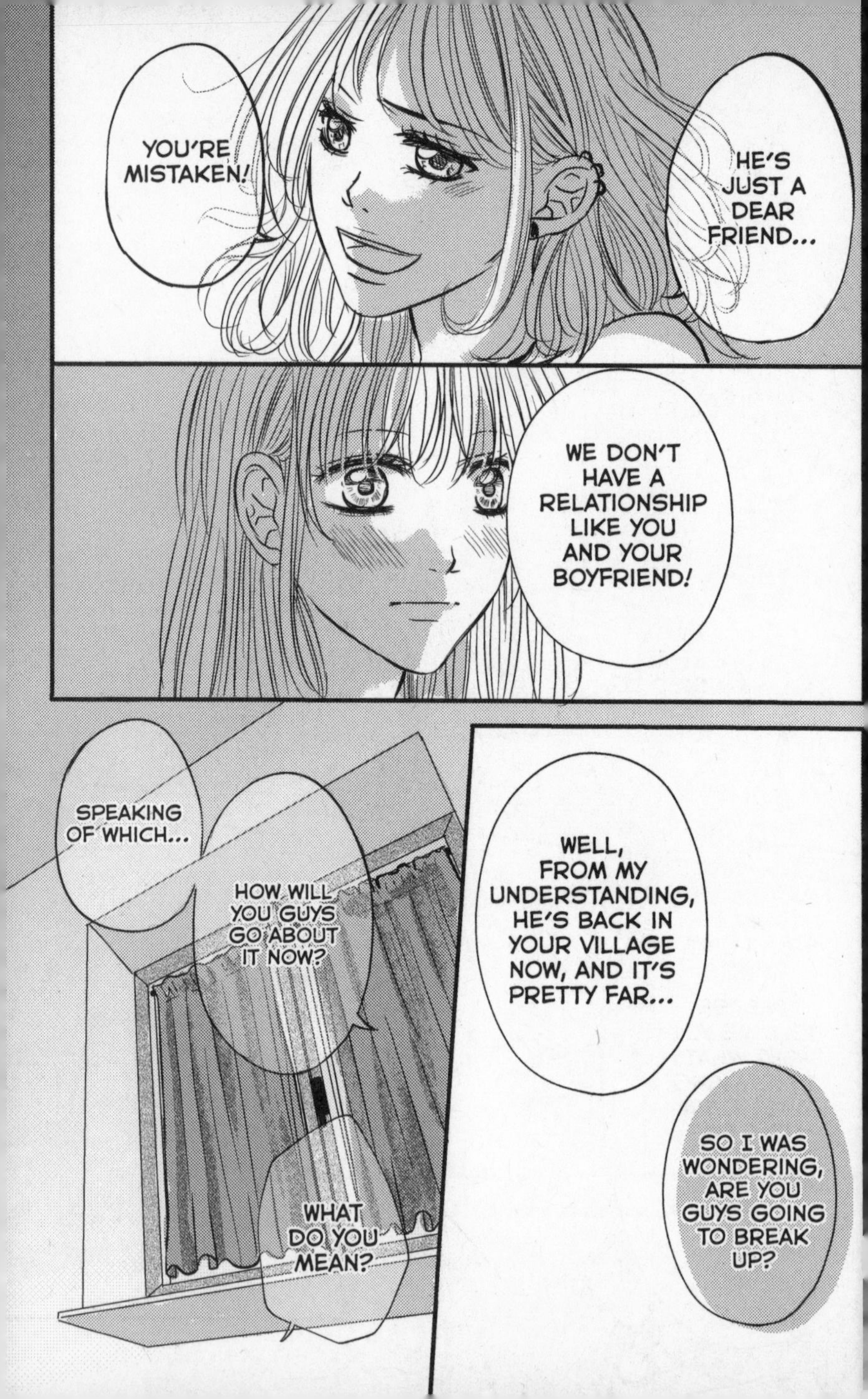
YOU'RE MISTAKEN!
HE'S JUST A DEAR FRIEND...
WE DON'T HAVE A RELATIONSHIP LIKE YOU AND YOUR BOYFRIEND!
SPEAKING OF WHICH...
HOW WILL YOU GUYS GO ABOUT IT NOW?
WHAT DO YOU MEAN?
WELL, FROM MY UNDERSTANDING, HE'S BACK IN YOUR VILLAGE NOW, AND IT'S PRETTY FAR...
SO I WAS WONDERING, ARE YOU GUYS GOING TO BREAK UP?

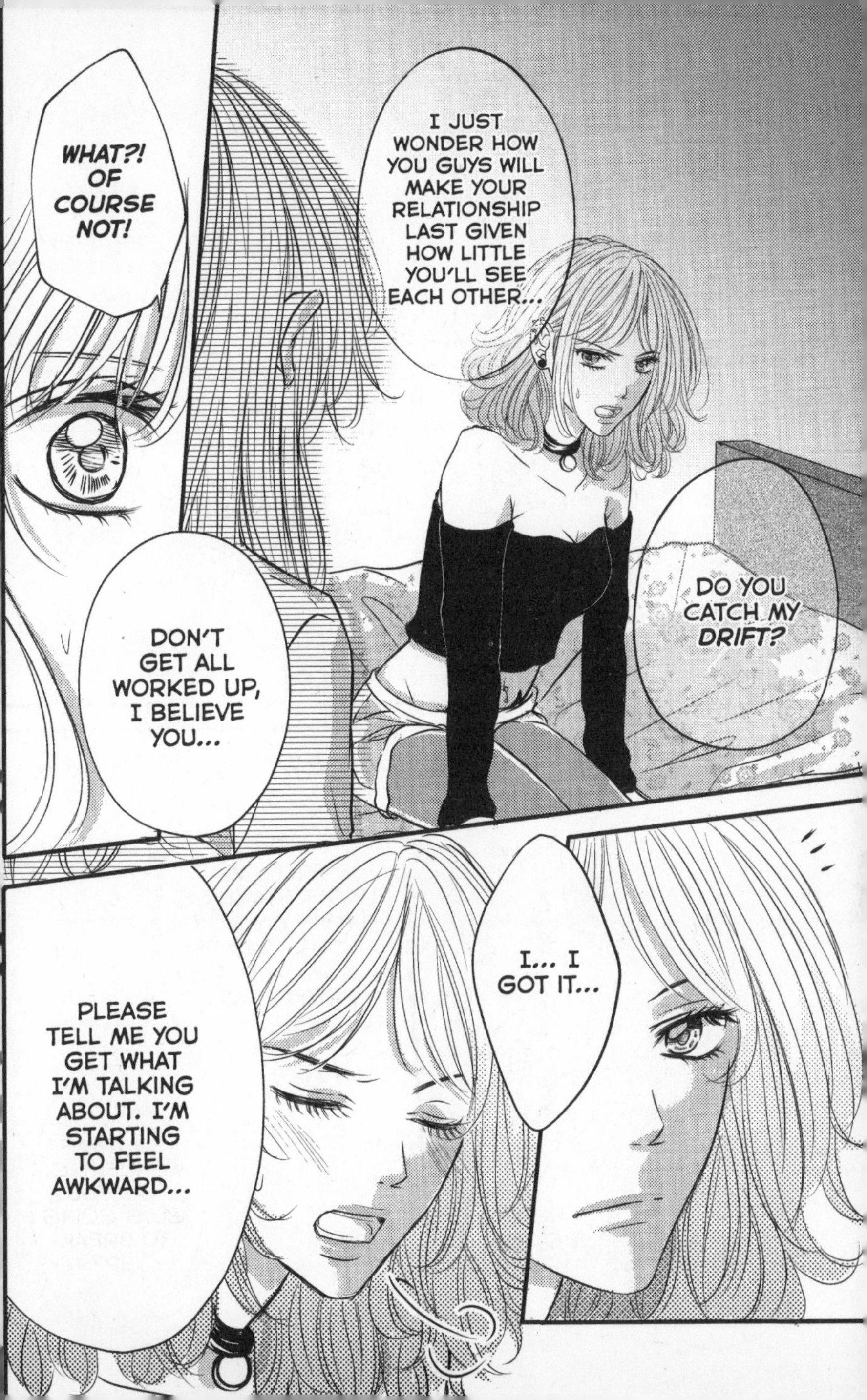
WHAT?! OF COURSE NOT!
DON'T GET ALL WORKED UP, I BELIEVE YOU...
I JUST WONDER HOW YOU GUYS WILL MAKE YOUR RELATIONSHIP LAST GIVEN HOW LITTLE YOU'LL SEE EACH OTHER...
DO YOU CATCH MY *DRIFT?*
PLEASE TELL ME YOU GET WHAT I'M TALKING ABOUT. I'M STARTING TO FEEL AWKWARD...
I... I GOT IT...

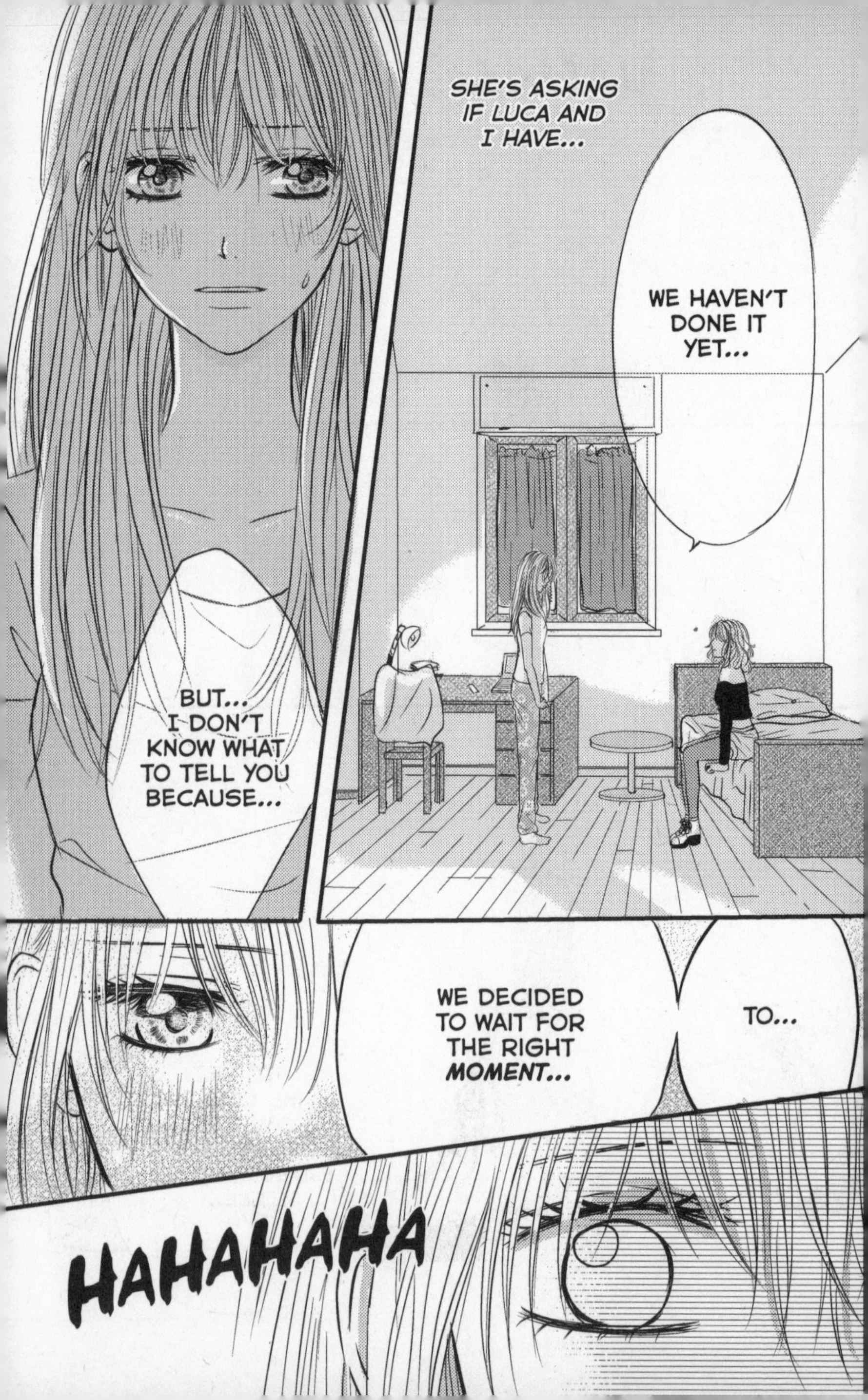
SHE'S ASKING IF LUCA AND I HAVE...
WE HAVEN'T DONE IT YET...
BUT... I DON'T KNOW WHAT TO TELL YOU BECAUSE...
WE DECIDED TO WAIT FOR THE RIGHT *MOMENT*...
TO...
HAHAHAHA

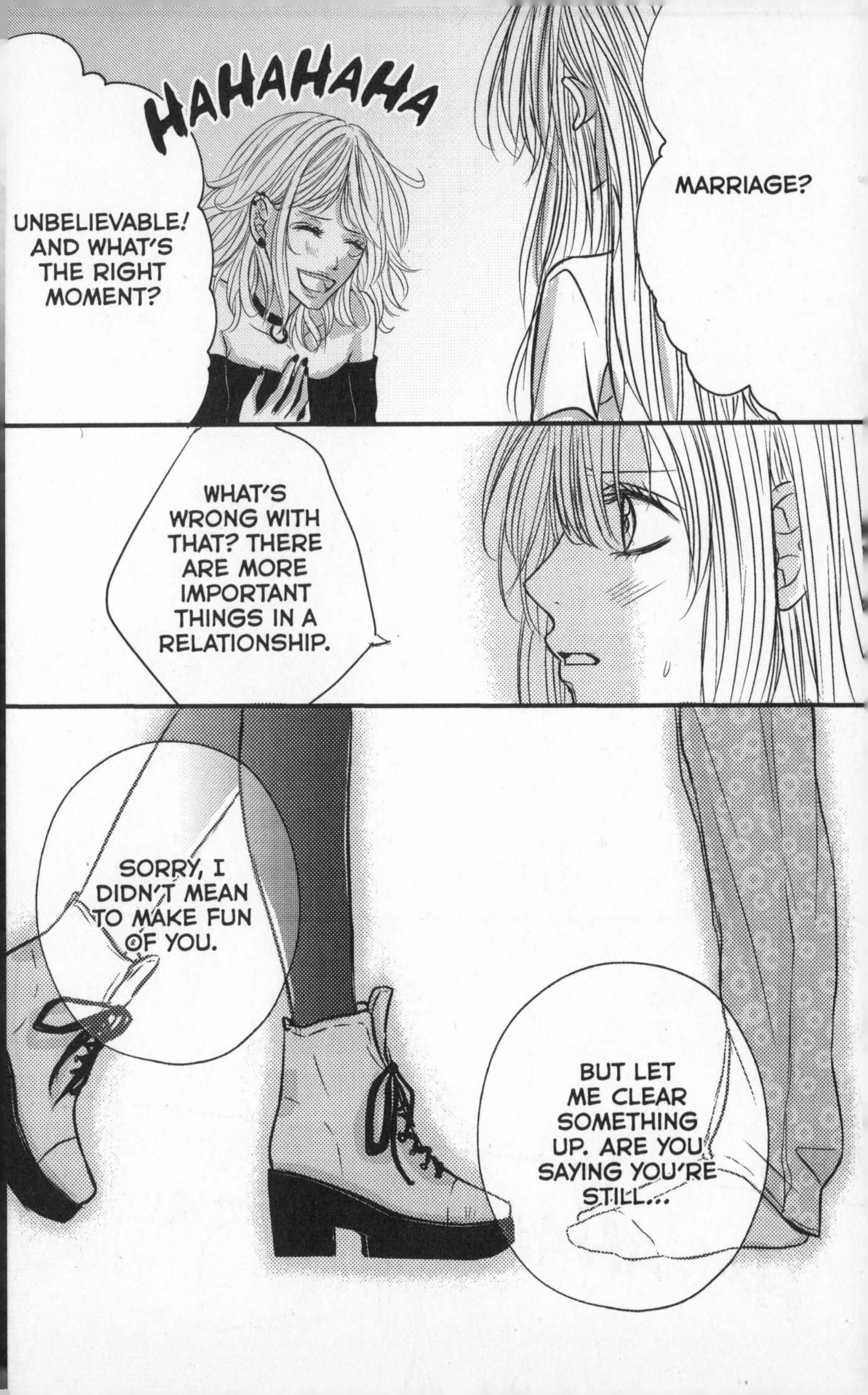
MARRIAGE?
HAHAHAHA
UNBELIEVABLE! AND WHAT'S THE RIGHT MOMENT?
WHAT'S WRONG WITH THAT? THERE ARE MORE IMPORTANT THINGS IN A RELATIONSHIP.
SORRY, I DIDN'T MEAN TO MAKE FUN OF YOU.
BUT LET ME CLEAR SOMETHING UP. ARE YOU SAYING YOU'RE STILL...

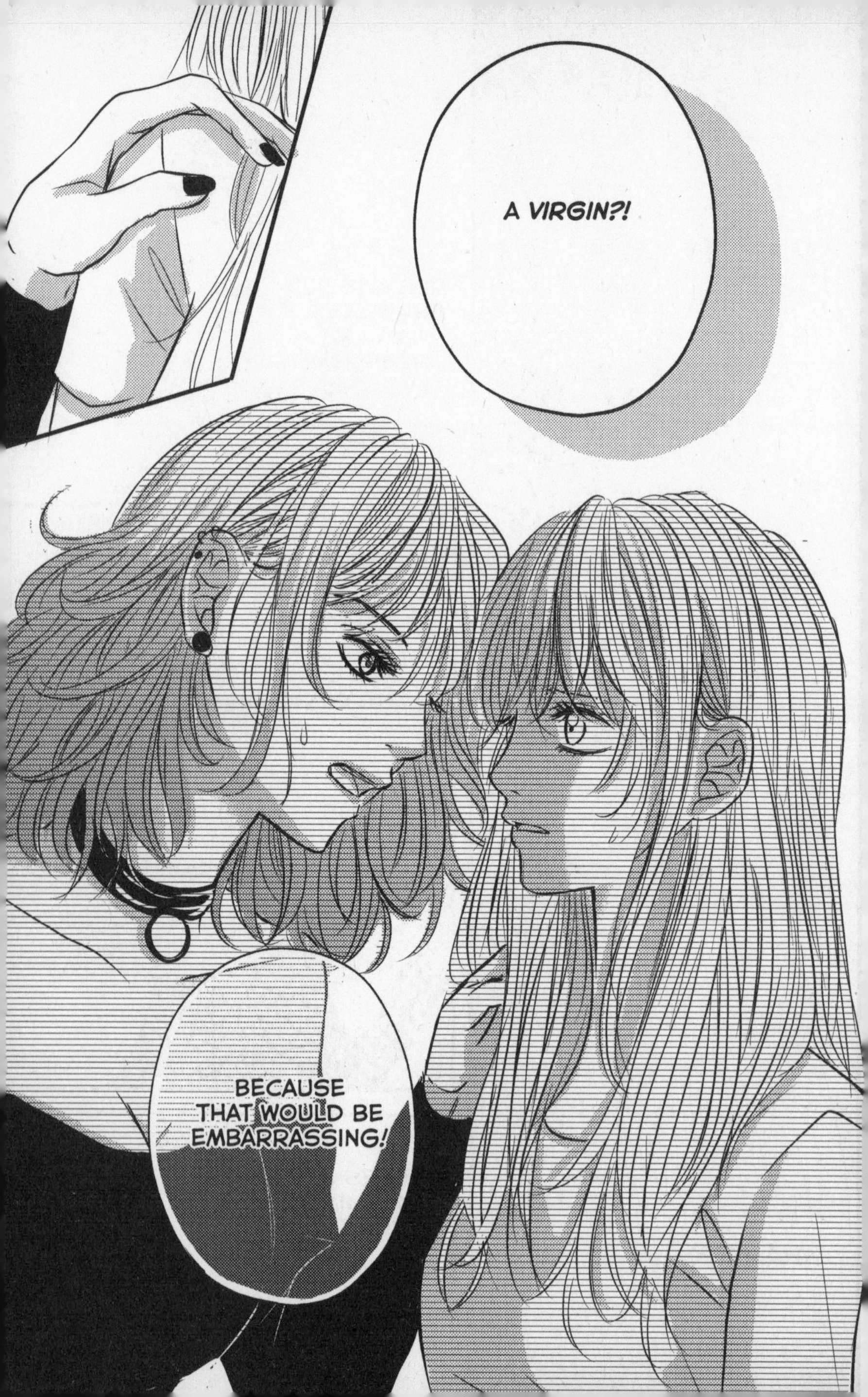
A VIRGIN?!
BECAUSE THAT WOULD BE EMBARRASSING!

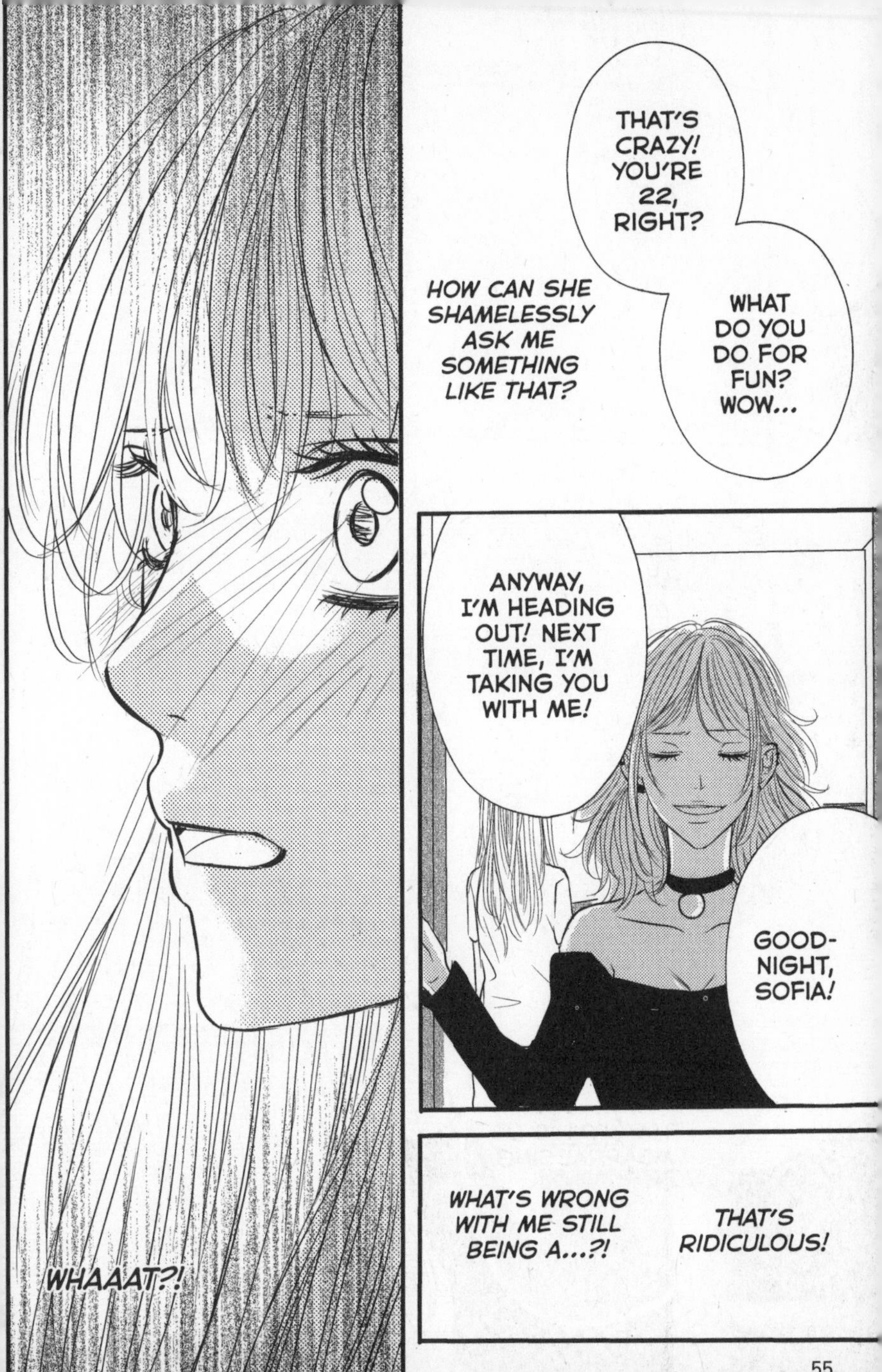
THAT'S CRAZY! YOU'RE 22, RIGHT?
WHAT DO YOU DO FOR FUN? WOW...
HOW CAN SHE SHAMELESSLY ASK ME SOMETHING LIKE THAT?
ANYWAY, I'M HEADING OUT! NEXT TIME, I'M TAKING YOU WITH ME!
GOOD-NIGHT, SOFIA!
THAT'S RIDICULOUS!
WHAT'S WRONG WITH ME STILL BEING A...?!
WHAAAT?!

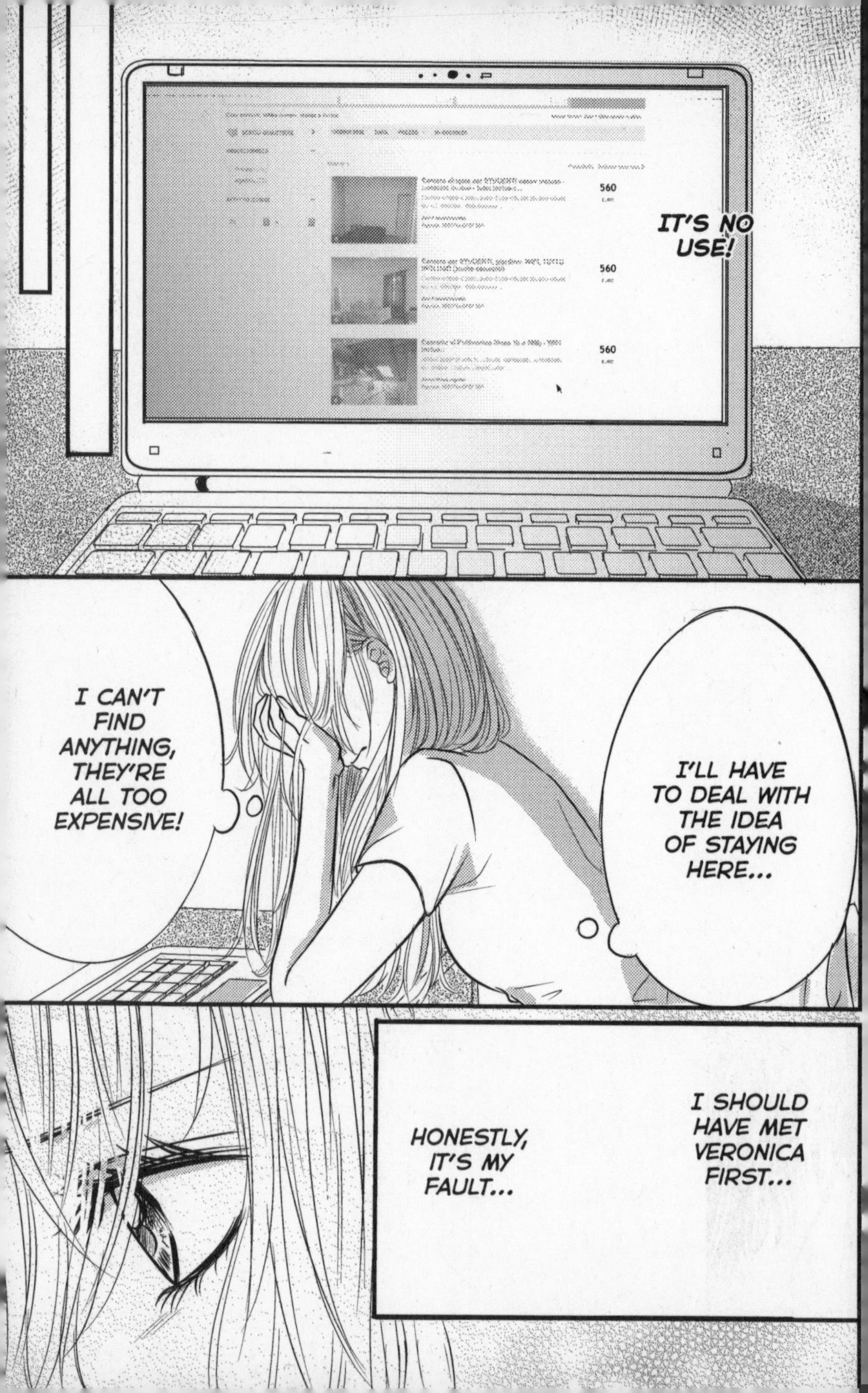
IT'S NO USE!
I CAN'T FIND ANYTHING, THEY'RE ALL TOO EXPENSIVE!
I'LL HAVE TO DEAL WITH THE IDEA OF STAYING HERE...
HONESTLY, IT'S MY FAULT...
I SHOULD HAVE MET VERONICA FIRST...

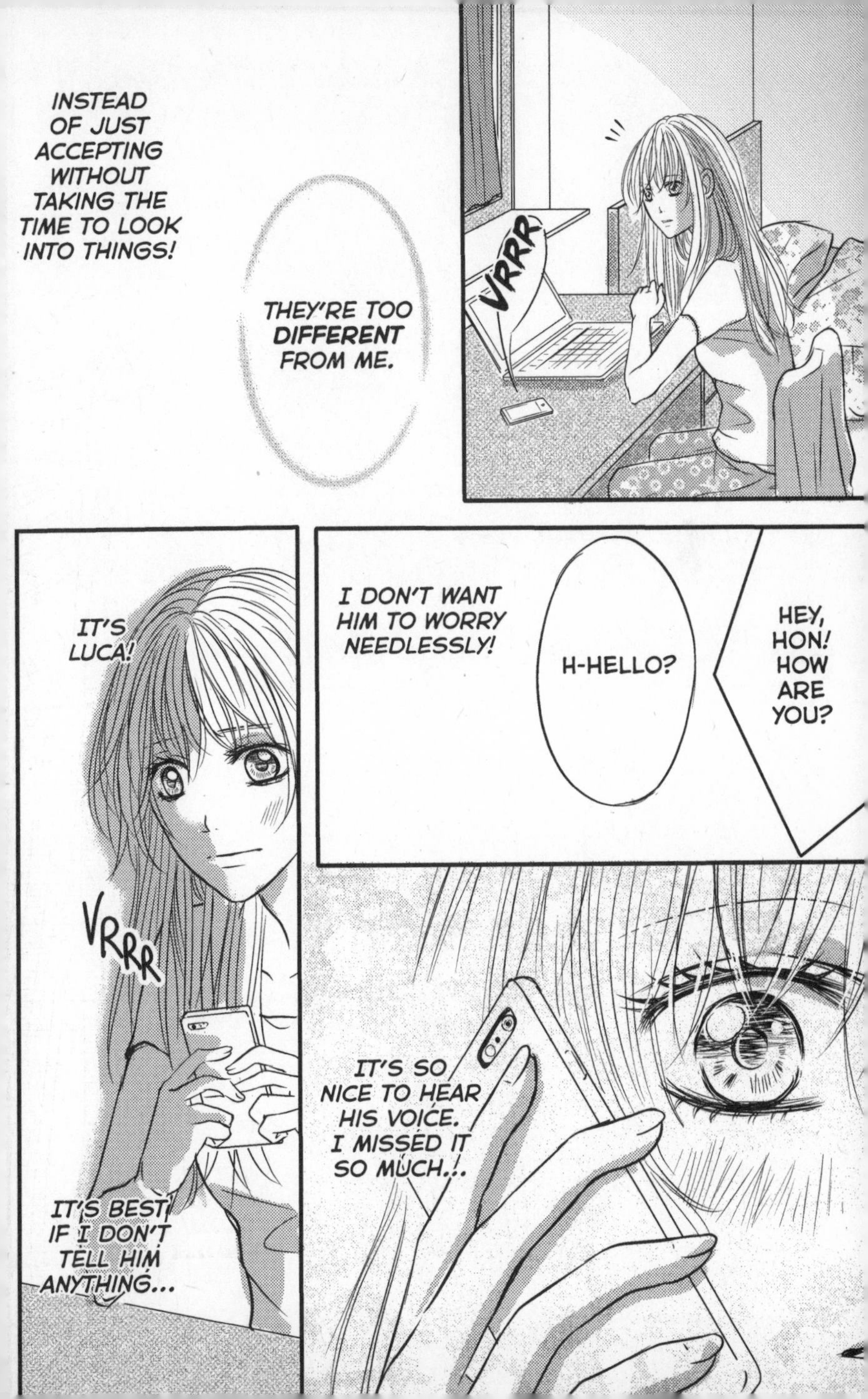
INSTEAD OF JUST ACCEPTING WITHOUT TAKING THE TIME TO LOOK INTO THINGS!
THEY'RE TOO DIFFERENT FROM ME.
VRRR
IT'S LUCA!
VRRR
IT'S BEST IF I DON'T TELL HIM ANYTHING...
HEY, HON! HOW ARE YOU?
H-HELLO?
I DON'T WANT HIM TO WORRY NEEDLESSLY!
IT'S SO NICE TO HEAR HIS VOICE. I MISSED IT SO MUCH...

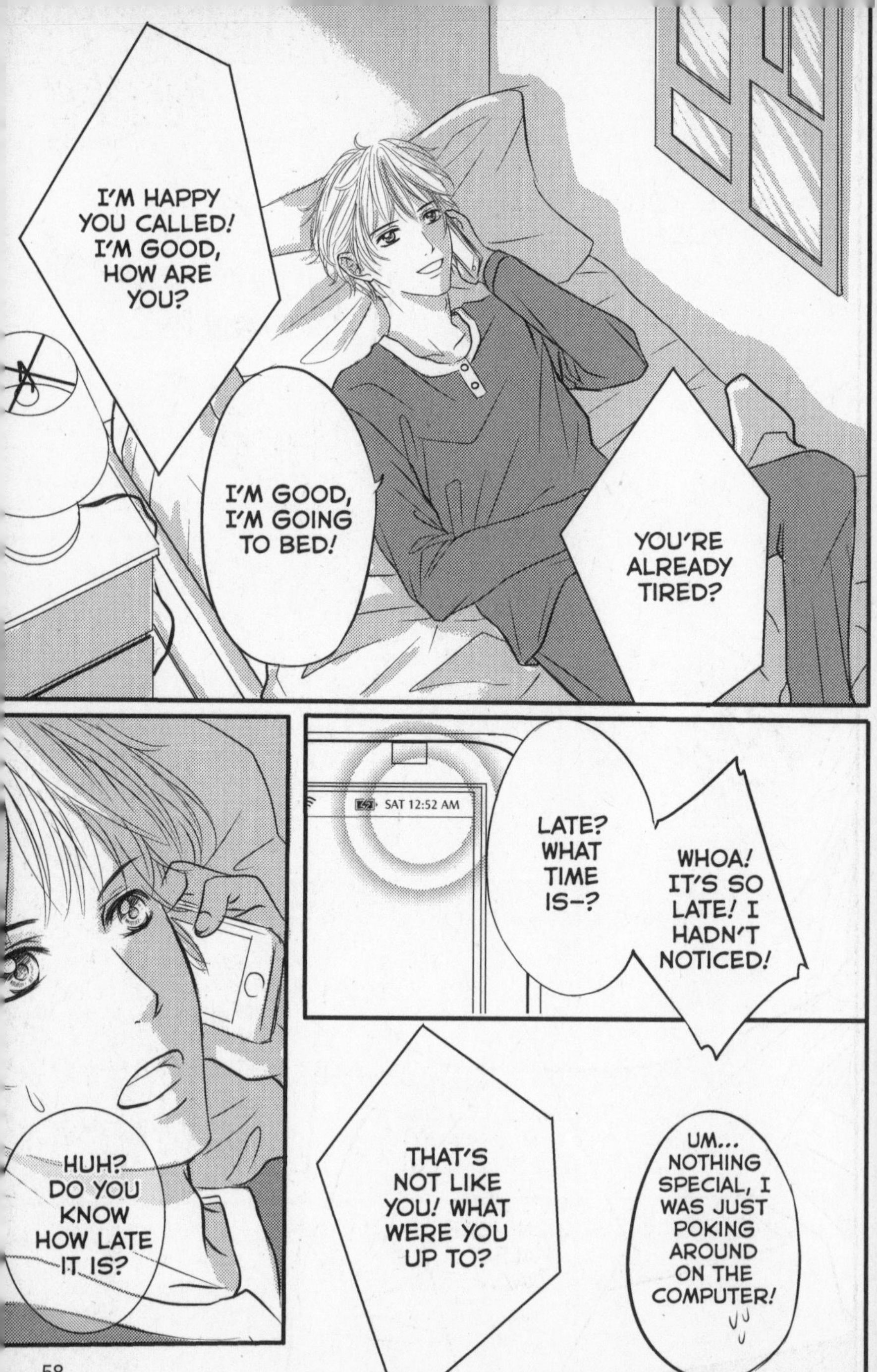
I'M HAPPY YOU CALLED! I'M GOOD, HOW ARE YOU?
I'M GOOD, I'M GOING TO BED!
YOU'RE ALREADY TIRED?
HUH? DO YOU KNOW HOW LATE IT IS?
SAT 12:52 AM
LATE? WHAT TIME IS–?
WHOA! IT'S SO LATE! I HADN'T NOTICED!
THAT'S NOT LIKE YOU! WHAT WERE YOU UP TO?
UM... NOTHING SPECIAL, I WAS JUST POKING AROUND ON THE COMPUTER!

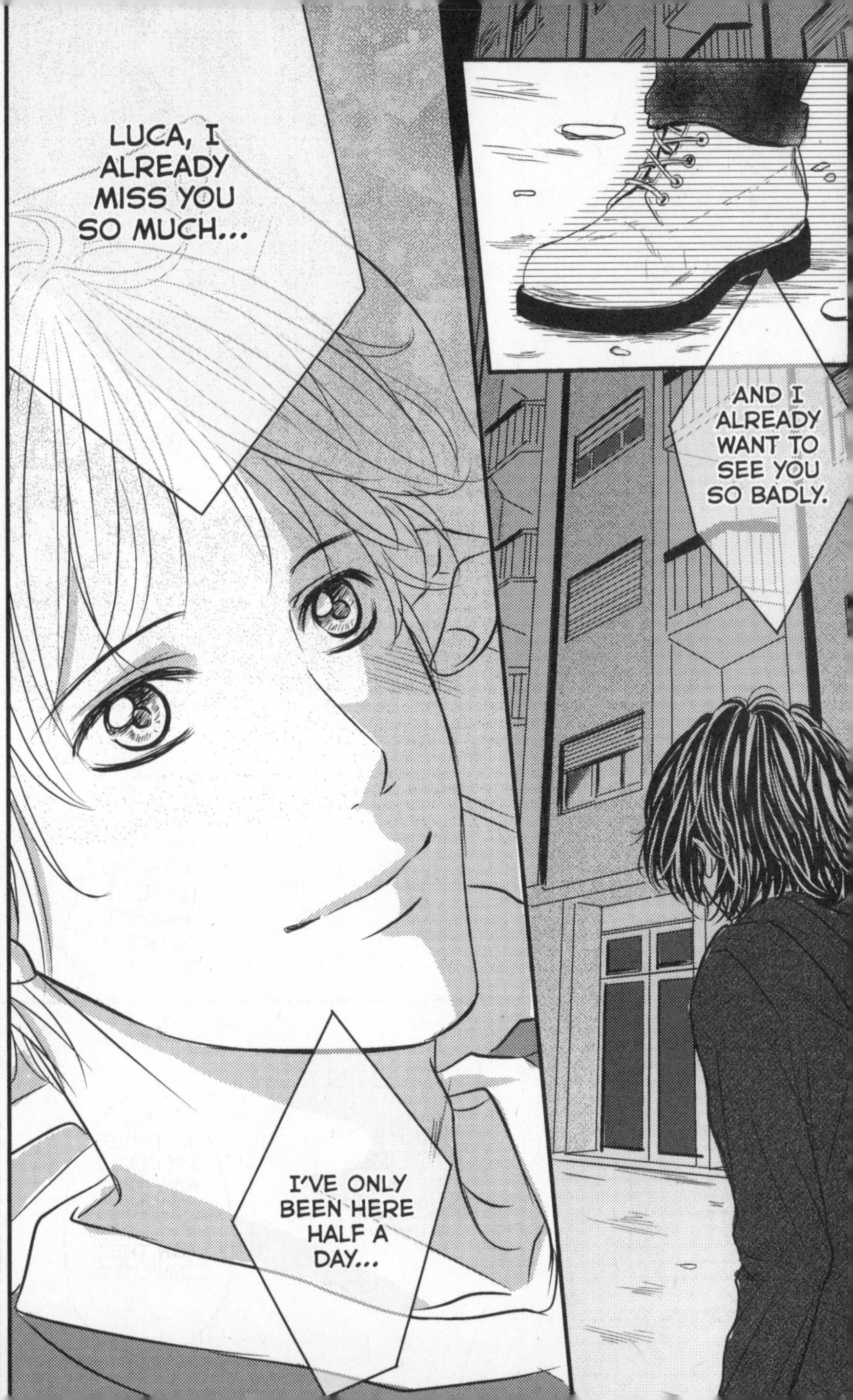
LUCA, I ALREADY MISS YOU SO MUCH...
AND I ALREADY WANT TO SEE YOU SO BADLY.
I'VE ONLY BEEN HERE HALF A DAY...

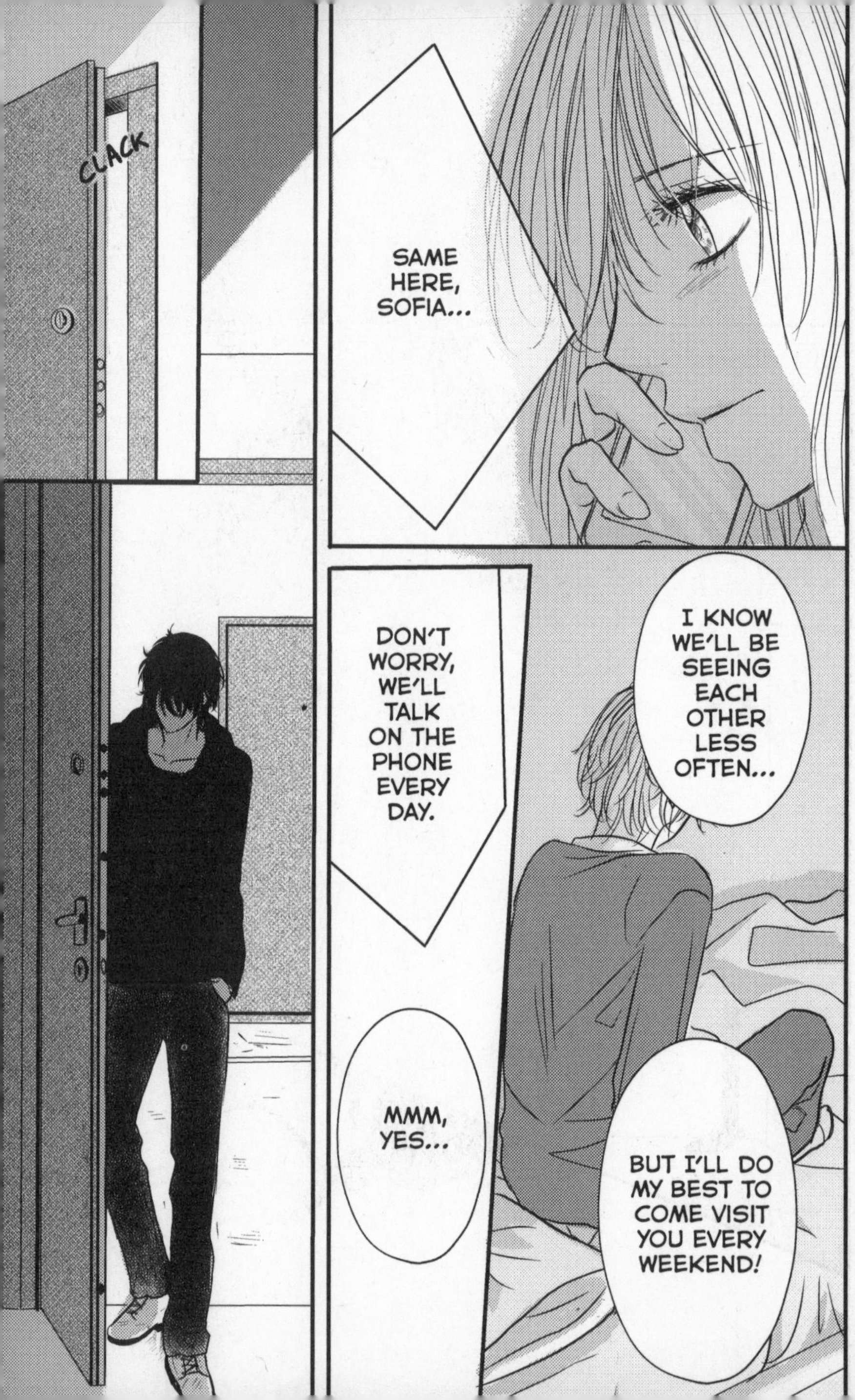
SAME HERE, SOFIA...
I KNOW WE'LL BE SEEING EACH OTHER LESS OFTEN...
BUT I'LL DO MY BEST TO COME VISIT YOU EVERY WEEKEND!
DON'T WORRY, WE'LL TALK ON THE PHONE EVERY DAY.
MMM, YES...
CLACK

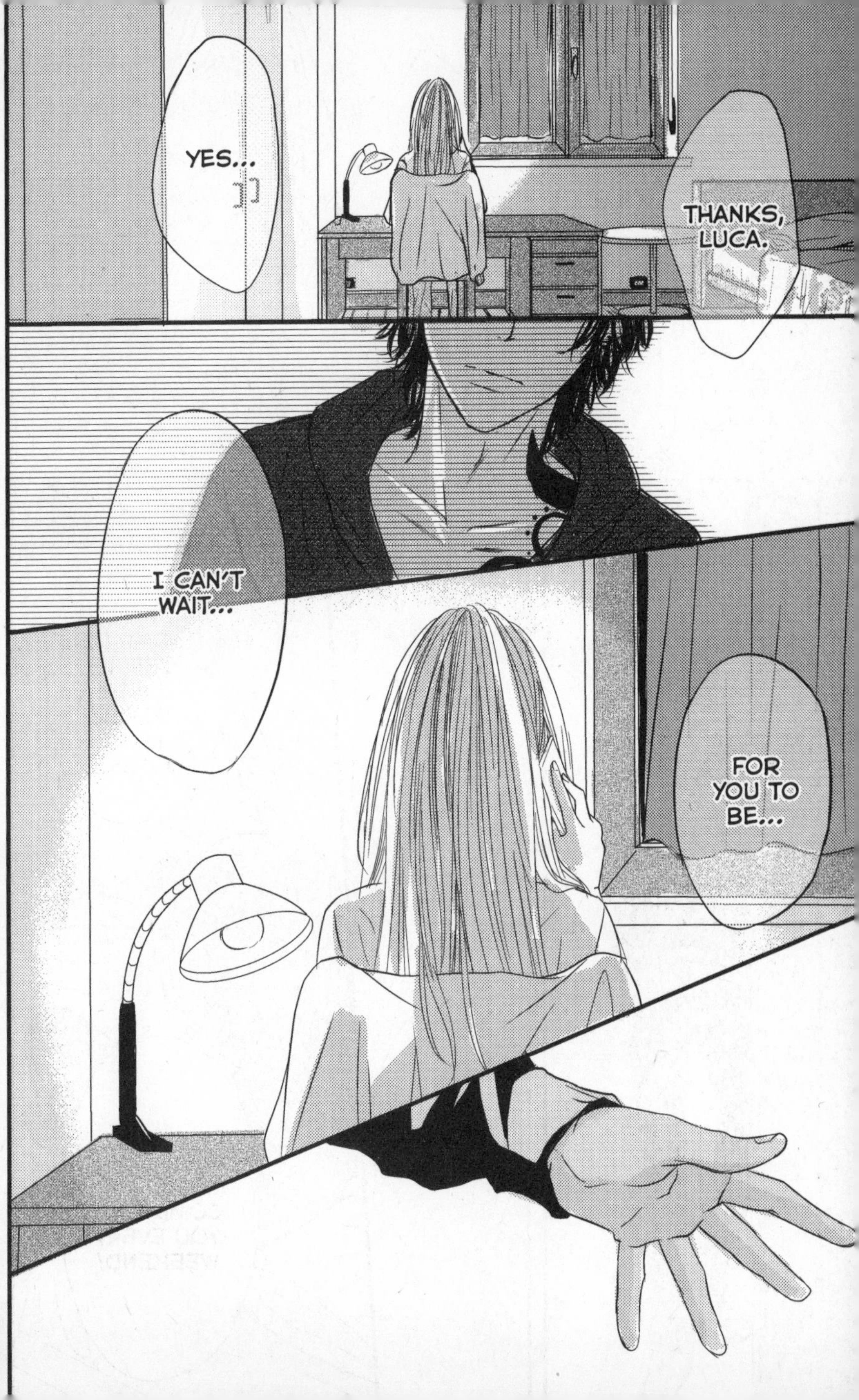
THANKS, LUCA.
YES...
I CAN'T WAIT...
FOR YOU TO BE...

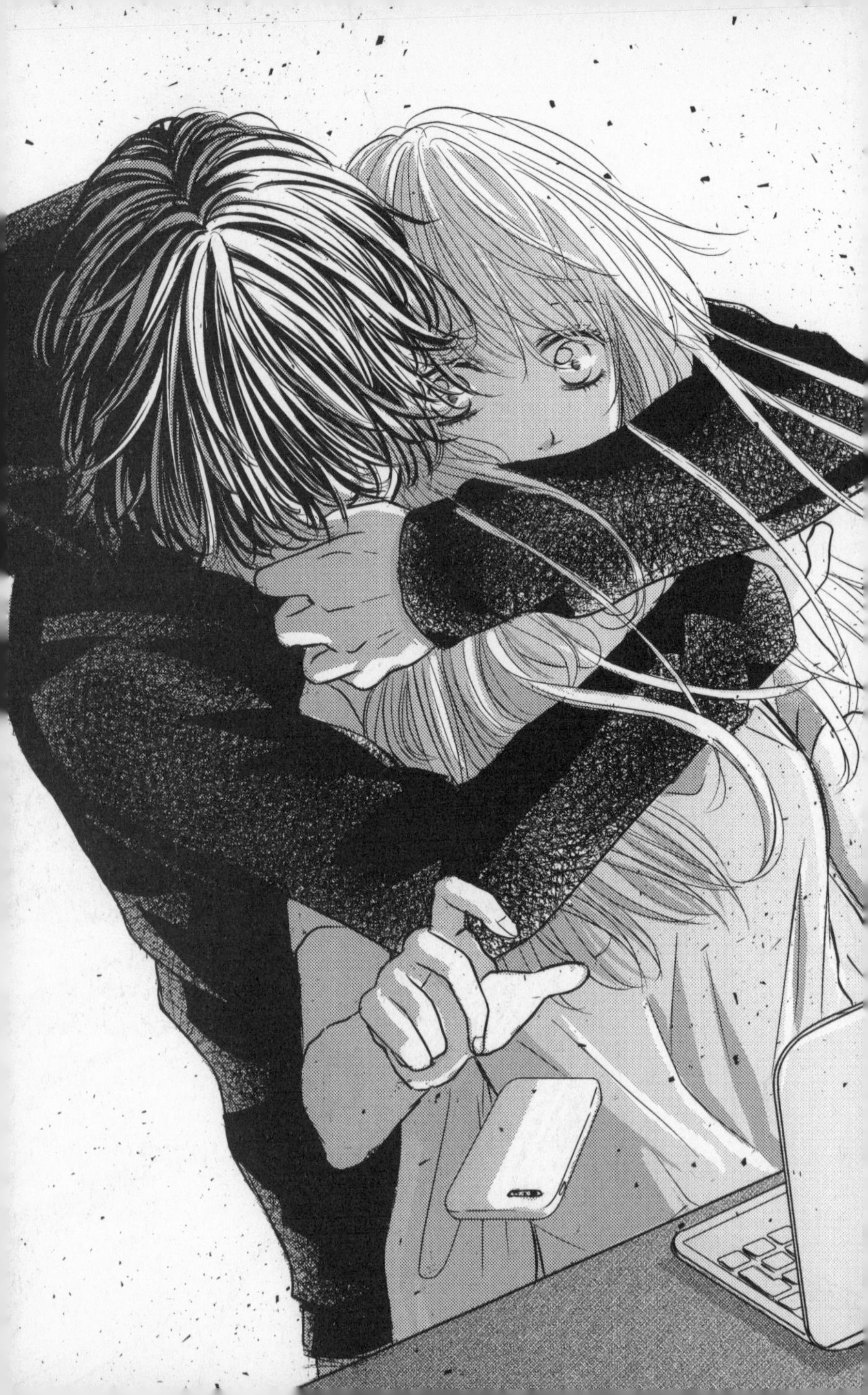

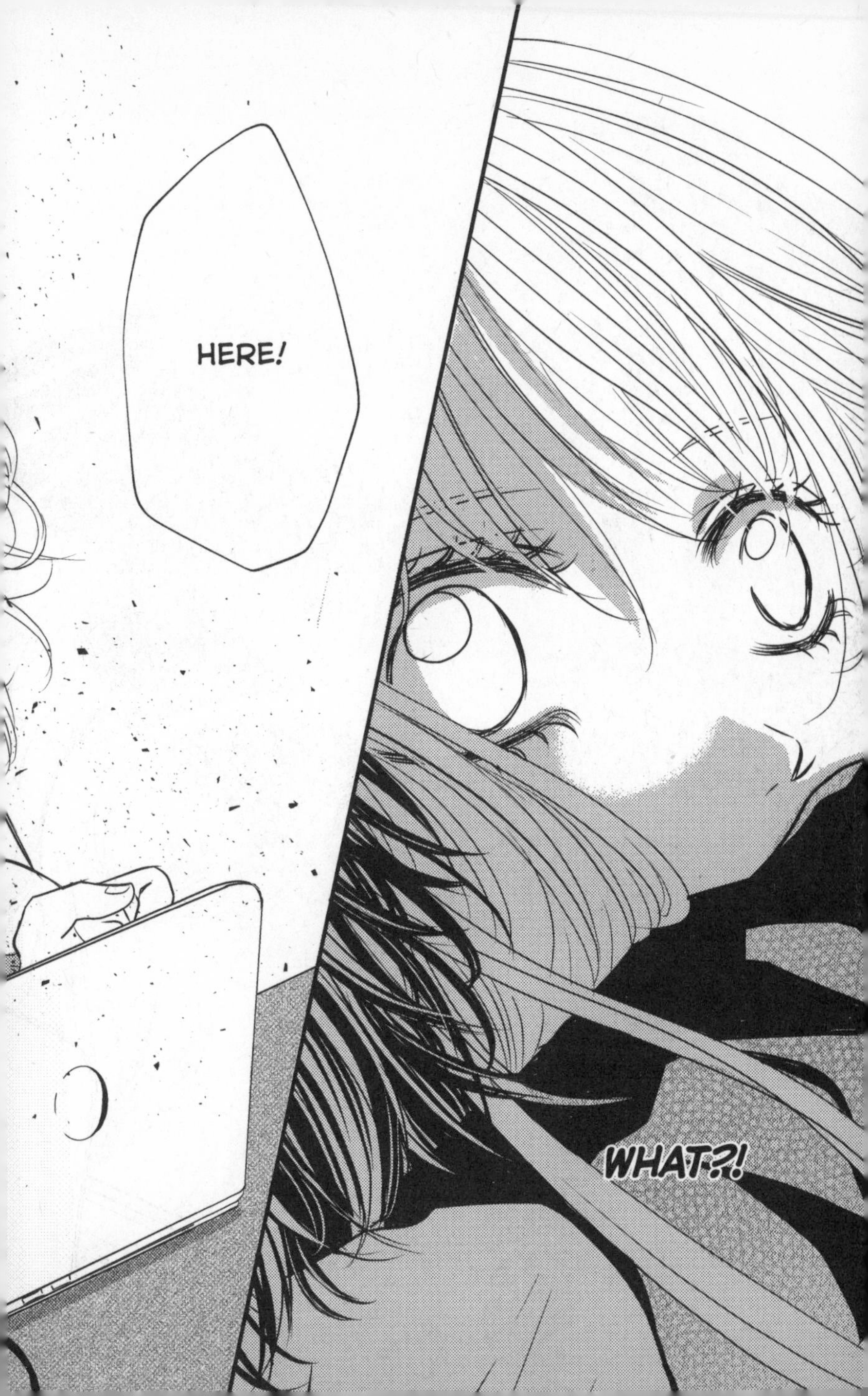
WHAT?!
HERE!

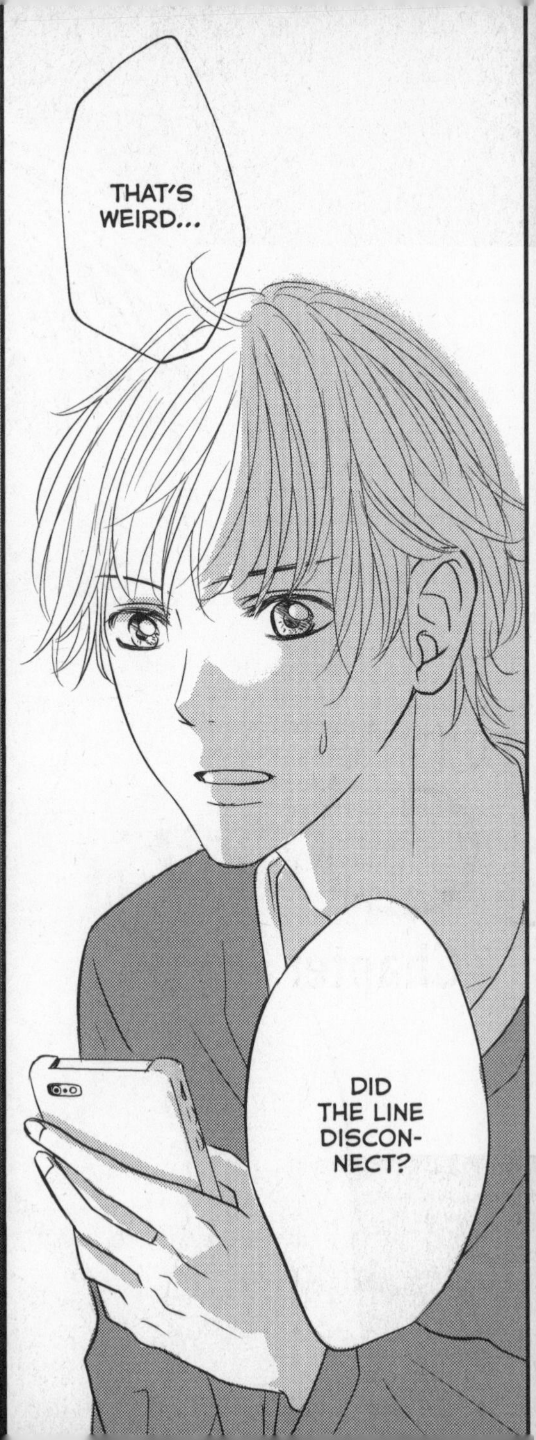
THAT'S WEIRD...
DID THE LINE DISCON-NECT?
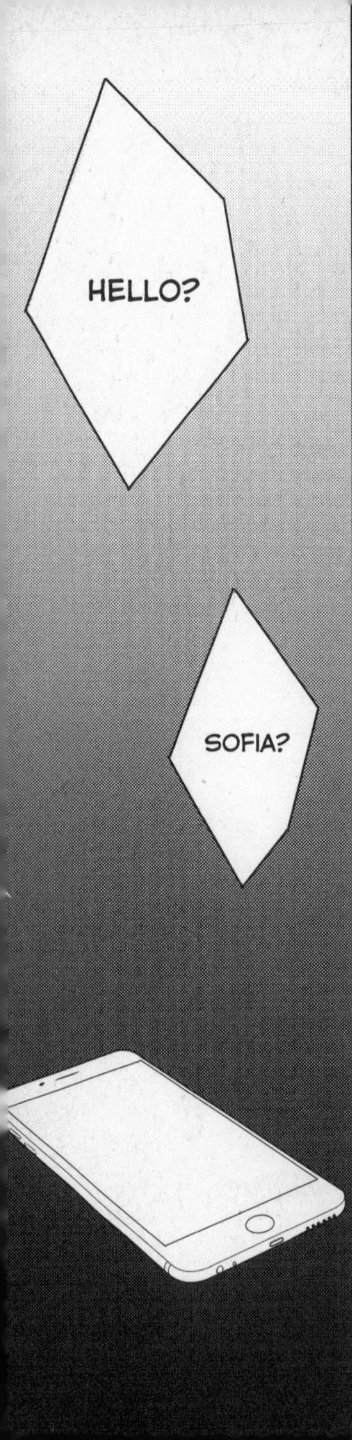
HELLO?
SOFIA?

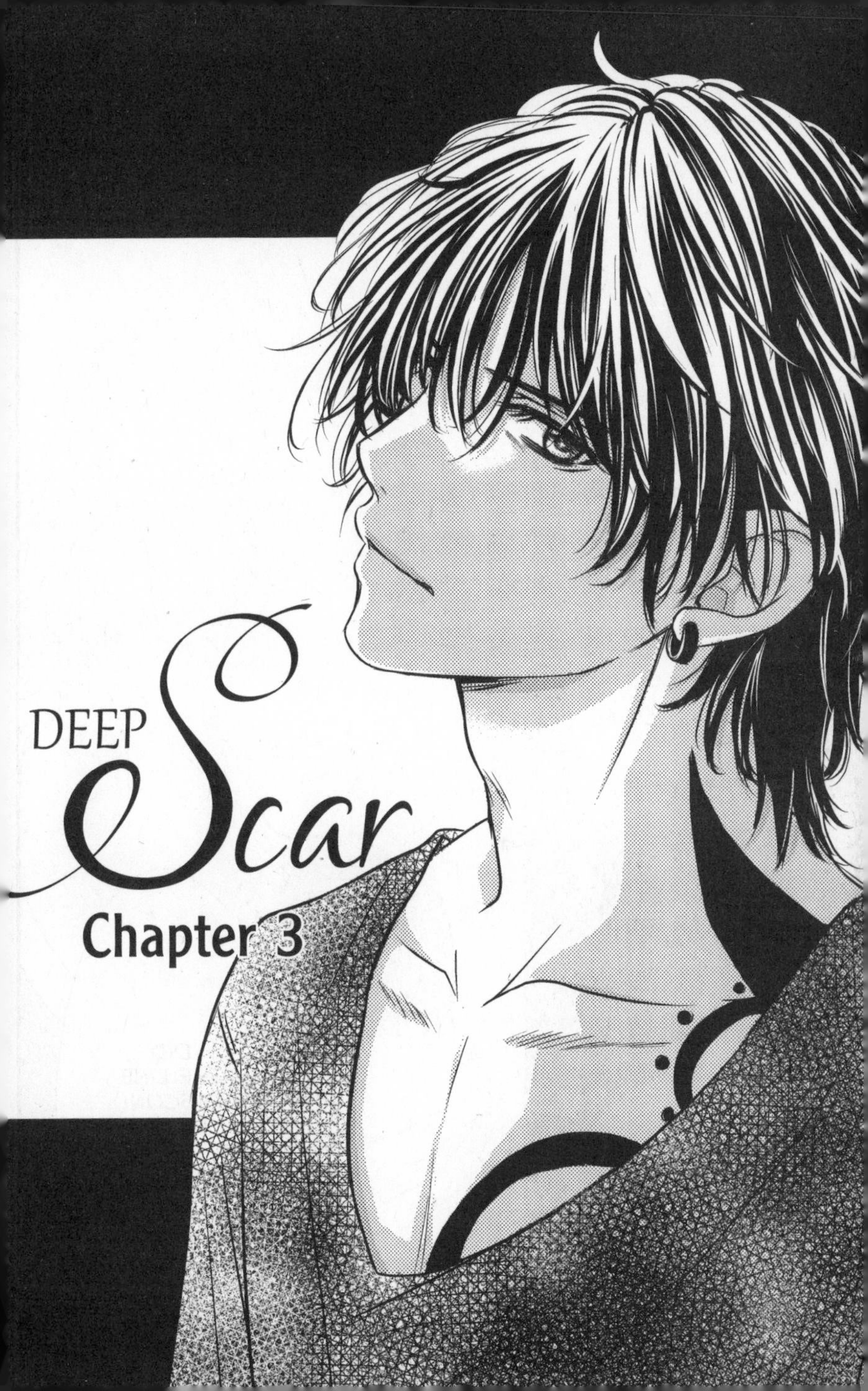
DEEP Scar
Chapter 3

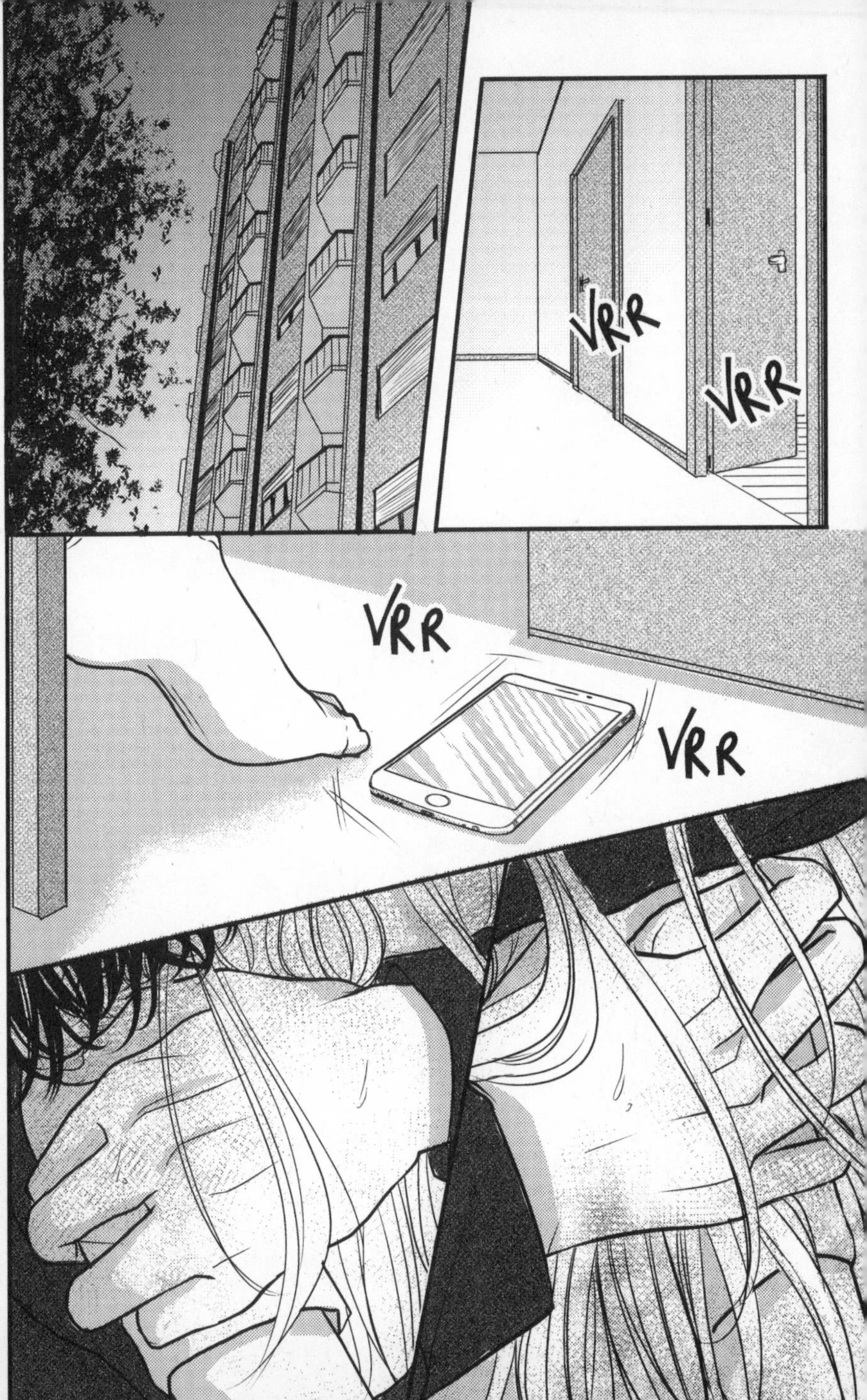
VRR
VRR
VRR
VRR

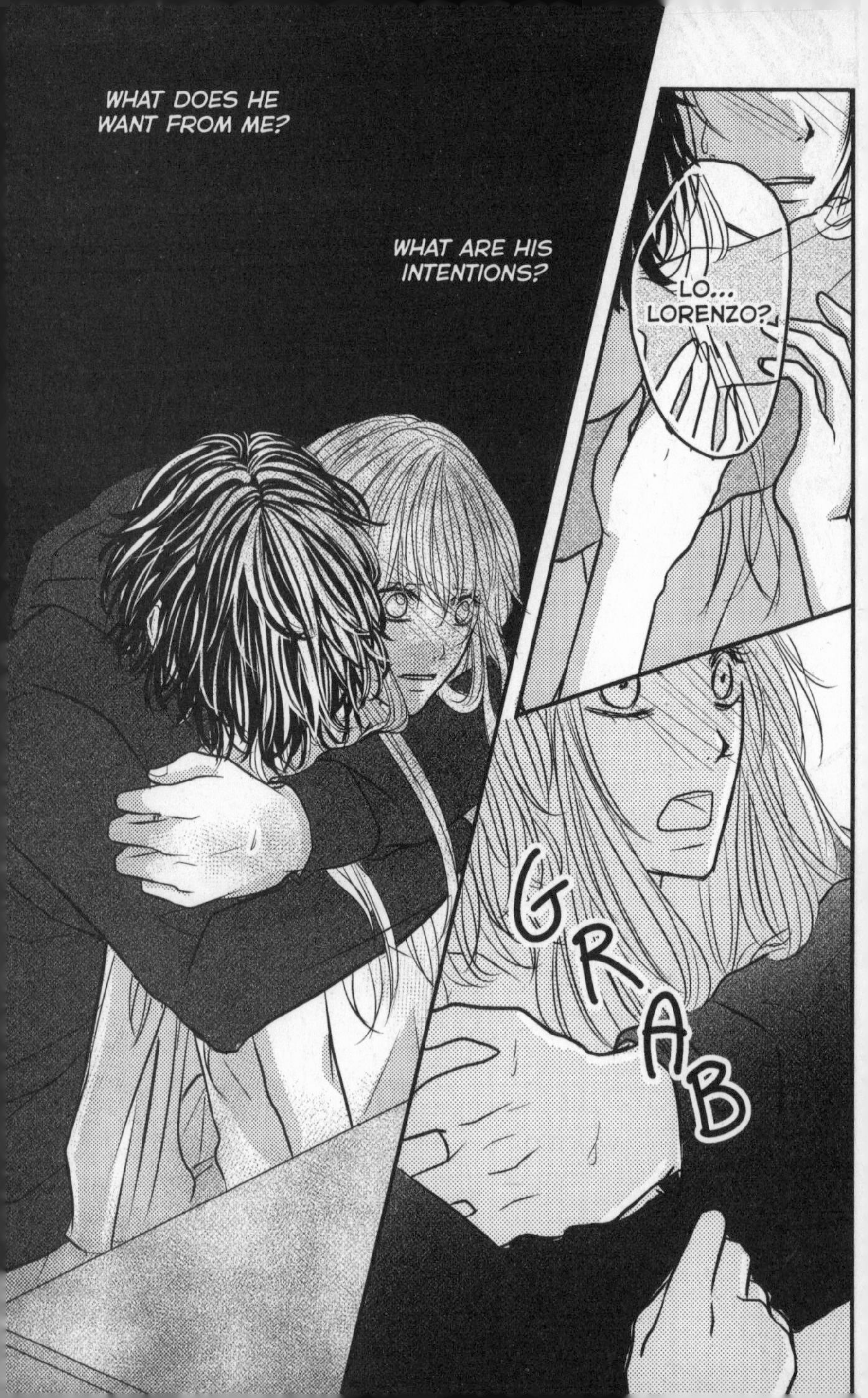
LO...
LORENZO?
GRAB
WHAT DOES HE WANT FROM ME?
WHAT ARE HIS INTENTIONS?

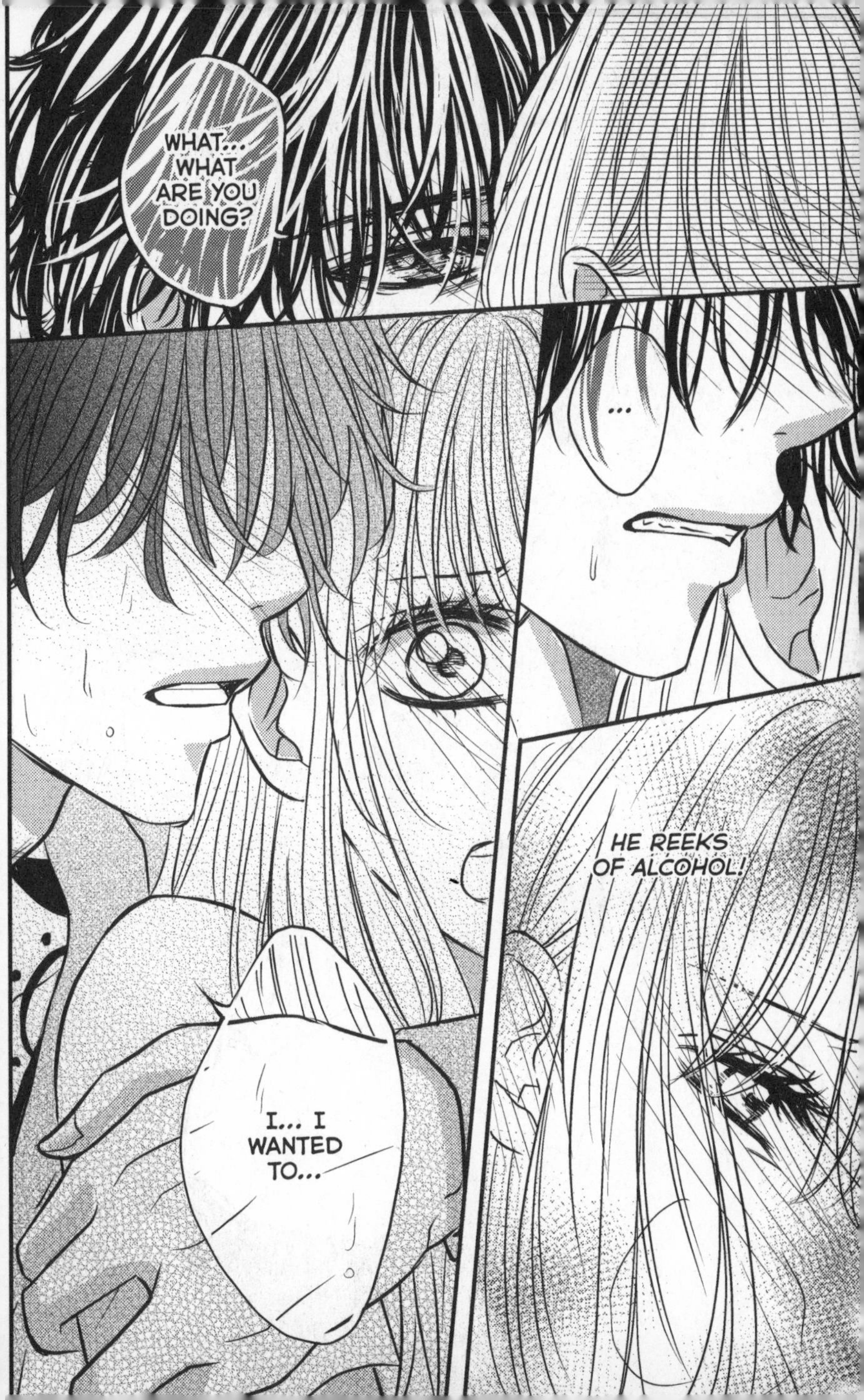
WHAT... WHAT ARE YOU DOING?
...
HE REEKS OF ALCOHOL!
I... I WANTED TO...

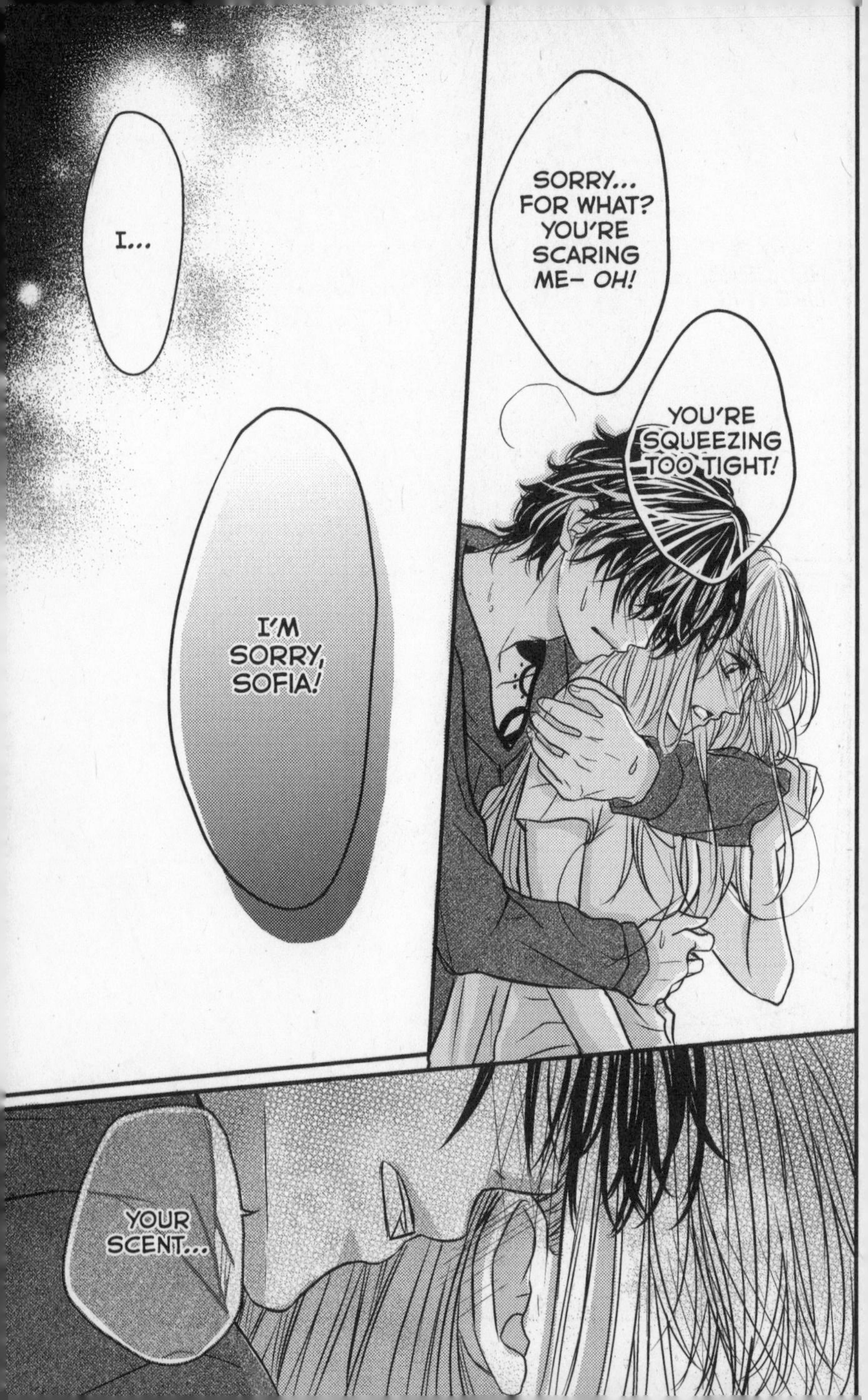
I...
I'M SORRY, SOFIA!
SORRY... FOR WHAT? YOU'RE SCARING ME— *OH!*
YOU'RE SQUEEZING TOO TIGHT!
YOUR SCENT...

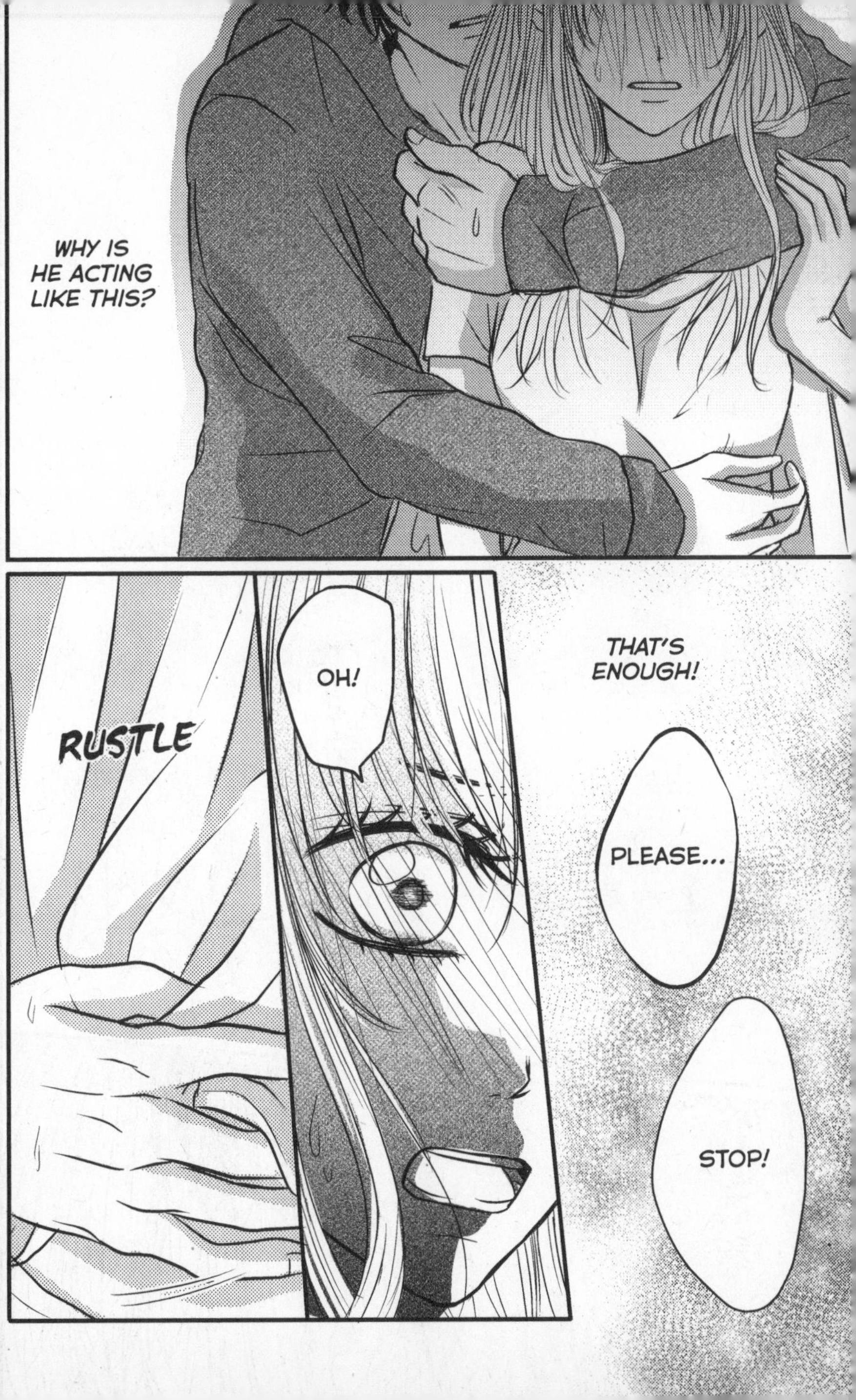
WHY IS HE ACTING LIKE THIS?
THAT'S ENOUGH!
PLEASE...
STOP!
OH!
RUSTLE

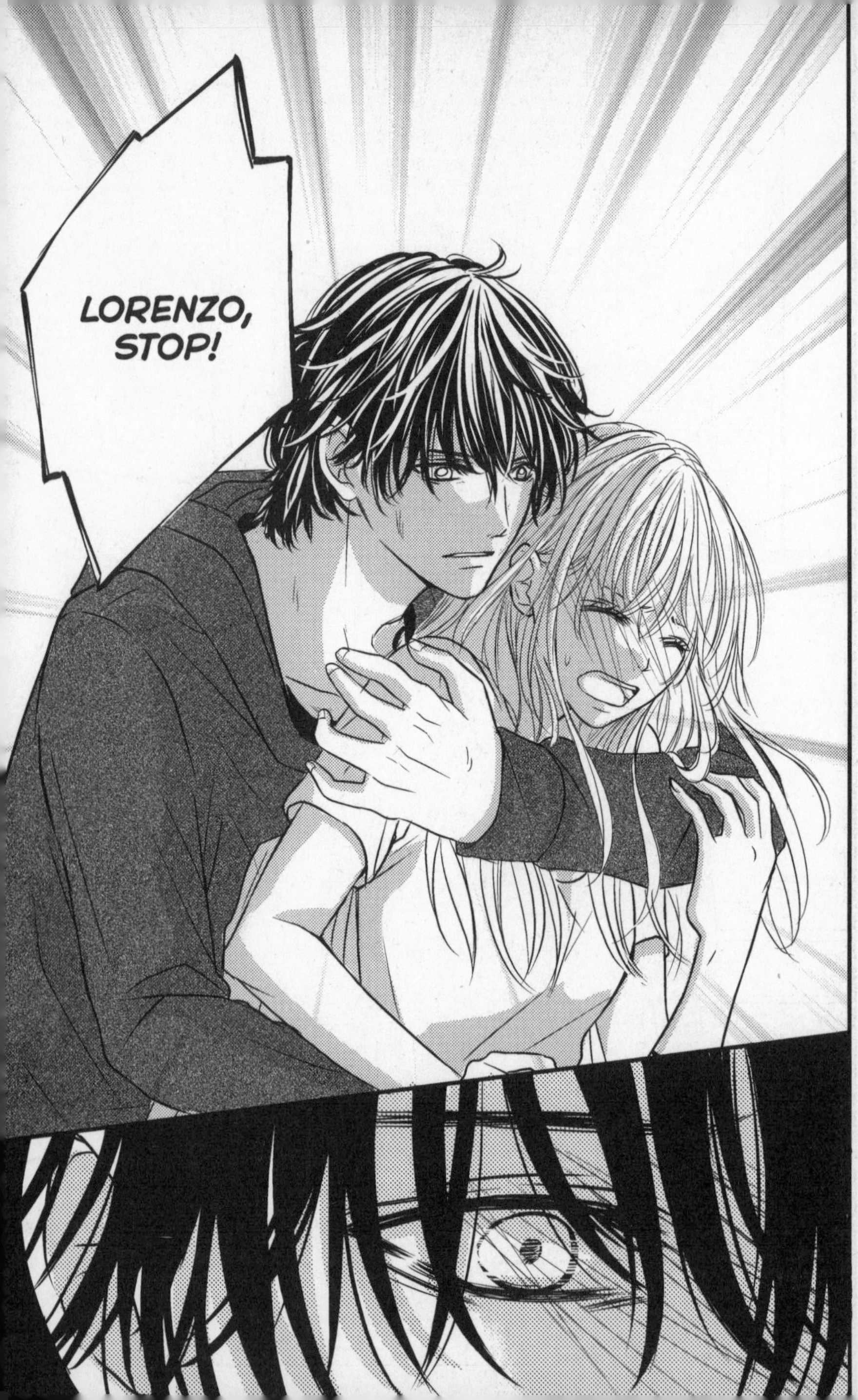
LORENZO, STOP!

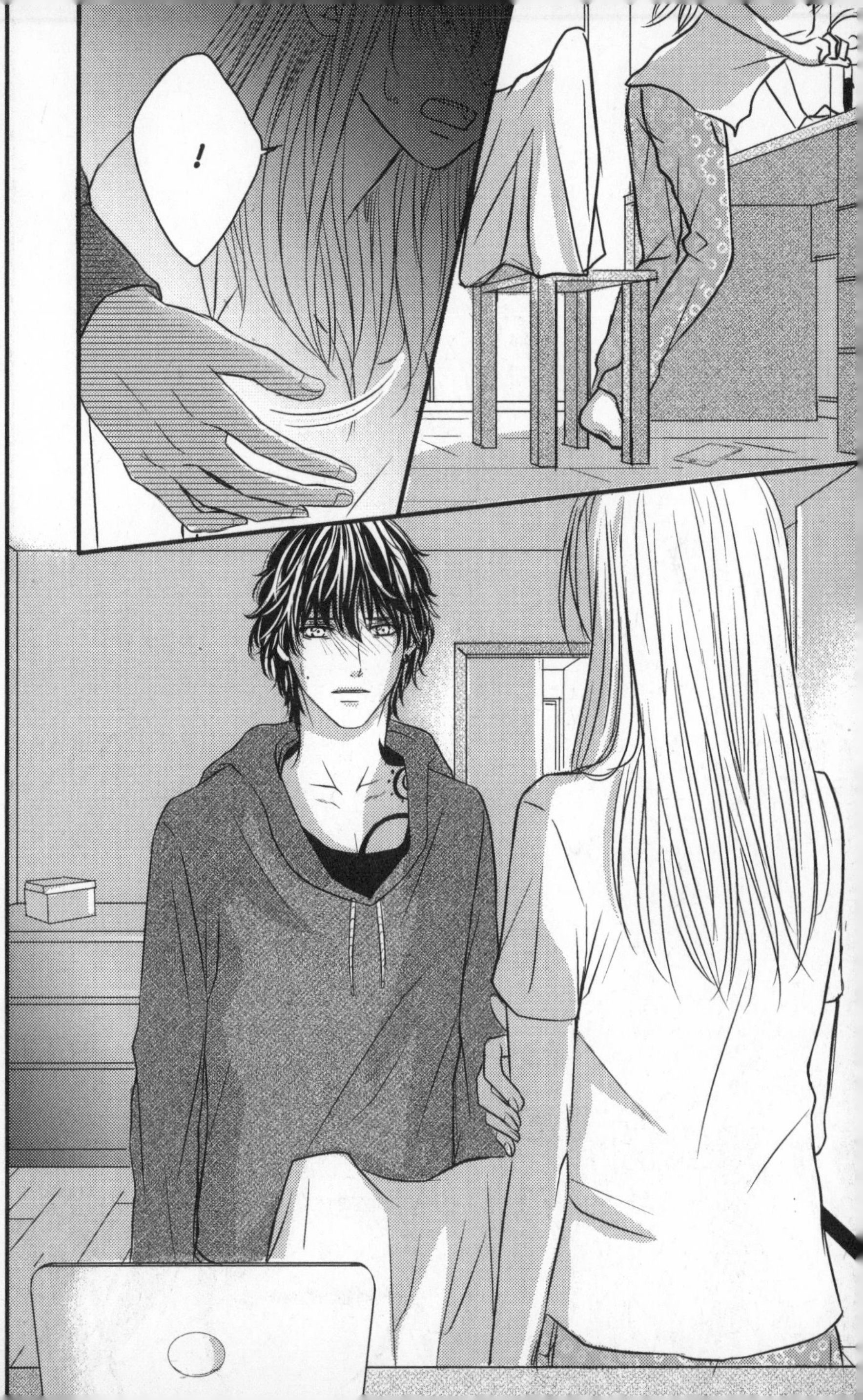
!

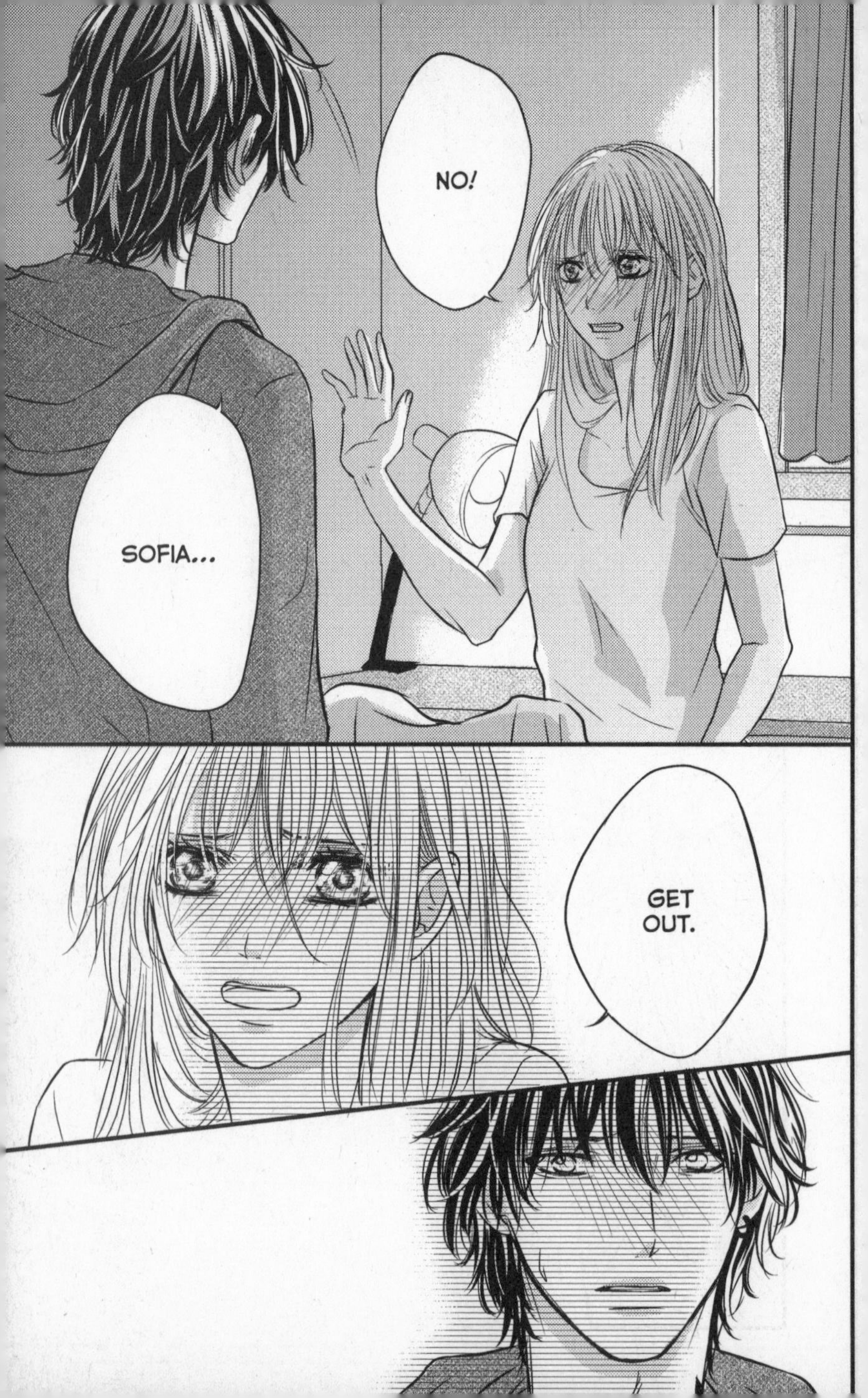
NO!
SOFIA...
GET OUT.

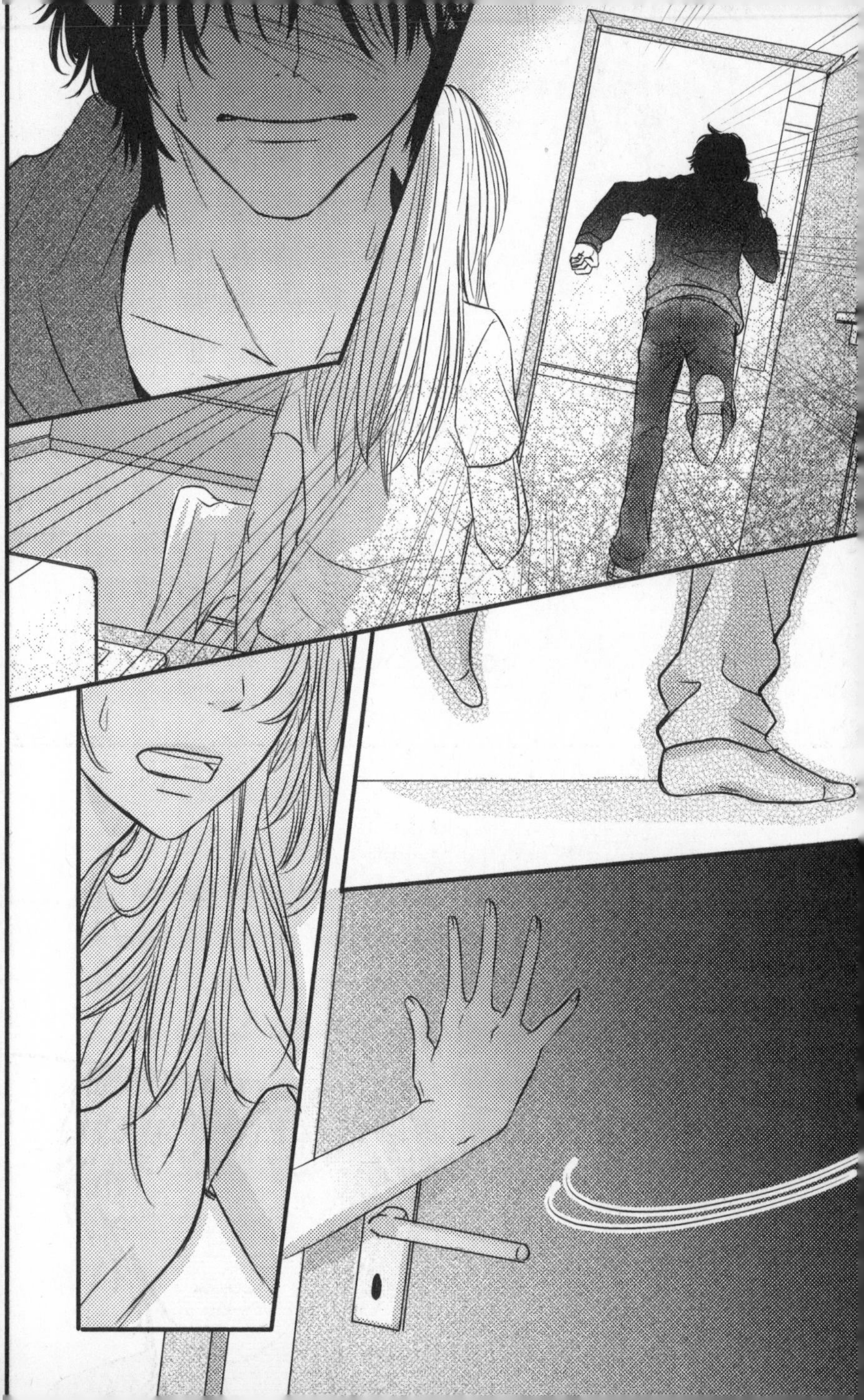

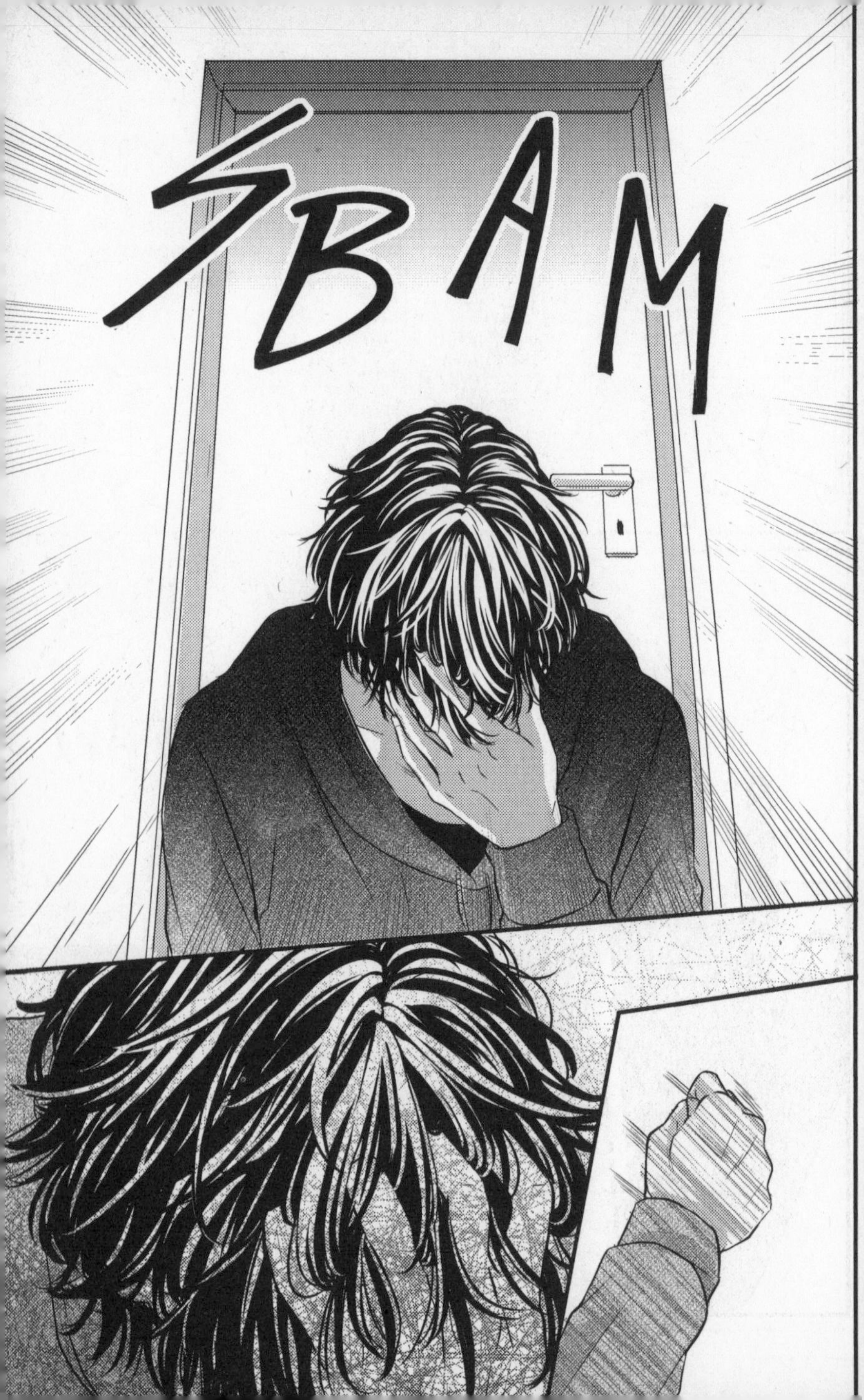
SBAM

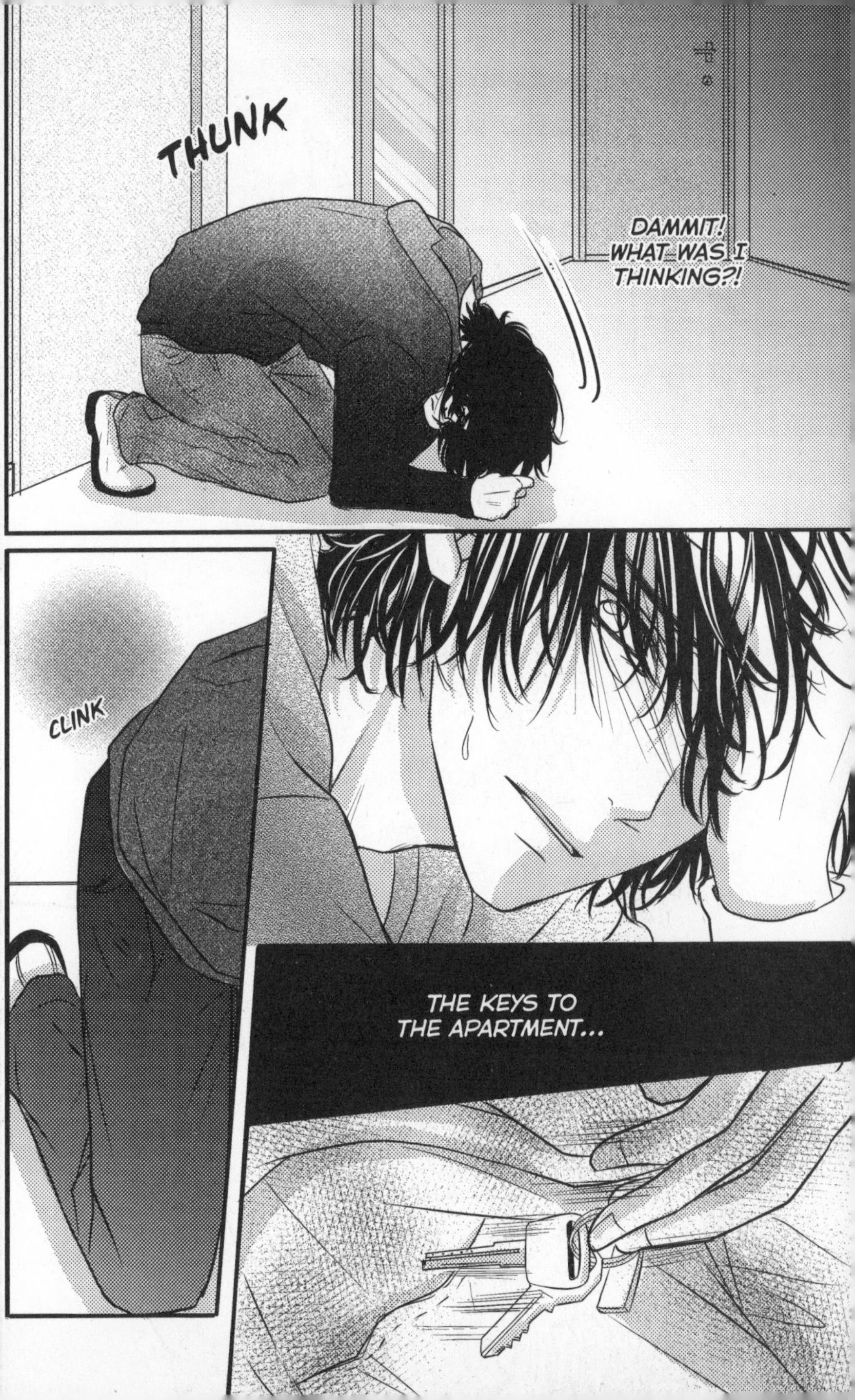
THUNK
DAMMIT! WHAT WAS I THINKING?!
THE KEYS TO THE APARTMENT...
CLINK

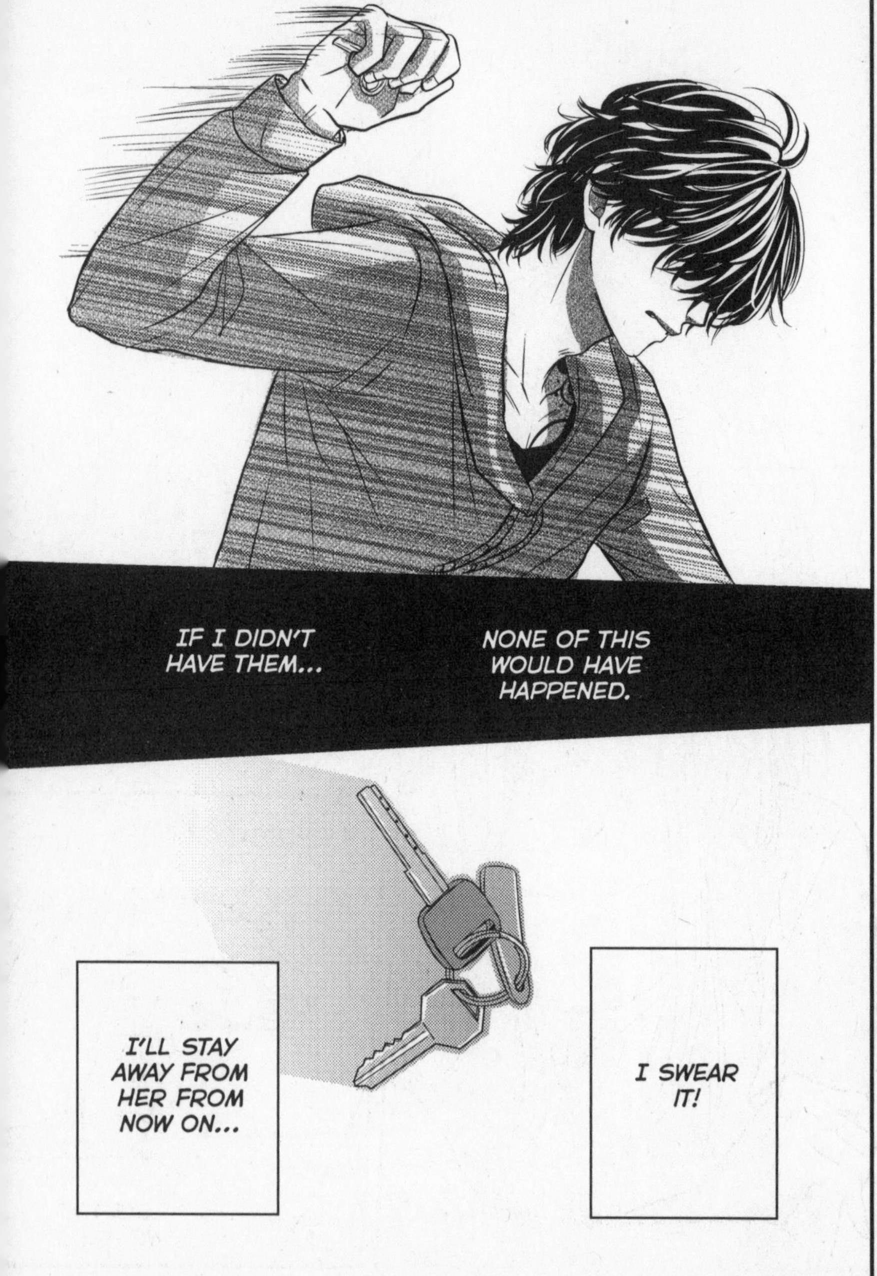
IF I DIDN'T HAVE THEM...
NONE OF THIS WOULD HAVE HAPPENED.
I'LL STAY AWAY FROM HER FROM NOW ON...
I SWEAR IT!

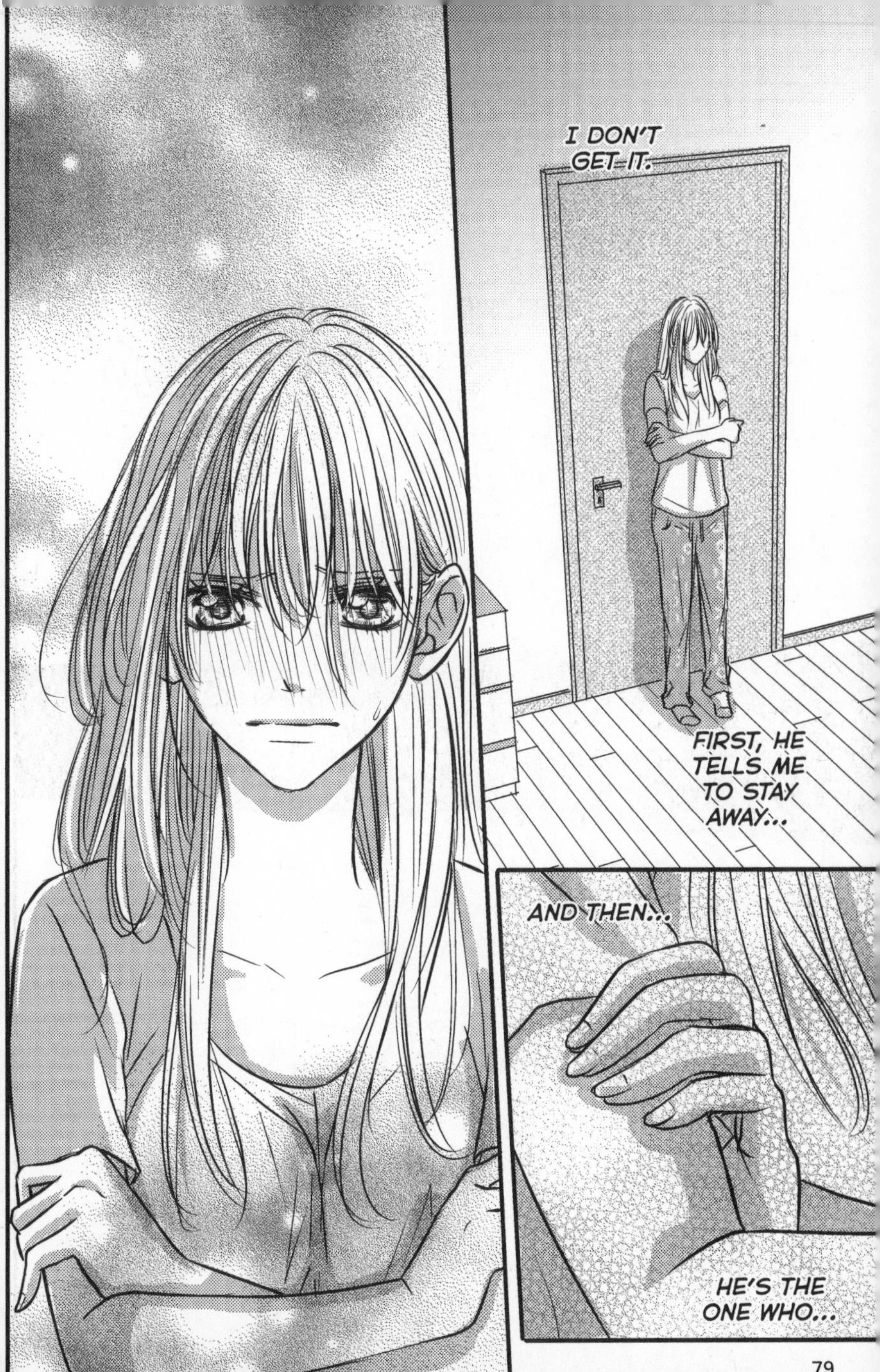
I DON'T GET IT.
FIRST, HE TELLS ME TO STAY AWAY...
AND THEN...
HE'S THE ONE WHO...

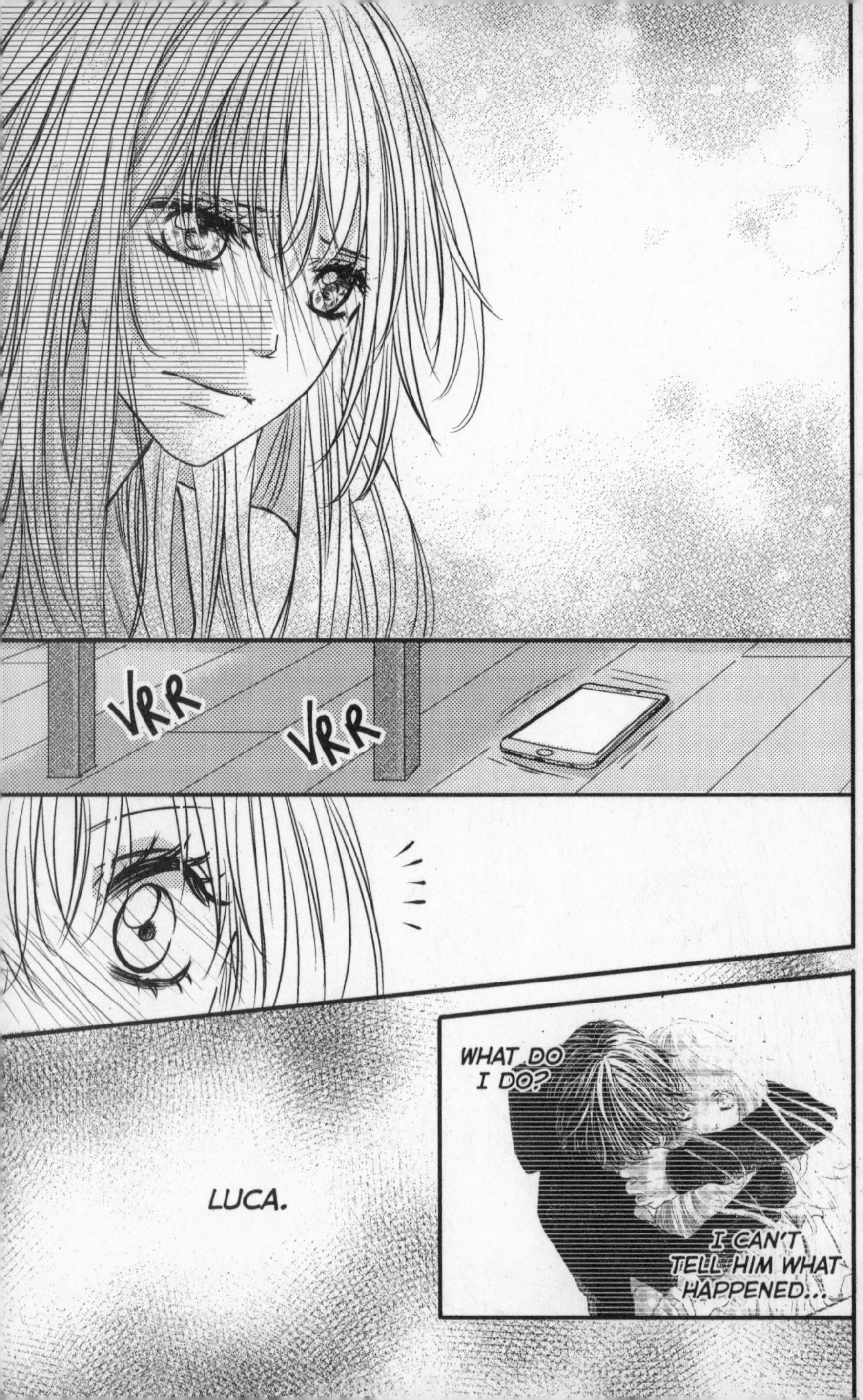
VRR
VRR
LUCA.
WHAT DO I DO?
I CAN'T TELL HIM WHAT HAPPENED...

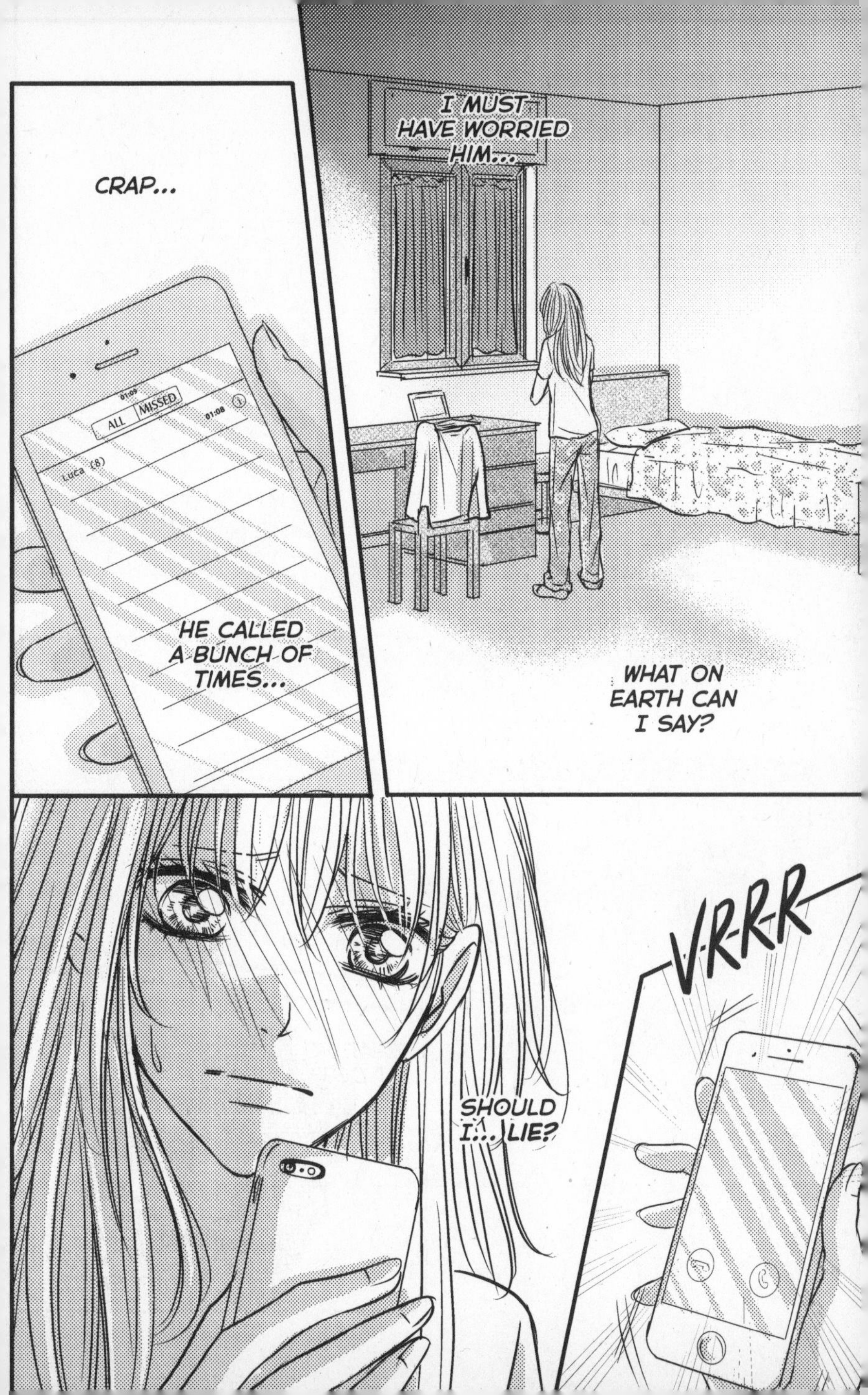
I MUST HAVE WORRIED HIM...
WHAT ON EARTH CAN I SAY?
CRAP...
ALL
MISSED
01:08
Luca (8)
HE CALLED A BUNCH OF TIMES...
V-R-R-R
SHOULD I... LIE?

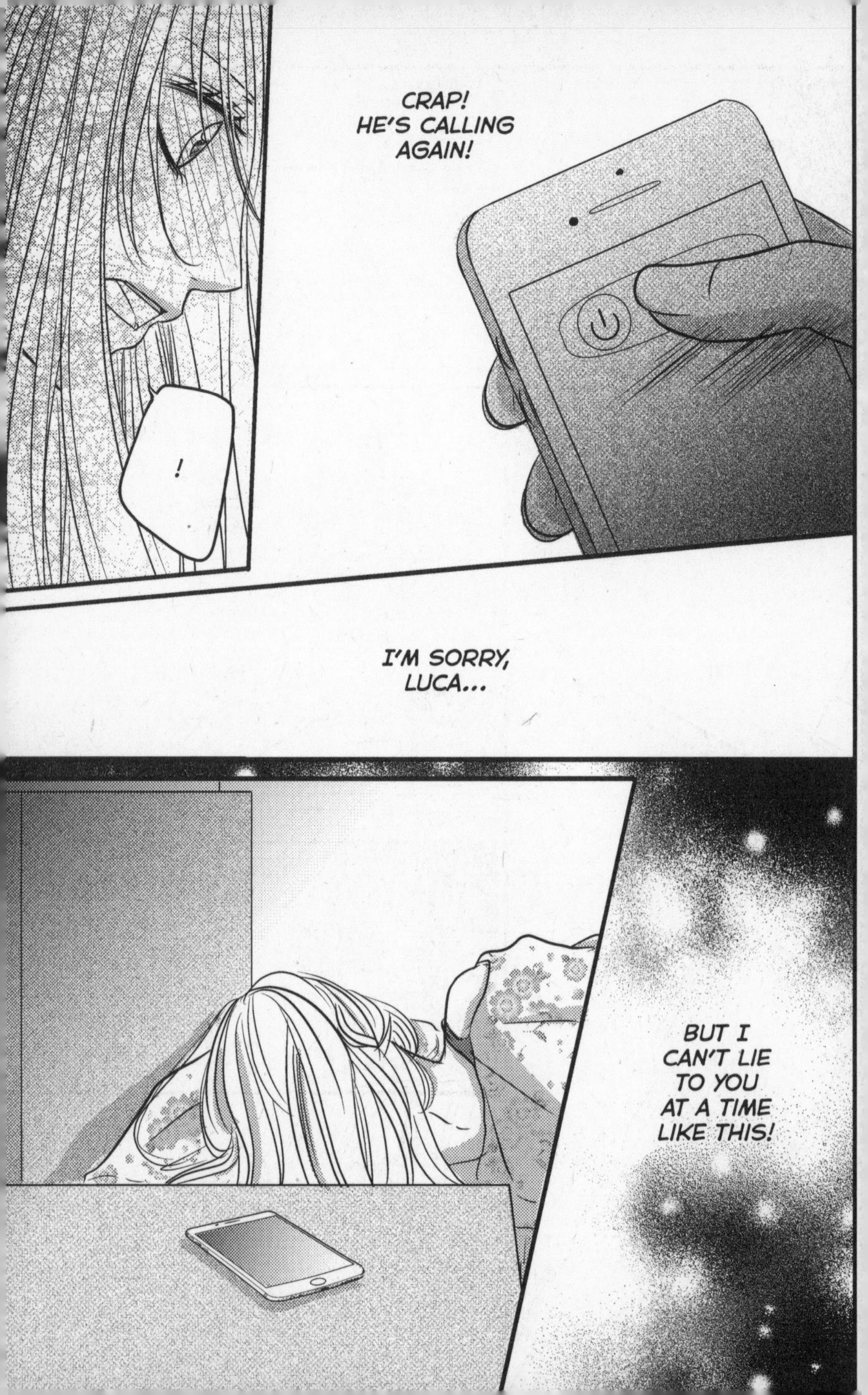
CRAP! HE'S CALLING AGAIN!
!
I'M SORRY, LUCA...
BUT I CAN'T LIE TO YOU AT A TIME LIKE THIS!

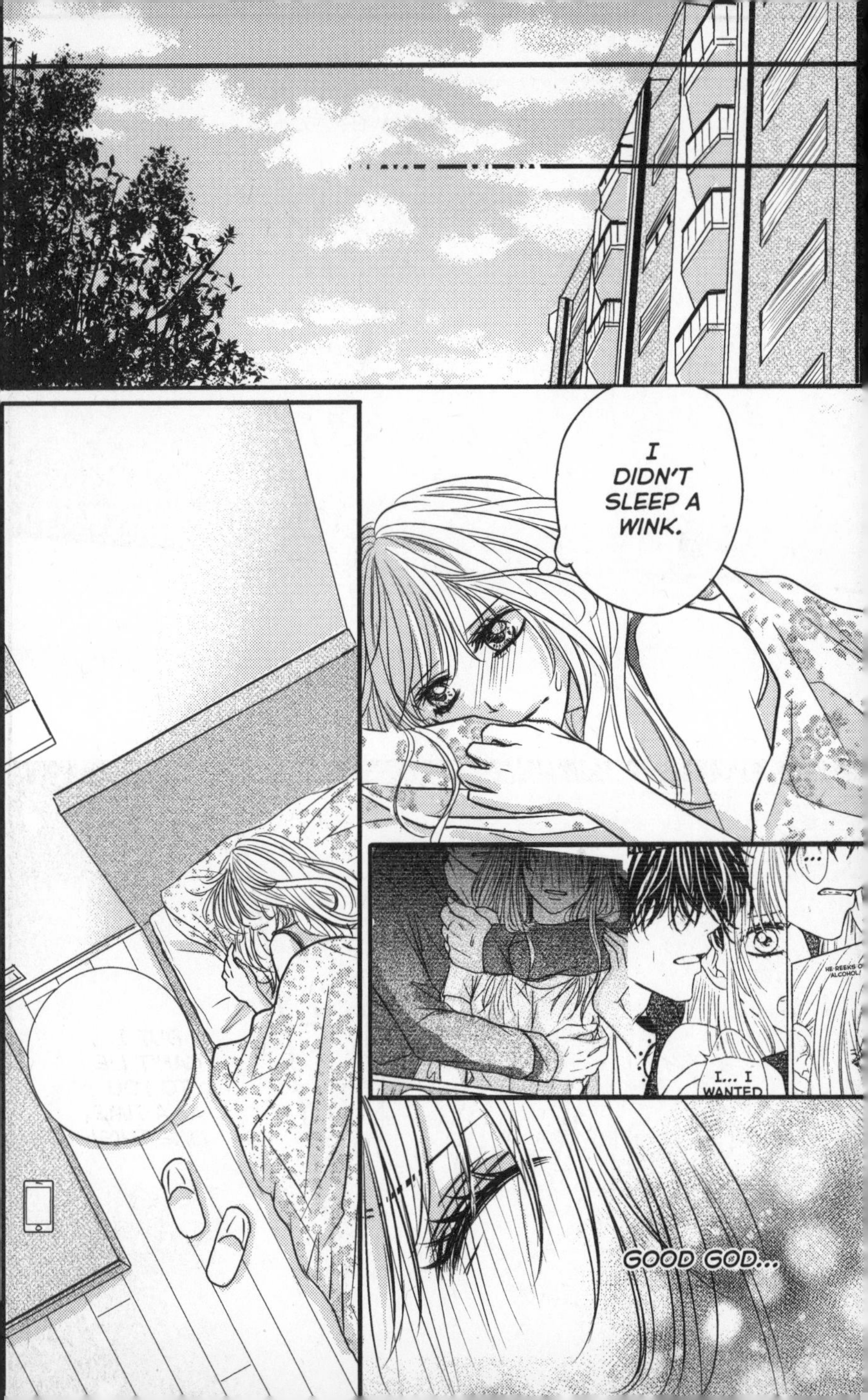
I DIDN'T SLEEP A WINK.
...
HE REEKS O
ALCOHOL!
I... I WANTED
GOOD GOD...

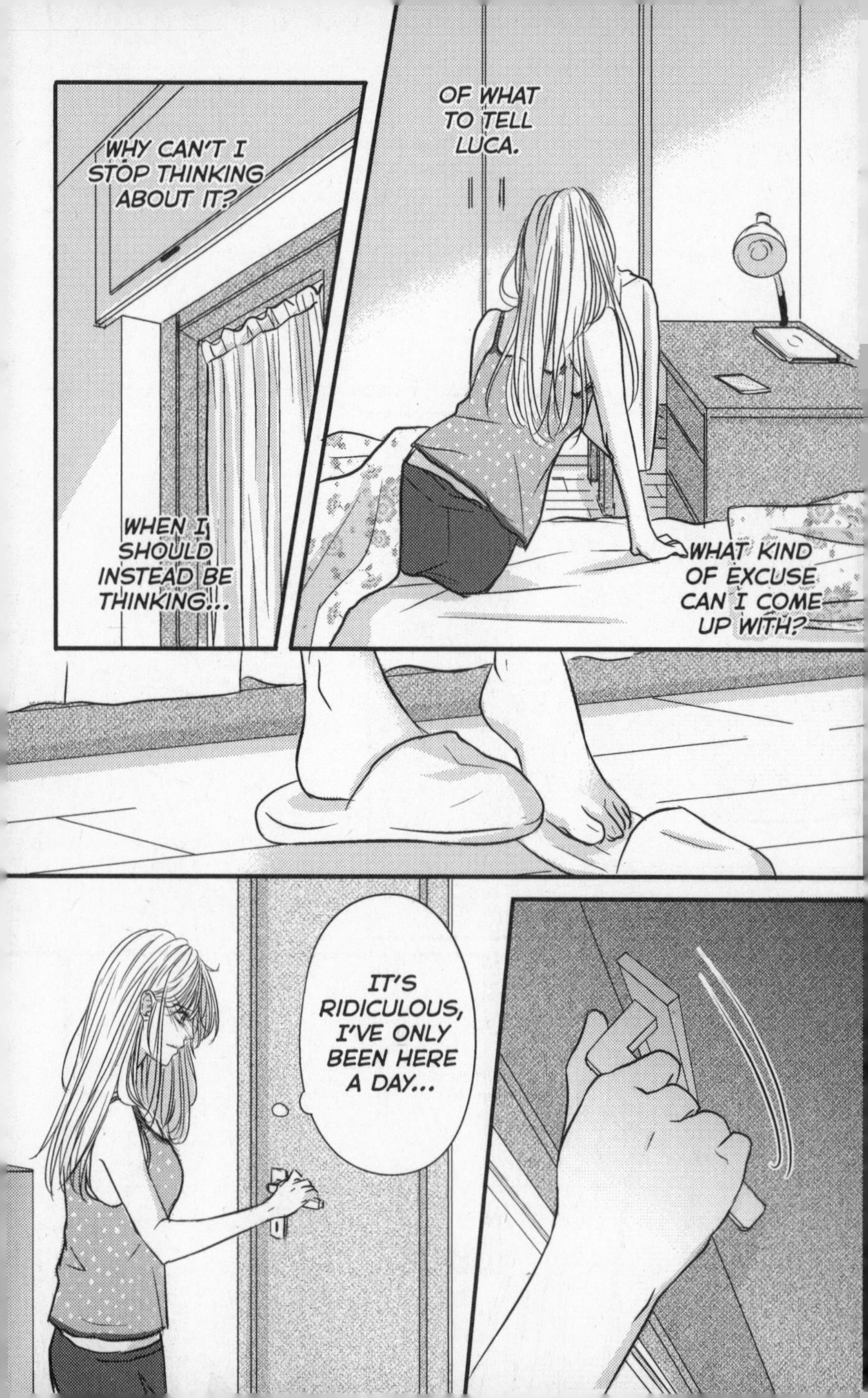
WHY CAN'T I STOP THINKING ABOUT IT?
WHEN I SHOULD INSTEAD BE THINKING...
OF WHAT TO TELL LUCA.
WHAT KIND OF EXCUSE CAN I COME UP WITH?
IT'S RIDICULOUS, I'VE ONLY BEEN HERE A DAY...

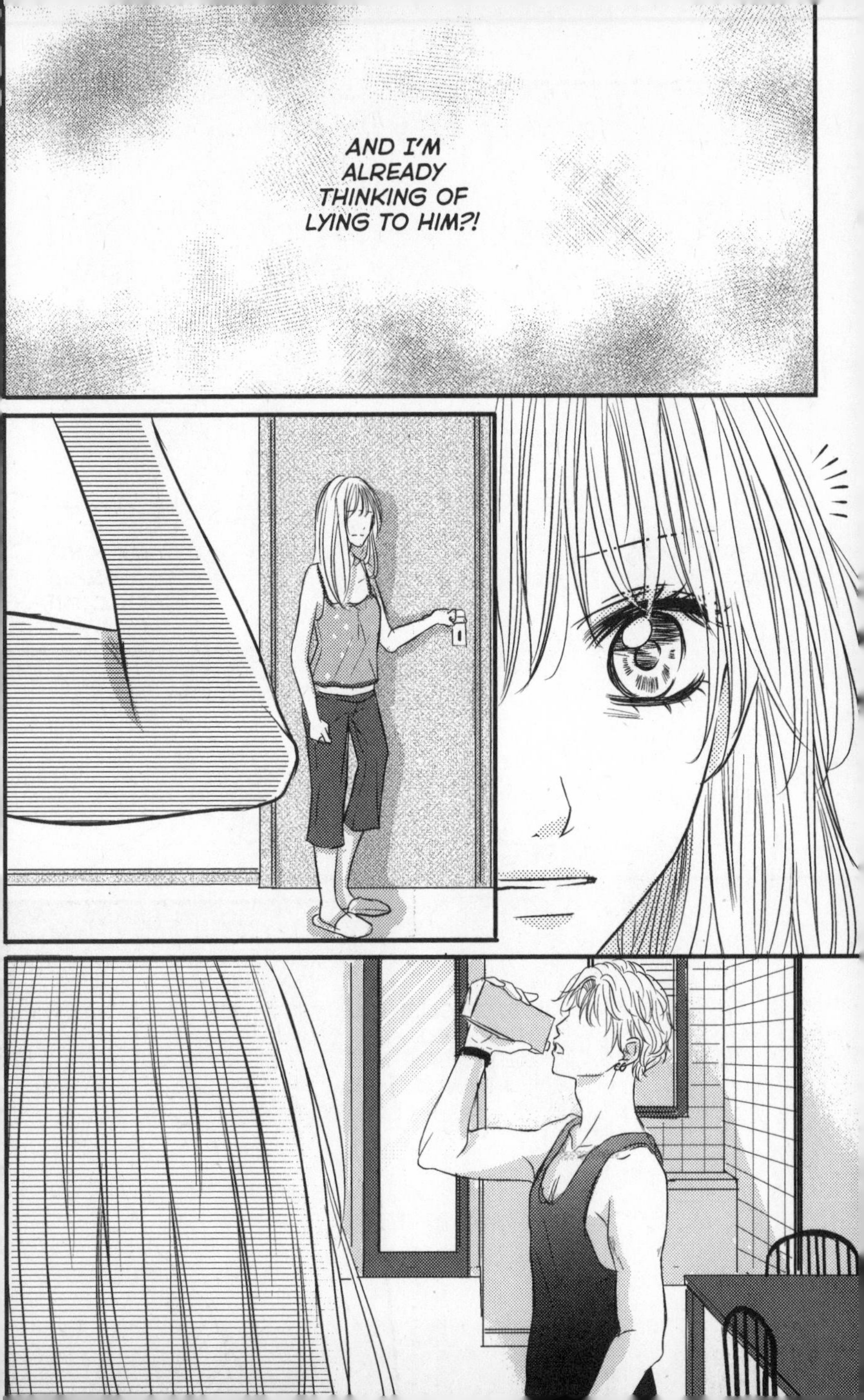
AND I'M ALREADY THINKING OF LYING TO HIM?!

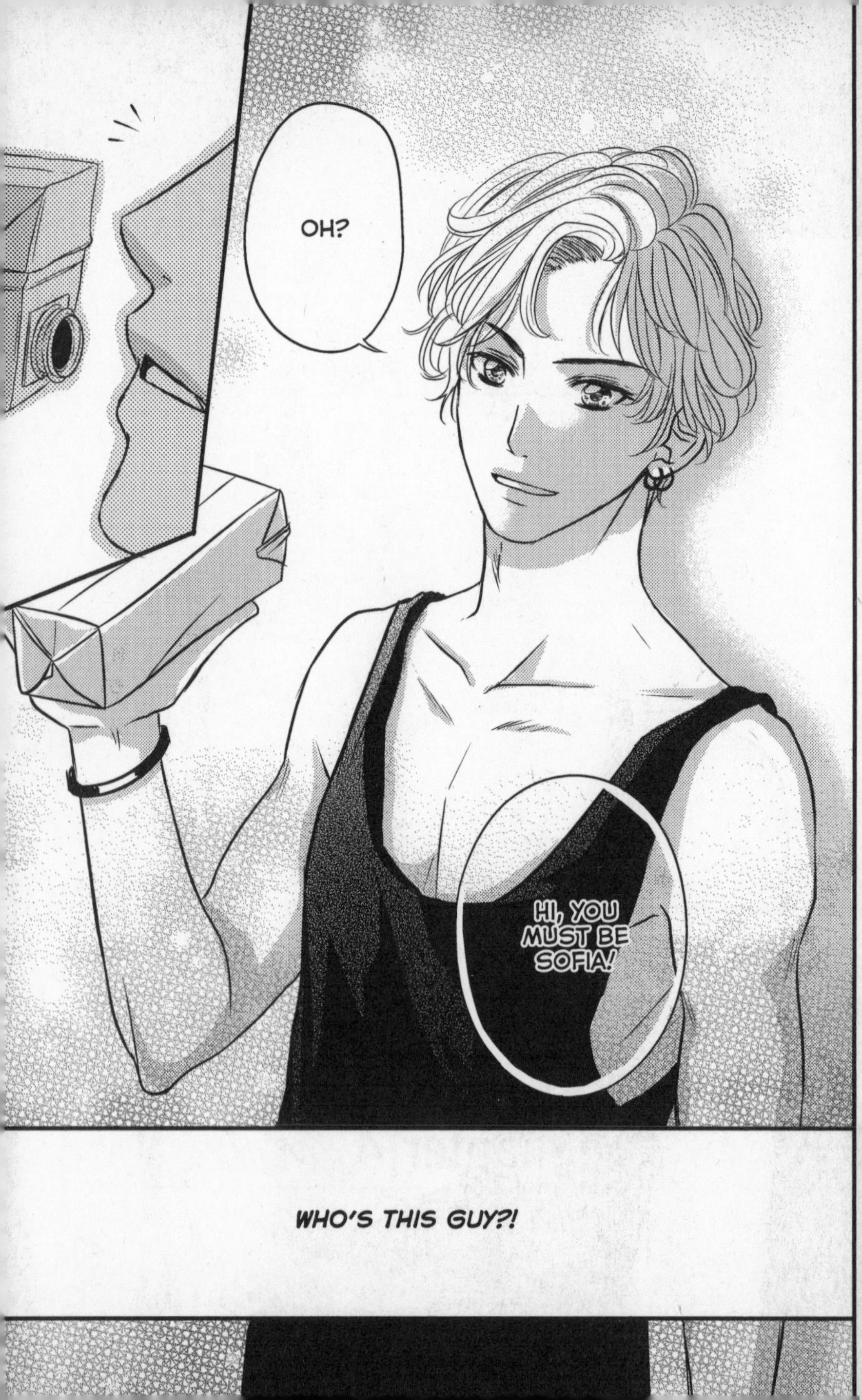
OH?
HI, YOU MUST BE SOFIA!
WHO'S THIS GUY?!

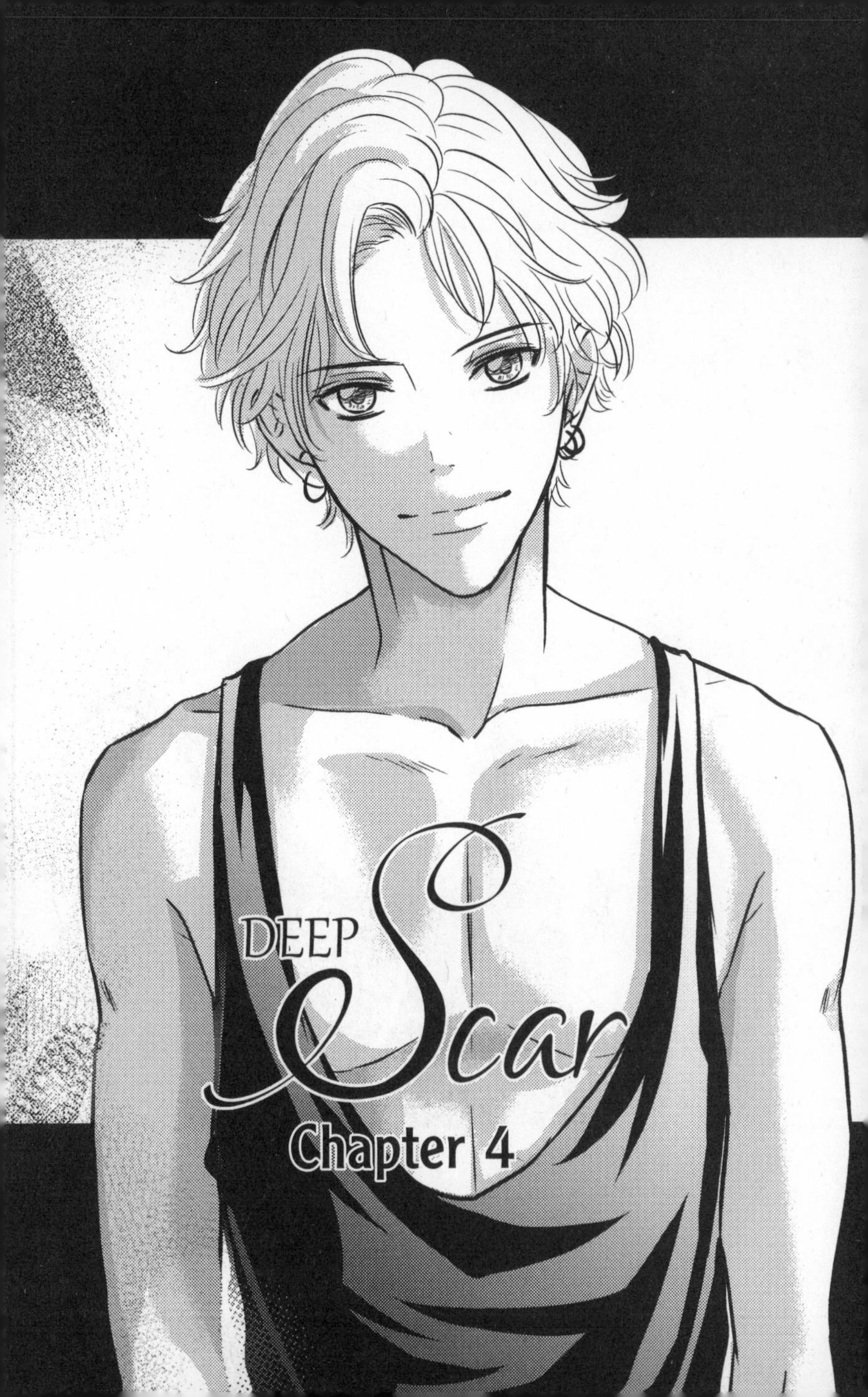
DEEP Scar
Chapter 4

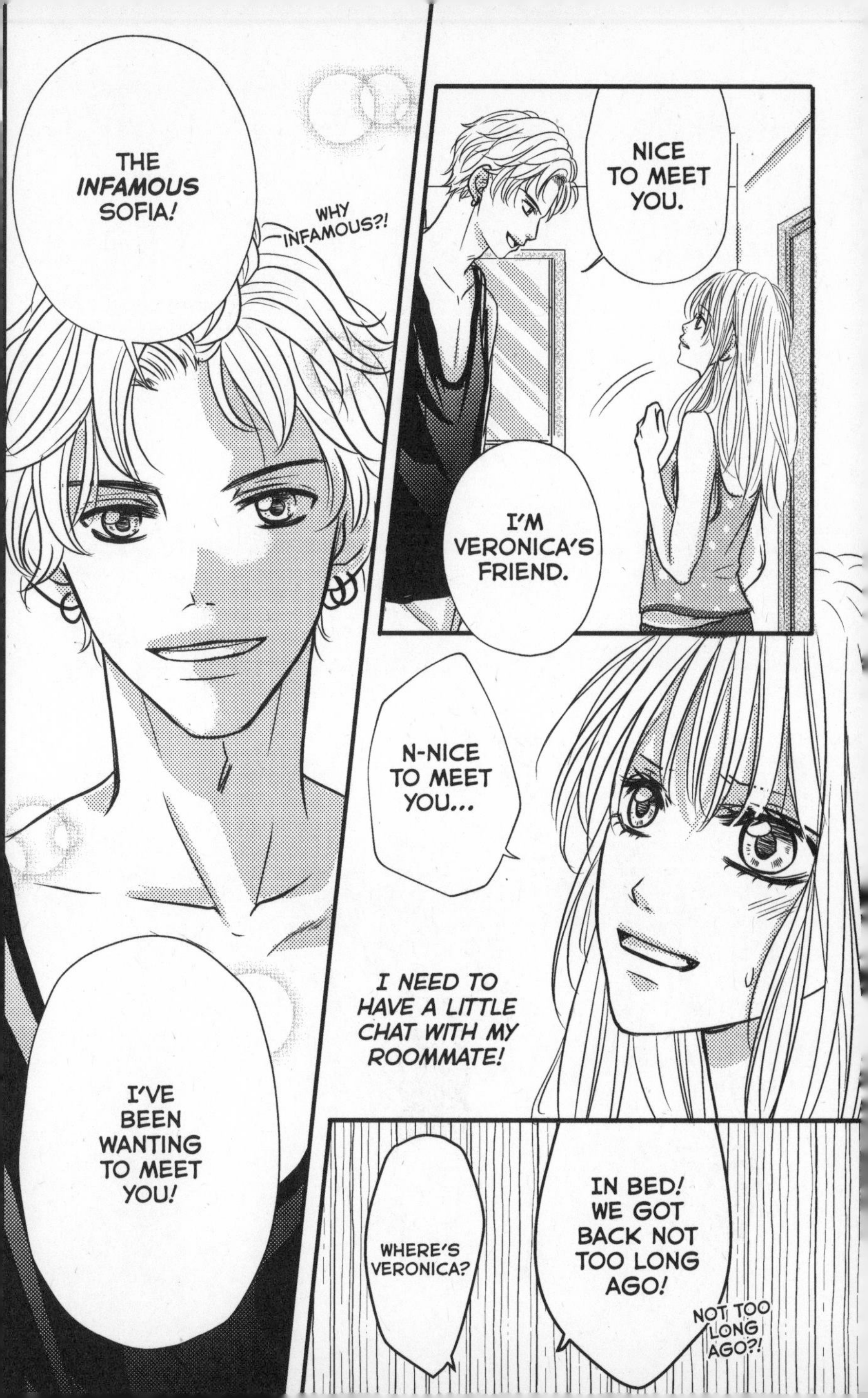
NICE TO MEET YOU.
I'M VERONICA'S FRIEND.
THE *INFAMOUS* SOFIA!
WHY INFAMOUS?!
I'VE BEEN WANTING TO MEET YOU!
N-NICE TO MEET YOU...
I NEED TO HAVE A LITTLE CHAT WITH MY ROOMMATE!
WHERE'S VERONICA?
IN BED! WE GOT BACK NOT TOO LONG AGO!
NOT TOO LONG AGO?!

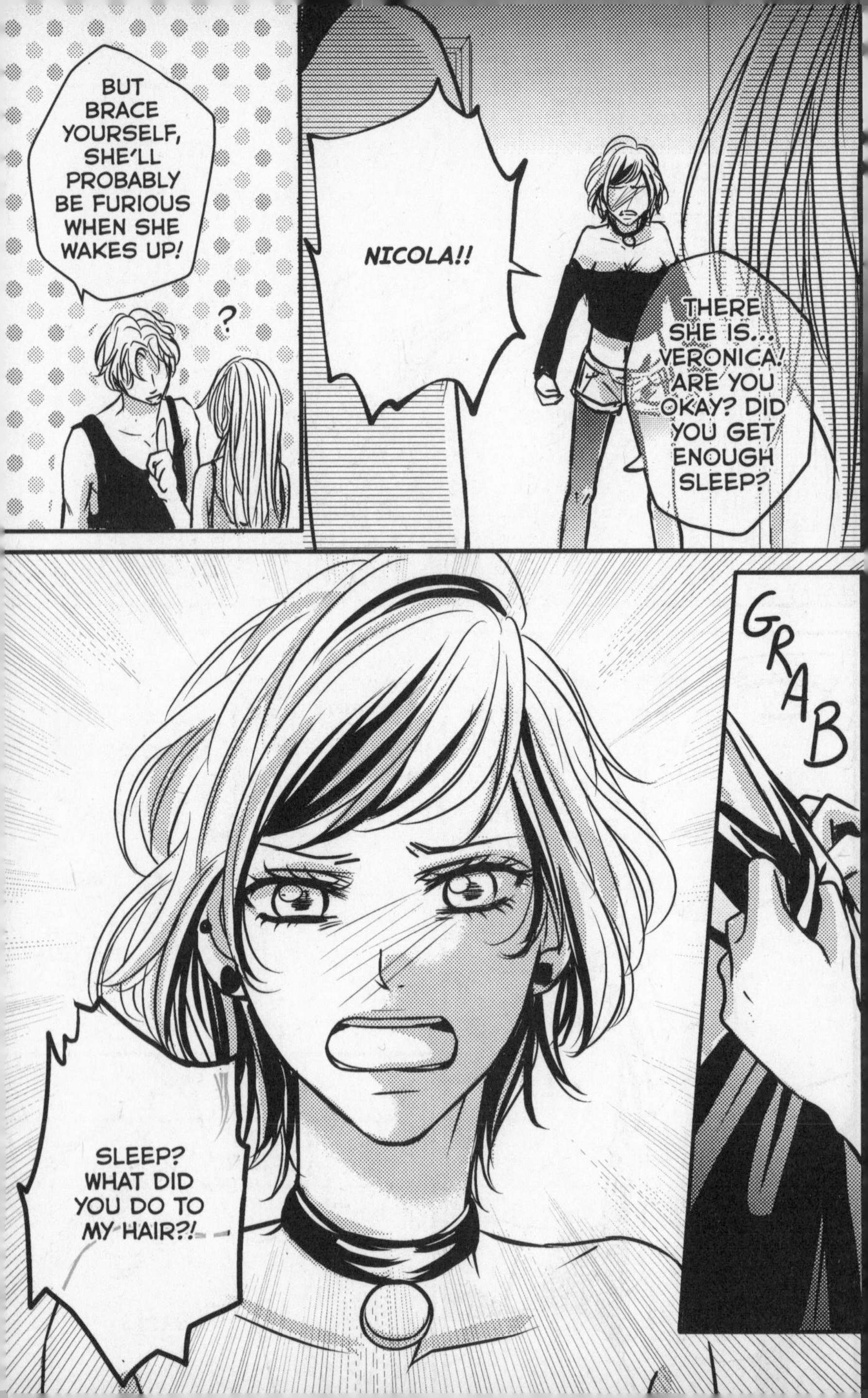
BUT BRACE YOURSELF, SHE'LL PROBABLY BE FURIOUS WHEN SHE WAKES UP!
?
NICOLA!!
THERE SHE IS... VERONICA! ARE YOU OKAY? DID YOU GET ENOUGH SLEEP?
GRAB
SLEEP? WHAT DID YOU DO TO MY HAIR?!

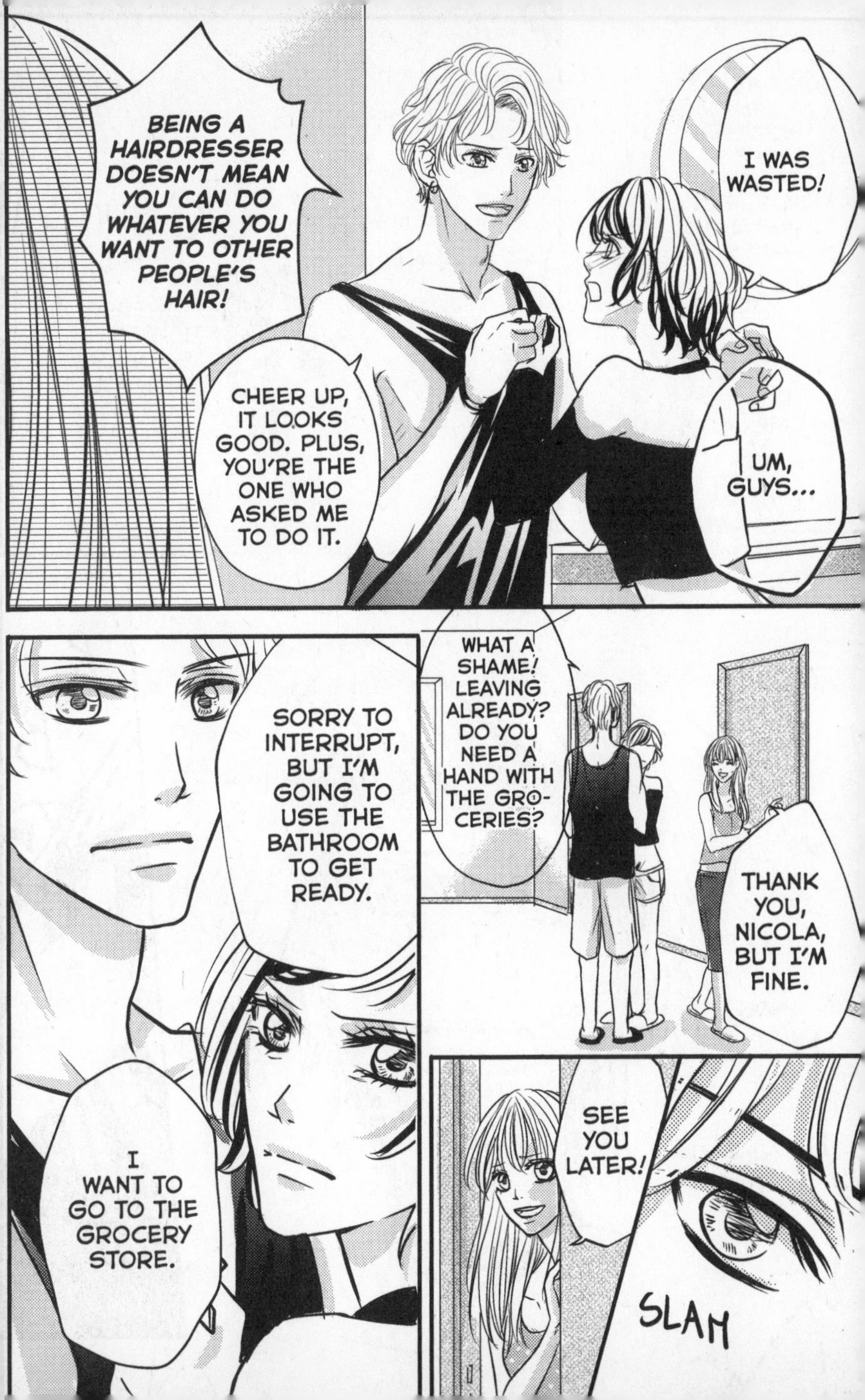
BEING A HAIRDRESSER DOESN'T MEAN YOU CAN DO WHATEVER YOU WANT TO OTHER PEOPLE'S HAIR!
CHEER UP, IT LOOKS GOOD. PLUS, YOU'RE THE ONE WHO ASKED ME TO DO IT.
I WAS WASTED!
UM, GUYS...
SORRY TO INTERRUPT, BUT I'M GOING TO USE THE BATHROOM TO GET READY.
I WANT TO GO TO THE GROCERY STORE.
WHAT A SHAME! LEAVING ALREADY? DO YOU NEED A HAND WITH THE GRO-CERIES?
THANK YOU, NICOLA, BUT I'M FINE.
SEE YOU LATER!
SLAM

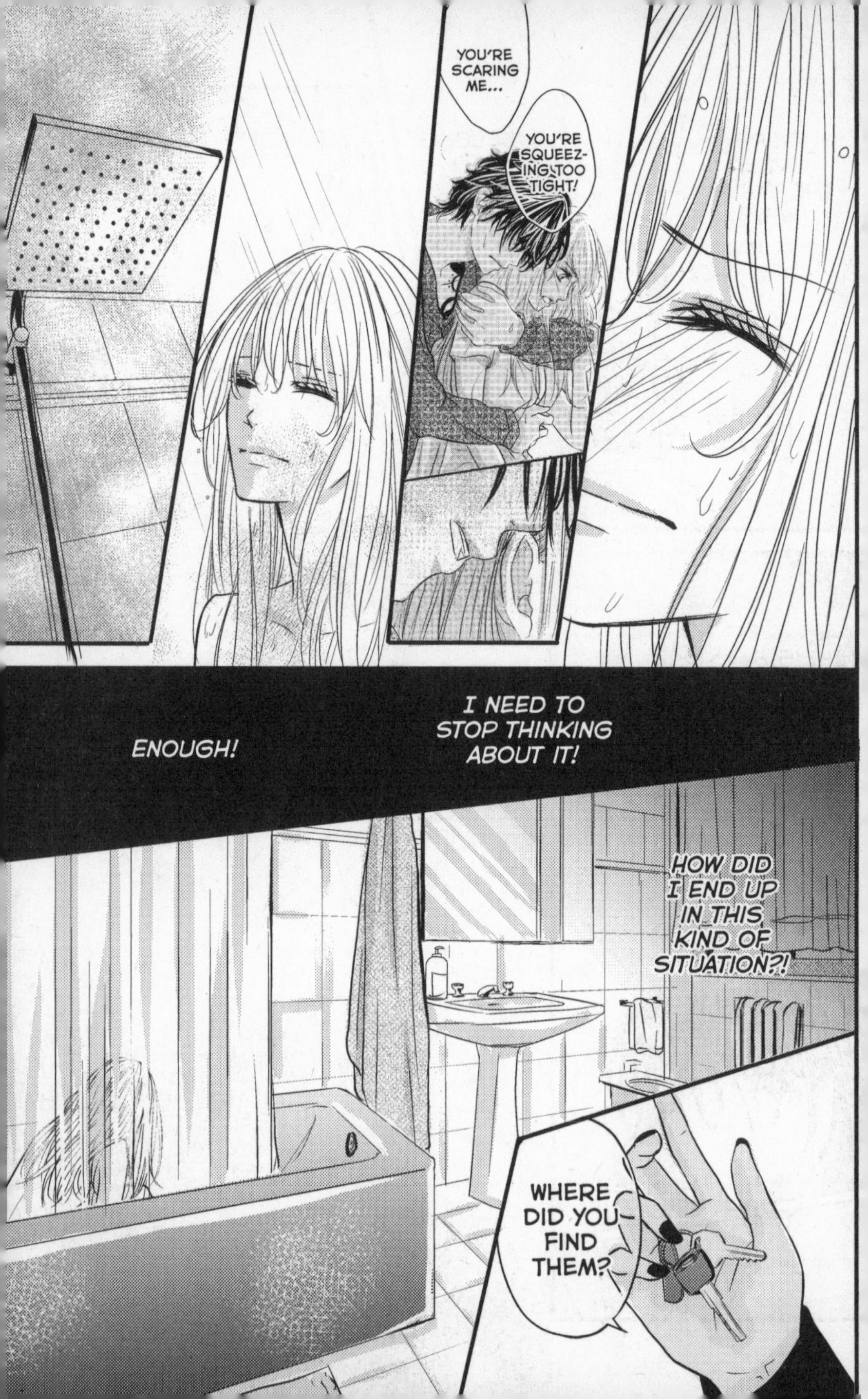
YOU'RE SCARING ME...
YOU'RE SQUEEZ-ING TOO TIGHT!
I NEED TO STOP THINKING ABOUT IT!
ENOUGH!
HOW DID I END UP IN THIS KIND OF SITUATION?!
WHERE DID YOU FIND THEM?

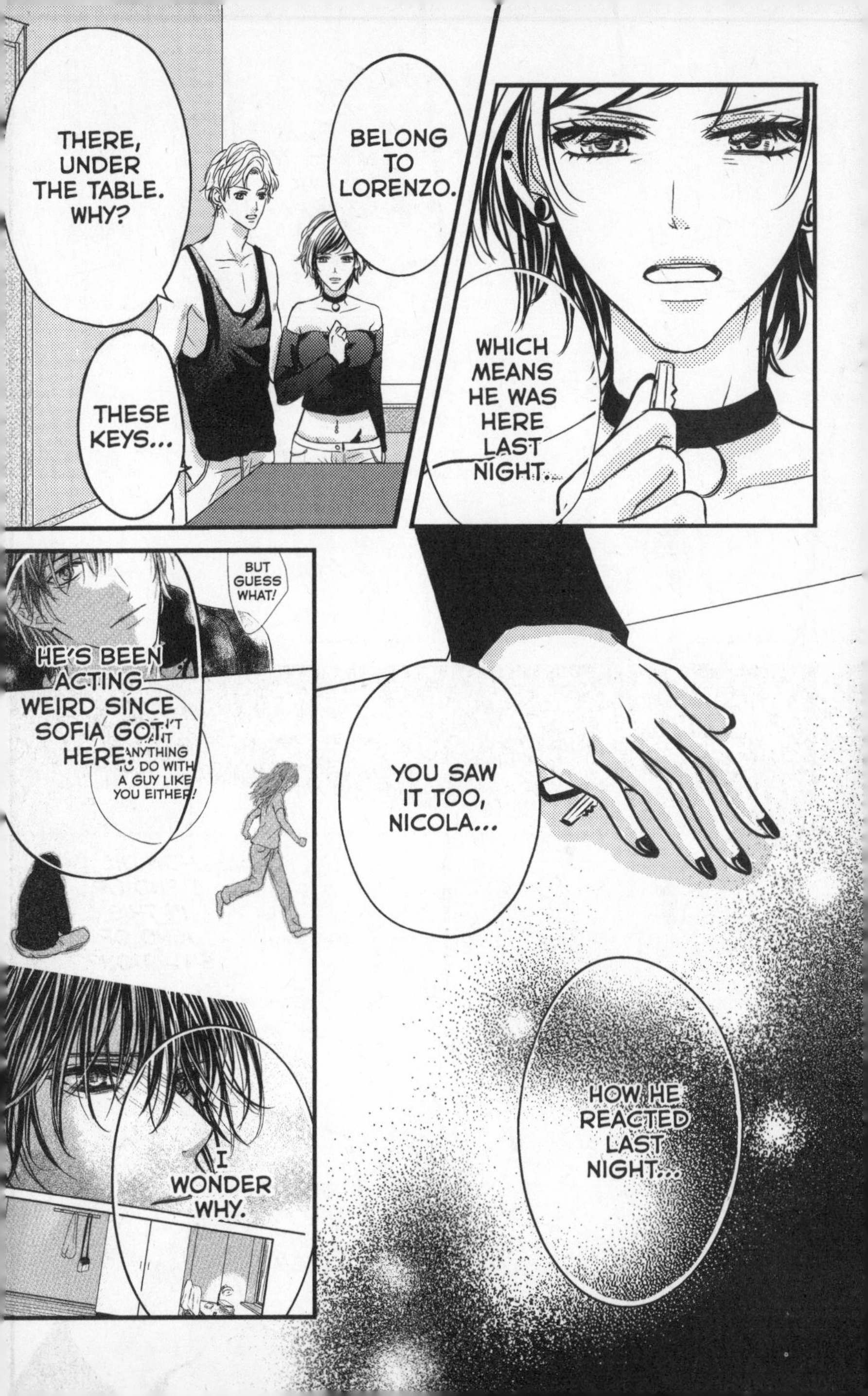
THERE, UNDER THE TABLE. WHY?
THESE KEYS...
BELONG TO LORENZO.
WHICH MEANS HE WAS HERE LAST NIGHT...
YOU SAW IT TOO, NICOLA...
HOW HE REACTED LAST NIGHT...
BUT GUESS WHAT!
ANYTHING TO DO WITH A GUY LIKE YOU EITHER!
HE'S BEEN ACTING WEIRD SINCE SOFIA GOT HERE.
I WONDER WHY.

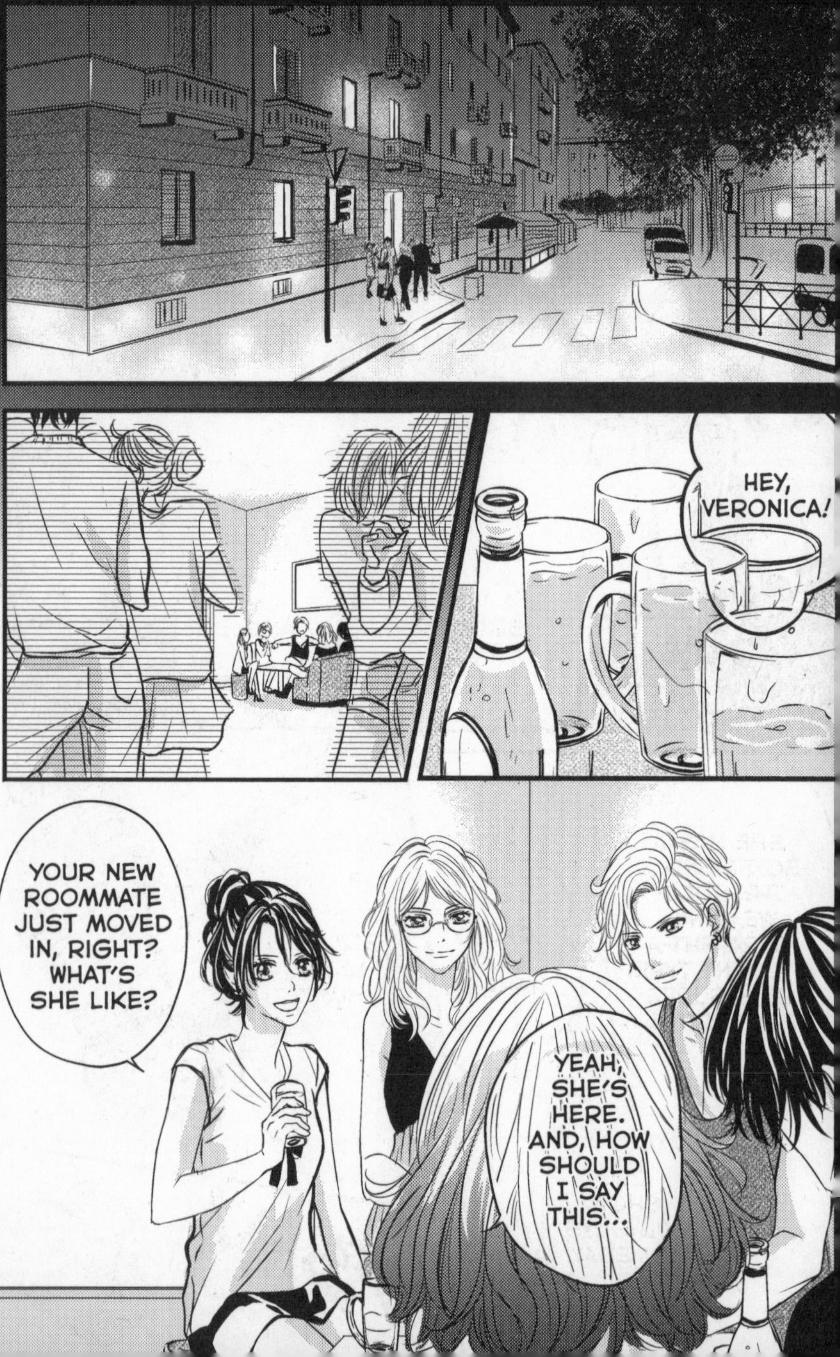
HEY, VERONICA!
YOUR NEW ROOMMATE JUST MOVED IN, RIGHT? WHAT'S SHE LIKE?
YEAH, SHE'S HERE. AND, HOW SHOULD I SAY THIS...

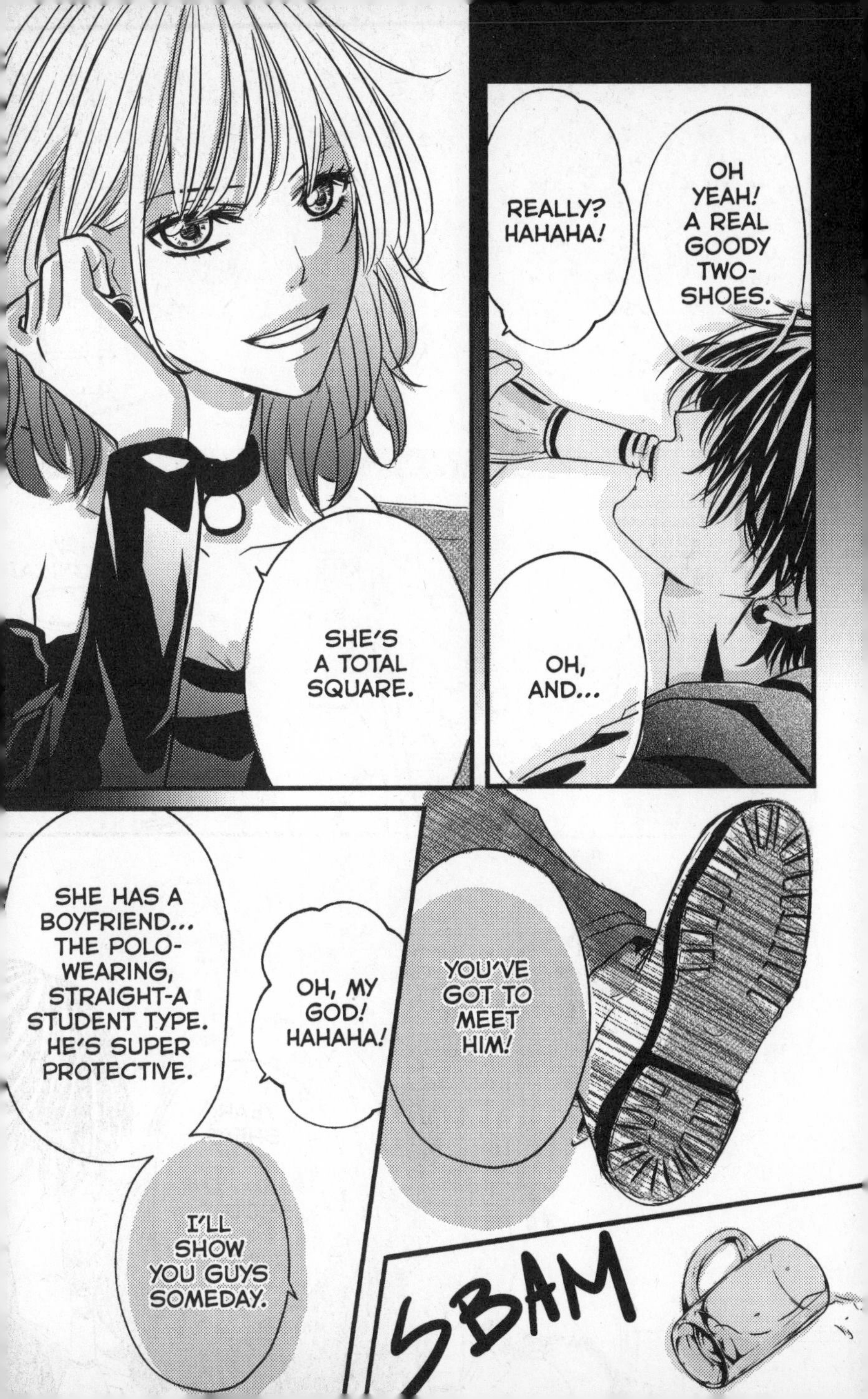
OH YEAH! A REAL GOODY TWO-SHOES.
REALLY? HAHAHA!
OH, AND...
SHE'S A TOTAL SQUARE.
SHE HAS A BOYFRIEND... THE POLO-WEARING, STRAIGHT-A STUDENT TYPE. HE'S SUPER PROTECTIVE.
OH, MY GOD! HAHAHA!
YOU'VE GOT TO MEET HIM!
I'LL SHOW YOU GUYS SOMEDAY.
SBAM

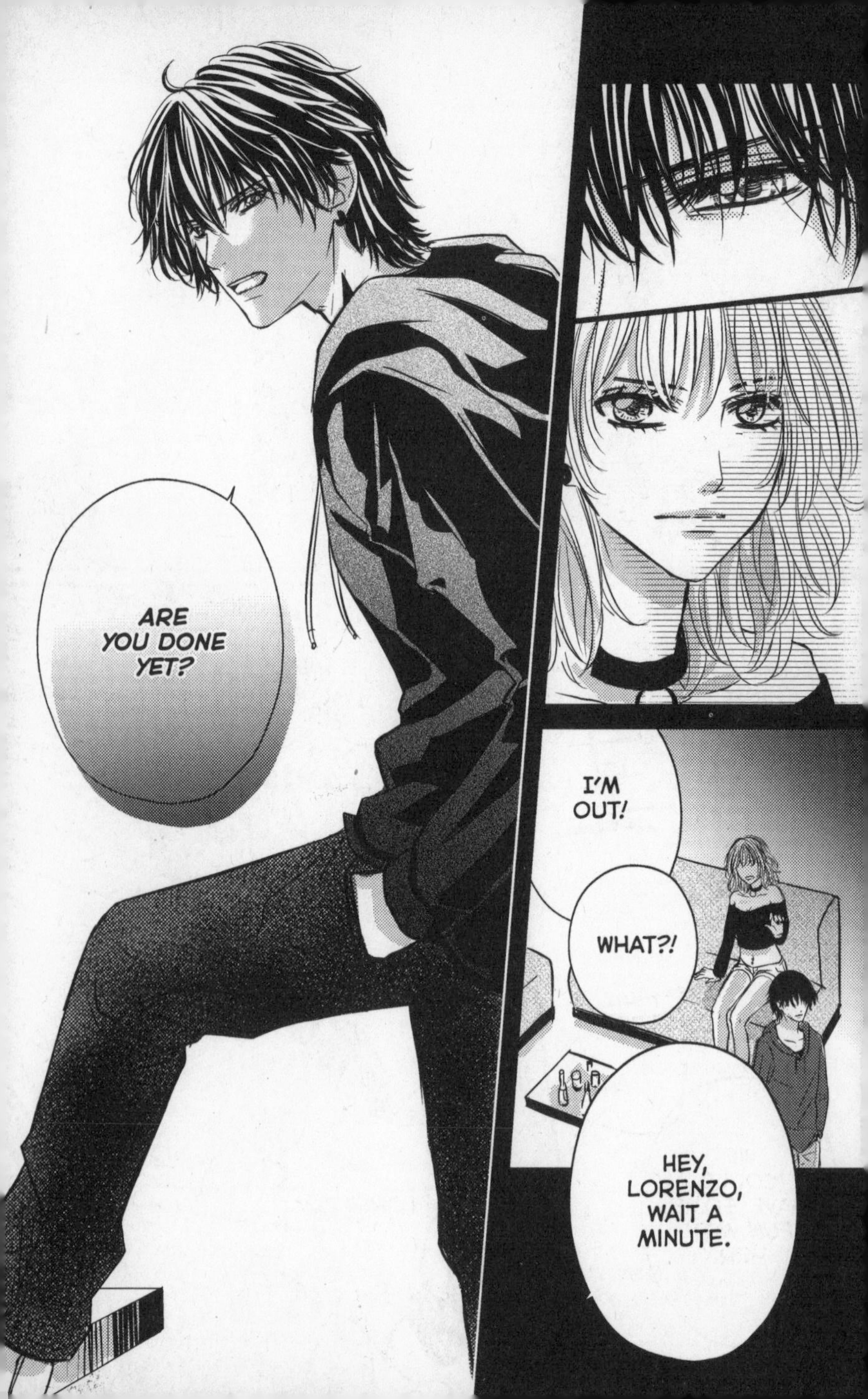
I'M OUT!
WHAT?!
HEY, LORENZO, WAIT A MINUTE.
ARE YOU DONE YET?

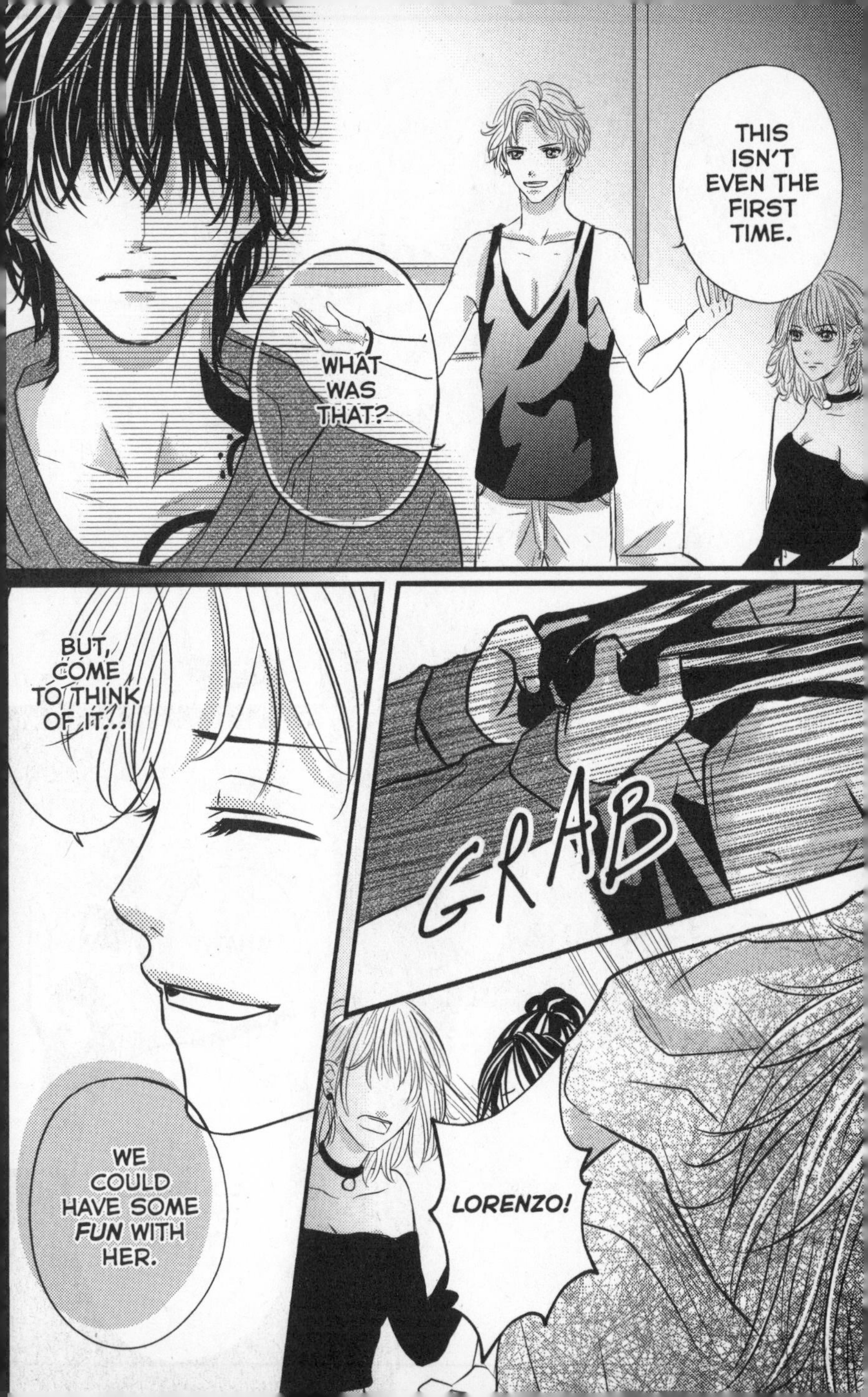
THIS ISN'T EVEN THE FIRST TIME.
WHAT WAS THAT?
GRAB
LORENZO!
BUT, COME TO THINK OF IT...
WE COULD HAVE SOME *FUN* WITH HER.

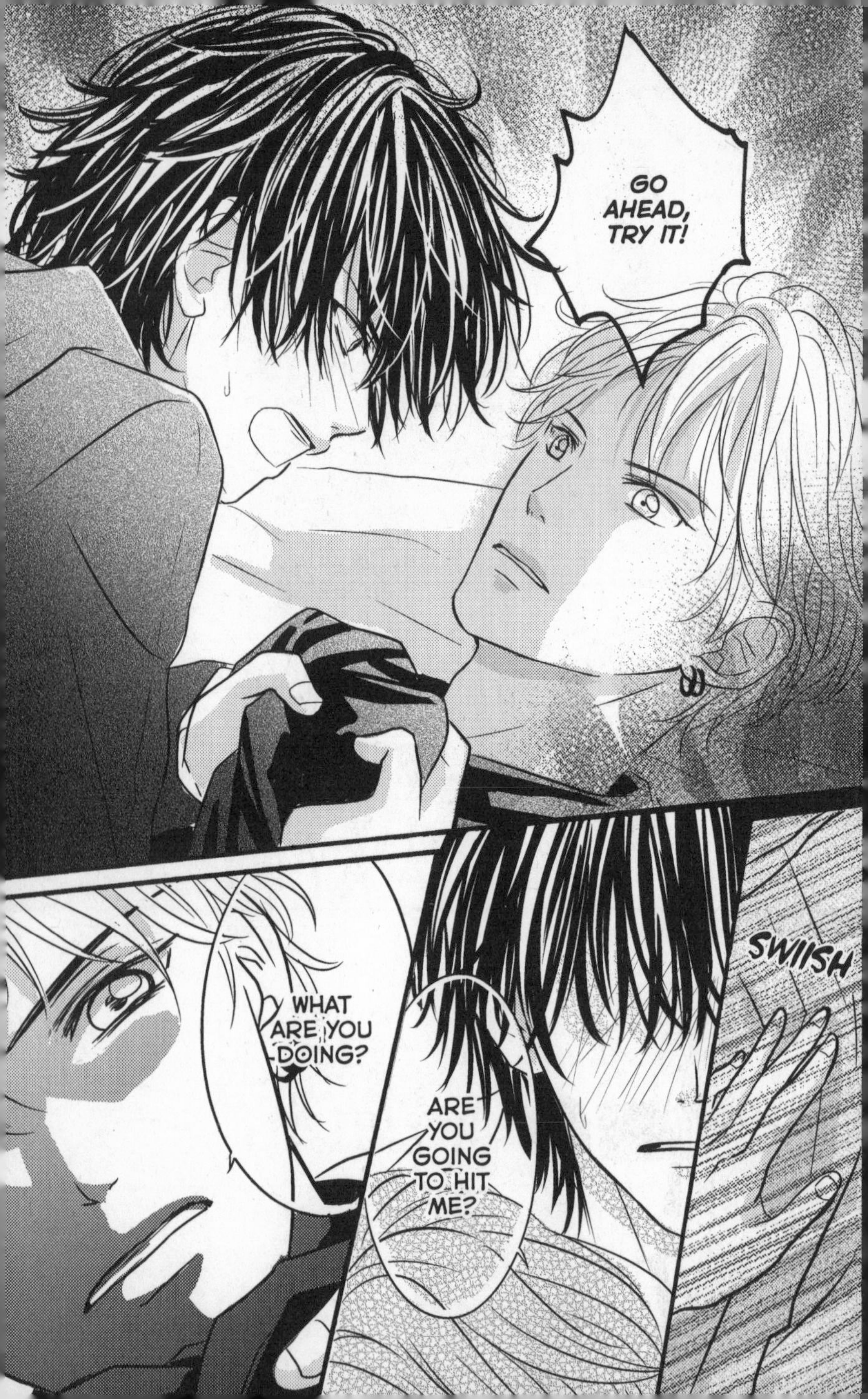
GO AHEAD, TRY IT!
SWIISH
WHAT ARE YOU DOING?
ARE YOU GOING TO HIT ME?

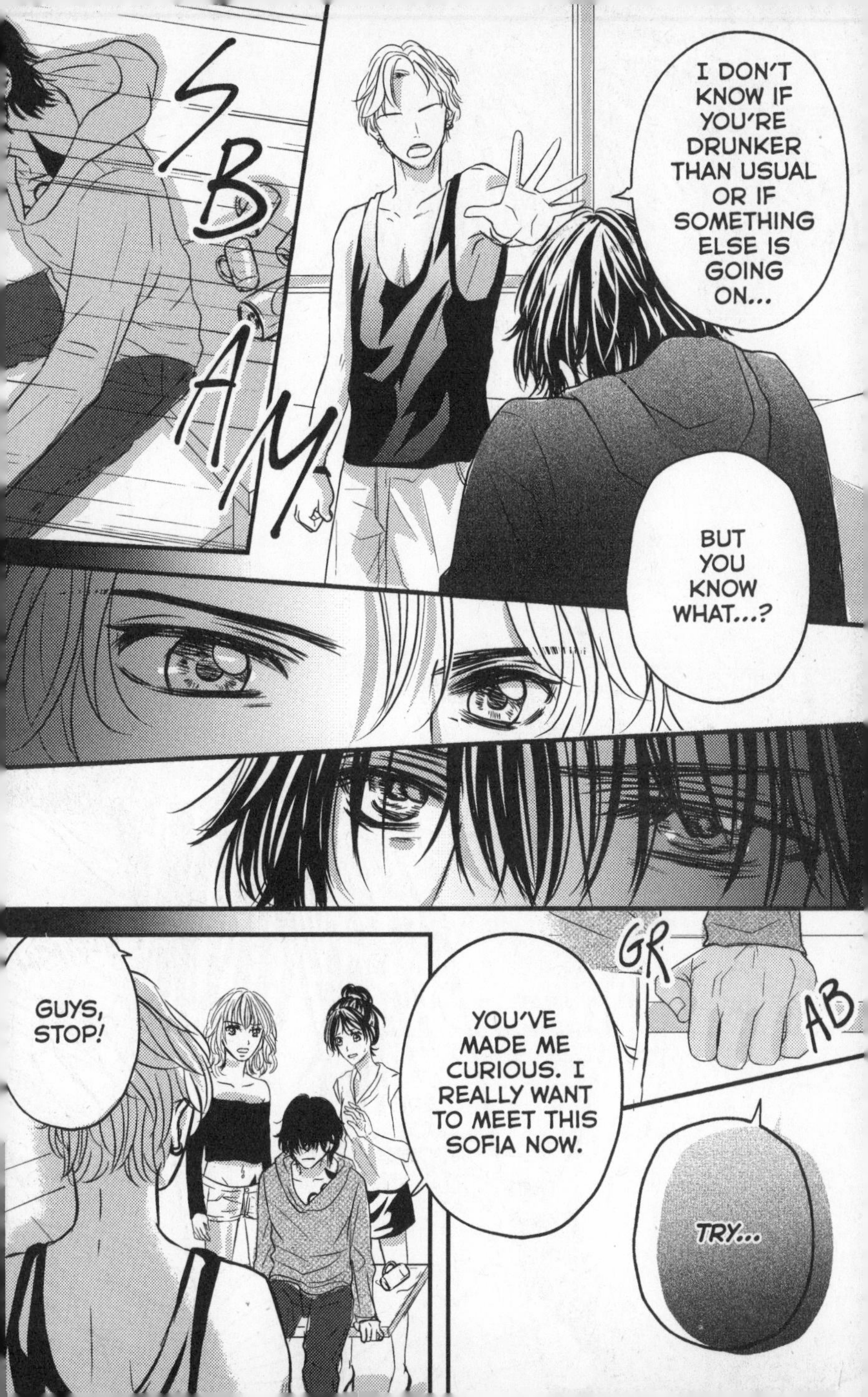
SBAM
I DON'T KNOW IF YOU'RE DRUNKER THAN USUAL OR IF SOMETHING ELSE IS GOING ON...
BUT YOU KNOW WHAT...?
GRAB
TRY...
YOU'VE MADE ME CURIOUS. I REALLY WANT TO MEET THIS SOFIA NOW.
GUYS, STOP!

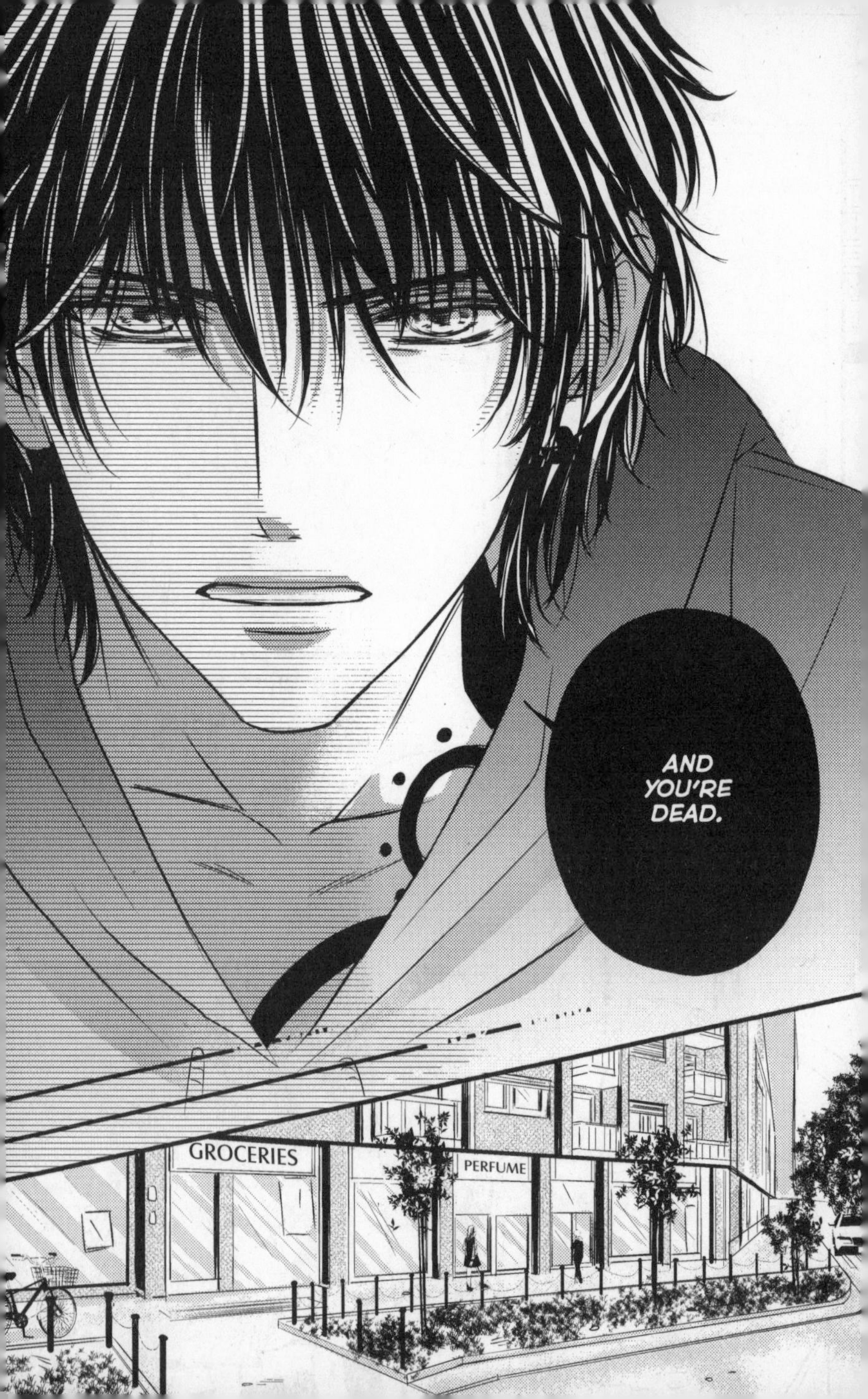
AND YOU'RE DEAD.
GROCERIES
PERFUME

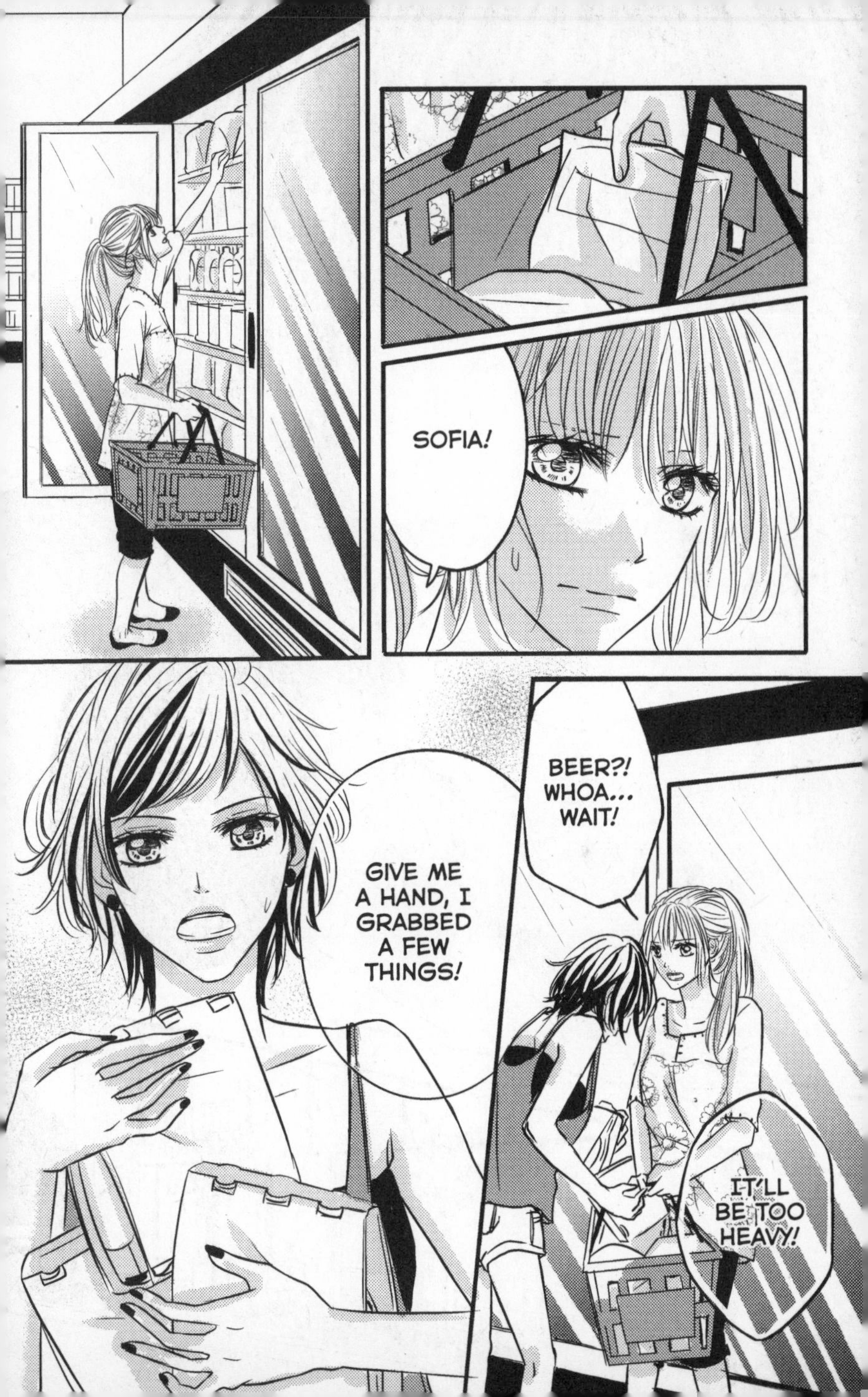
SOFIA!
BEER?! WHOA... WAIT!
IT'LL BE TOO HEAVY!
GIVE ME A HAND, I GRABBED A FEW THINGS!

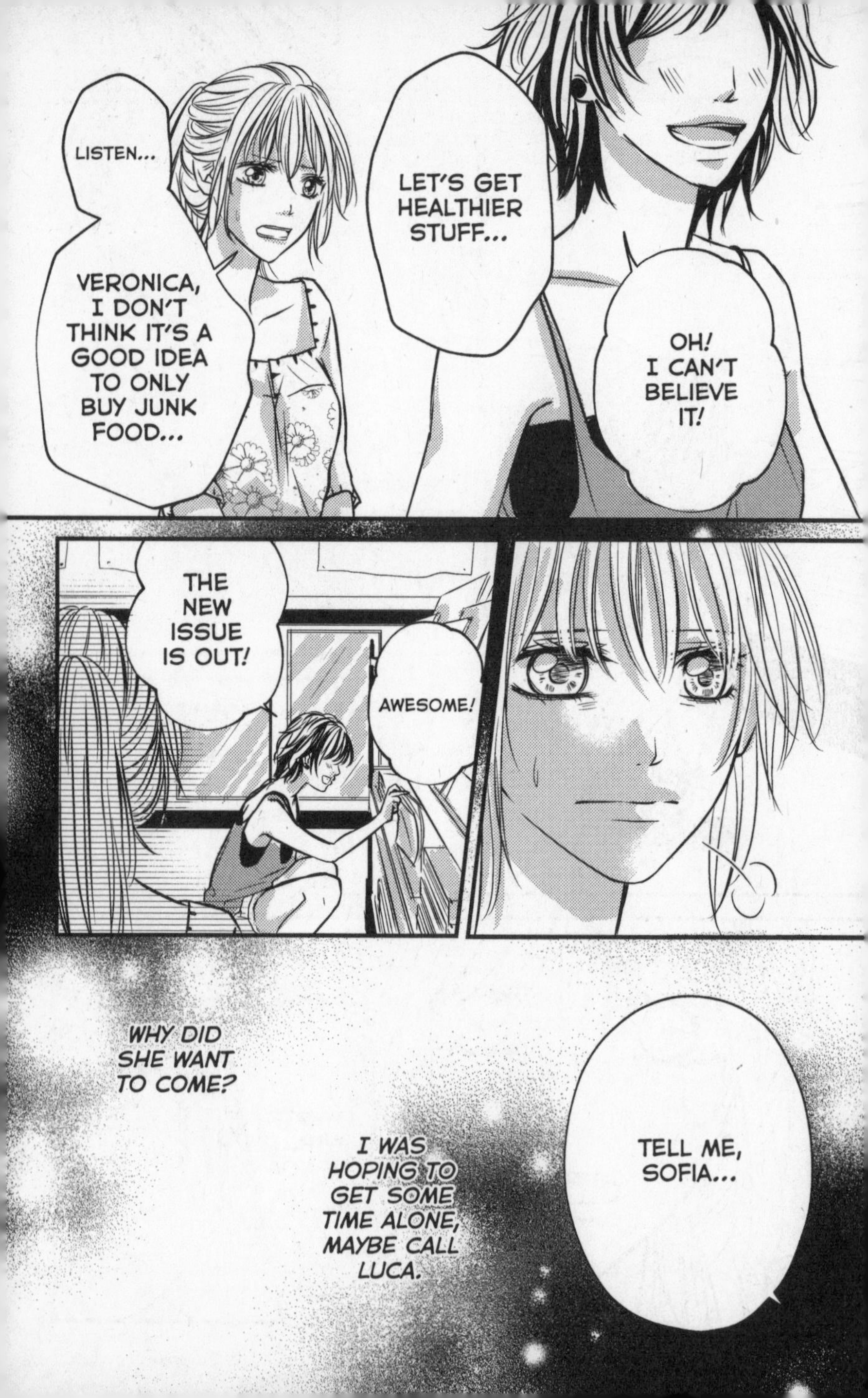
LISTEN...
VERONICA, I DON'T THINK IT'S A GOOD IDEA TO ONLY BUY JUNK FOOD...
LET'S GET HEALTHIER STUFF...
OH! I CAN'T BELIEVE IT!
THE NEW ISSUE IS OUT!
AWESOME!
WHY DID SHE WANT TO COME?
I WAS HOPING TO GET SOME TIME ALONE, MAYBE CALL LUCA.
TELL ME, SOFIA...

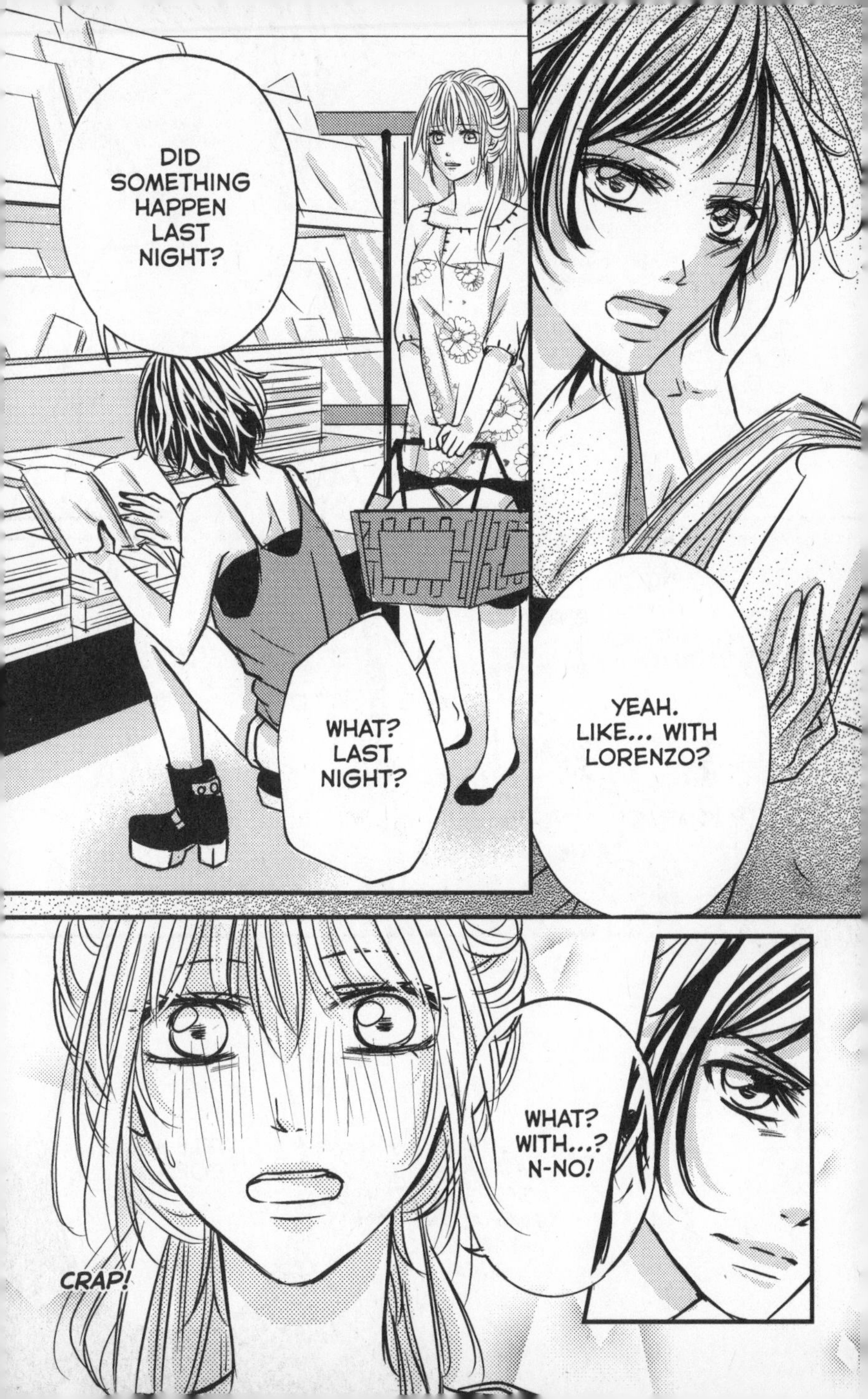
DID SOMETHING HAPPEN LAST NIGHT?
WHAT? LAST NIGHT?
YEAH. LIKE... WITH LORENZO?
WHAT? WITH...? N-NO!
CRAP!

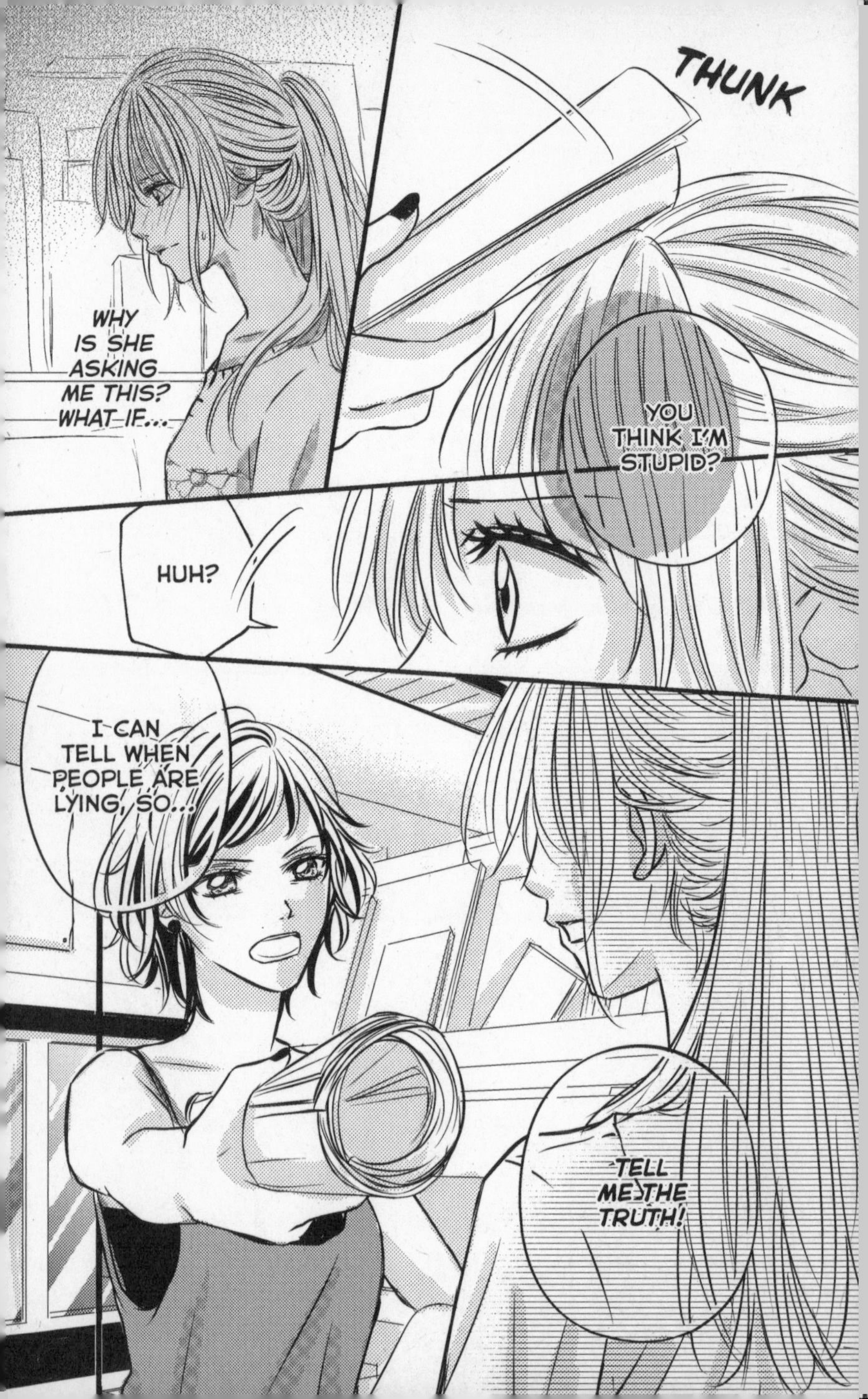
THUNK
YOU THINK I'M STUPID?
WHY IS SHE ASKING ME THIS? WHAT IF...
HUH?
I CAN TELL WHEN PEOPLE ARE LYING, SO...
TELL ME THE TRUTH!

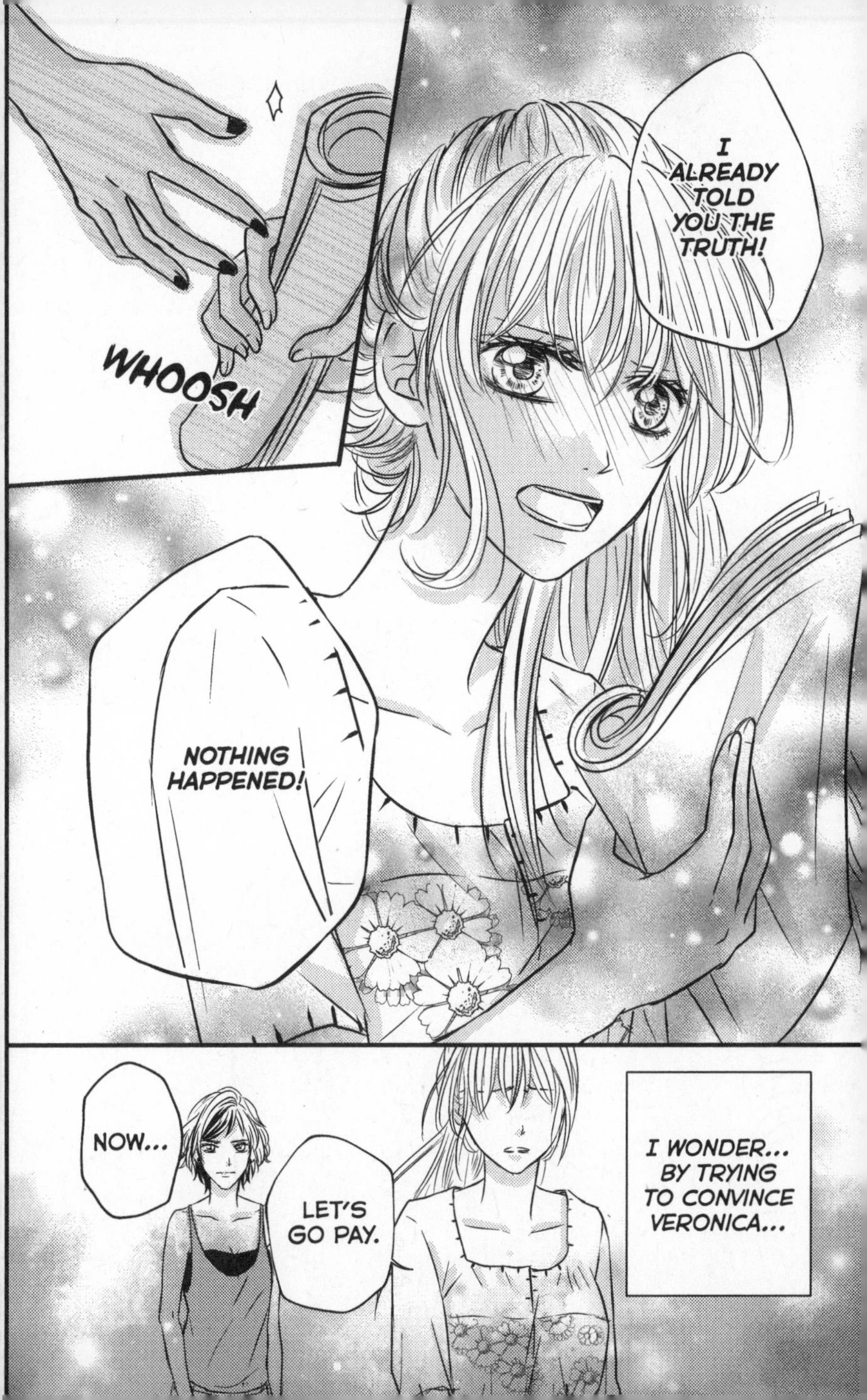
I ALREADY TOLD YOU THE TRUTH!
WHOOSH
NOTHING HAPPENED!
I WONDER... BY TRYING TO CONVINCE VERONICA...
NOW...
LET'S GO PAY.

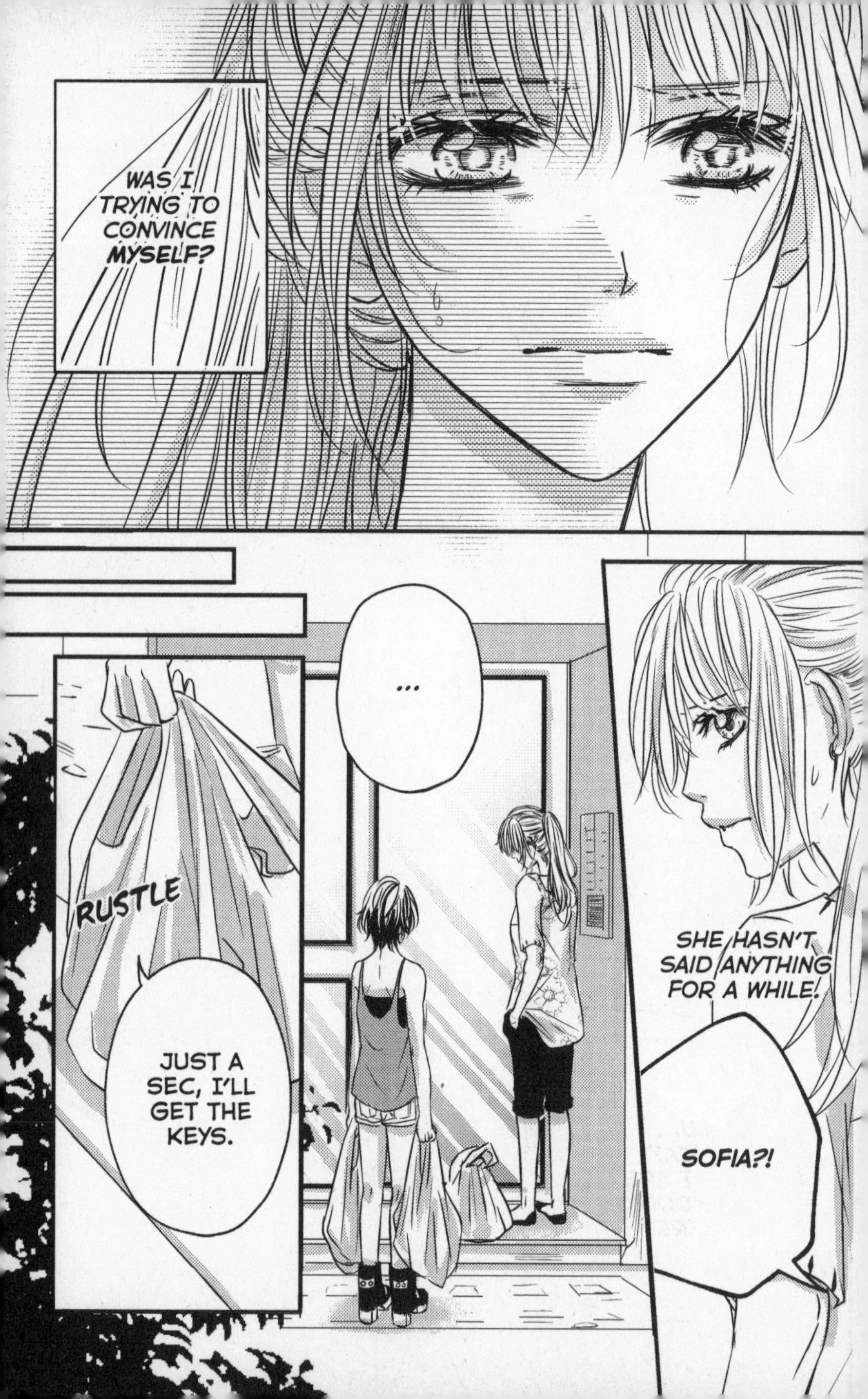
WAS I TRYING TO CONVINCE MYSELF?
SHE HASN'T SAID ANYTHING FOR A WHILE!
SOFIA?!
...
RUSTLE
JUST A SEC, I'LL GET THE KEYS.

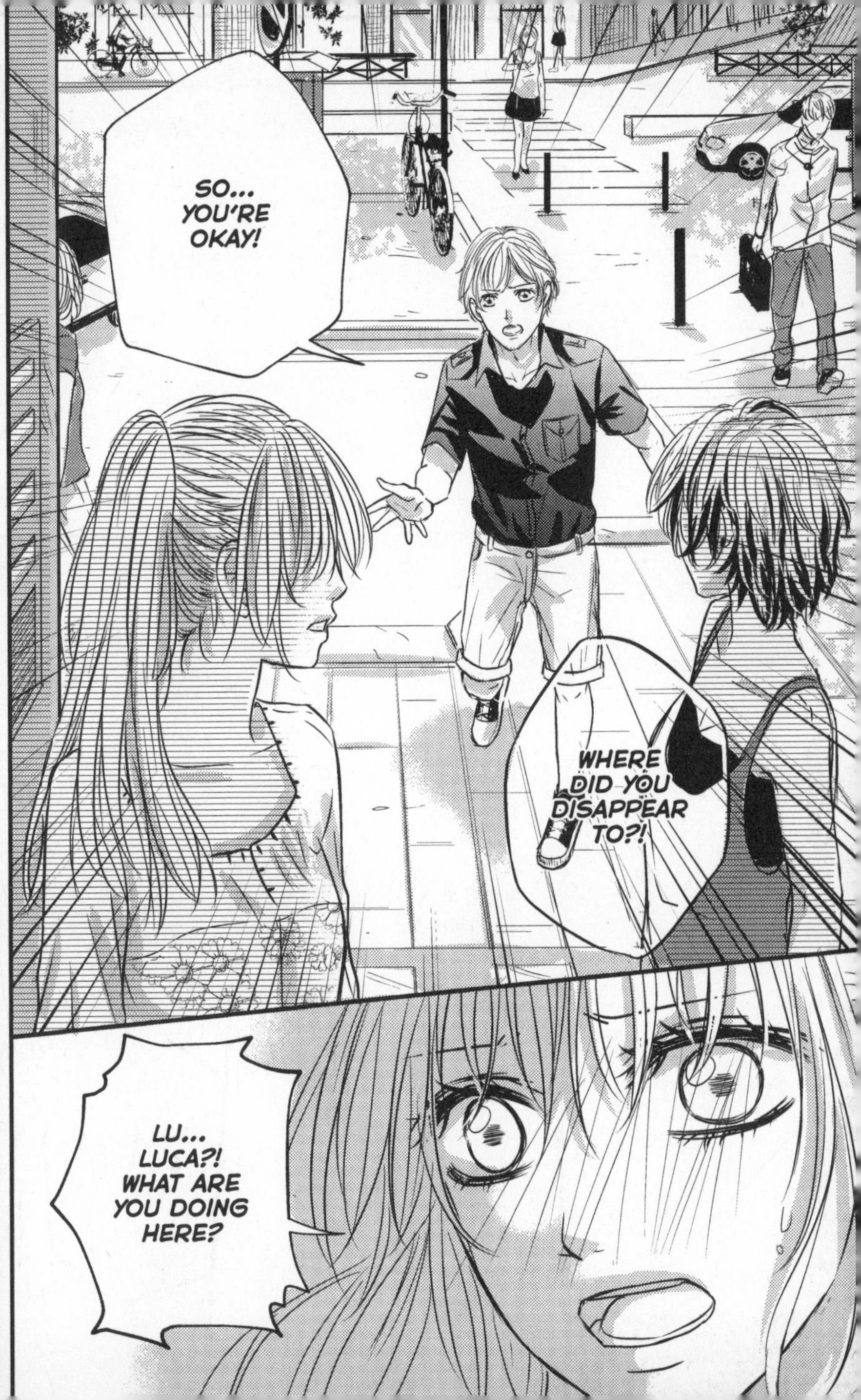
SO... YOU'RE OKAY!
WHERE DID YOU DISAPPEAR TO?!
LU... LUCA?! WHAT ARE YOU DOING HERE?

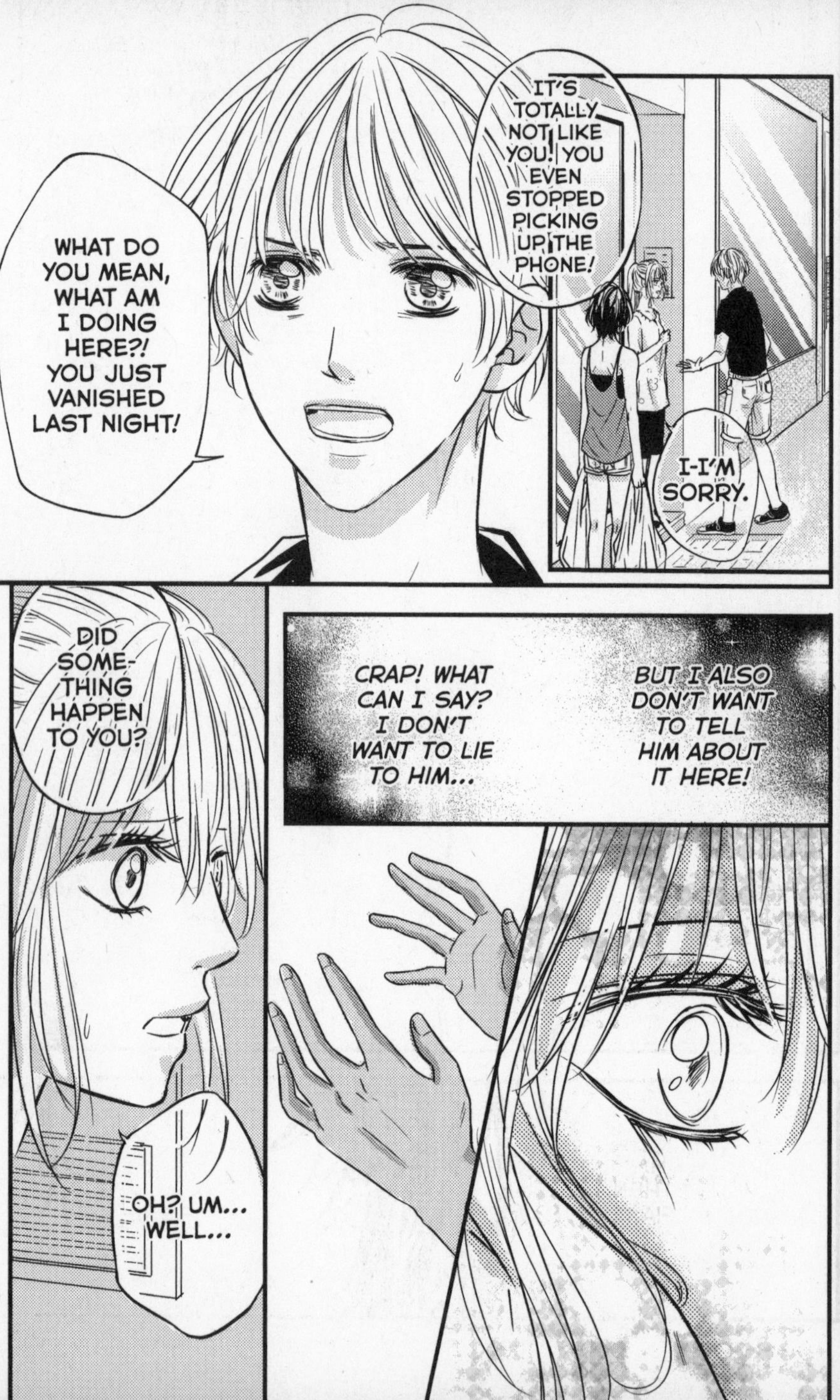
WHAT DO YOU MEAN, WHAT AM I DOING HERE?! YOU JUST VANISHED LAST NIGHT!
IT'S TOTALLY NOT LIKE YOU! YOU EVEN STOPPED PICKING UP THE PHONE!
I-I'M SORRY.
DID SOME-THING HAPPEN TO YOU?
OH? UM... WELL...
CRAP! WHAT CAN I SAY? I DON'T WANT TO LIE TO HIM...
BUT I ALSO DON'T WANT TO TELL HIM ABOUT IT HERE!

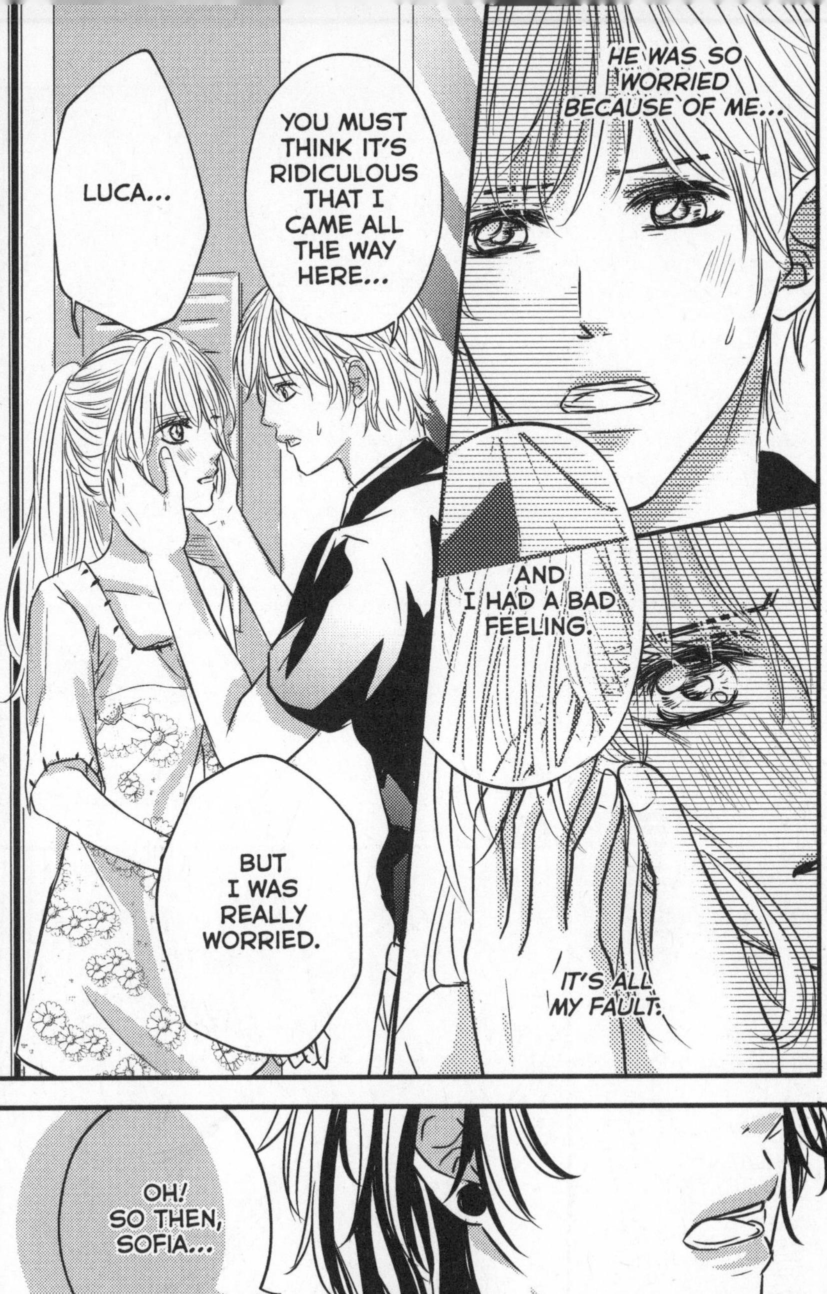
HE WAS SO WORRIED BECAUSE OF ME...
AND I HAD A BAD FEELING.
IT'S ALL MY FAULT.
YOU MUST THINK IT'S RIDICULOUS THAT I CAME ALL THE WAY HERE...
LUCA...
BUT I WAS REALLY WORRIED.
OH! SO THEN, SOFIA...

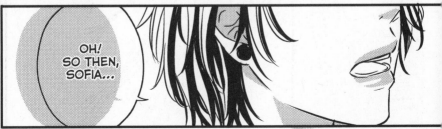

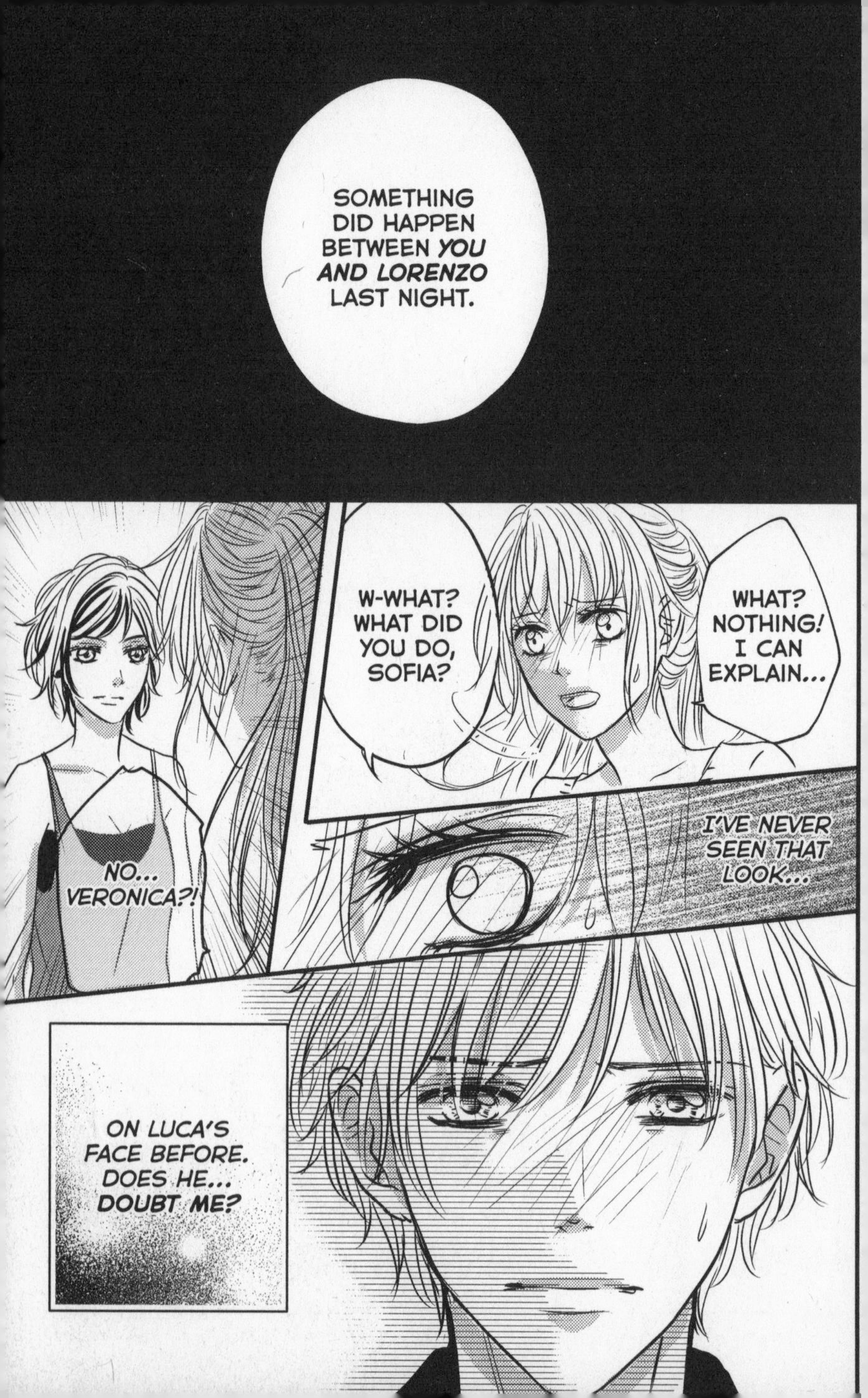
SOMETHING DID HAPPEN BETWEEN *YOU AND LORENZO* LAST NIGHT.
NO... VERONICA?!
W-WHAT? WHAT DID YOU DO, SOFIA?
WHAT? NOTHING! I CAN EXPLAIN...
I'VE NEVER SEEN THAT LOOK...
ON LUCA'S FACE BEFORE. DOES HE... DOUBT ME?

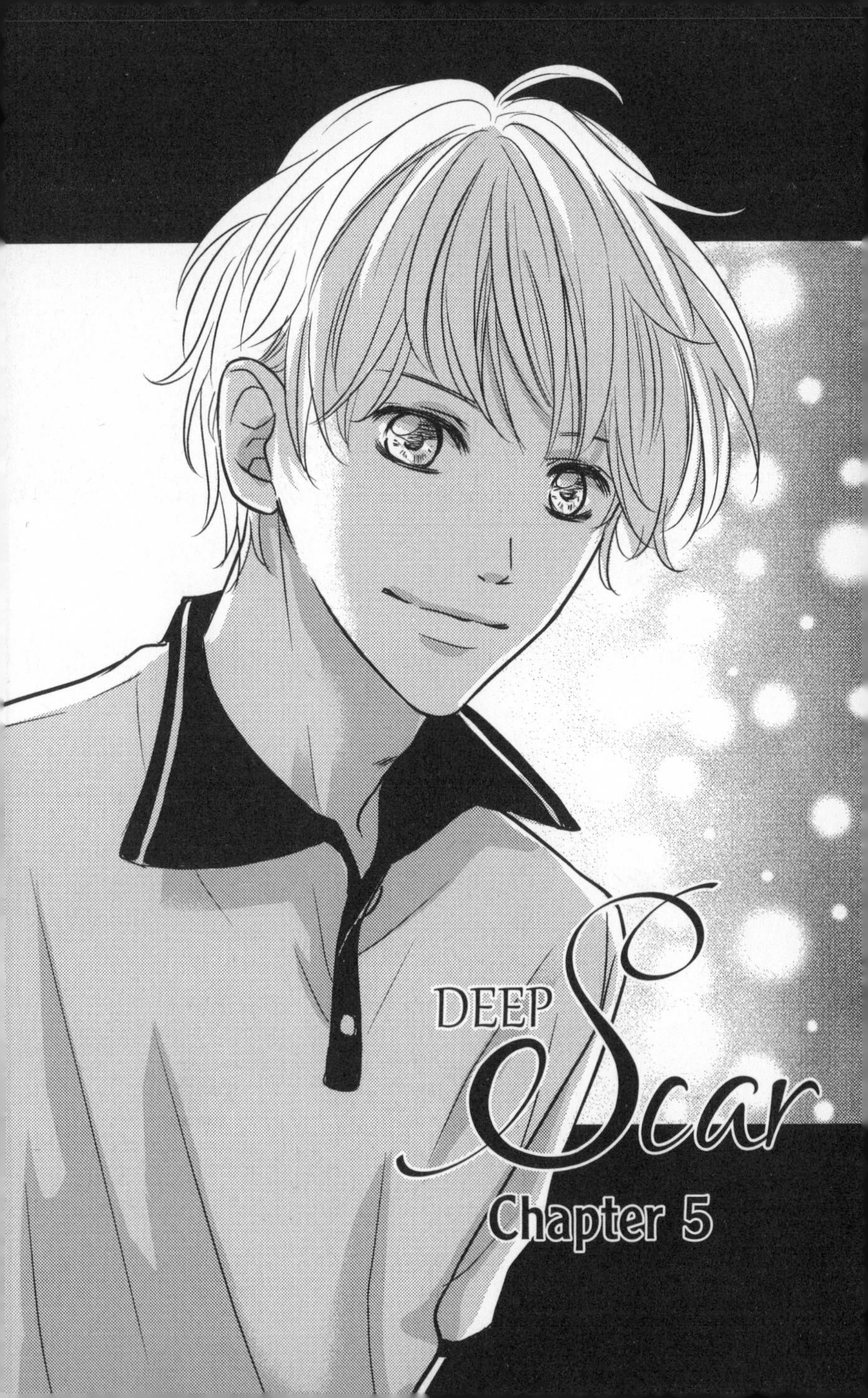
DEEP Scar
Chapter 5

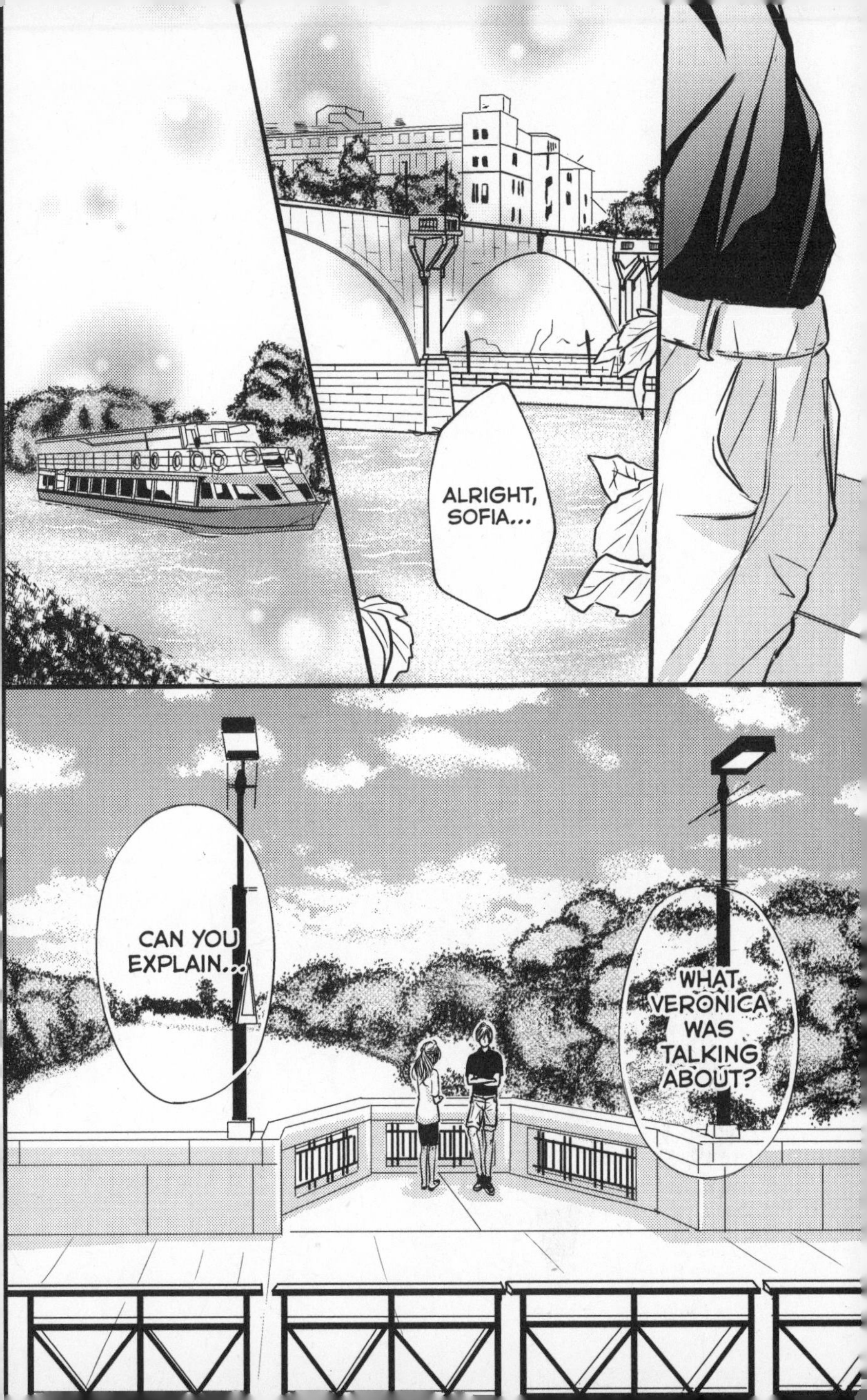
ALRIGHT, SOFIA...
CAN YOU EXPLAIN...
WHAT VERONICA WAS TALKING ABOUT?

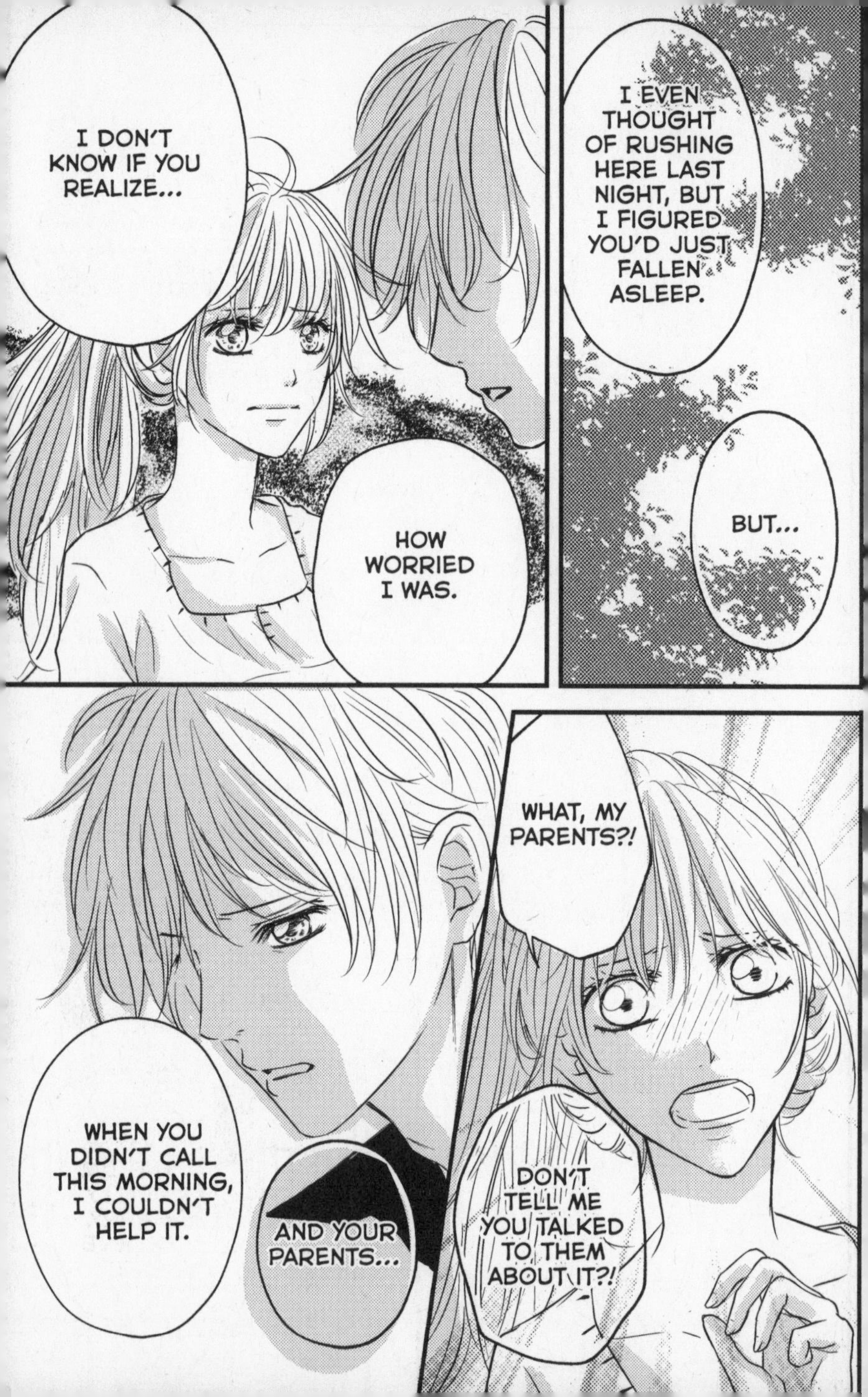
I DON'T KNOW IF YOU REALIZE...
HOW WORRIED I WAS.
I EVEN THOUGHT OF RUSHING HERE LAST NIGHT, BUT I FIGURED YOU'D JUST FALLEN ASLEEP.
BUT...
WHEN YOU DIDN'T CALL THIS MORNING, I COULDN'T HELP IT.
AND YOUR PARENTS...
WHAT, MY PARENTS?!
DON'T TELL ME YOU TALKED TO THEM ABOUT IT?!

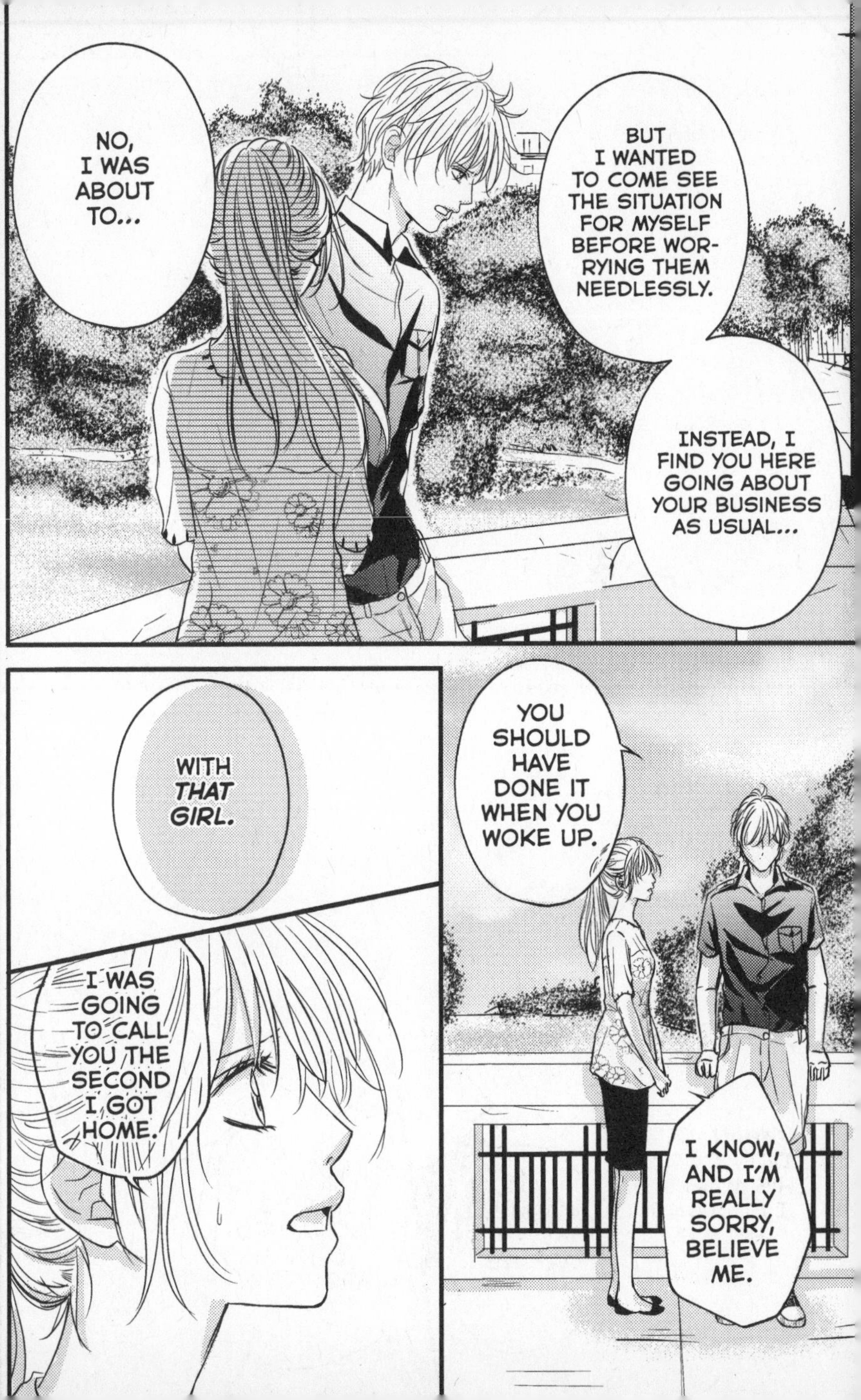
NO, I WAS ABOUT TO...
BUT I WANTED TO COME SEE THE SITUATION FOR MYSELF BEFORE WOR-RYING THEM NEEDLESSLY.
INSTEAD, I FIND YOU HERE GOING ABOUT YOUR BUSINESS AS USUAL...
WITH *THAT* GIRL.
I WAS GOING TO CALL YOU THE SECOND I GOT HOME.
YOU SHOULD HAVE DONE IT WHEN YOU WOKE UP.
I KNOW, AND I'M REALLY SORRY, BELIEVE ME.

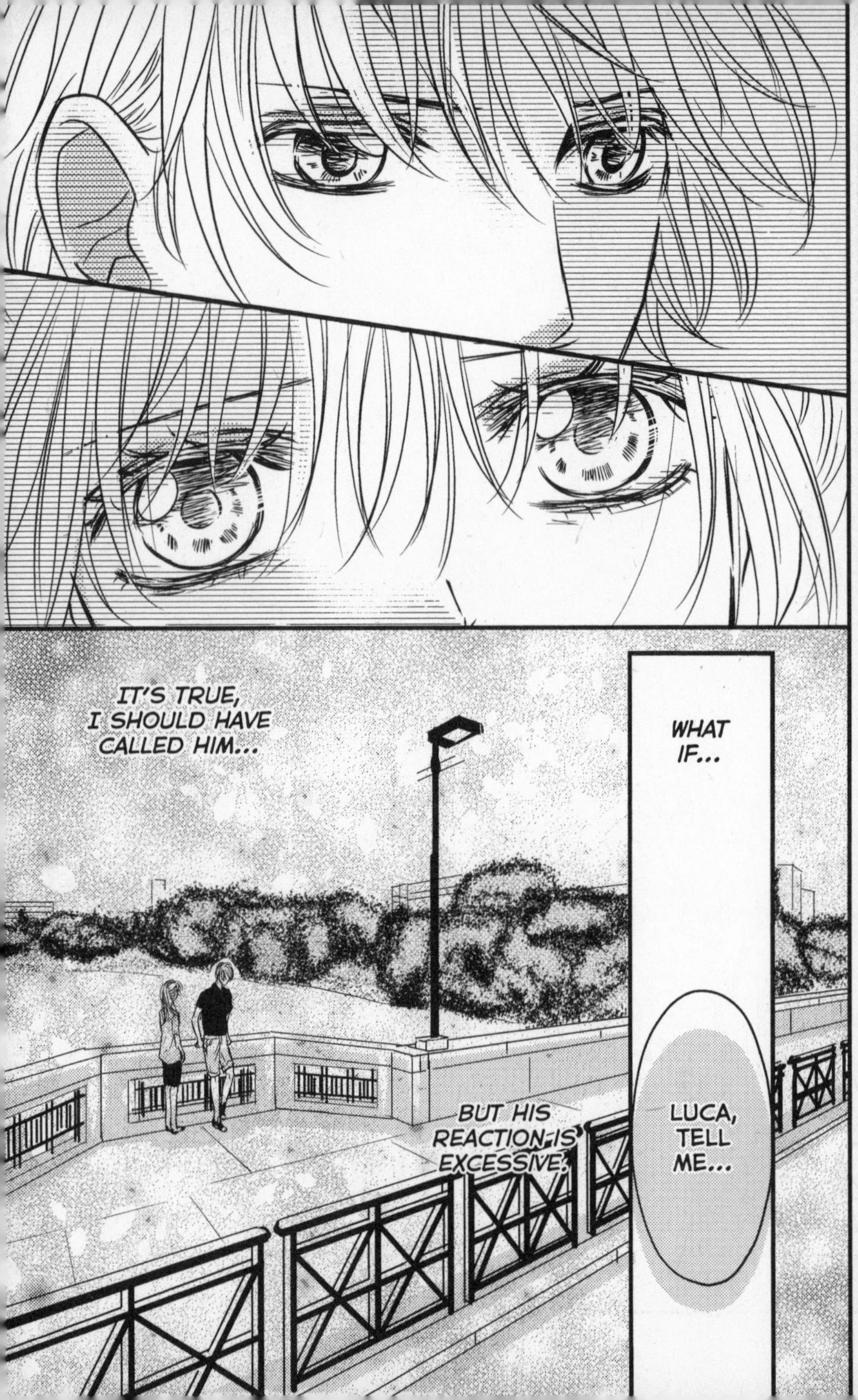
IT'S TRUE, I SHOULD HAVE CALLED HIM...
BUT HIS REACTION IS EXCESSIVE.
WHAT IF...
LUCA, TELL ME...

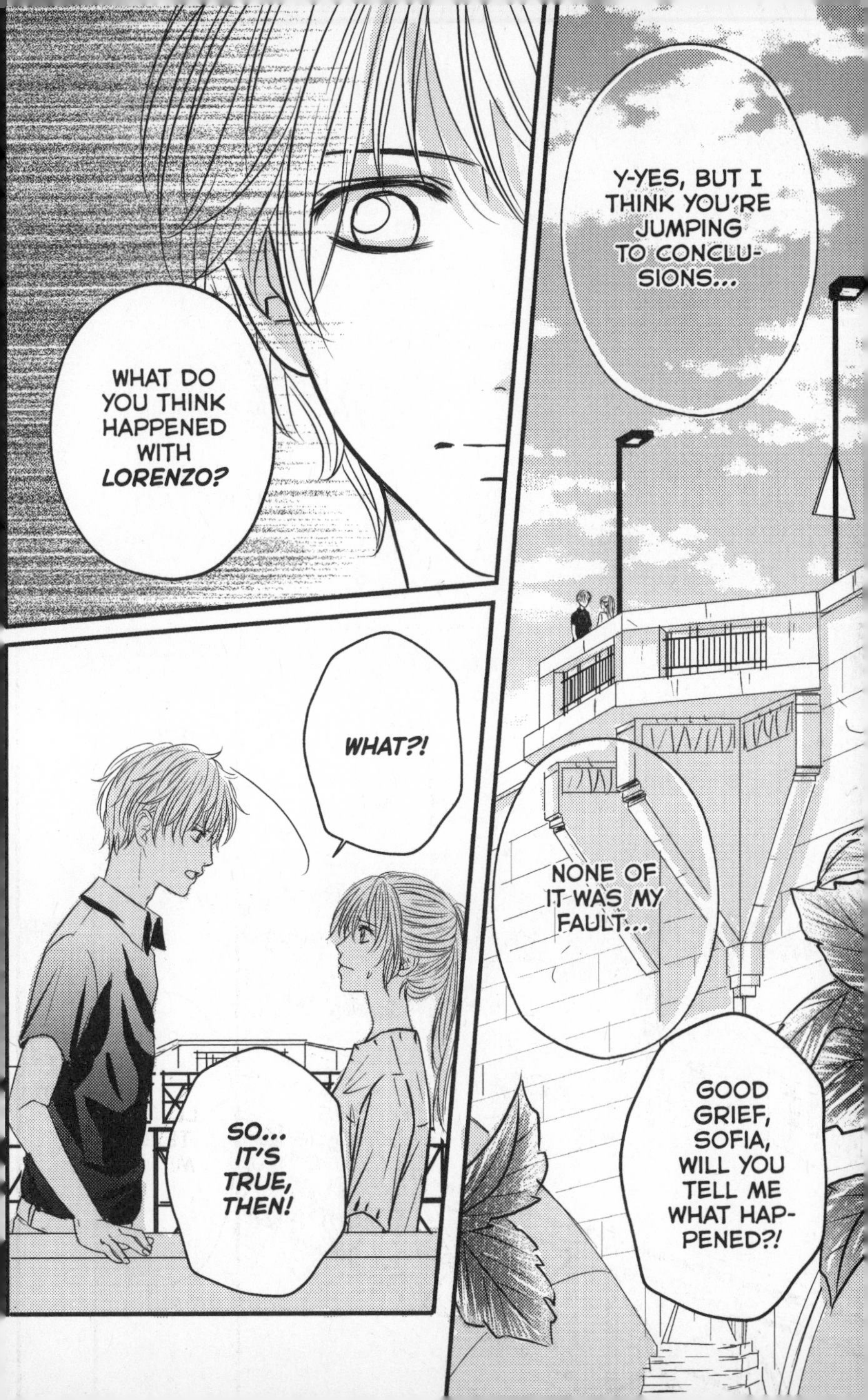
Y-YES, BUT I THINK YOU'RE JUMPING TO CONCLU-SIONS...
NONE OF IT WAS MY FAULT...
GOOD GRIEF, SOFIA, WILL YOU TELL ME WHAT HAP-PENED?!
WHAT DO YOU THINK HAPPENED WITH *LORENZO?*
*WHAT?!*
*SO... IT'S TRUE, THEN!*

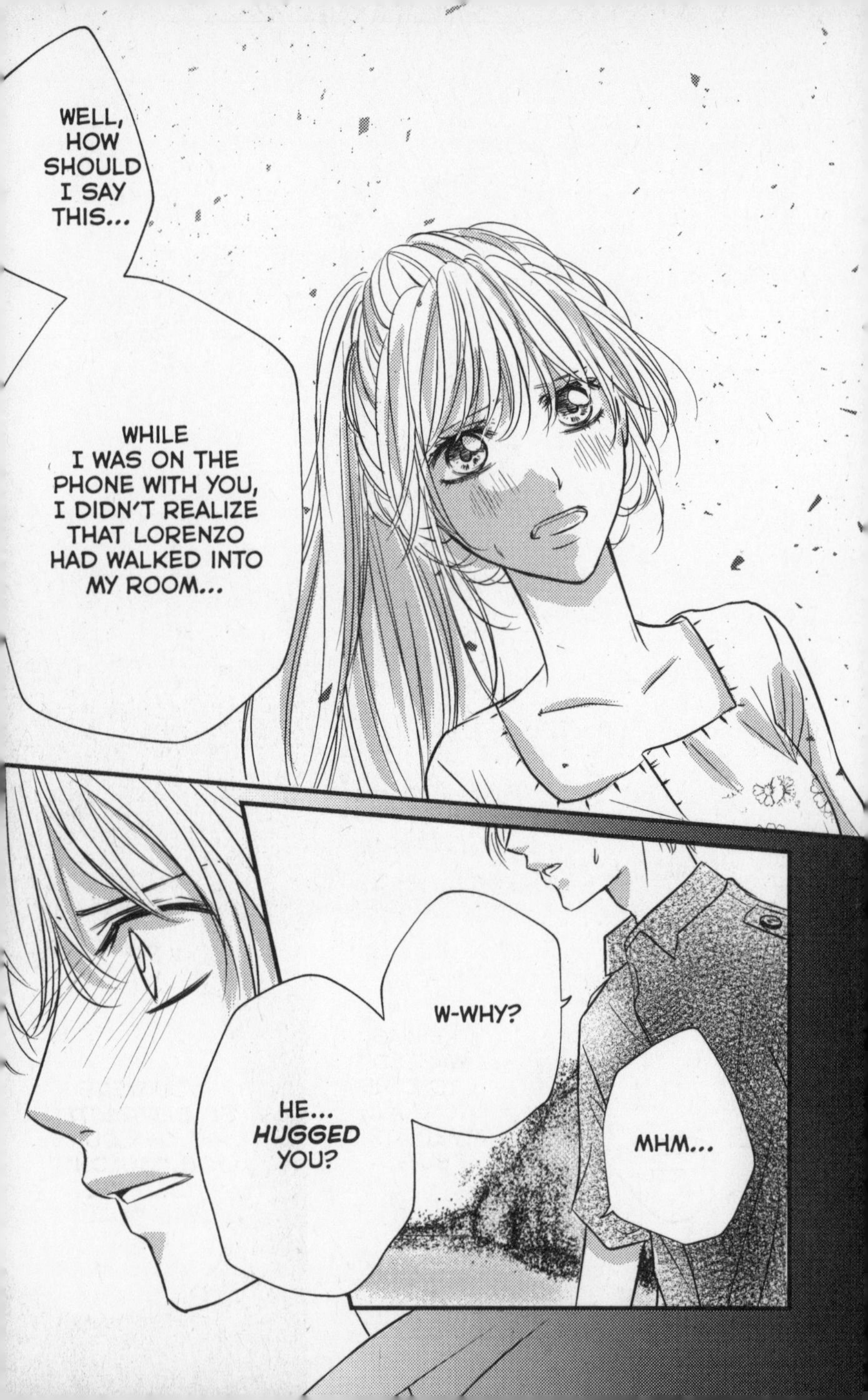
WELL, HOW SHOULD I SAY THIS...
WHILE I WAS ON THE PHONE WITH YOU, I DIDN'T REALIZE THAT LORENZO HAD WALKED INTO MY ROOM...
HE... *HUGGED* YOU?
MHM...
W-WHY?

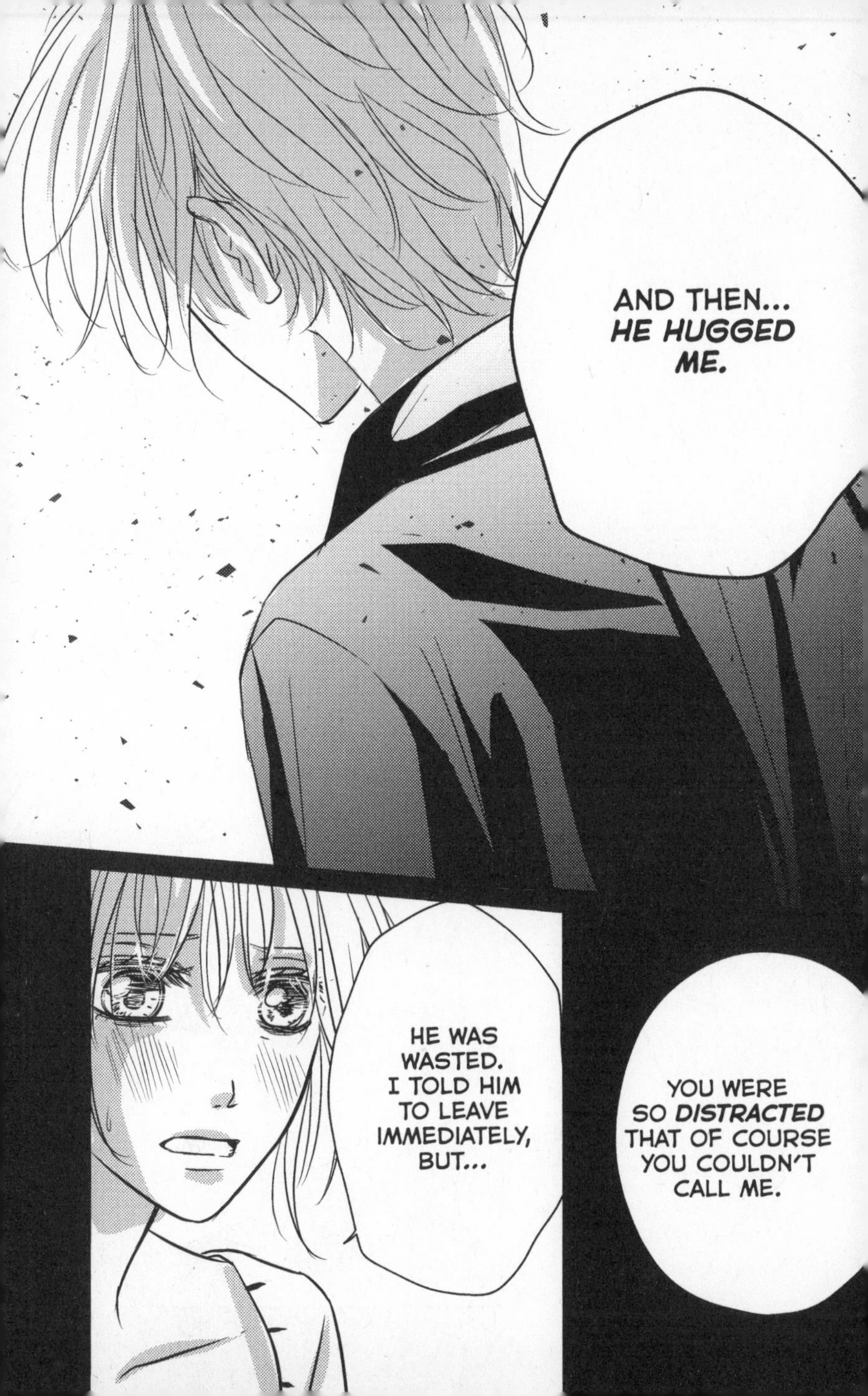
AND THEN... *HE HUGGED* *ME.*
YOU WERE SO *DISTRACTED* THAT OF COURSE YOU COULDN'T CALL ME.
HE WAS WASTED. I TOLD HIM TO LEAVE IMMEDIATELY, BUT...

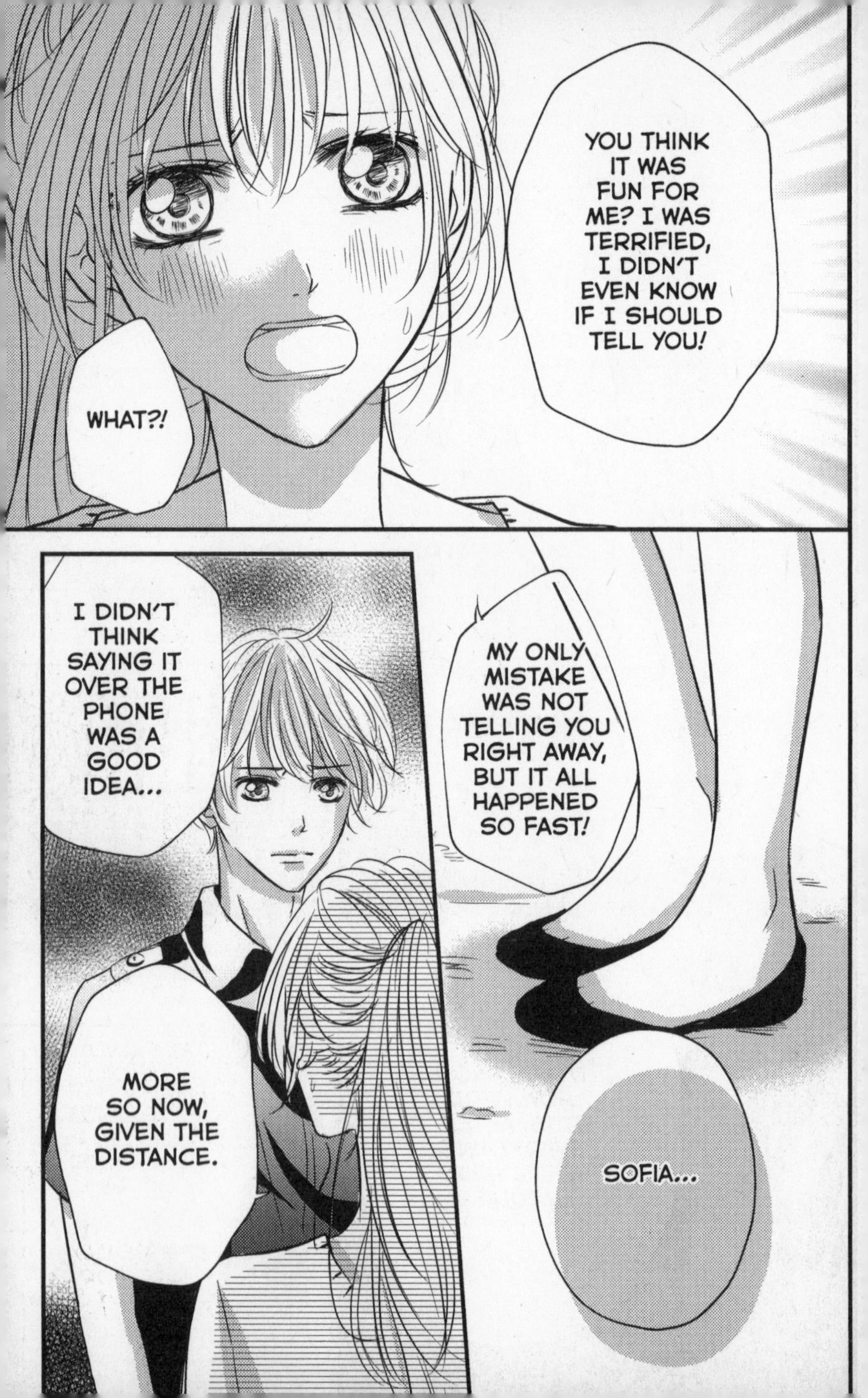
YOU THINK IT WAS FUN FOR ME? I WAS TERRIFIED, I DIDN'T EVEN KNOW IF I SHOULD TELL YOU!
WHAT?!
MY ONLY MISTAKE WAS NOT TELLING YOU RIGHT AWAY, BUT IT ALL HAPPENED SO FAST!
SOFIA...
I DIDN'T THINK SAYING IT OVER THE PHONE WAS A GOOD IDEA...
MORE SO NOW, GIVEN THE DISTANCE.

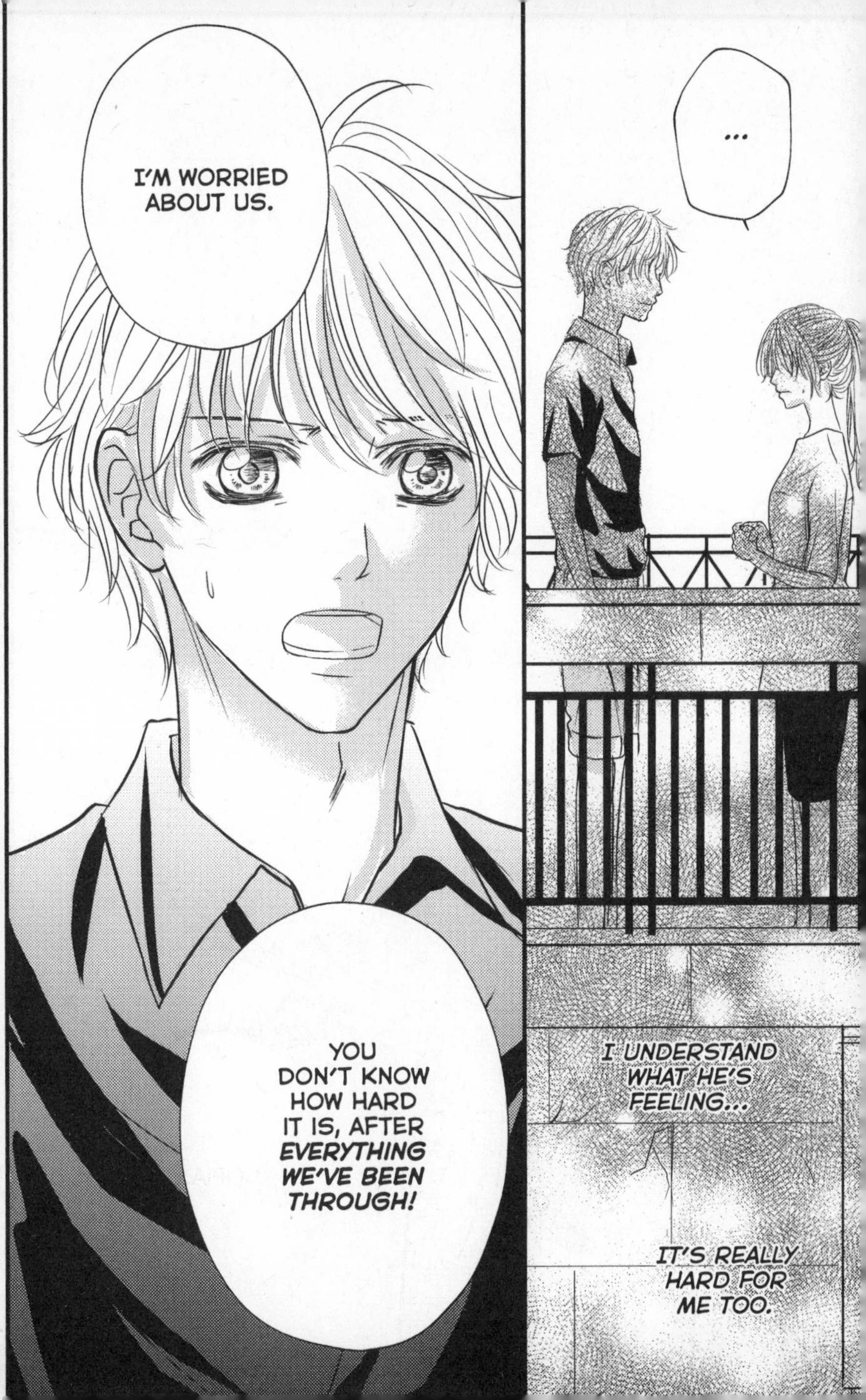
...
I UNDERSTAND WHAT HE'S FEELING...
IT'S REALLY HARD FOR ME TOO.
I'M WORRIED ABOUT US.
YOU DON'T KNOW HOW HARD IT IS, AFTER *EVERYTHING* *WE'VE BEEN* *THROUGH!*

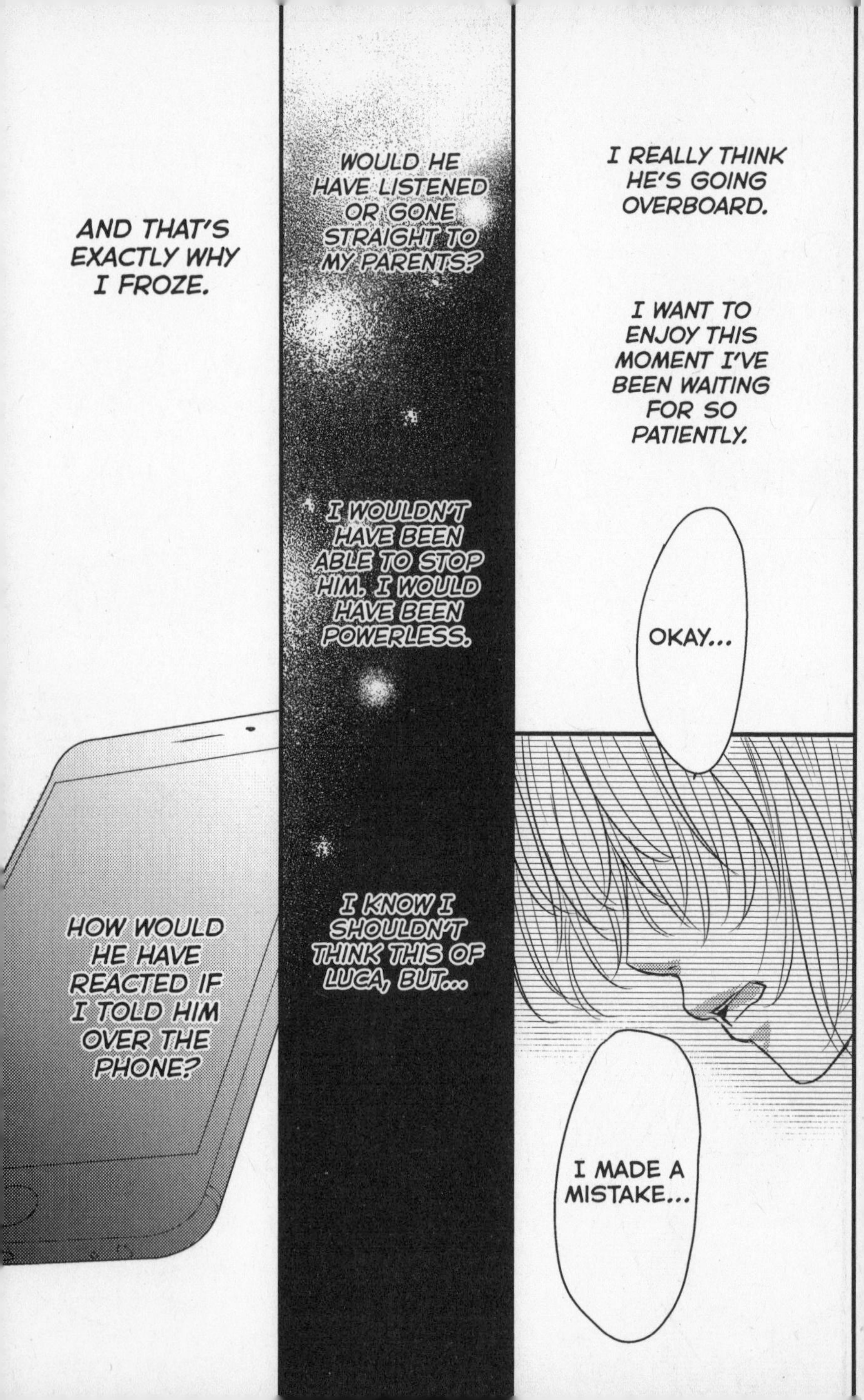
I REALLY THINK HE'S GOING OVERBOARD.
I WANT TO ENJOY THIS MOMENT I'VE BEEN WAITING FOR SO PATIENTLY.
OKAY...
I MADE A MISTAKE...
WOULD HE HAVE LISTENED OR GONE STRAIGHT TO MY PARENTS?
I WOULDN'T HAVE BEEN ABLE TO STOP HIM. I WOULD HAVE BEEN POWERLESS.
I KNOW I SHOULDN'T THINK THIS OF LUCA, BUT...
AND THAT'S EXACTLY WHY I FROZE.
HOW WOULD HE HAVE REACTED IF I TOLD HIM OVER THE PHONE?

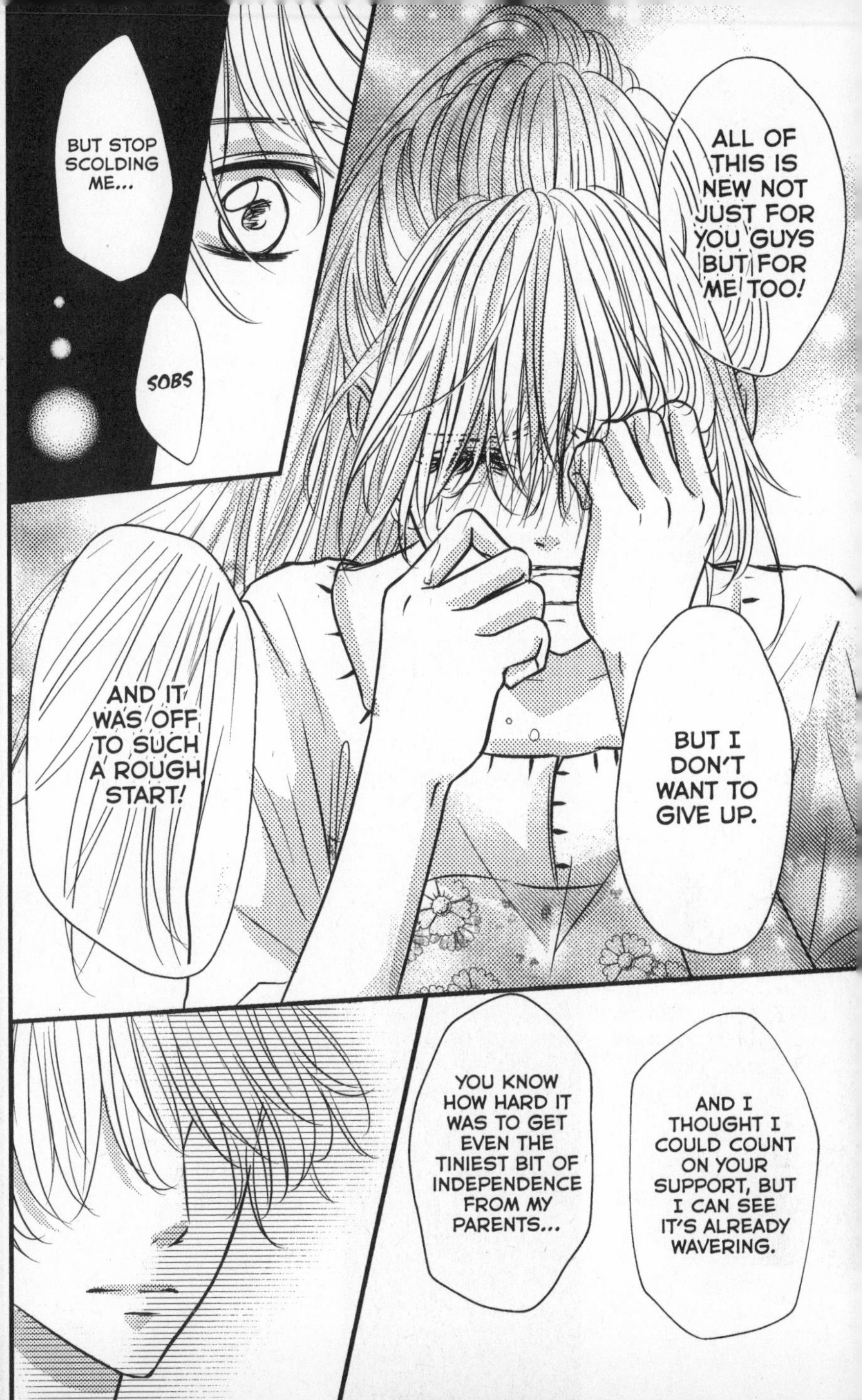
ALL OF THIS IS NEW NOT JUST FOR YOU GUYS BUT FOR ME TOO!
BUT STOP SCOLDING ME...
SOBS
BUT I DON'T WANT TO GIVE UP.
AND IT WAS OFF TO SUCH A ROUGH START!
AND I THOUGHT I COULD COUNT ON YOUR SUPPORT, BUT I CAN SEE IT'S ALREADY WAVERING.
YOU KNOW HOW HARD IT WAS TO GET EVEN THE TINIEST BIT OF INDEPENDENCE FROM MY PARENTS...

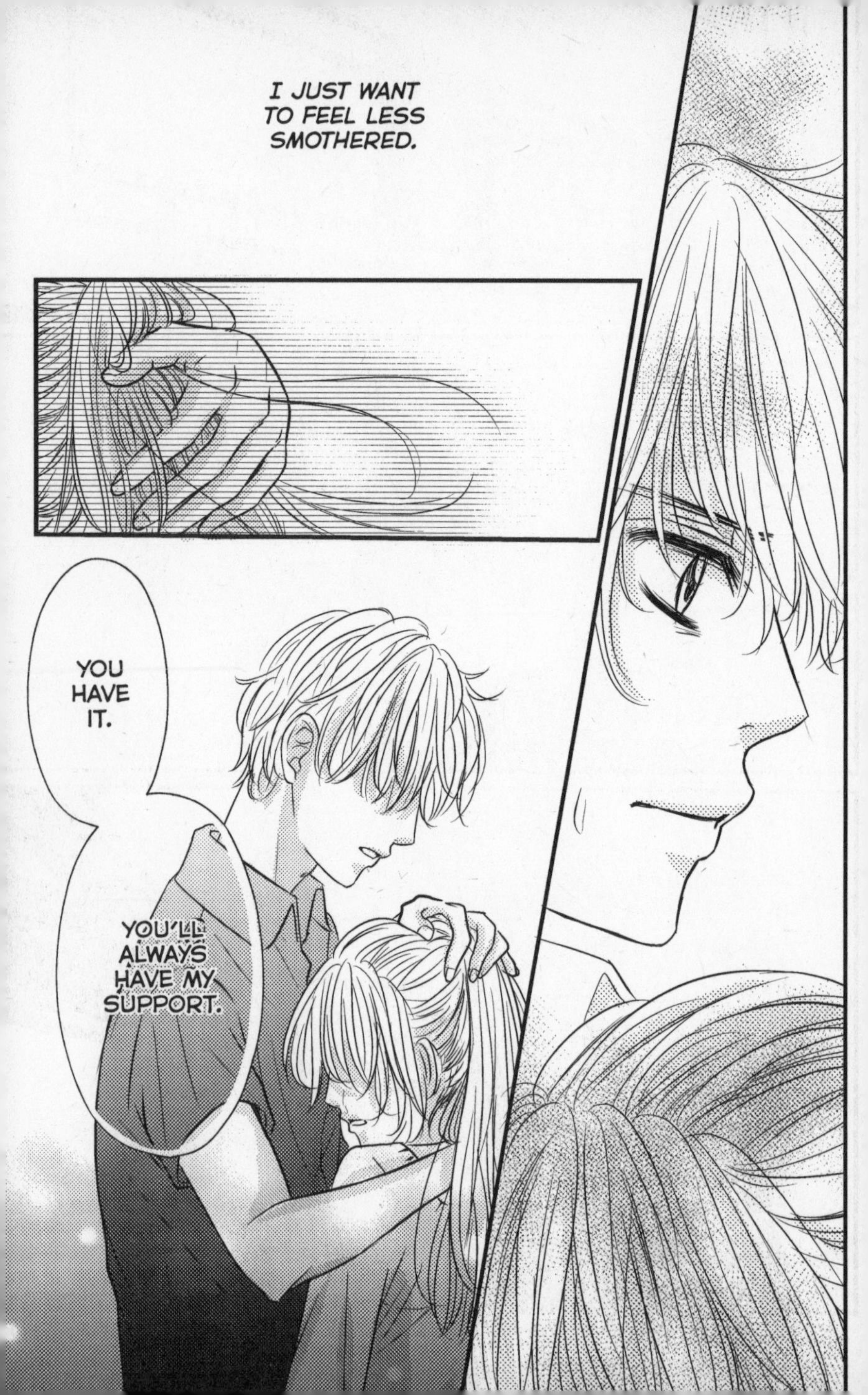
I JUST WANT TO FEEL LESS SMOTHERED.
YOU HAVE IT.
YOU'LL ALWAYS HAVE MY SUPPORT.

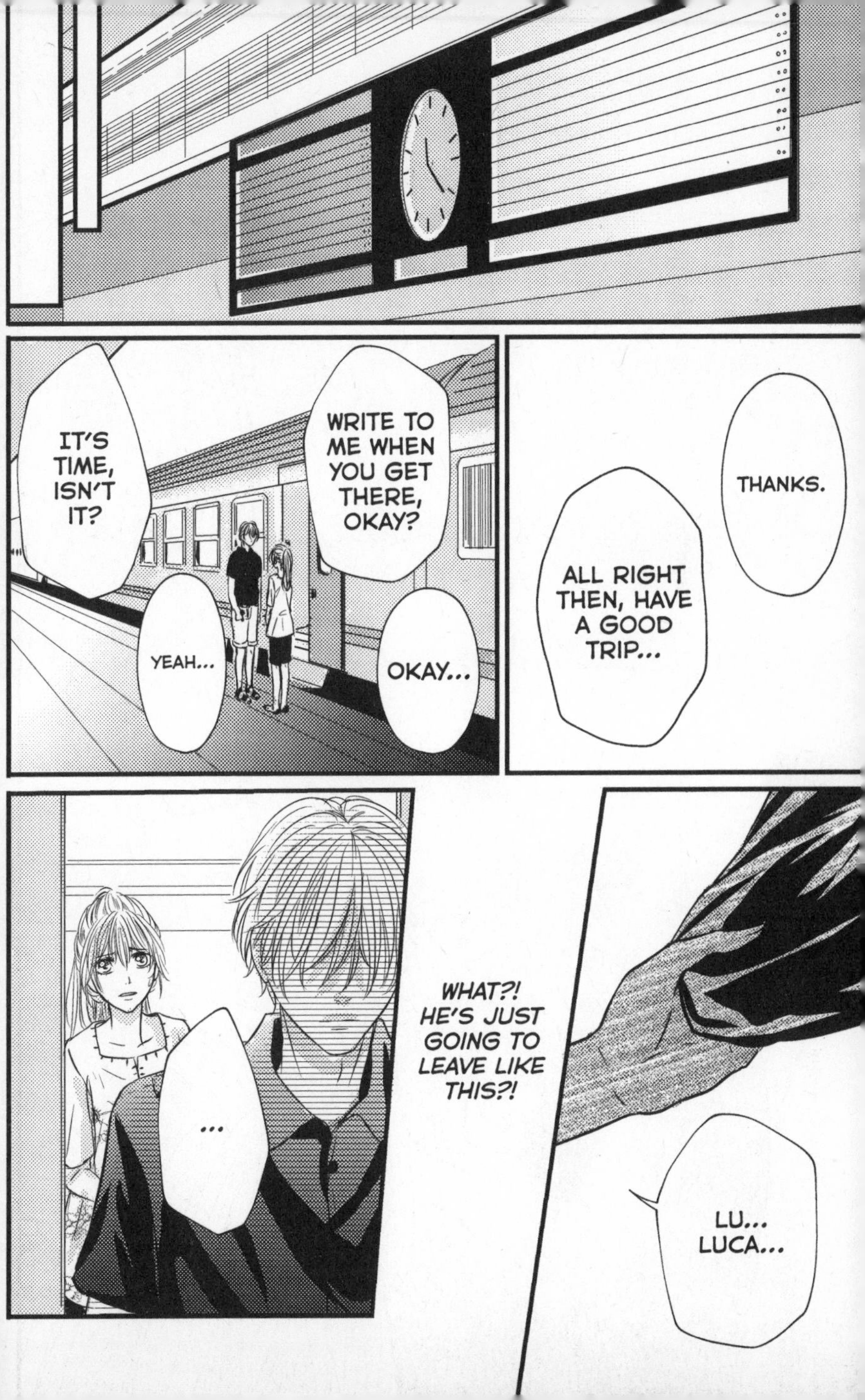
IT'S TIME, ISN'T IT?
YEAH...
WRITE TO ME WHEN YOU GET THERE, OKAY?
OKAY...
ALL RIGHT THEN, HAVE A GOOD TRIP...
THANKS.
...
WHAT?! HE'S JUST GOING TO LEAVE LIKE THIS?!
LU... LUCA...

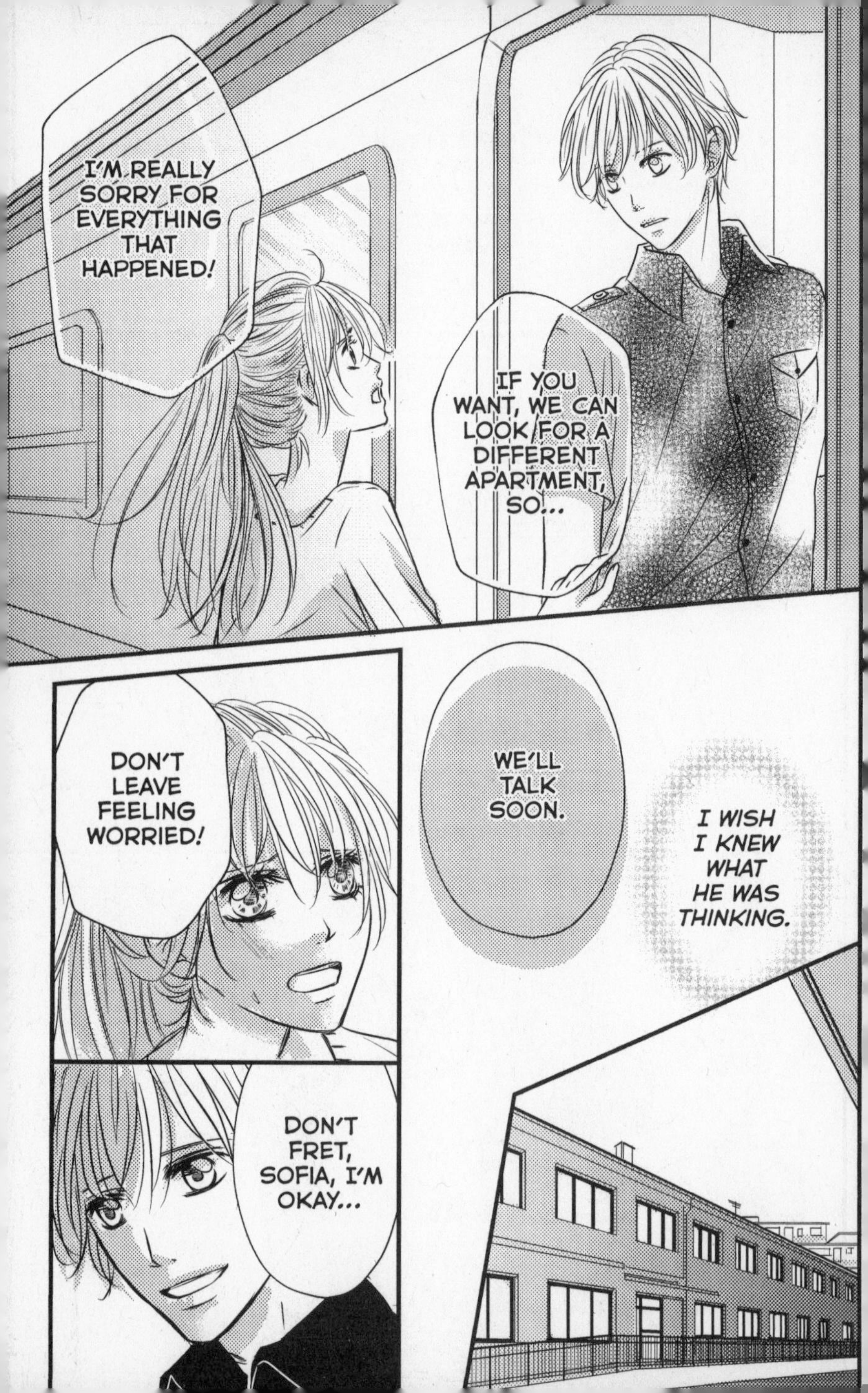
IF YOU WANT, WE CAN LOOK FOR A DIFFERENT APARTMENT, SO...
I'M REALLY SORRY FOR EVERYTHING THAT HAPPENED!
DON'T LEAVE FEELING WORRIED!
DON'T FRET, SOFIA, I'M OKAY...
WE'LL TALK SOON.
I WISH I KNEW WHAT HE WAS THINKING.

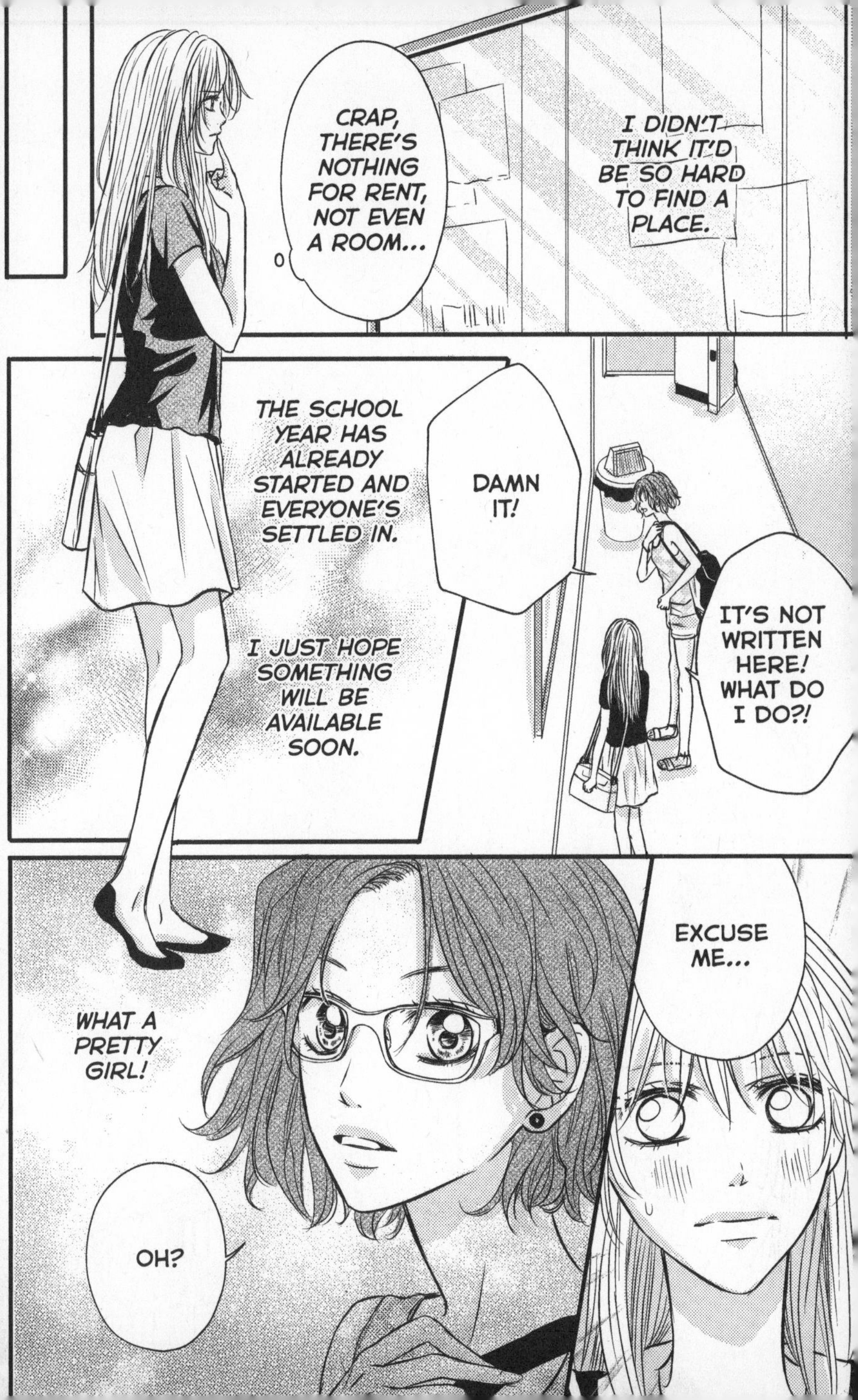
I DIDN'T THINK IT'D BE SO HARD TO FIND A PLACE.
CRAP, THERE'S NOTHING FOR RENT, NOT EVEN A ROOM...
DAMN IT!
IT'S NOT WRITTEN HERE! WHAT DO I DO?!
THE SCHOOL YEAR HAS ALREADY STARTED AND EVERYONE'S SETTLED IN.
I JUST HOPE SOMETHING WILL BE AVAILABLE SOON.
EXCUSE ME...
WHAT A PRETTY GIRL!
OH?

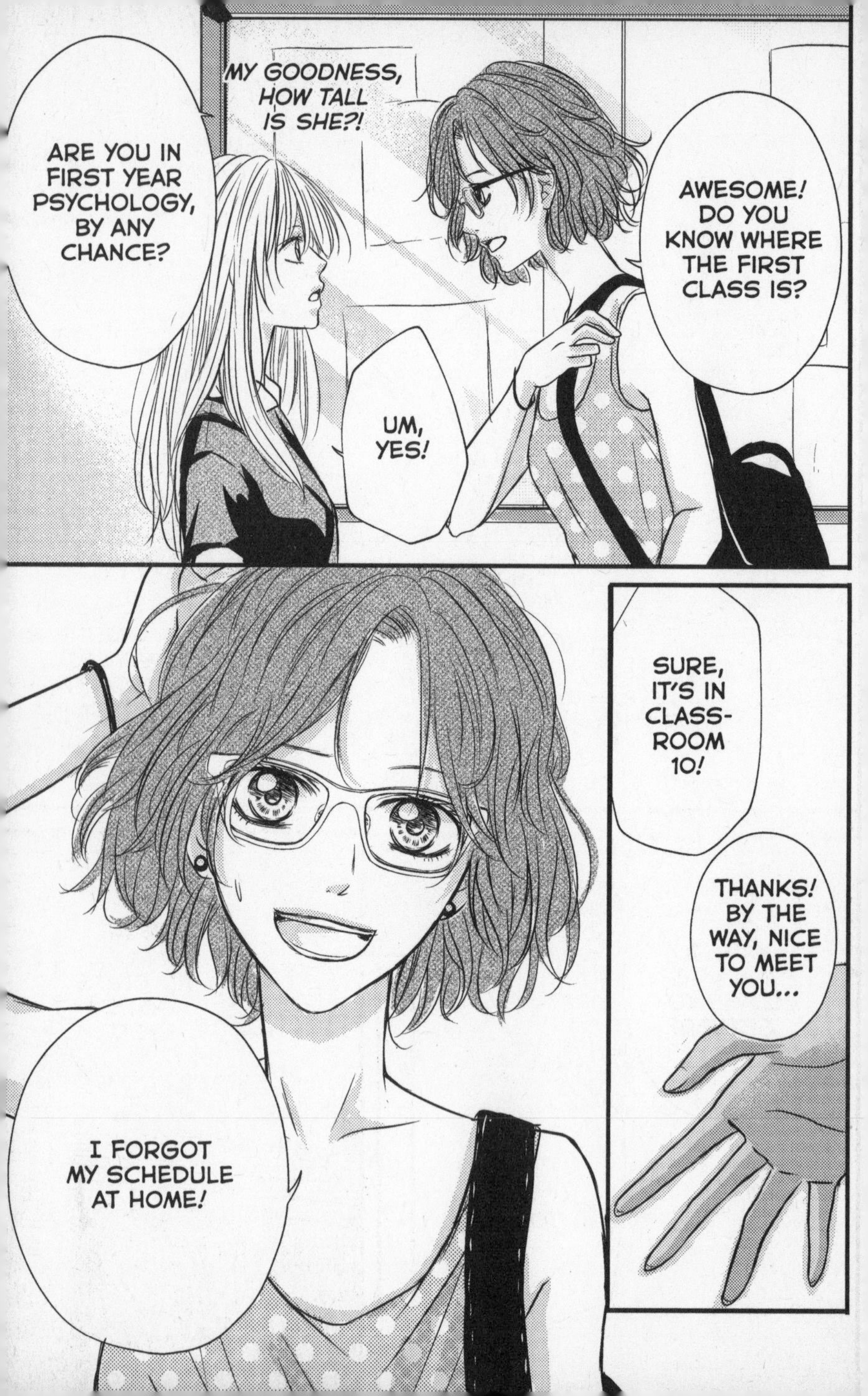
ARE YOU IN FIRST YEAR PSYCHOLOGY, BY ANY CHANCE?
MY GOODNESS, HOW TALL IS SHE?!
UM, YES!
AWESOME! DO YOU KNOW WHERE THE FIRST CLASS IS?
I FORGOT MY SCHEDULE AT HOME!
SURE, IT'S IN CLASS-ROOM 10!
THANKS! BY THE WAY, NICE TO MEET YOU...

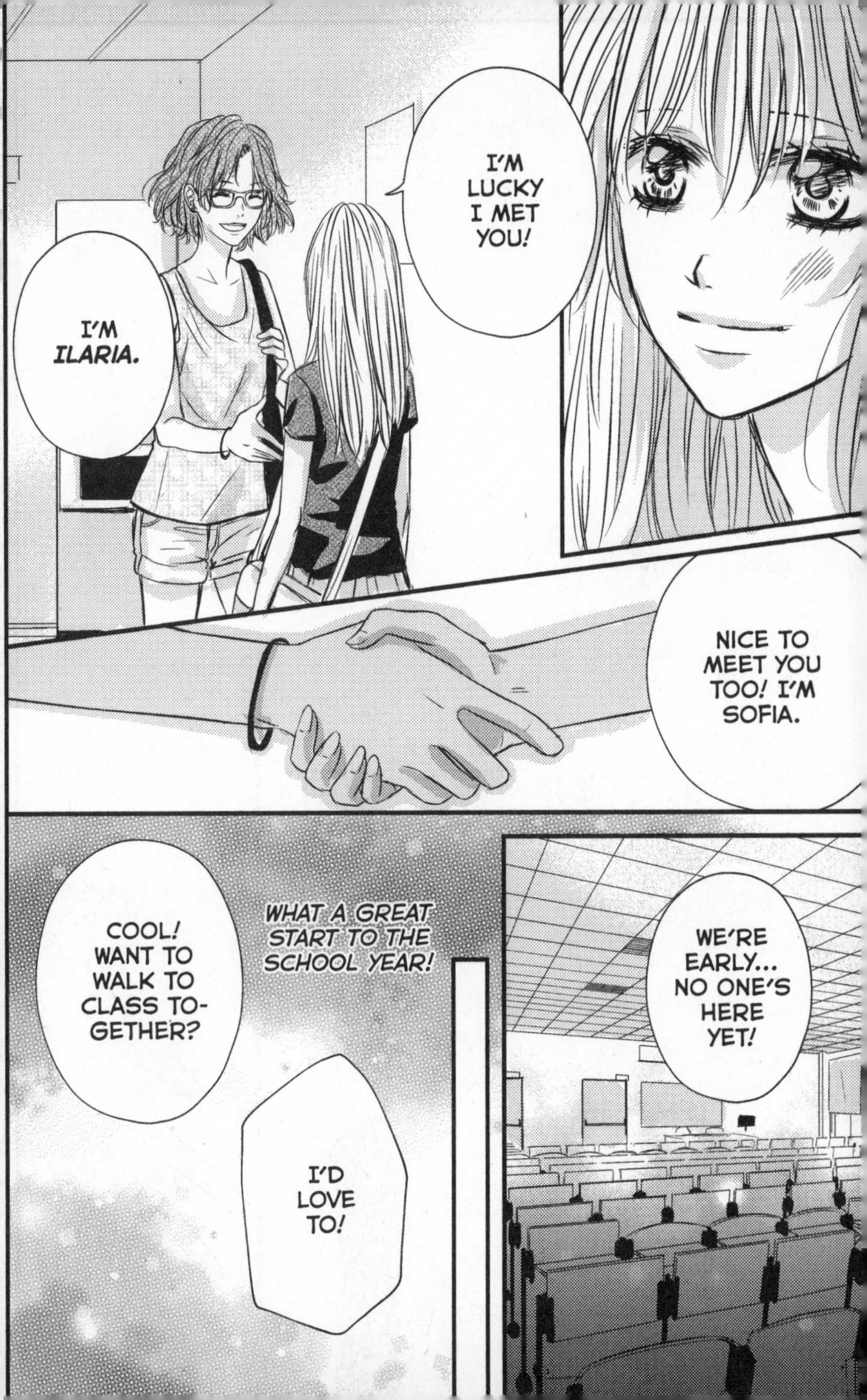
I'M ILARIA.
I'M LUCKY I MET YOU!
NICE TO MEET YOU TOO! I'M SOFIA.
COOL! WANT TO WALK TO CLASS TO-GETHER?
WHAT A GREAT START TO THE SCHOOL YEAR!
I'D LOVE TO!
WE'RE EARLY... NO ONE'S HERE YET!

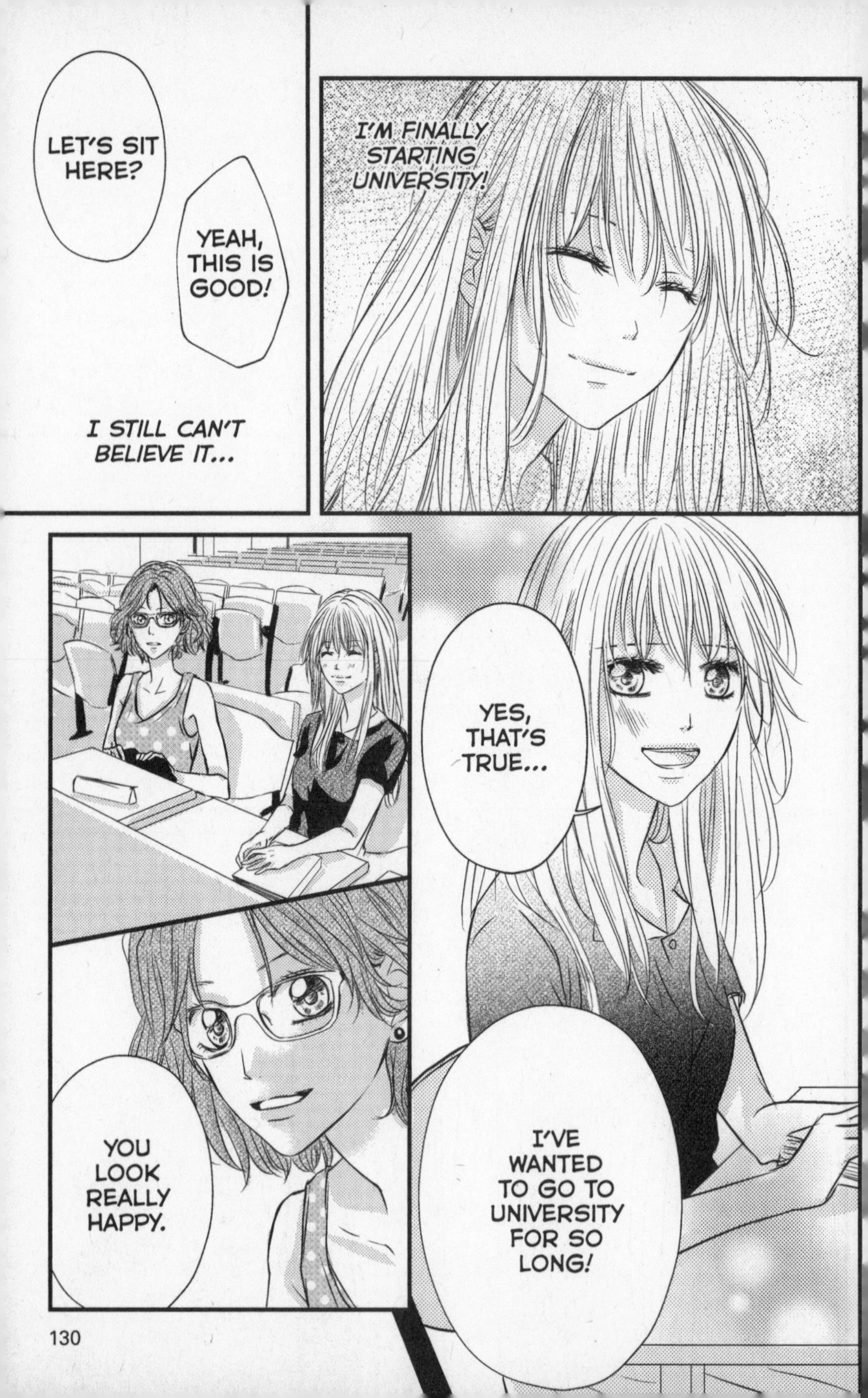
LET'S SIT HERE?
YEAH, THIS IS GOOD!
I STILL CAN'T BELIEVE IT...
I'M FINALLY STARTING UNIVERSITY!
YOU LOOK REALLY HAPPY.
YES, THAT'S TRUE...
I'VE WANTED TO GO TO UNIVERSITY FOR SO LONG!

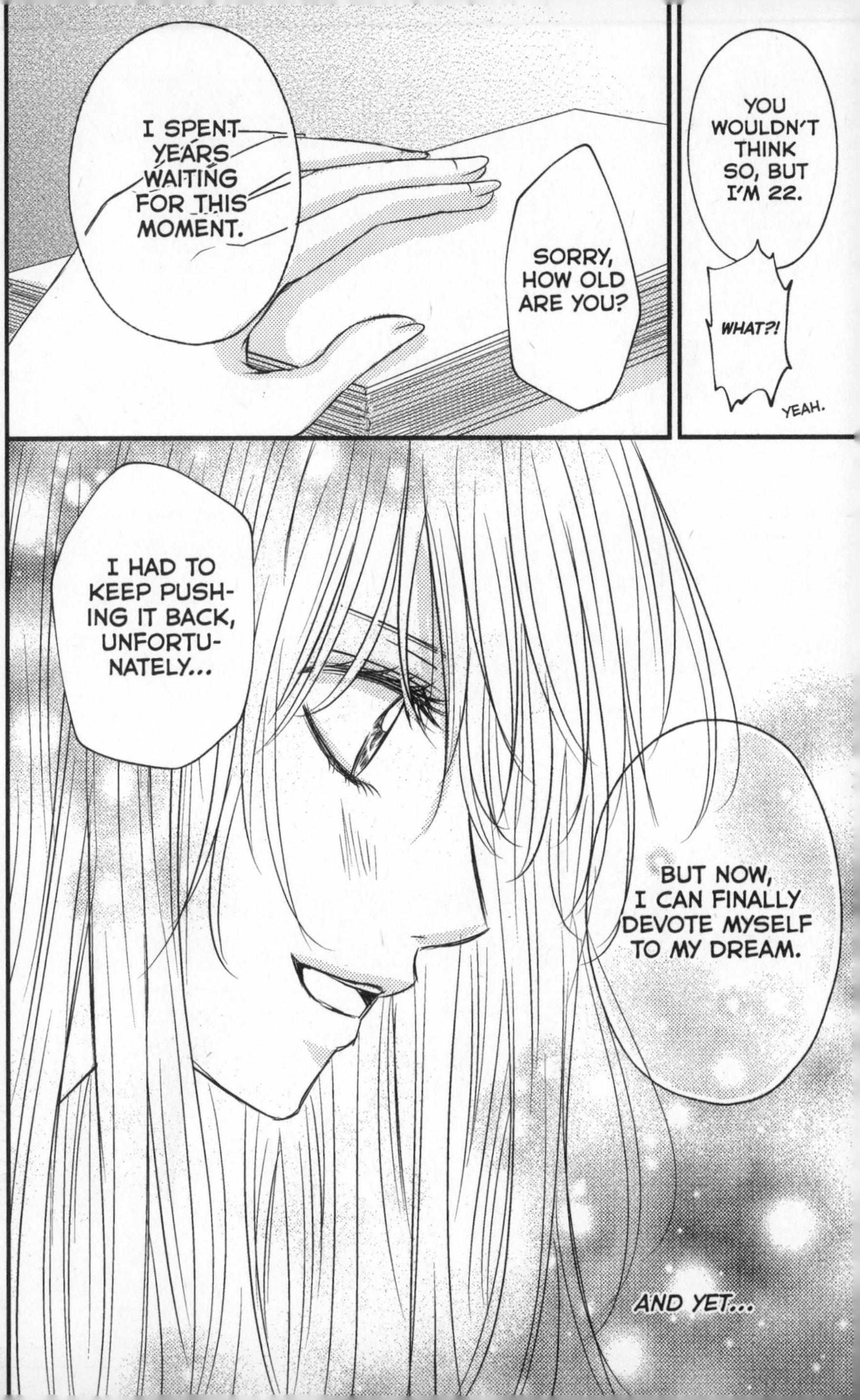
I SPENT YEARS WAITING FOR THIS MOMENT.
SORRY, HOW OLD ARE YOU?
YOU WOULDN'T THINK SO, BUT I'M 22.
WHAT?!
YEAH.
I HAD TO KEEP PUSHING IT BACK, UNFORTUNATELY...
BUT NOW, I CAN FINALLY DEVOTE MYSELF TO MY DREAM.
AND YET...

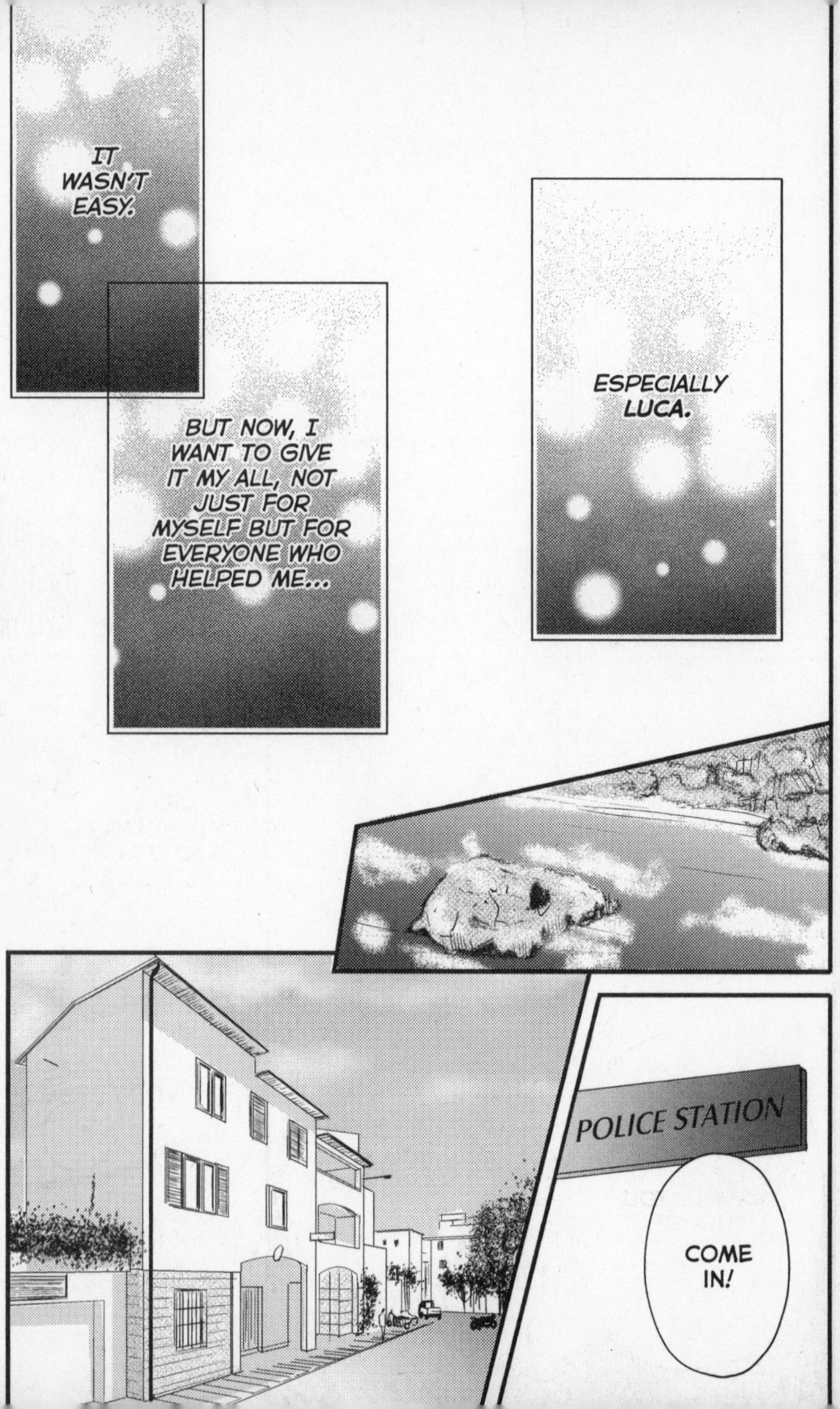
ESPECIALLY LUCA.
IT WASN'T EASY.
BUT NOW, I WANT TO GIVE IT MY ALL, NOT JUST FOR MYSELF BUT FOR EVERYONE WHO HELPED ME...
POLICE STATION
COME IN!

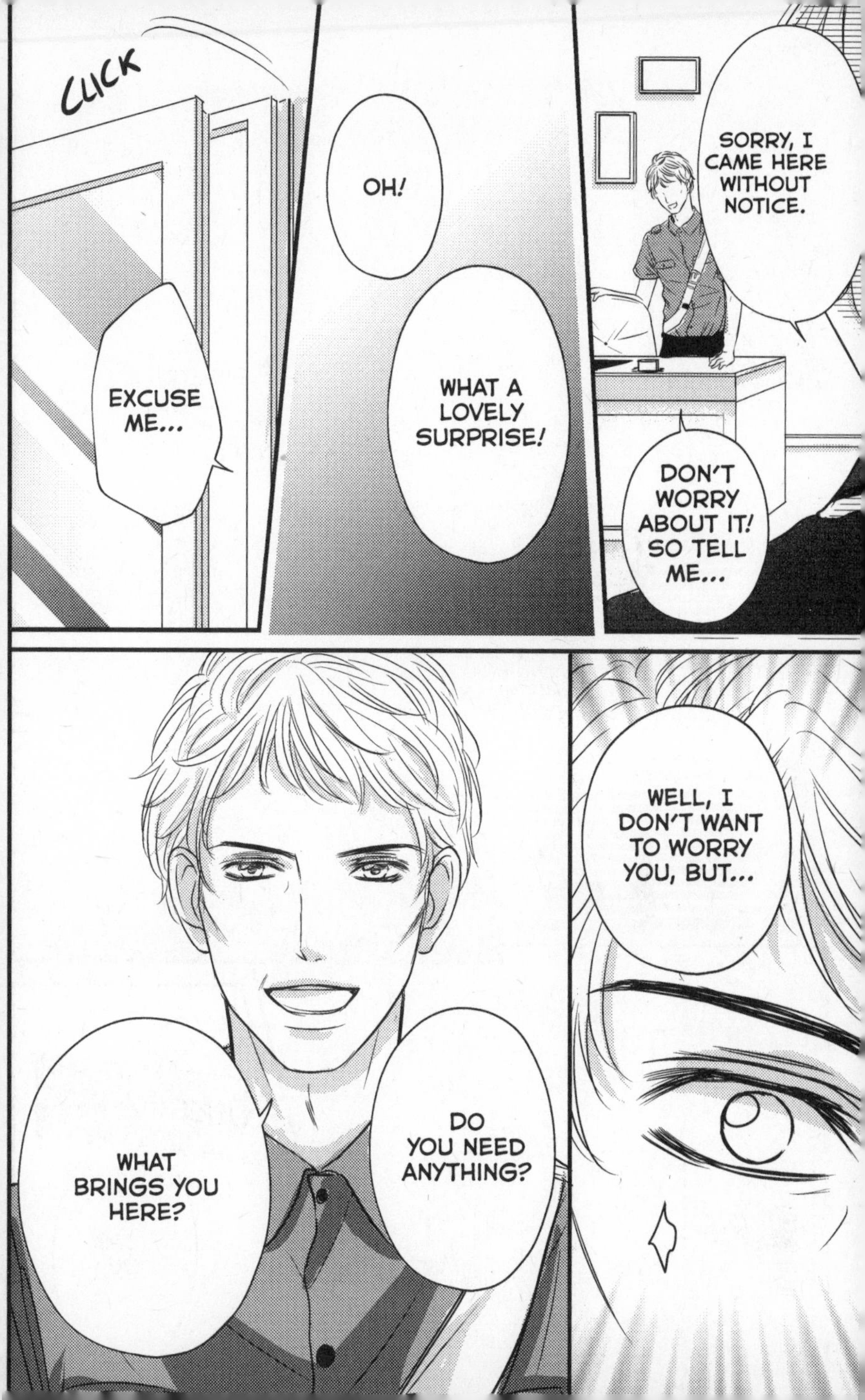
CLICK
EXCUSE ME...
OH!
WHAT A LOVELY SURPRISE!
SORRY, I CAME HERE WITHOUT NOTICE.
DON'T WORRY ABOUT IT! SO TELL ME...
WHAT BRINGS YOU HERE?
DO YOU NEED ANYTHING?
WELL, I DON'T WANT TO WORRY YOU, BUT...

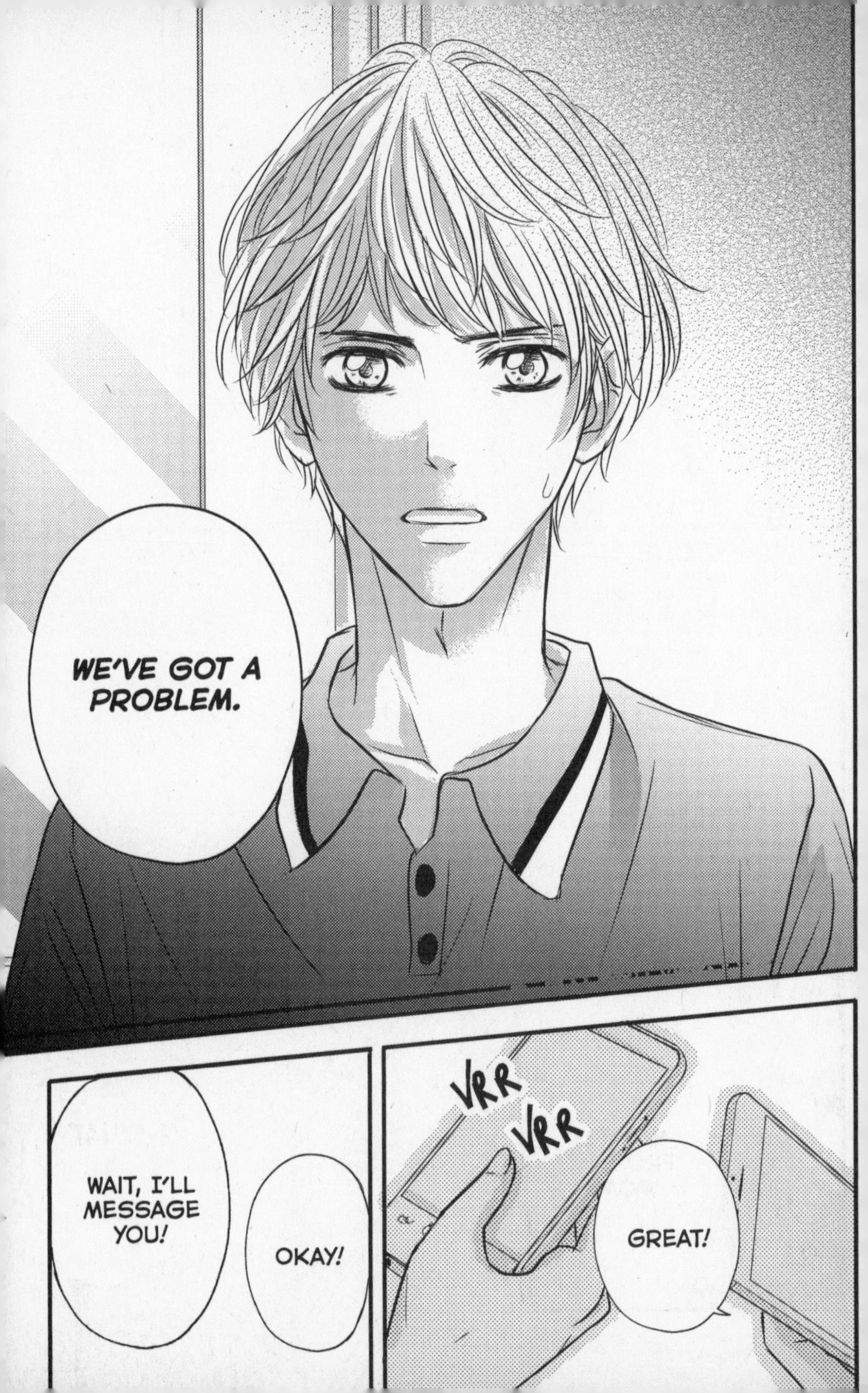
WE'VE GOT A PROBLEM.
VRR
VRR
GREAT!
WAIT, I'LL MESSAGE YOU!
OKAY!

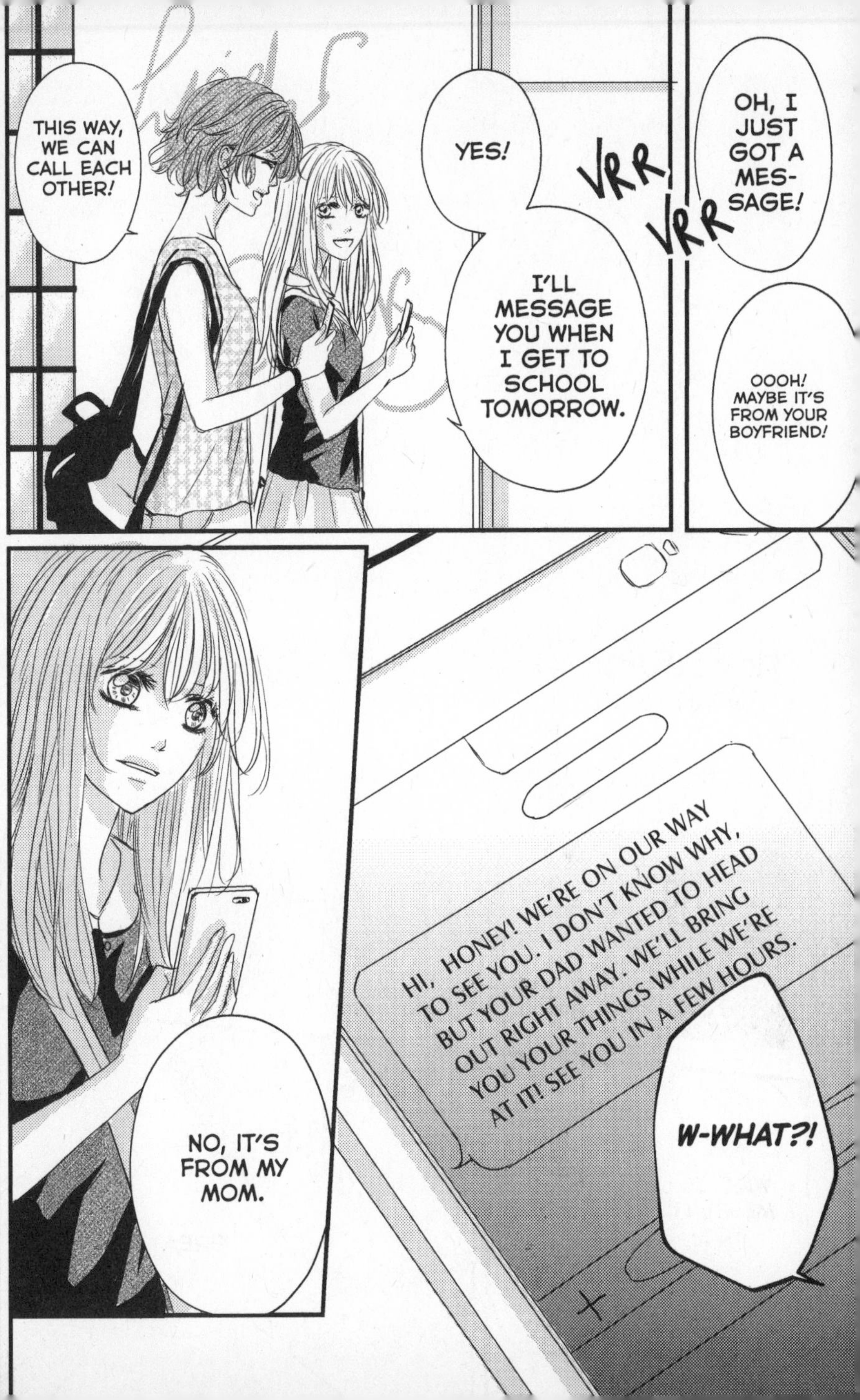
THIS WAY, WE CAN CALL EACH OTHER!
YES!
I'LL MESSAGE YOU WHEN I GET TO SCHOOL TOMORROW.
VRR VRR
OH, I JUST GOT A MES-SAGE!
OOOH! MAYBE IT'S FROM YOUR BOYFRIEND!
NO, IT'S FROM MY MOM.
HI, HONEY! WE'RE ON OUR WAY TO SEE YOU. I DON'T KNOW WHY, BUT YOUR DAD WANTED TO HEAD OUT RIGHT AWAY. WE'LL BRING YOU YOUR THINGS WHILE WE'RE AT IT! SEE YOU IN A FEW HOURS.
W-WHAT?!

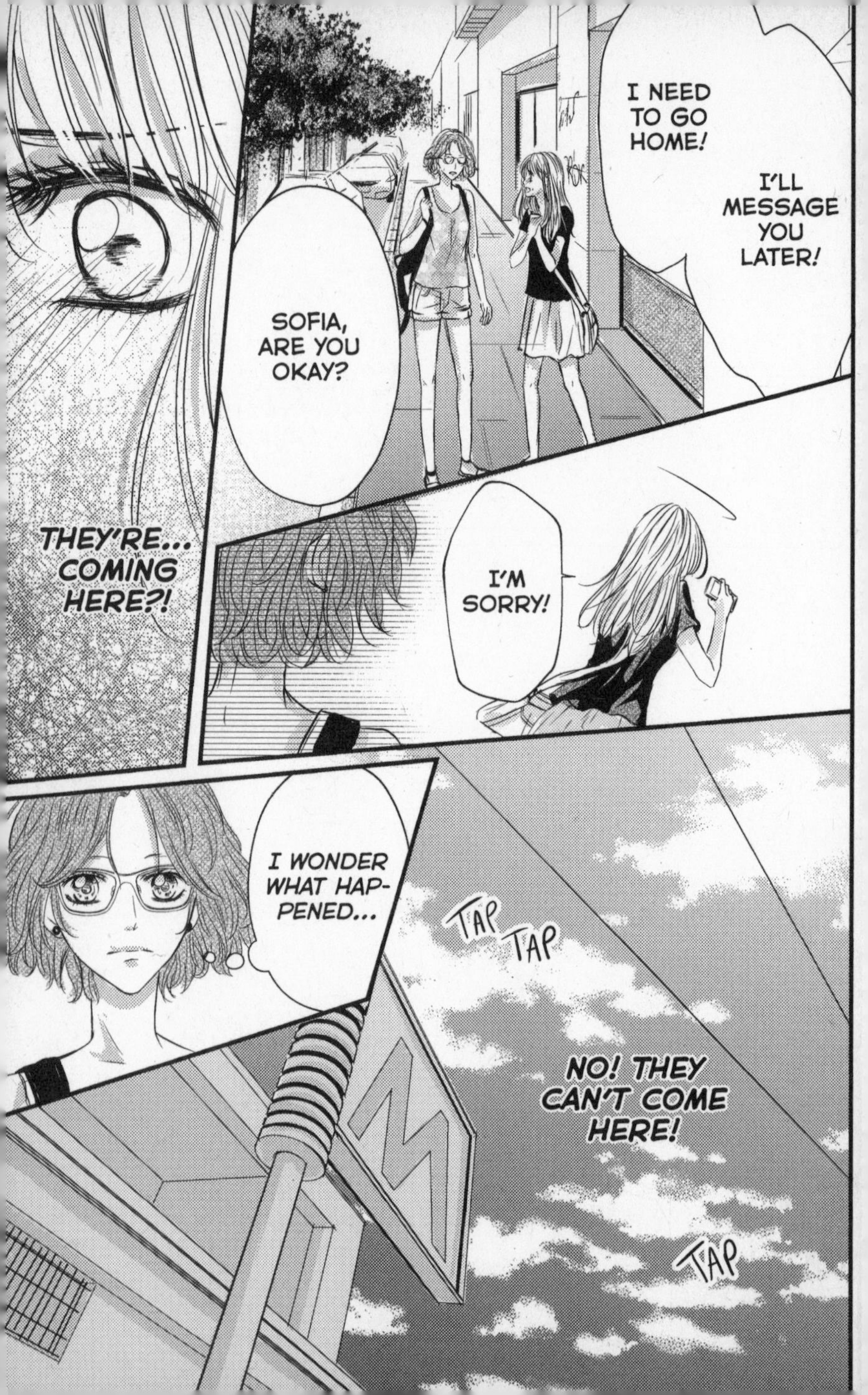
I NEED TO GO HOME!
I'LL MESSAGE YOU LATER!
SOFIA, ARE YOU OKAY?
I'M SORRY!
THEY'RE... COMING HERE?!
I WONDER WHAT HAP-PENED...
TAP TAP
NO! THEY CAN'T COME HERE!
TAP

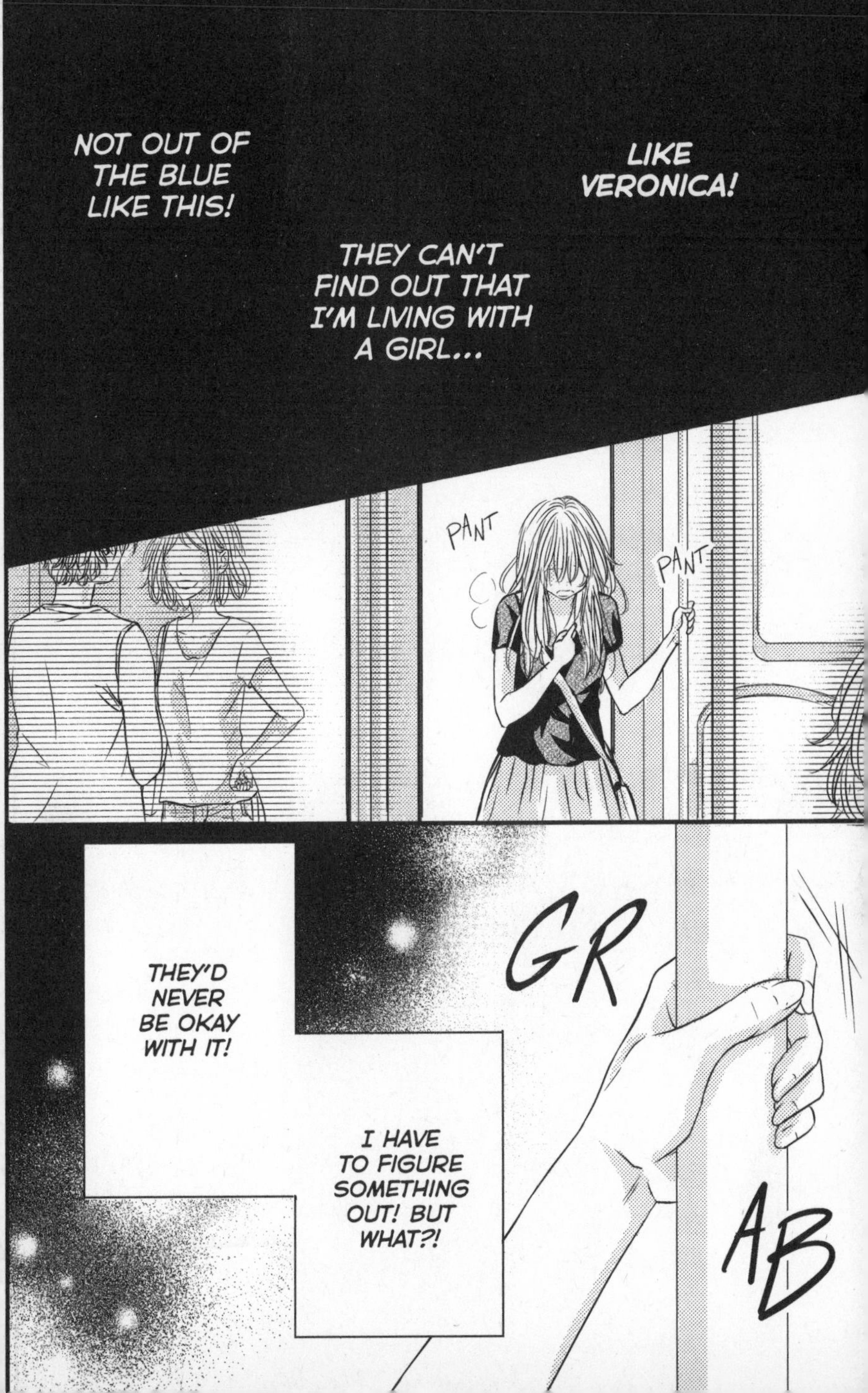
LIKE VERONICA!
THEY CAN'T FIND OUT THAT I'M LIVING WITH A GIRL...
NOT OUT OF THE BLUE LIKE THIS!
PANT
PANT
GR
AB
I HAVE TO FIGURE SOMETHING OUT! BUT WHAT?!
THEY'D NEVER BE OKAY WITH IT!

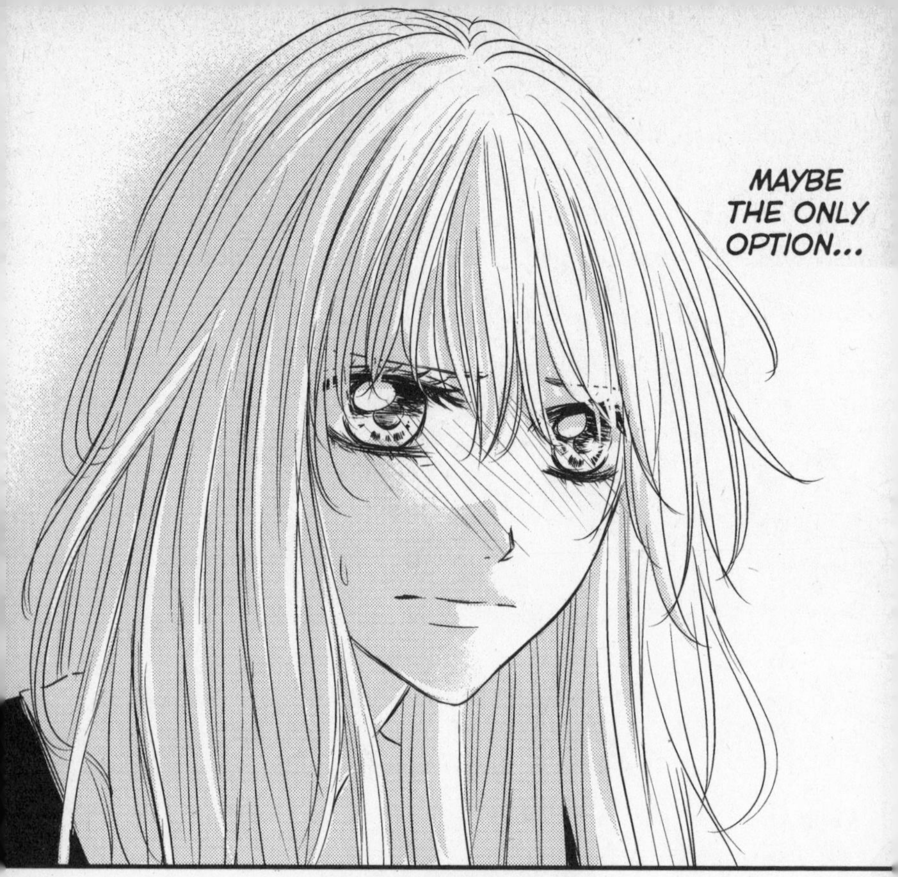
MAYBE THE ONLY OPTION...
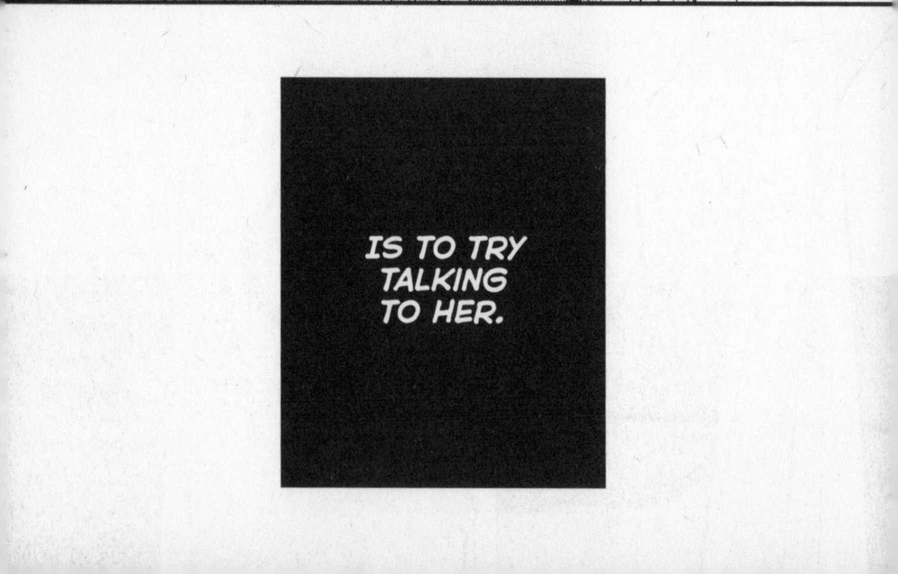
IS TO TRY TALKING TO HER.

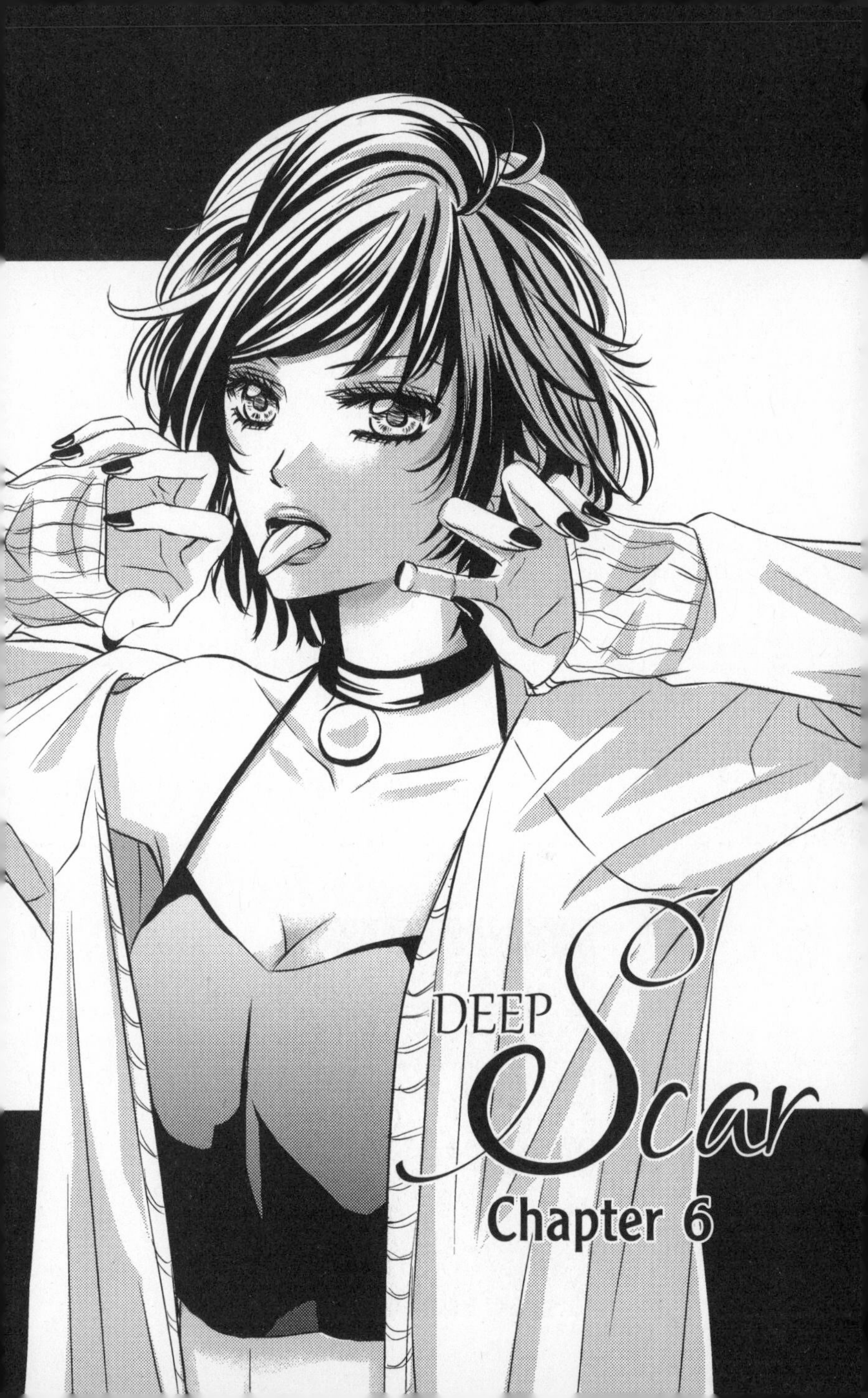
DEEP Scar
Chapter 6

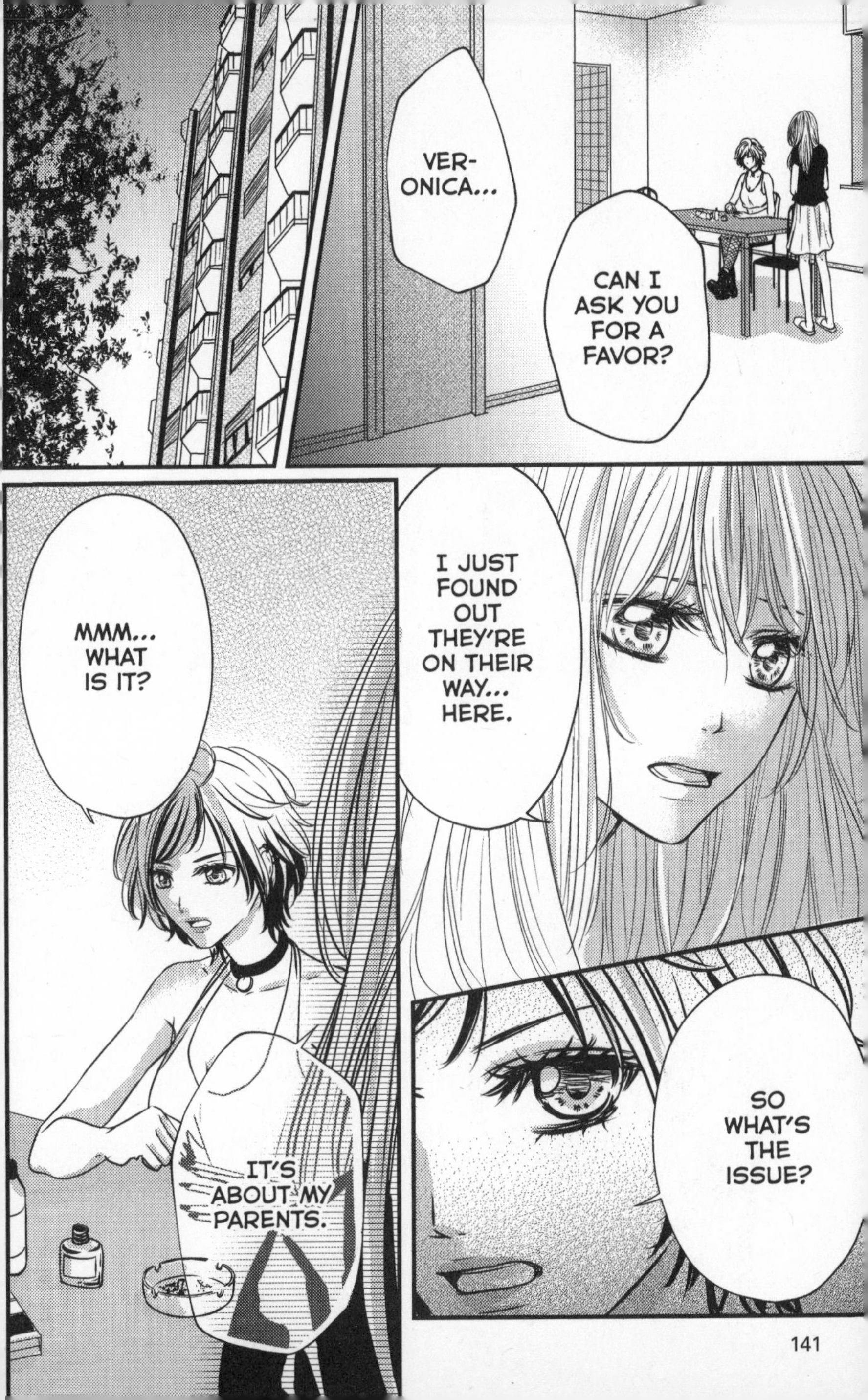
CAN I ASK YOU FOR A FAVOR?
VER-ONICA...
I JUST FOUND OUT THEY'RE ON THEIR WAY... HERE.
MMM... WHAT IS IT?
SO WHAT'S THE ISSUE?
IT'S ABOUT MY PARENTS.

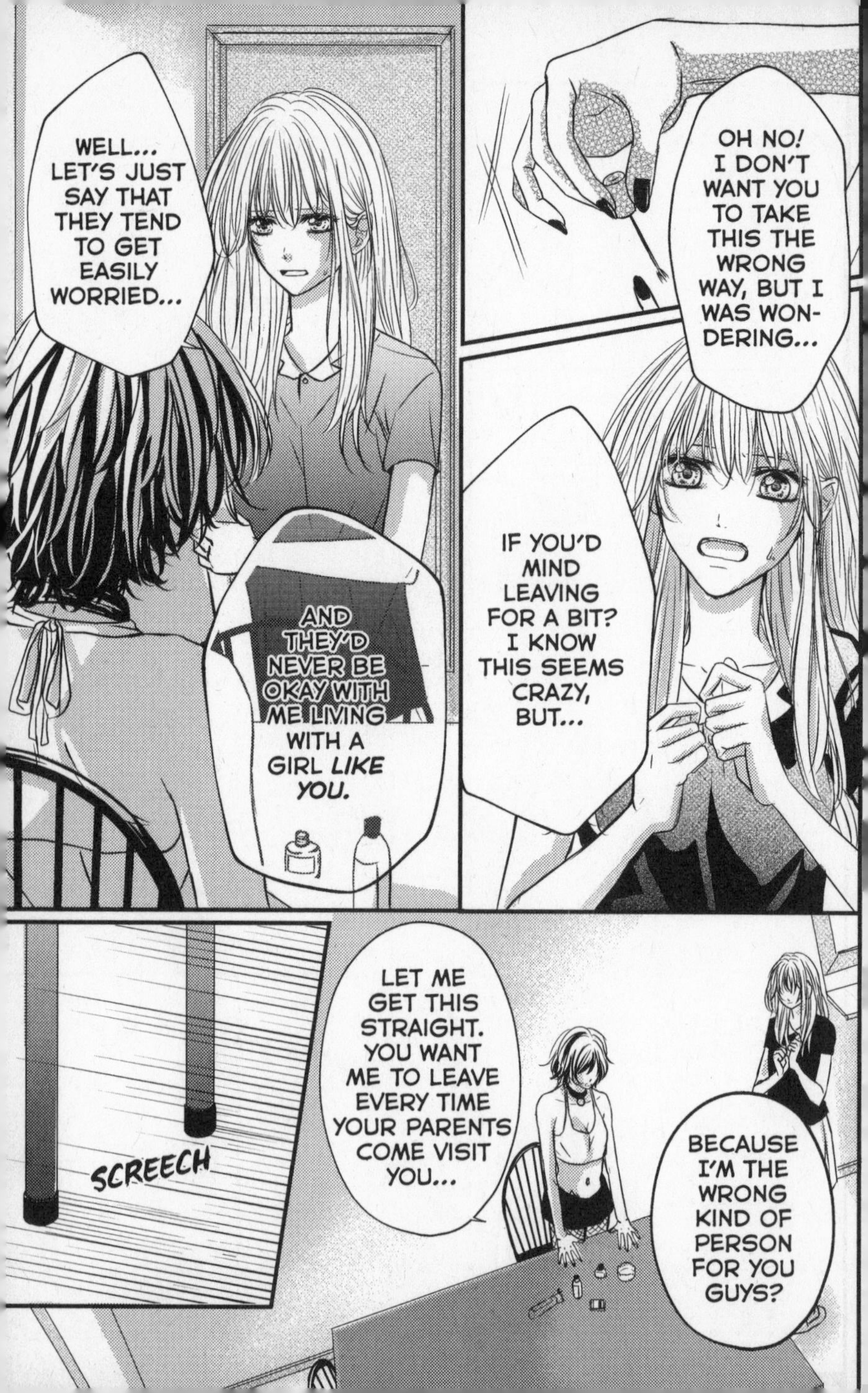
OH NO! I DON'T WANT YOU TO TAKE THIS THE WRONG WAY, BUT I WAS WON-DERING...
IF YOU'D MIND LEAVING FOR A BIT? I KNOW THIS SEEMS CRAZY, BUT...
WELL... LET'S JUST SAY THAT THEY TEND TO GET EASILY WORRIED...
AND THEY'D NEVER BE OKAY WITH ME LIVING WITH A GIRL *LIKE YOU.*
LET ME GET THIS STRAIGHT. YOU WANT ME TO LEAVE EVERY TIME YOUR PARENTS COME VISIT YOU...
BECAUSE I'M THE WRONG KIND OF PERSON FOR YOU GUYS?
SCREECH

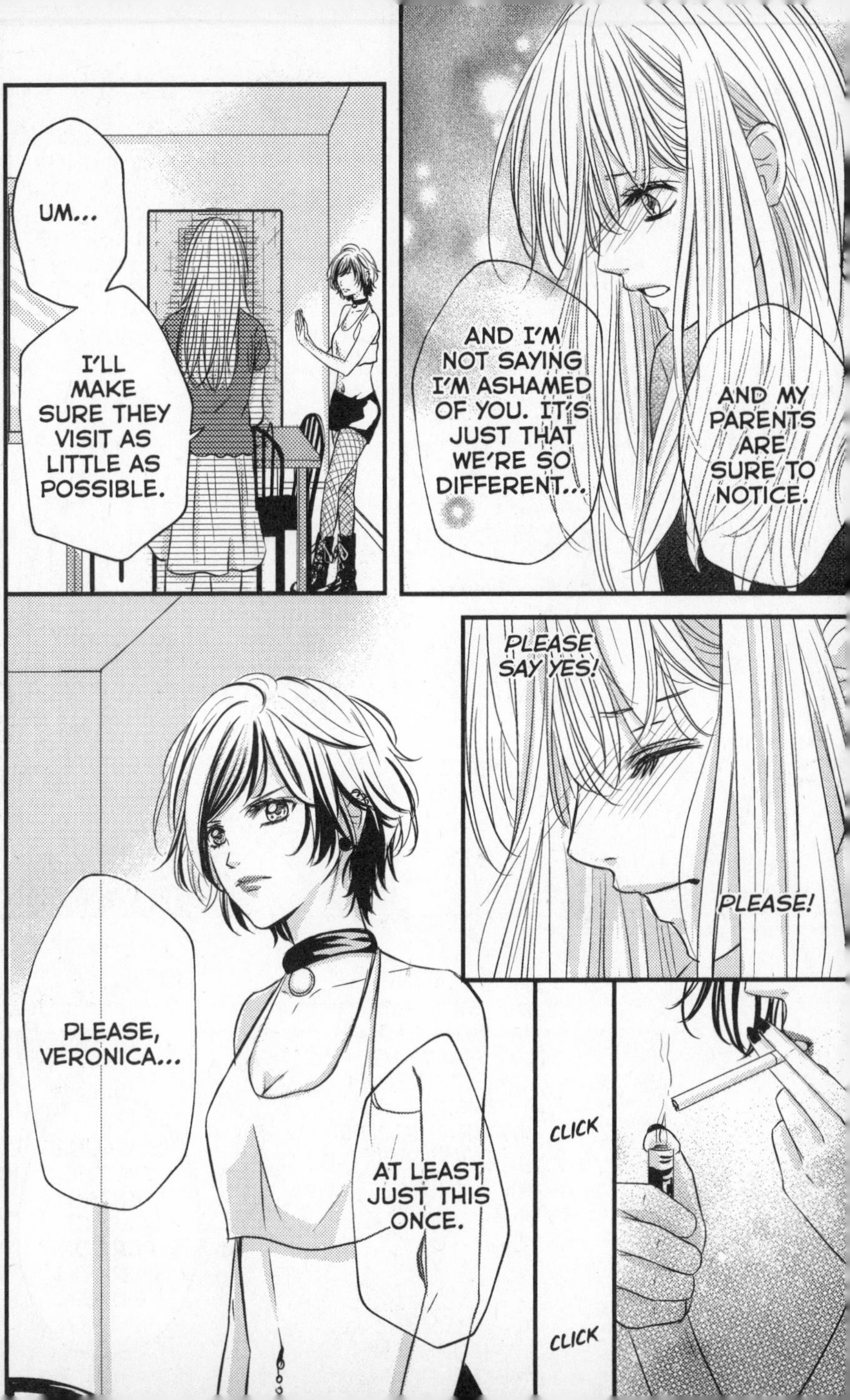
AND I'M NOT SAYING I'M ASHAMED OF YOU. IT'S JUST THAT WE'RE SO DIFFERENT...
AND MY PARENTS ARE SURE TO NOTICE.
UM...
I'LL MAKE SURE THEY VISIT AS LITTLE AS POSSIBLE.
PLEASE SAY YES!
PLEASE!
CLICK
CLICK
PLEASE, VERONICA...
AT LEAST JUST THIS ONCE.

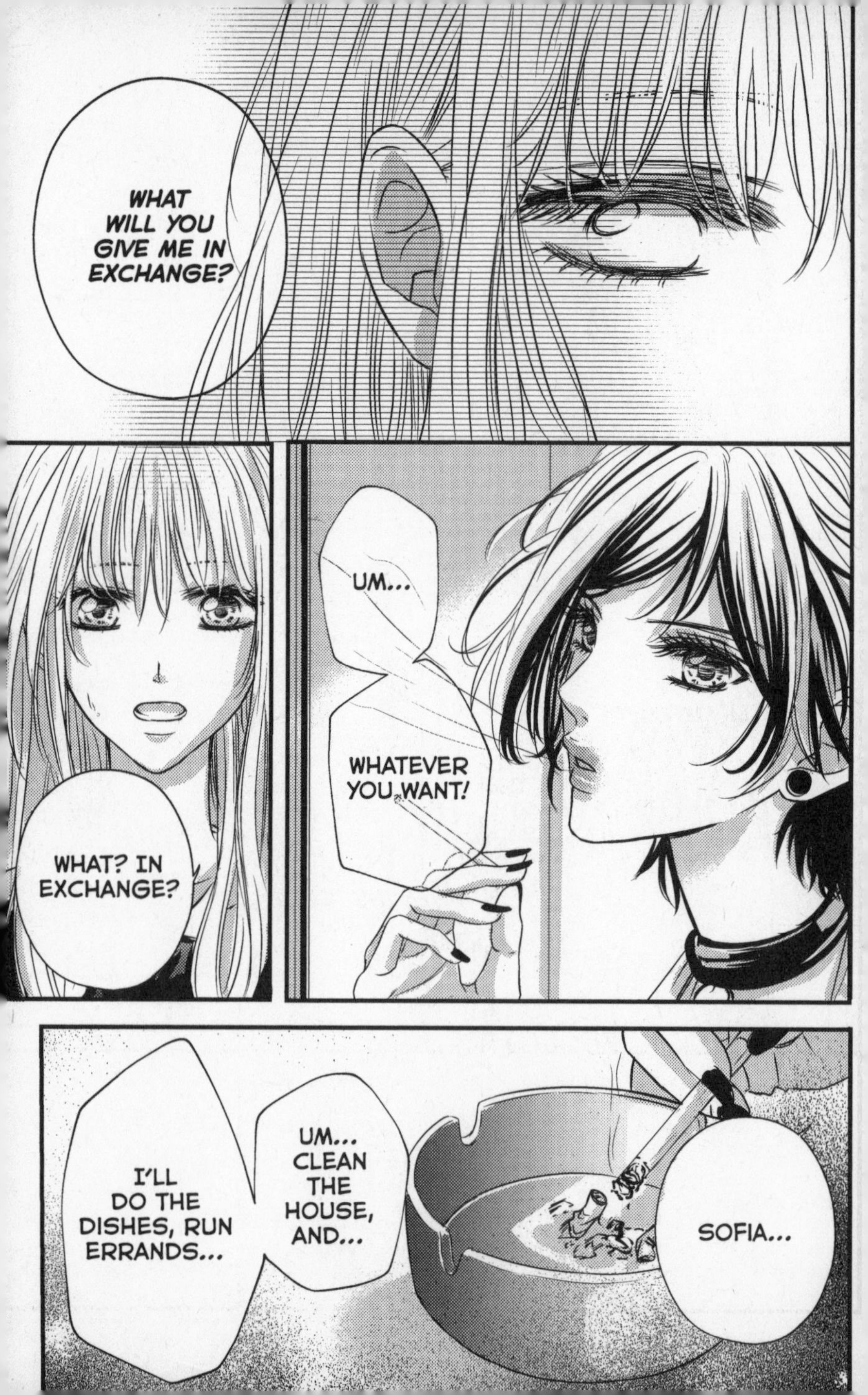
WHAT WILL YOU GIVE ME IN EXCHANGE?
UM...
WHATEVER YOU WANT!
WHAT? IN EXCHANGE?
SOFIA...
UM... CLEAN THE HOUSE, AND...
I'LL DO THE DISHES, RUN ERRANDS...

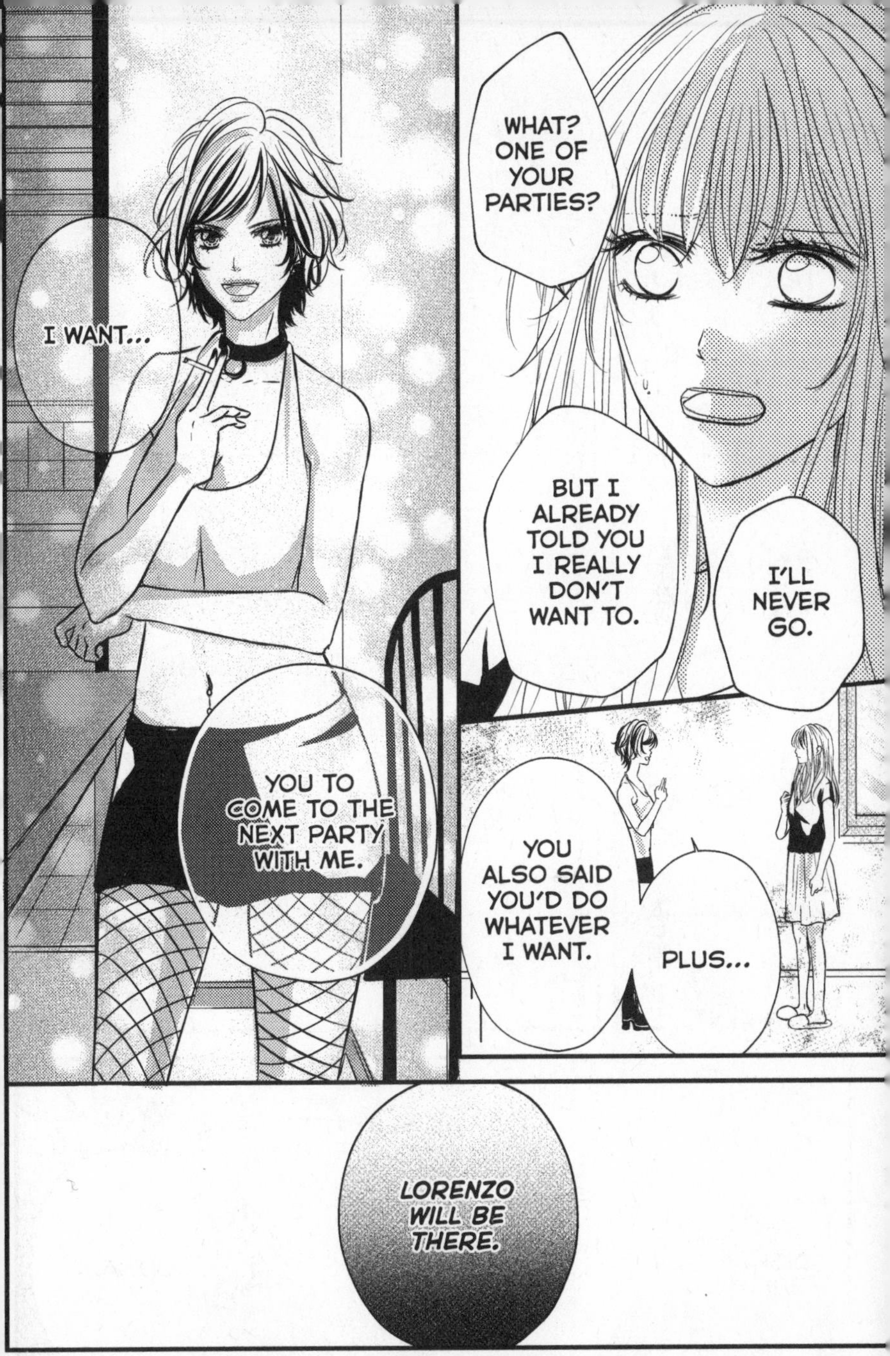
I WANT...
YOU TO COME TO THE NEXT PARTY WITH ME.
WHAT? ONE OF YOUR PARTIES?
BUT I ALREADY TOLD YOU I REALLY DON'T WANT TO.
I'LL NEVER GO.
YOU ALSO SAID YOU'D DO WHATEVER I WANT.
PLUS...
LORENZO WILL BE THERE.

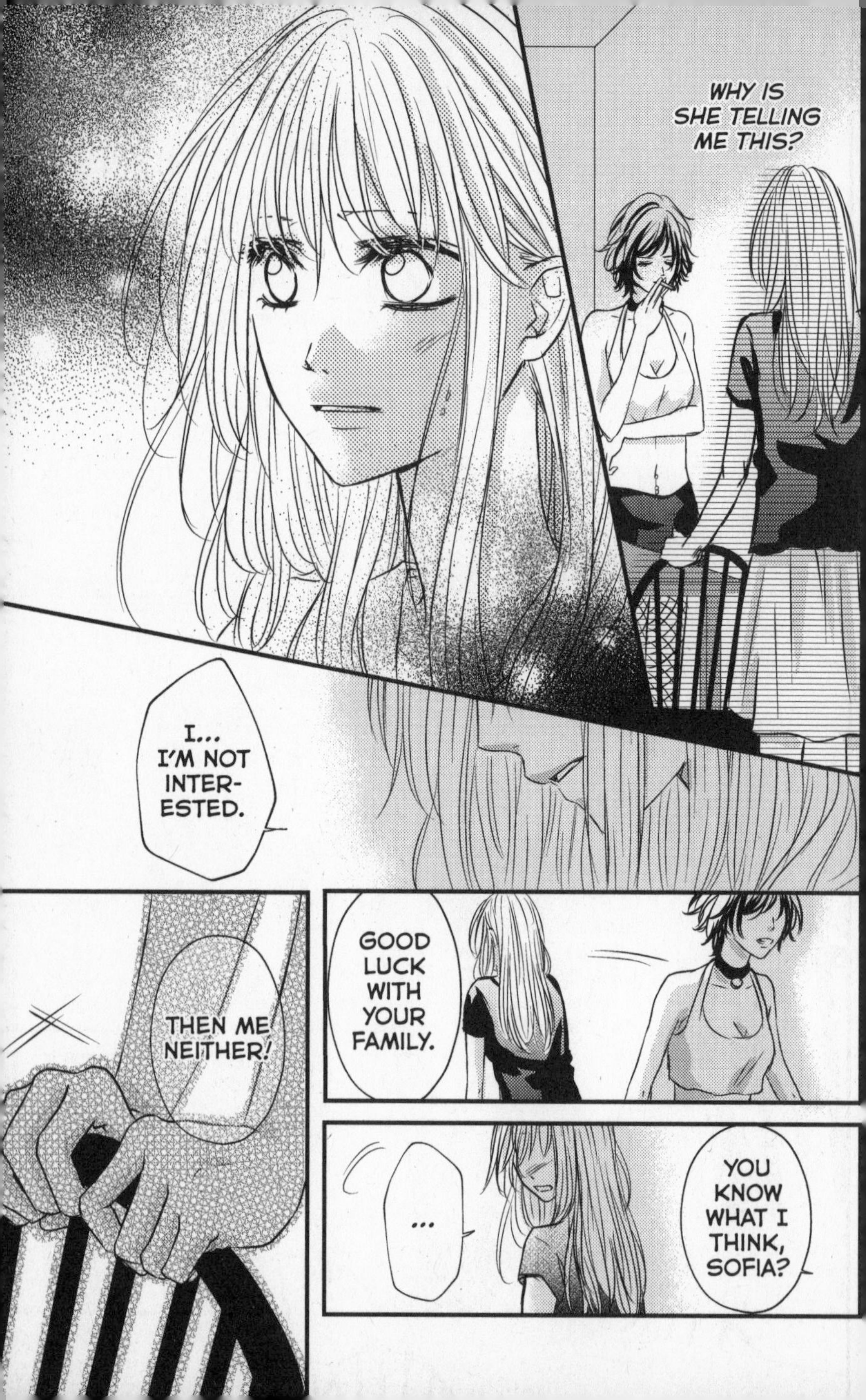
WHY IS SHE TELLING ME THIS?
I... I'M NOT INTER-ESTED.
GOOD LUCK WITH YOUR FAMILY.
YOU KNOW WHAT I THINK, SOFIA?
...
THEN ME NEITHER!

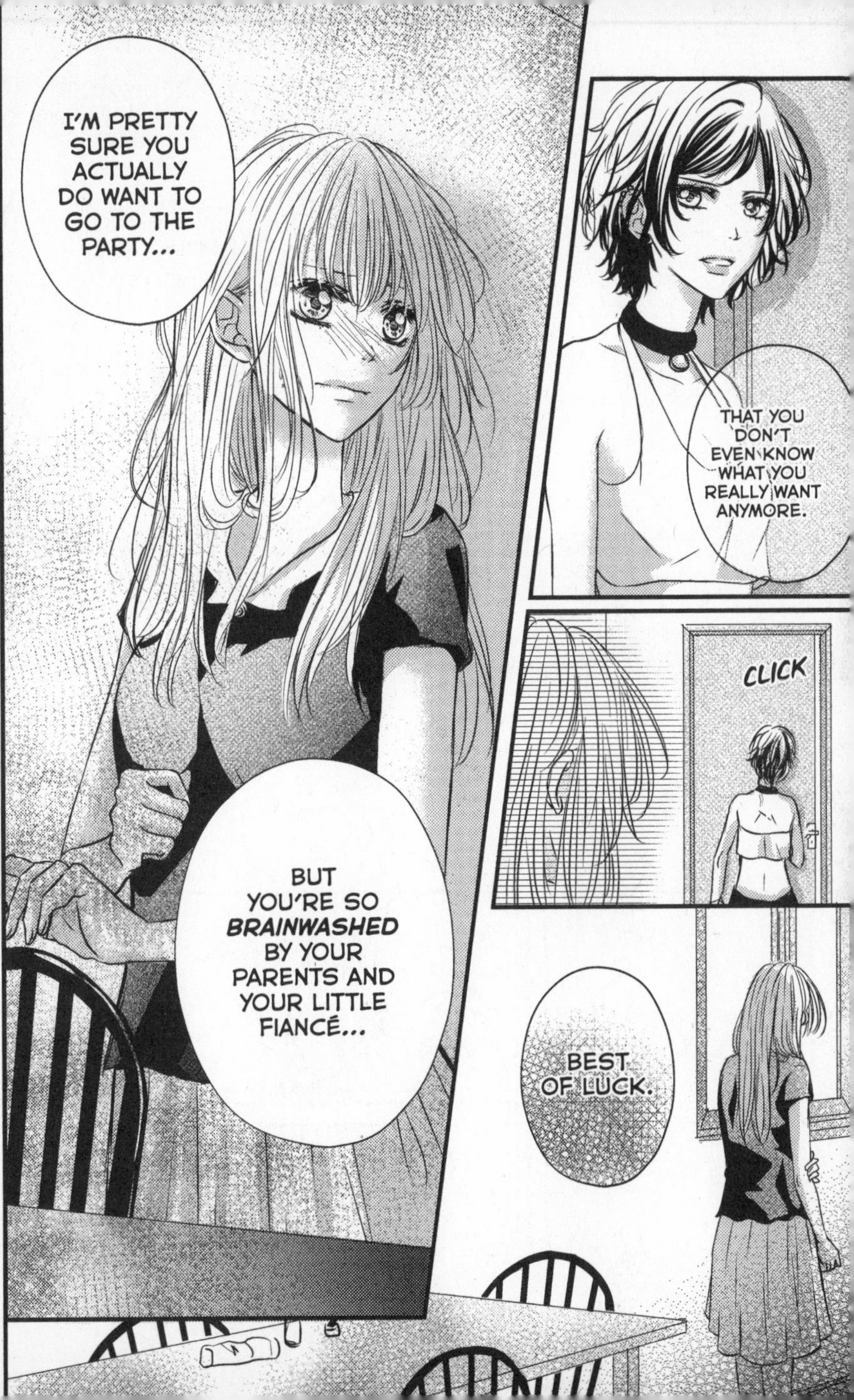
I'M PRETTY SURE YOU ACTUALLY DO WANT TO GO TO THE PARTY...
BUT YOU'RE SO *BRAINWASHED* BY YOUR PARENTS AND YOUR LITTLE FIANCÉ...
THAT YOU DON'T EVEN KNOW WHAT YOU REALLY WANT ANYMORE.
CLICK
BEST OF LUCK.

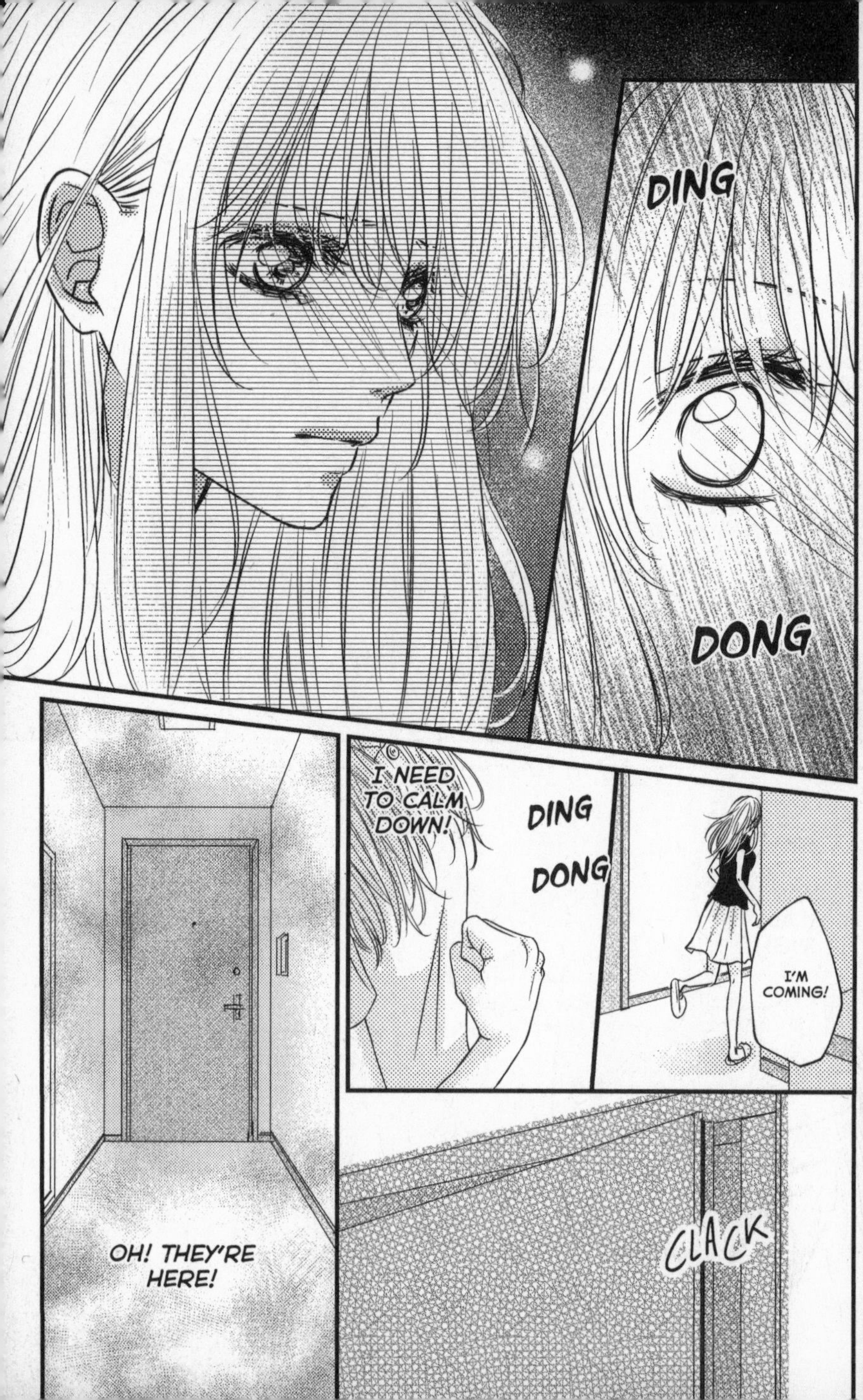
DING
DONG
I'M COMING!
DING
DONG
I NEED TO CALM DOWN!
CLACK
OH! THEY'RE HERE!

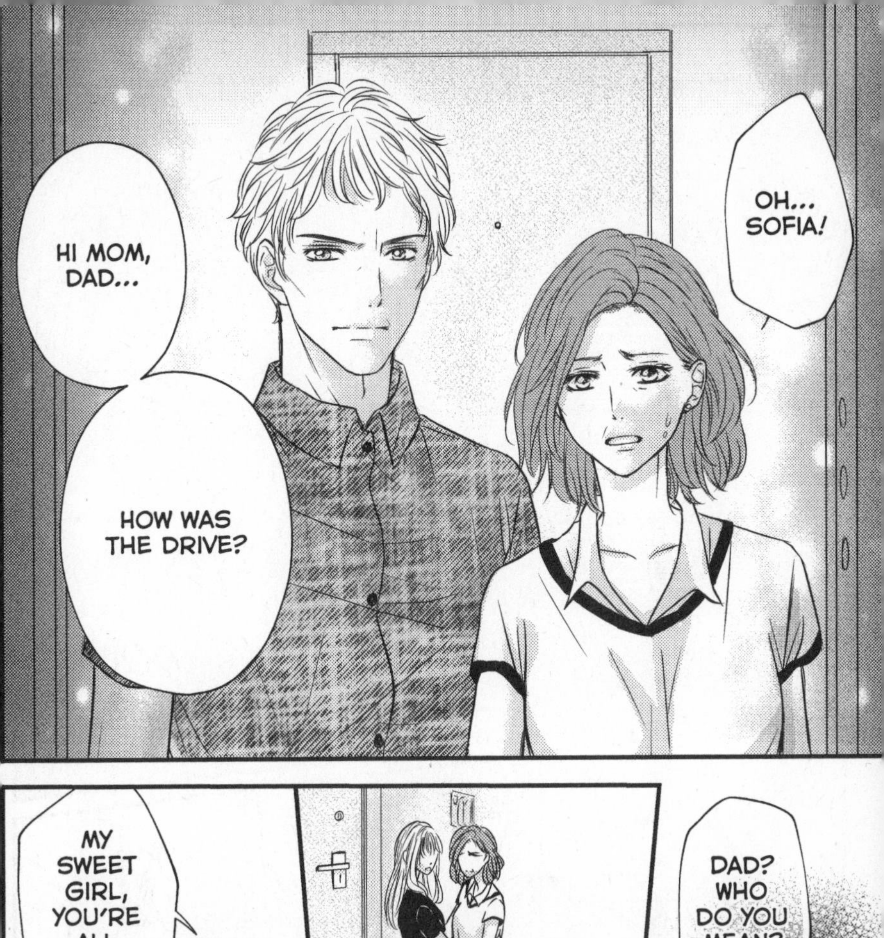
HI MOM, DAD...
HOW WAS THE DRIVE?
OH... SOFIA!

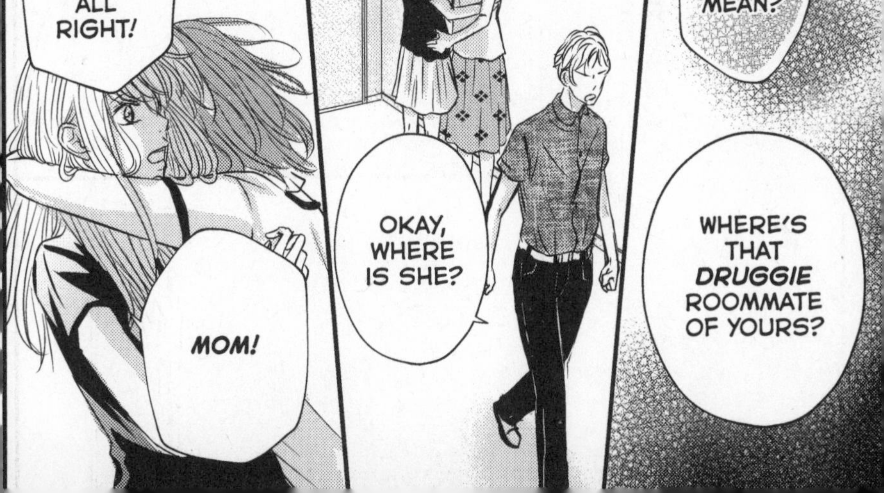
MY SWEET GIRL, YOU'RE ALL RIGHT!
MOM!
OKAY, WHERE IS SHE?
WHERE'S THAT *DRUGGIE* ROOMMATE OF YOURS?
DAD? WHO DO YOU MEAN?

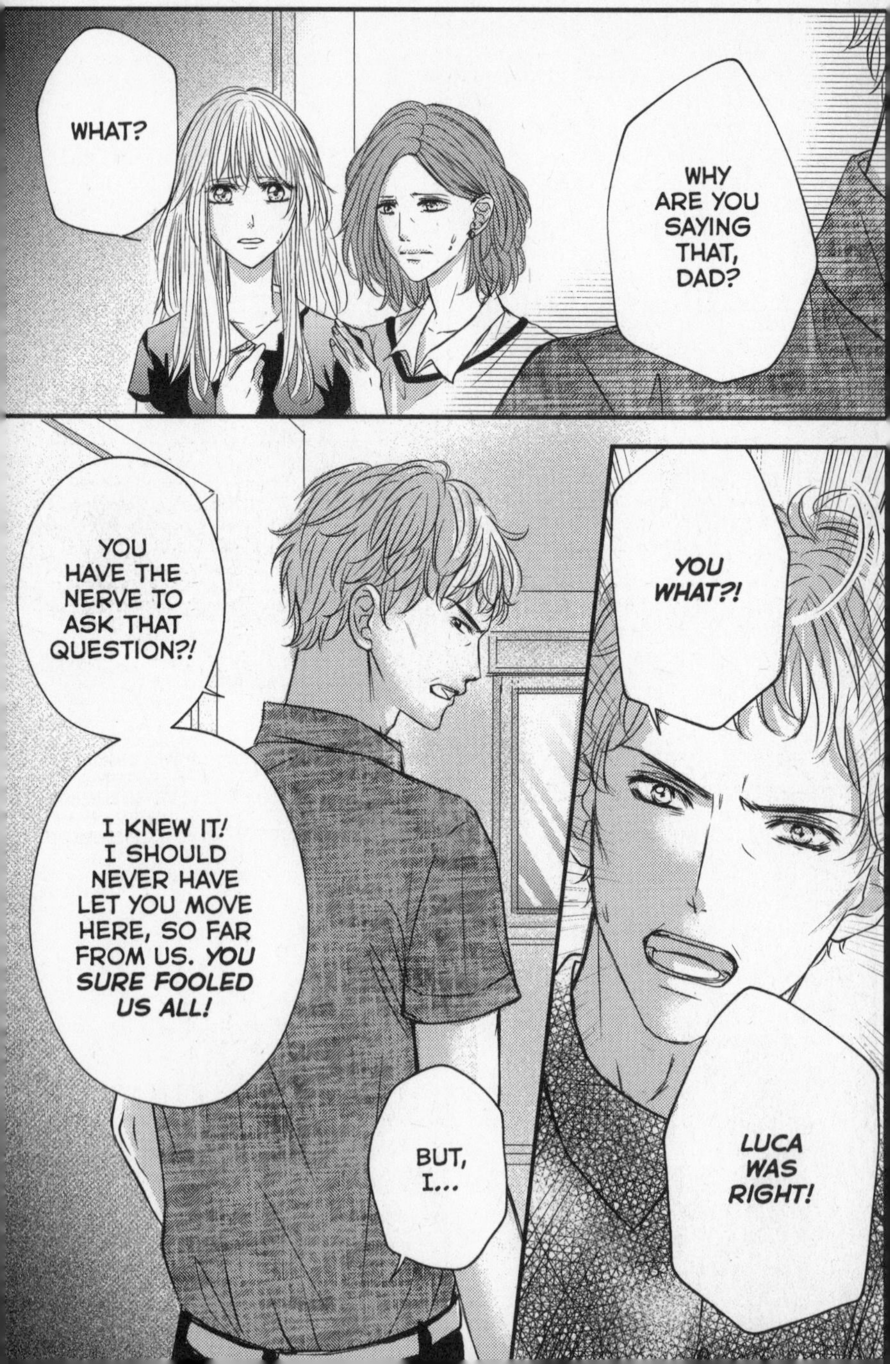
WHY ARE YOU SAYING THAT, DAD?
WHAT?
YOU WHAT?!
LUCA WAS RIGHT!
YOU HAVE THE NERVE TO ASK THAT QUESTION?!
I KNEW IT! I SHOULD NEVER HAVE LET YOU MOVE HERE, SO FAR FROM US. YOU SURE FOOLED US ALL!
BUT, I...

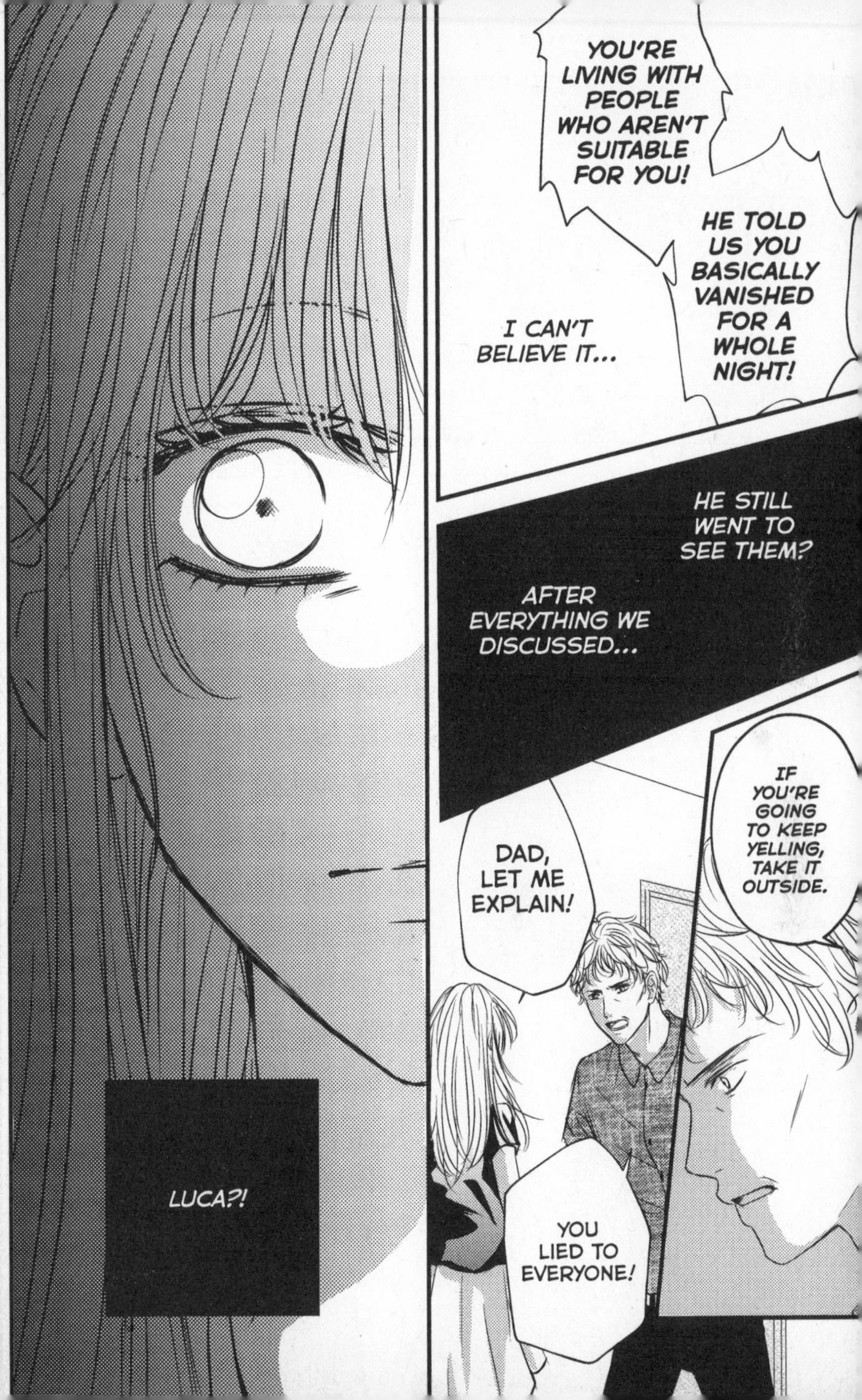
YOU'RE LIVING WITH PEOPLE WHO AREN'T SUITABLE FOR YOU!
HE TOLD US YOU BASICALLY VANISHED FOR A WHOLE NIGHT!
I CAN'T BELIEVE IT...
HE STILL WENT TO SEE THEM?
AFTER EVERYTHING WE DISCUSSED...
IF YOU'RE GOING TO KEEP YELLING, TAKE IT OUTSIDE.
DAD, LET ME EXPLAIN!
YOU LIED TO EVERYONE!
LUCA?!

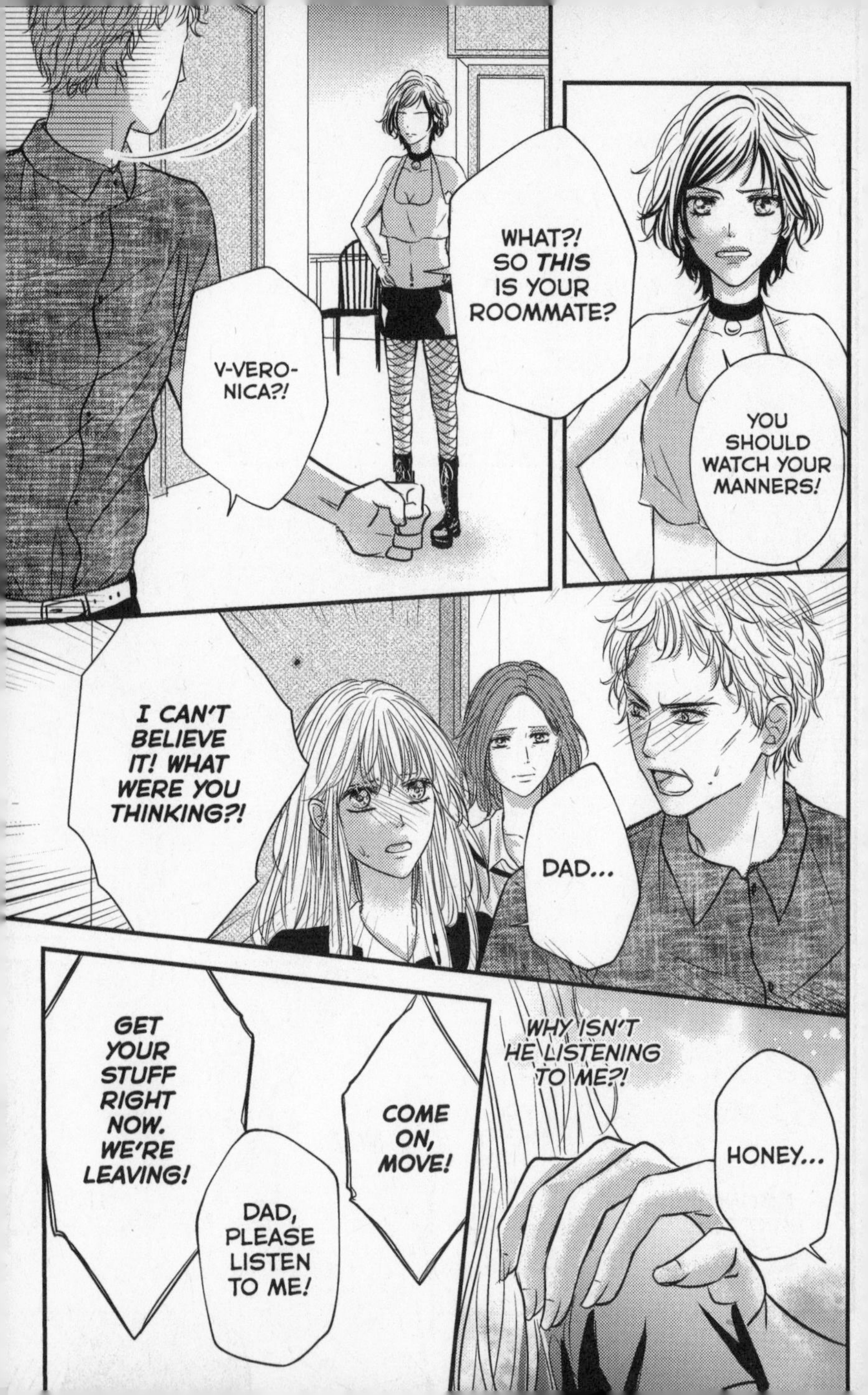
V-VERONICA?!
WHAT?! SO THIS IS YOUR ROOMMATE?
YOU SHOULD WATCH YOUR MANNERS!
I CAN'T BELIEVE IT! WHAT WERE YOU THINKING?!
DAD...
GET YOUR STUFF RIGHT NOW. WE'RE LEAVING!
COME ON, MOVE!
DAD, PLEASE LISTEN TO ME!
WHY ISN'T HE LISTENING TO ME?!
HONEY...

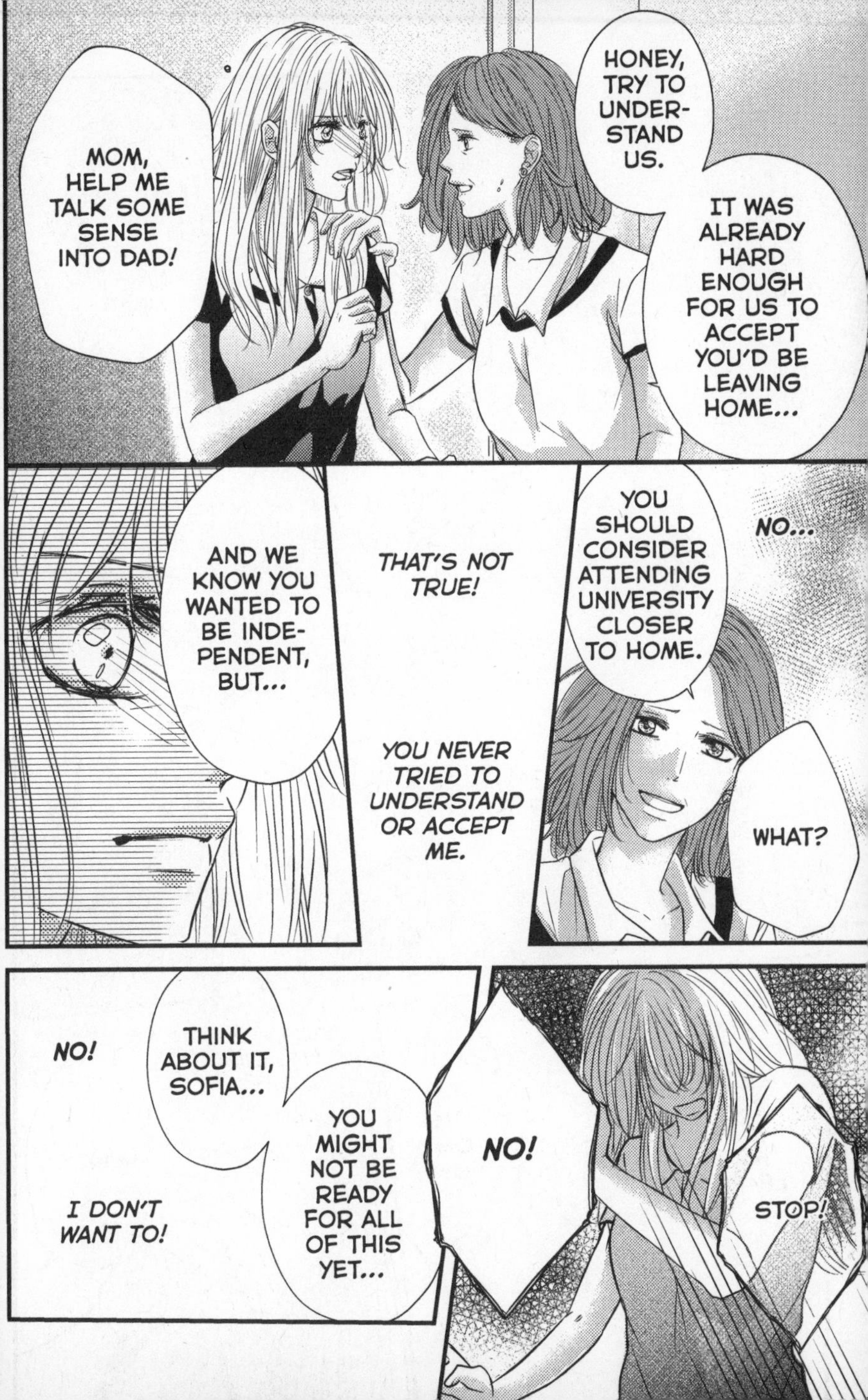
MOM, HELP ME TALK SOME SENSE INTO DAD!
HONEY, TRY TO UNDER-STAND US.
IT WAS ALREADY HARD ENOUGH FOR US TO ACCEPT YOU'D BE LEAVING HOME...
AND WE KNOW YOU WANTED TO BE INDE-PENDENT, BUT...
YOU SHOULD CONSIDER ATTENDING UNIVERSITY CLOSER TO HOME.
NO...
WHAT?
THAT'S NOT TRUE!
YOU NEVER TRIED TO UNDERSTAND OR ACCEPT ME.
THINK ABOUT IT, SOFIA...
YOU MIGHT NOT BE READY FOR ALL OF THIS YET...
NO!
I DON'T WANT TO!
NO!
STOP!

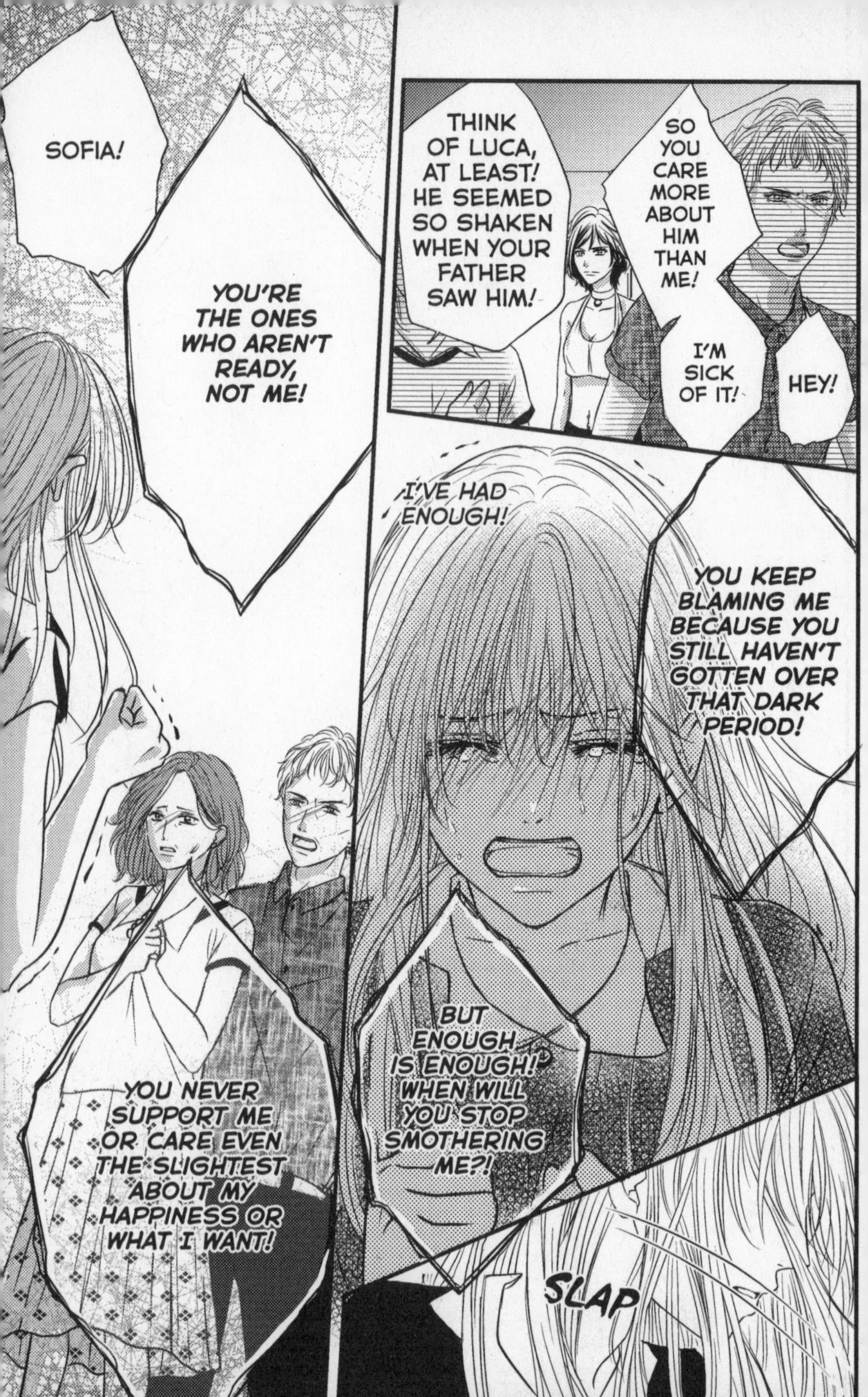
THINK OF LUCA, AT LEAST! HE SEEMED SO SHAKEN WHEN YOUR FATHER SAW HIM!
SO YOU CARE MORE ABOUT HIM THAN ME!
HEY!
I'M SICK OF IT!
I'VE HAD ENOUGH!
YOU KEEP BLAMING ME BECAUSE YOU STILL HAVEN'T GOTTEN OVER THAT DARK PERIOD!
BUT ENOUGH IS ENOUGH! WHEN WILL YOU STOP SMOTHERING ME?!
SLAP
SOFIA!
YOU'RE THE ONES WHO AREN'T READY, NOT ME!
YOU NEVER SUPPORT ME OR CARE EVEN THE SLIGHTEST ABOUT MY HAPPINESS OR WHAT I WANT!

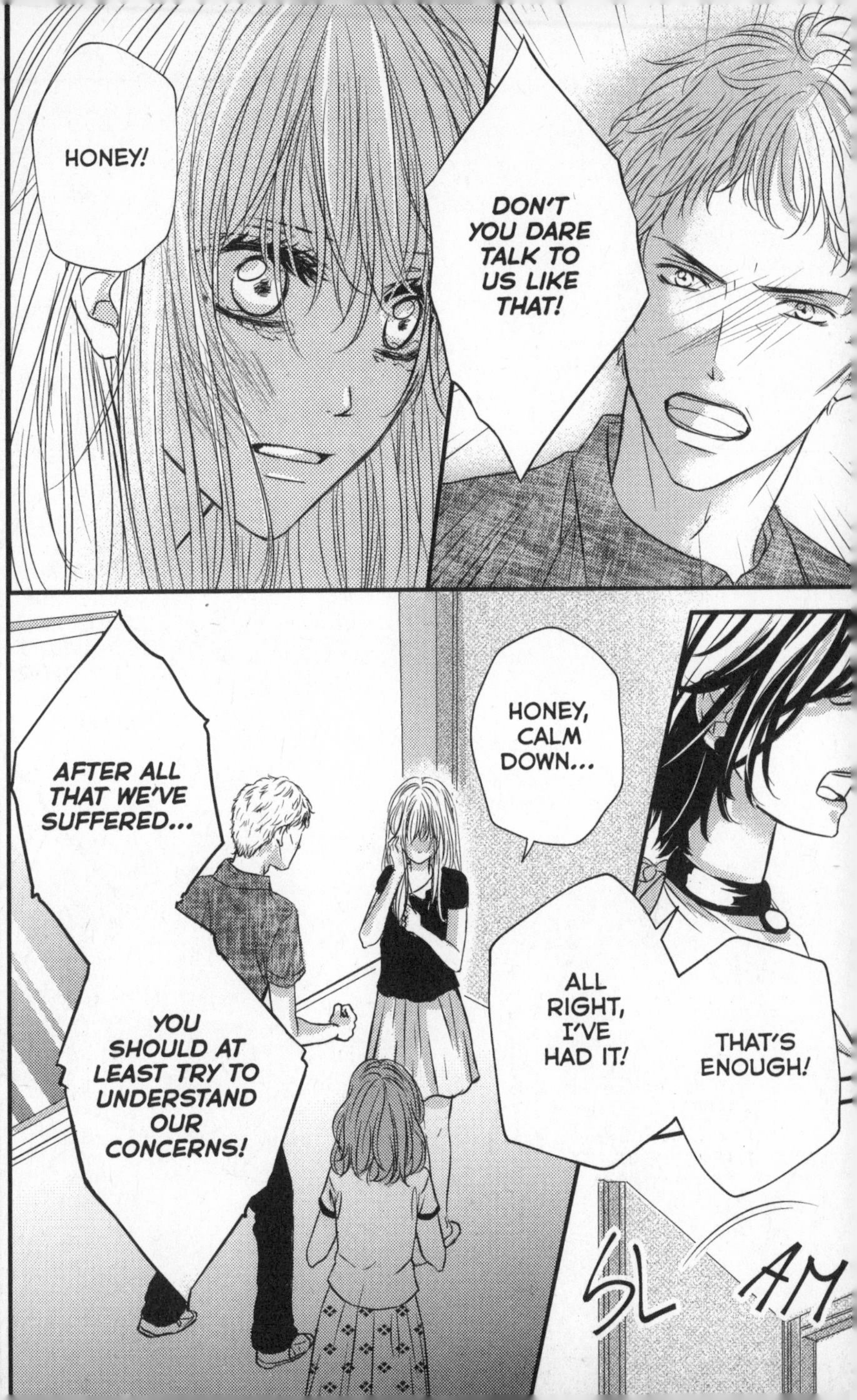
DON'T YOU DARE TALK TO US LIKE THAT!
HONEY!
HONEY, CALM DOWN...
AFTER ALL THAT WE'VE SUFFERED...
YOU SHOULD AT LEAST TRY TO UNDERSTAND OUR CONCERNS!
THAT'S ENOUGH!
ALL RIGHT, I'VE HAD IT!
SL AM

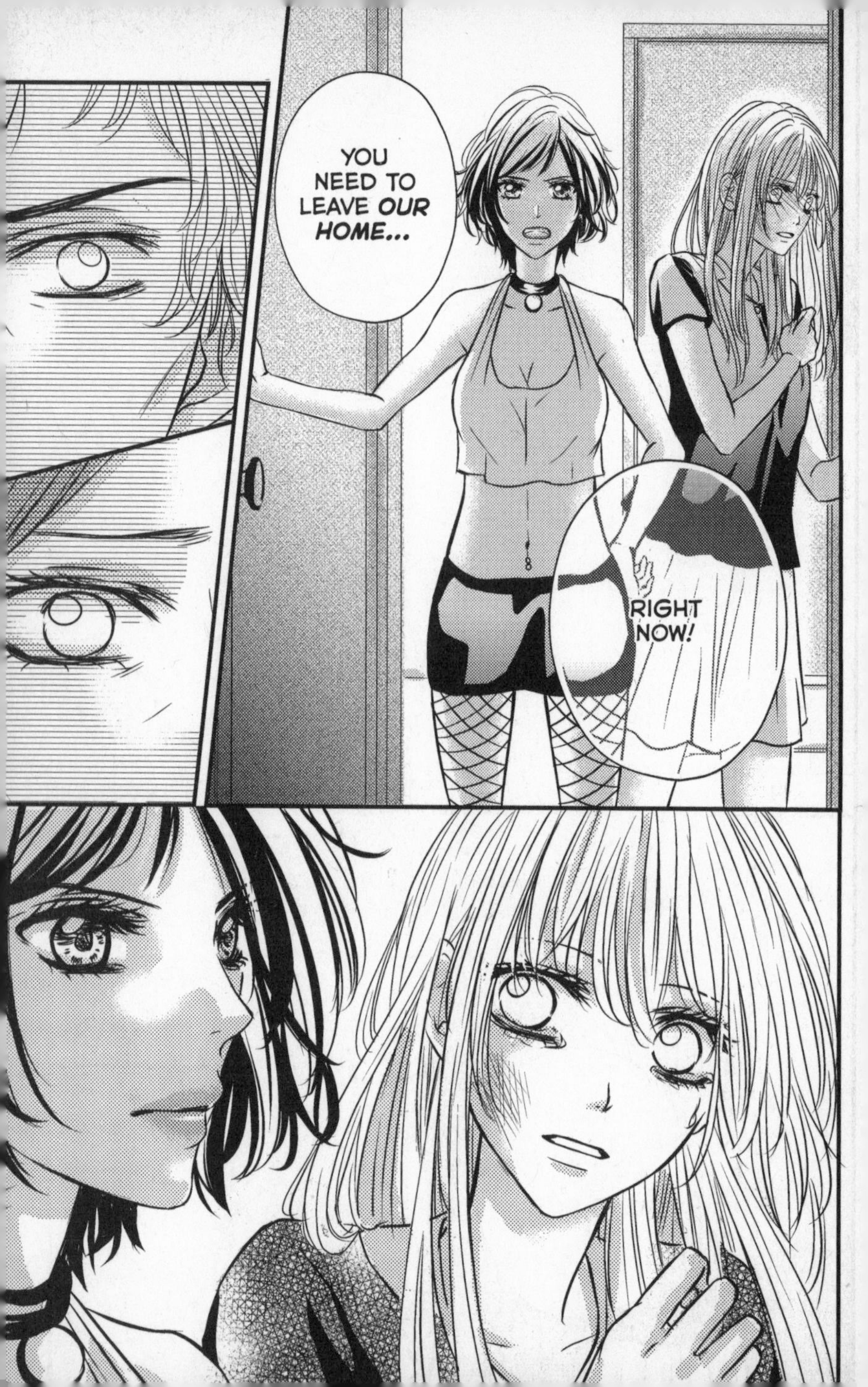
YOU NEED TO LEAVE *OUR HOME*...
RIGHT NOW!

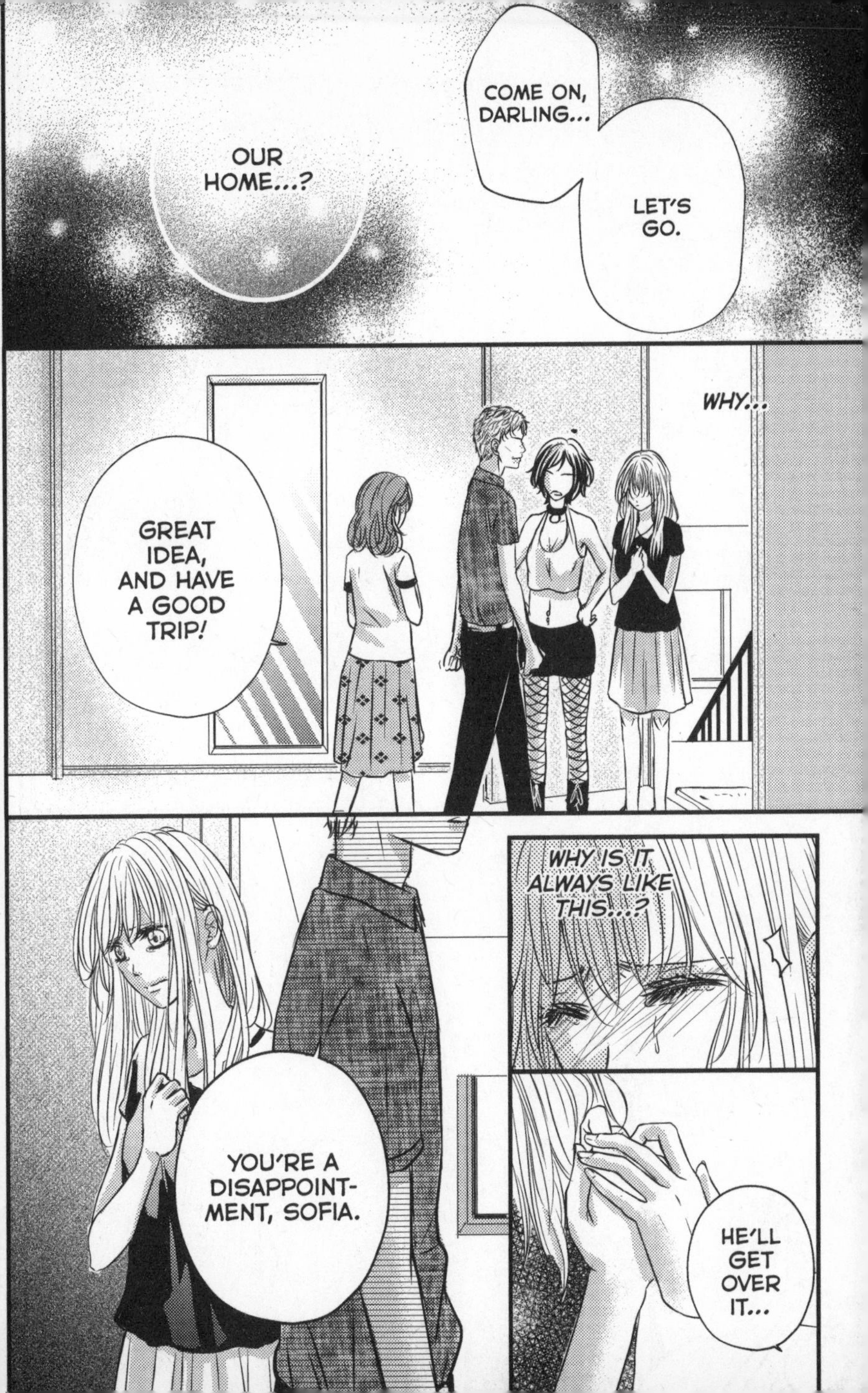
COME ON, DARLING...
LET'S GO.
OUR HOME...?
WHY...
GREAT IDEA, AND HAVE A GOOD TRIP!
WHY IS IT ALWAYS LIKE THIS...?
HE'LL GET OVER IT...
YOU'RE A DISAPPOINT-MENT, SOFIA.

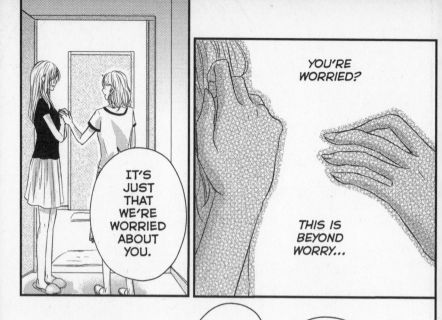

IT'S JUST THAT WE'RE WORRIED ABOUT YOU.

YOU'RE WORRIED?

THIS IS BEYOND WORRY...

IT'S PROOF THAT THEY DON'T HAVE ANY FAITH IN ME!

IF YOU CAN...

PLEASE TRY TO FIND A SOLUTION, SOFIA.

TAP

TAP

WHAT LOVELY PARENTS...

N-NO...

SO... SOFIA?!

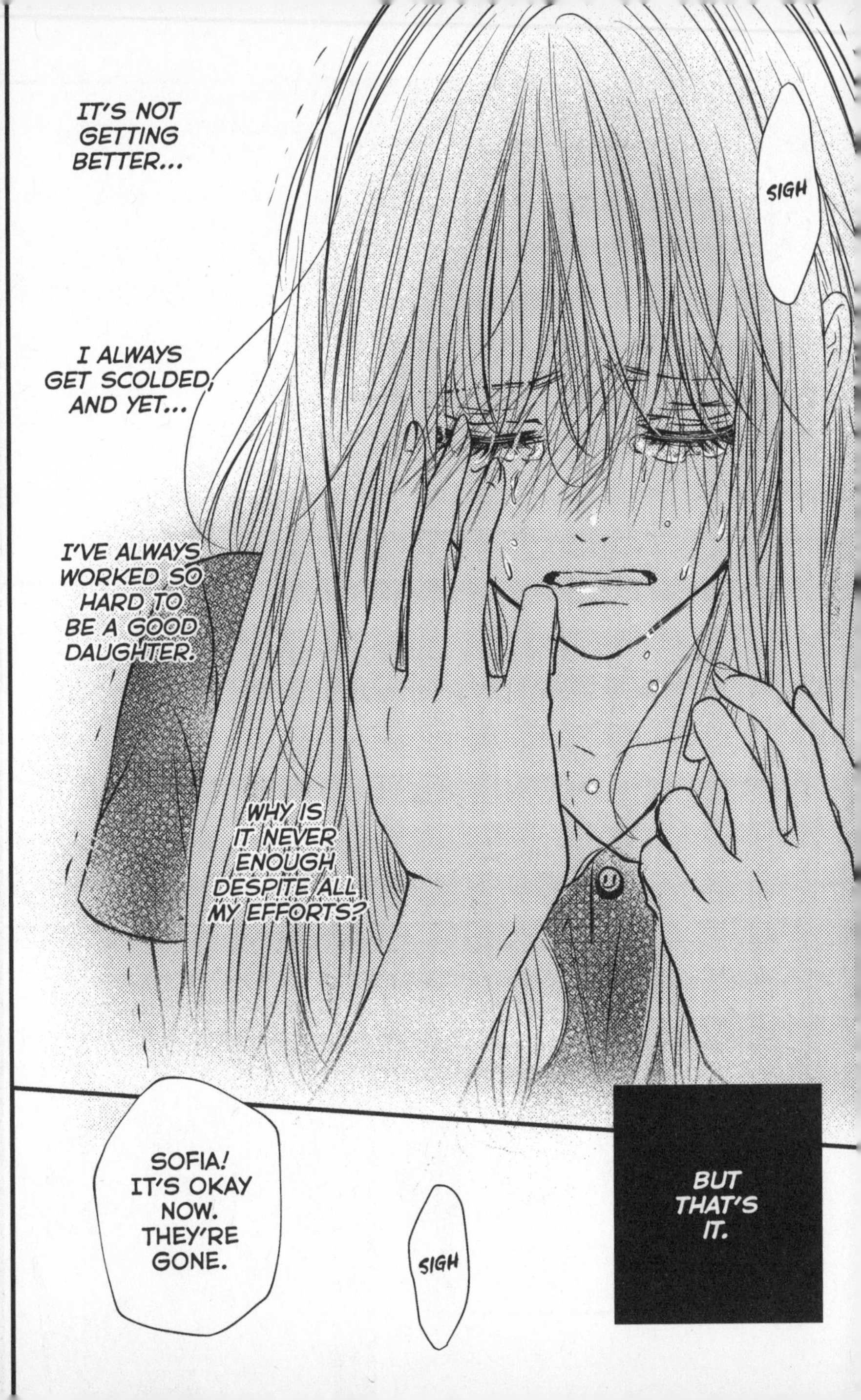
SIGH
IT'S NOT GETTING BETTER...
I ALWAYS GET SCOLDED, AND YET...
I'VE ALWAYS WORKED SO HARD TO BE A GOOD DAUGHTER.
WHY IS IT NEVER ENOUGH DESPITE ALL MY EFFORTS?
BUT THAT'S IT.
SIGH
SOFIA! IT'S OKAY NOW. THEY'RE GONE.

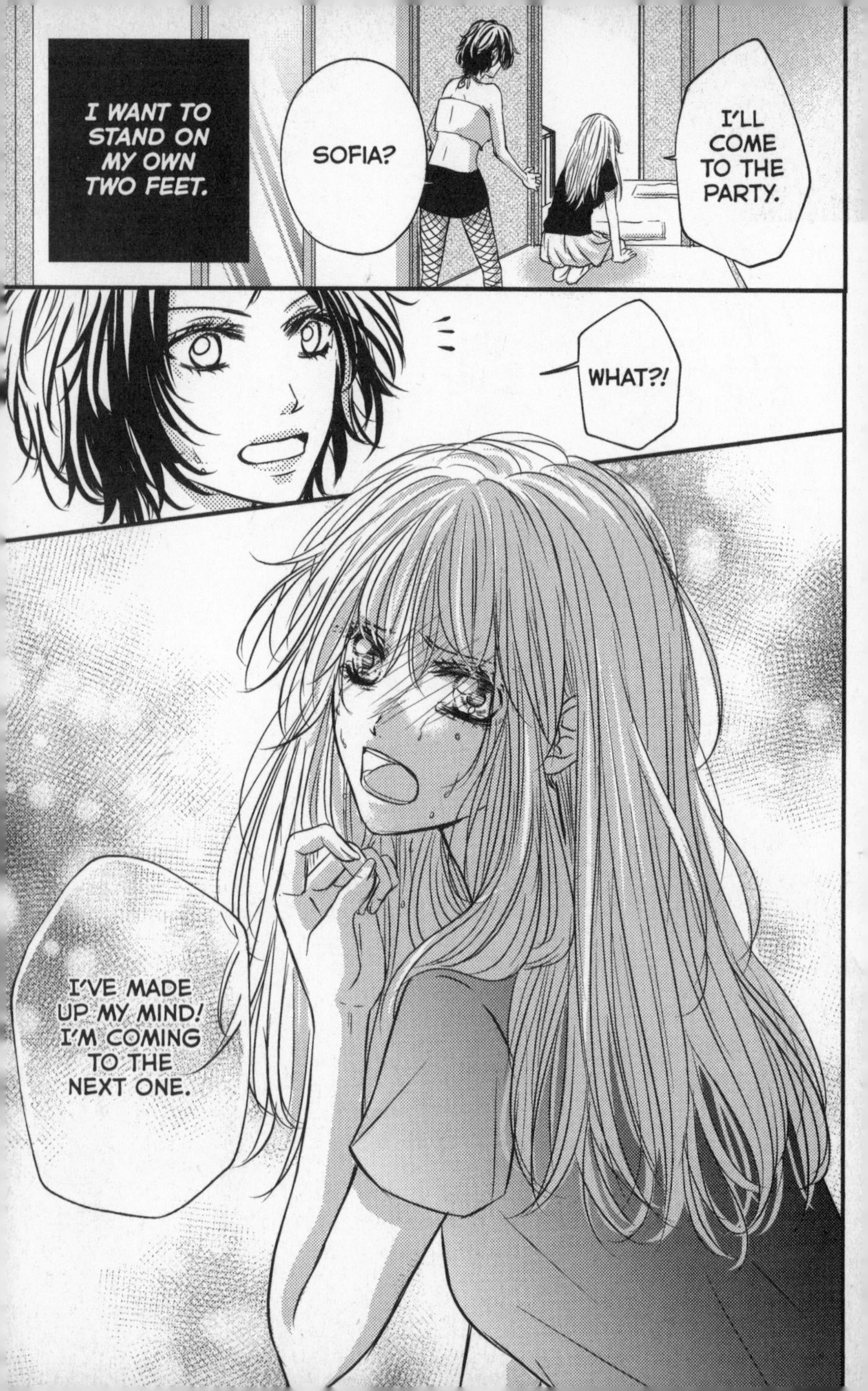
I'LL COME TO THE PARTY.
SOFIA?
I WANT TO STAND ON MY OWN TWO FEET.
WHAT?!
I'VE MADE UP MY MIND! I'M COMING TO THE NEXT ONE.

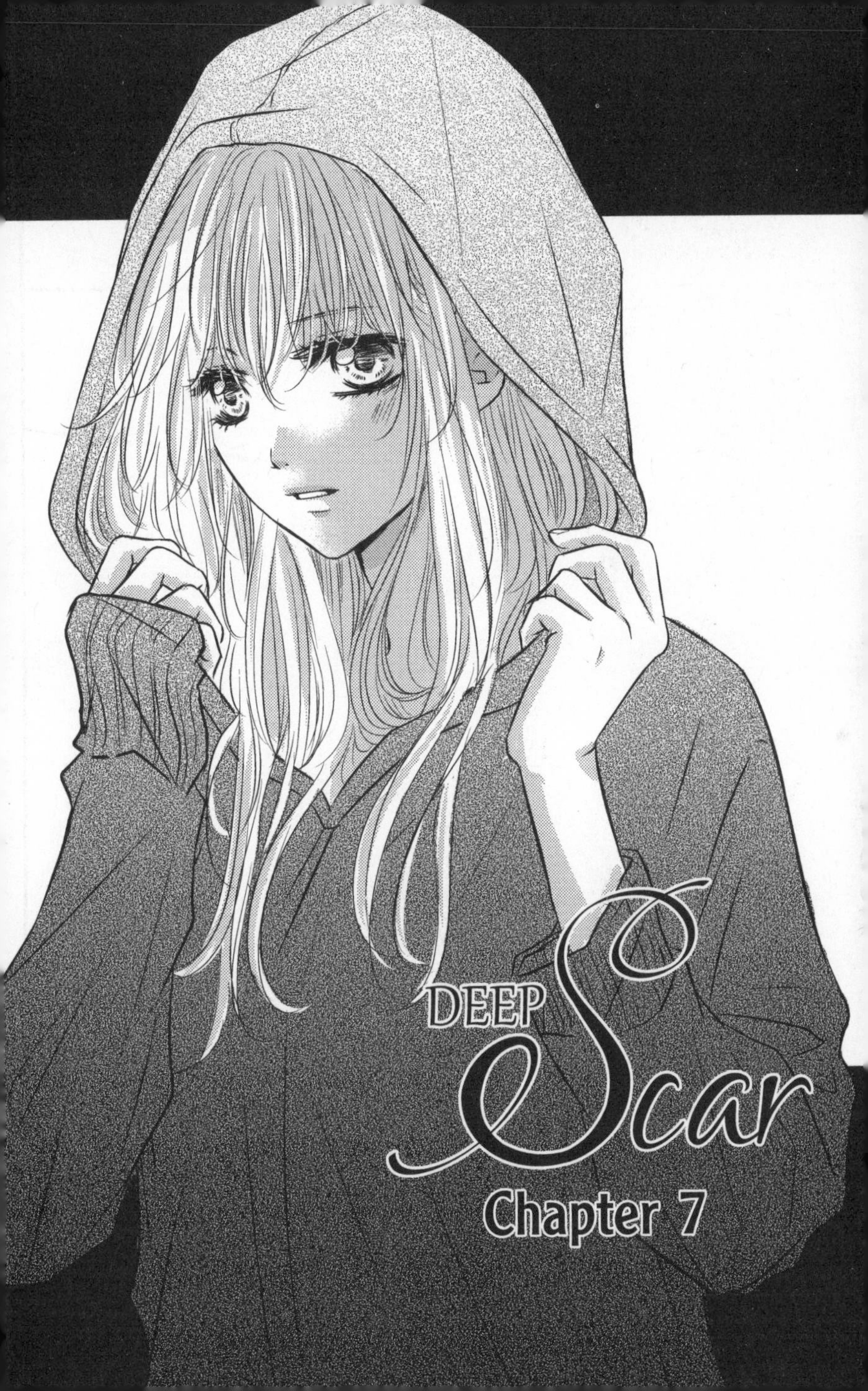
DEEP
Scar
Chapter 7

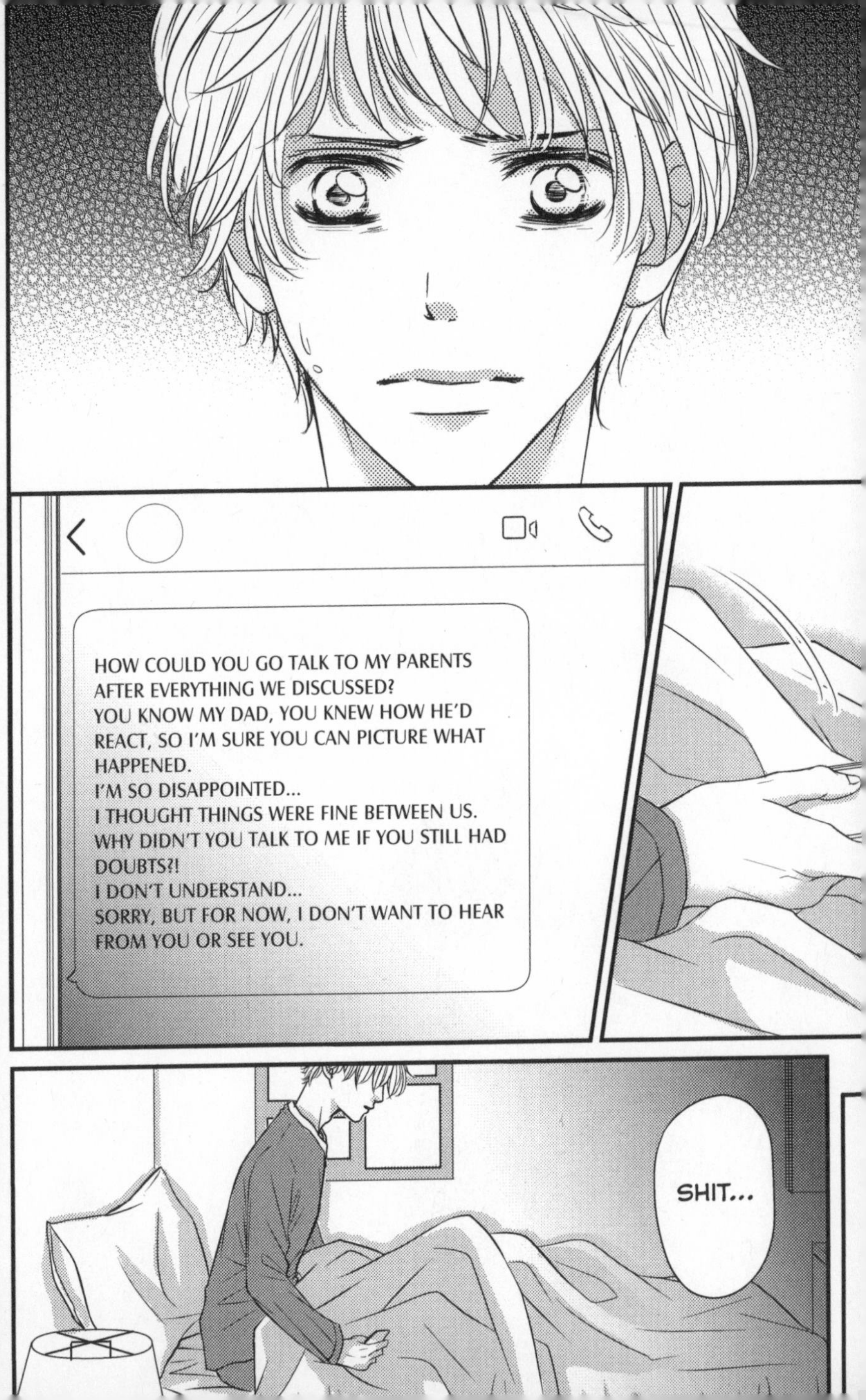
HOW COULD YOU GO TALK TO MY PARENTS AFTER EVERYTHING WE DISCUSSED?
YOU KNOW MY DAD, YOU KNEW HOW HE'D REACT, SO I'M SURE YOU CAN PICTURE WHAT HAPPENED.
I'M SO DISAPPOINTED...
I THOUGHT THINGS WERE FINE BETWEEN US.
WHY DIDN'T YOU TALK TO ME IF YOU STILL HAD DOUBTS?!
I DON'T UNDERSTAND...
SORRY, BUT FOR NOW, I DON'T WANT TO HEAR FROM YOU OR SEE YOU.
SHIT...

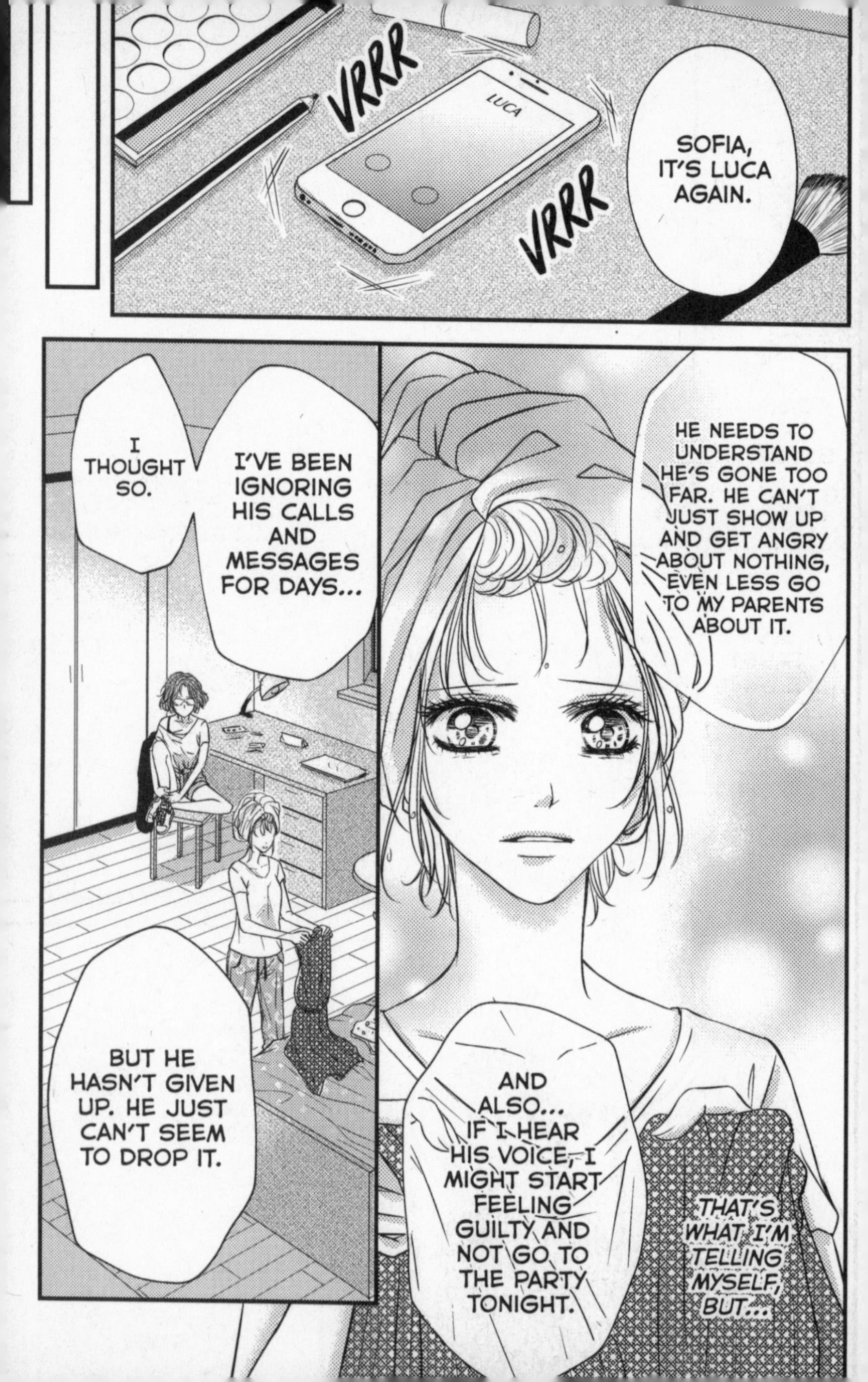
LUCA
VRRR
VRRR
SOFIA, IT'S LUCA AGAIN.
I THOUGHT SO.
I'VE BEEN IGNORING HIS CALLS AND MESSAGES FOR DAYS...
BUT HE HASN'T GIVEN UP. HE JUST CAN'T SEEM TO DROP IT.
HE NEEDS TO UNDERSTAND HE'S GONE TOO FAR. HE CAN'T JUST SHOW UP AND GET ANGRY ABOUT NOTHING, EVEN LESS GO TO MY PARENTS ABOUT IT.
AND ALSO... IF I HEAR HIS VOICE, I MIGHT START FEELING GUILTY AND NOT GO TO THE PARTY TONIGHT.
THAT'S WHAT I'M TELLING MYSELF, BUT...

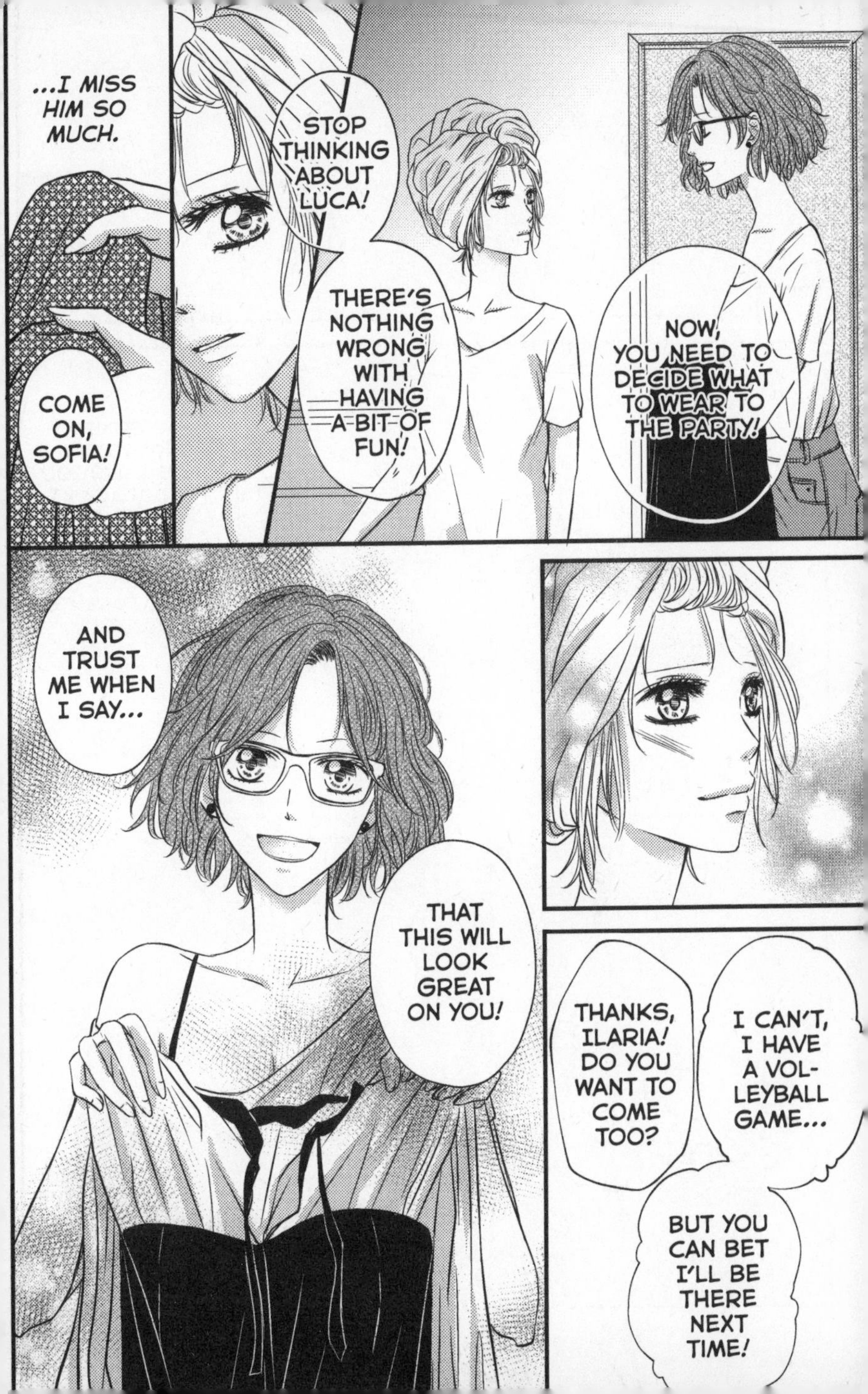
...I MISS HIM SO MUCH.
COME ON, SOFIA!
STOP THINKING ABOUT LUCA!
THERE'S NOTHING WRONG WITH HAVING A BIT OF FUN!
NOW, YOU NEED TO DECIDE WHAT TO WEAR TO THE PARTY!
AND TRUST ME WHEN I SAY...
THAT THIS WILL LOOK GREAT ON YOU!
THANKS, ILARIA! DO YOU WANT TO COME TOO?
I CAN'T, I HAVE A VOL-LEYBALL GAME...
BUT YOU CAN BET I'LL BE THERE NEXT TIME!

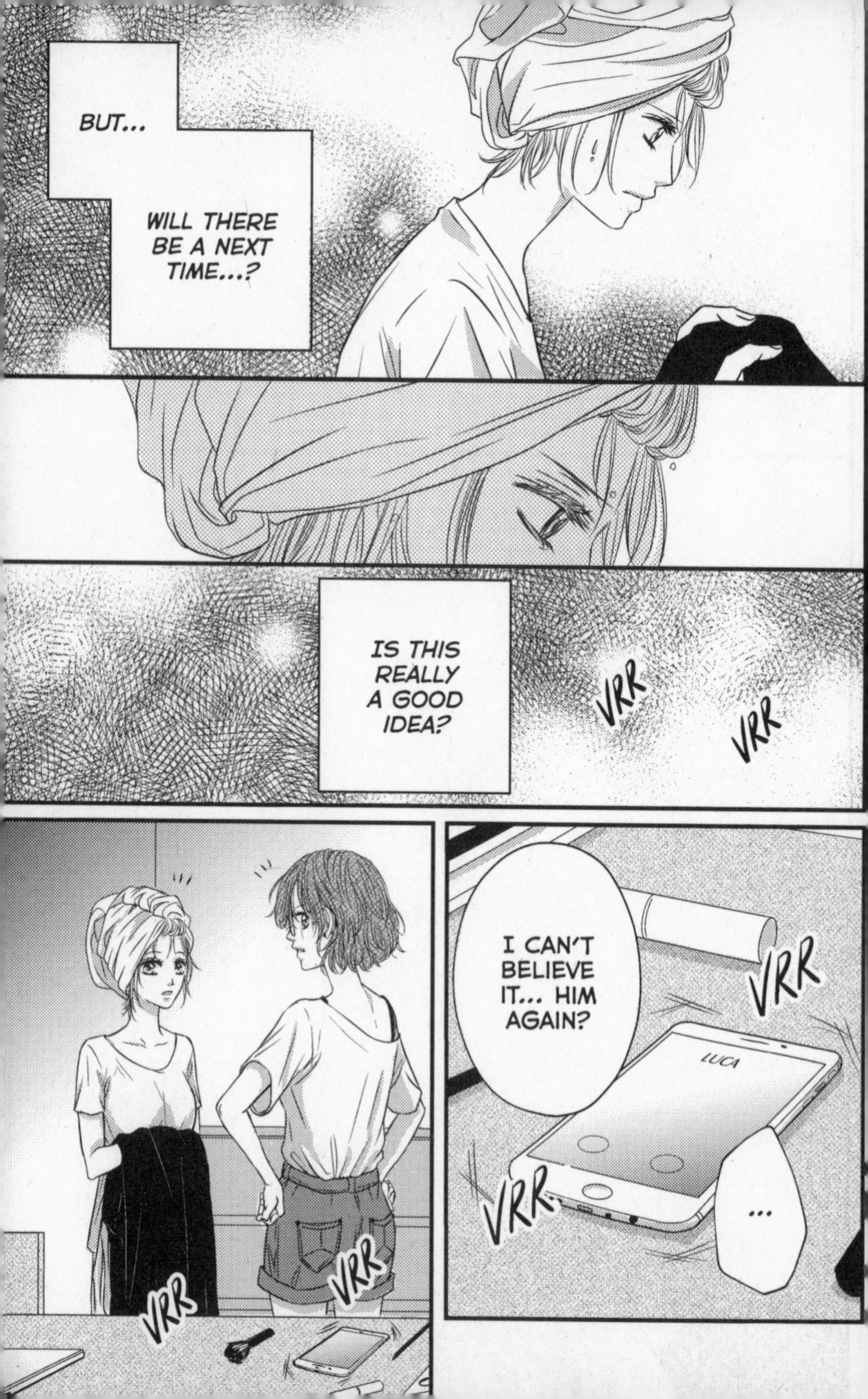
BUT...
WILL THERE BE A NEXT TIME...?
IS THIS REALLY A GOOD IDEA?
VRR
VRR
I CAN'T BELIEVE IT... HIM AGAIN?
VRR
LUCA
VRR
...
VRR
VRR

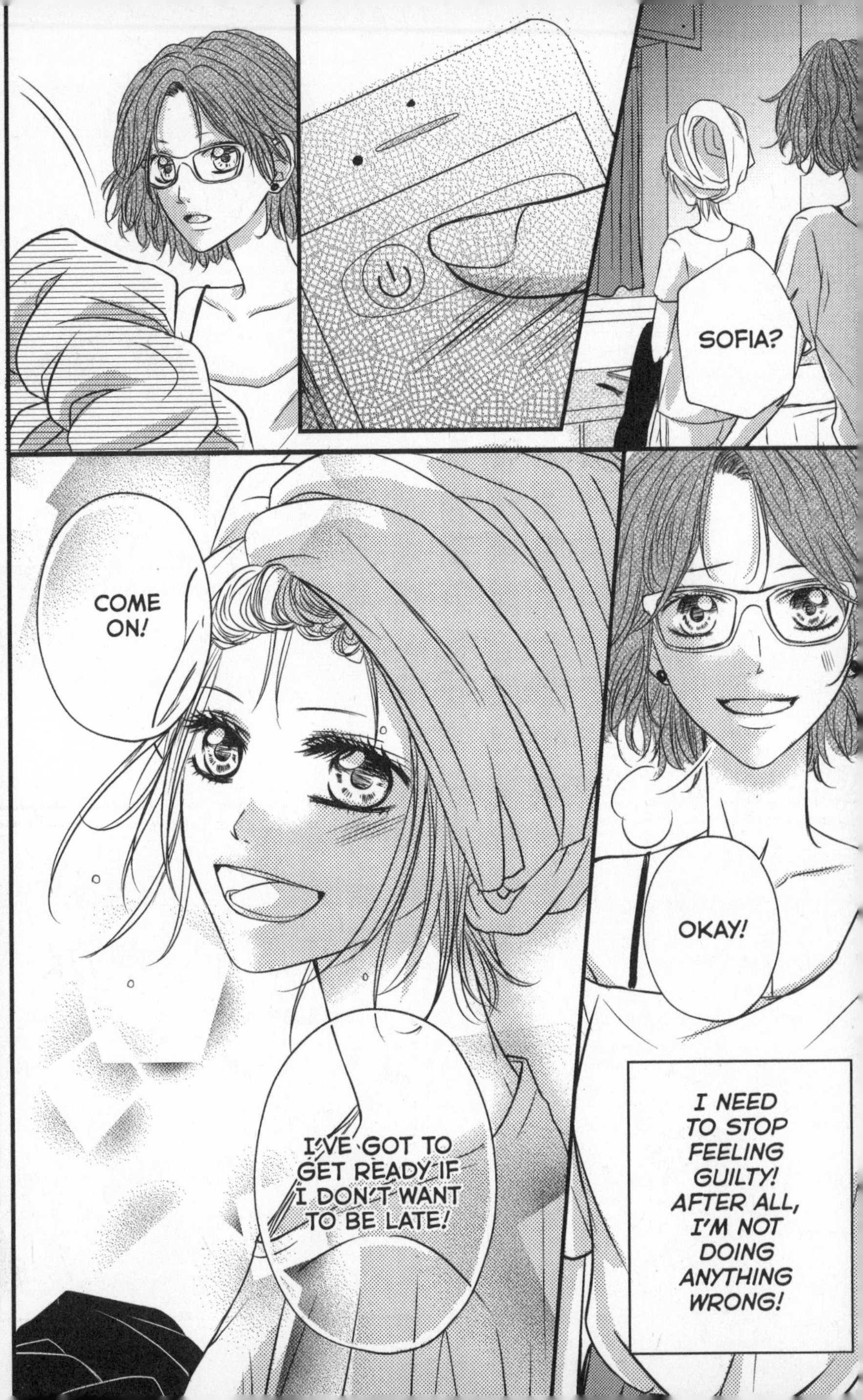
SOFIA?
COME ON!
I'VE GOT TO GET READY IF I DON'T WANT TO BE LATE!
OKAY!
I NEED TO STOP FEELING GUILTY! AFTER ALL, I'M NOT DOING ANYTHING WRONG!

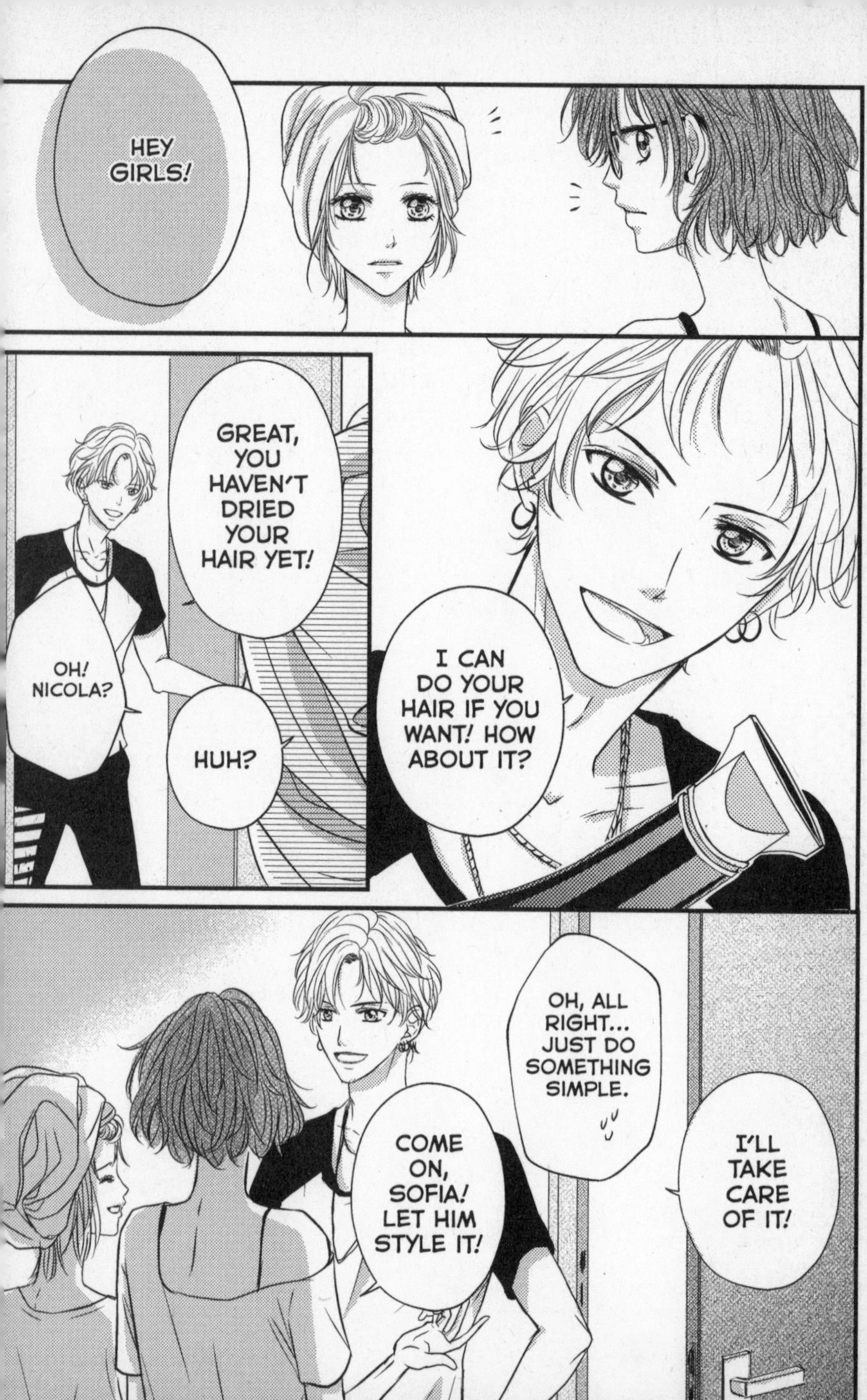
HEY GIRLS!
OH! NICOLA?
HUH?
GREAT, YOU HAVEN'T DRIED YOUR HAIR YET!
I CAN DO YOUR HAIR IF YOU WANT! HOW ABOUT IT?
COME ON, SOFIA! LET HIM STYLE IT!
OH, ALL RIGHT... JUST DO SOMETHING SIMPLE.
I'LL TAKE CARE OF IT!

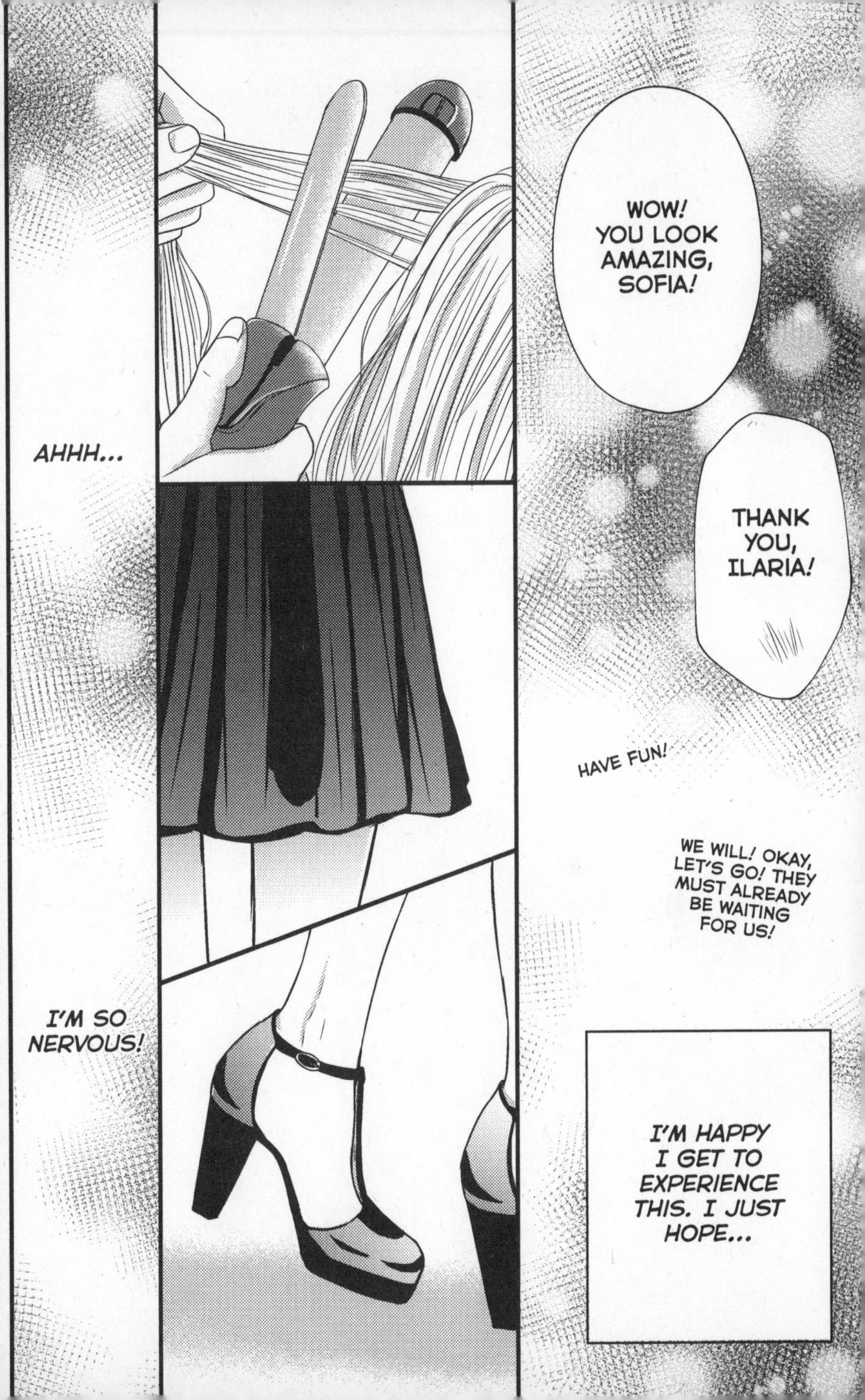
WOW! YOU LOOK AMAZING, SOFIA!
THANK YOU, ILARIA!
HAVE FUN!
WE WILL! OKAY, LET'S GO! THEY MUST ALREADY BE WAITING FOR US!
I'M HAPPY I GET TO EXPERIENCE THIS. I JUST HOPE...
AHHH...
I'M SO NERVOUS!

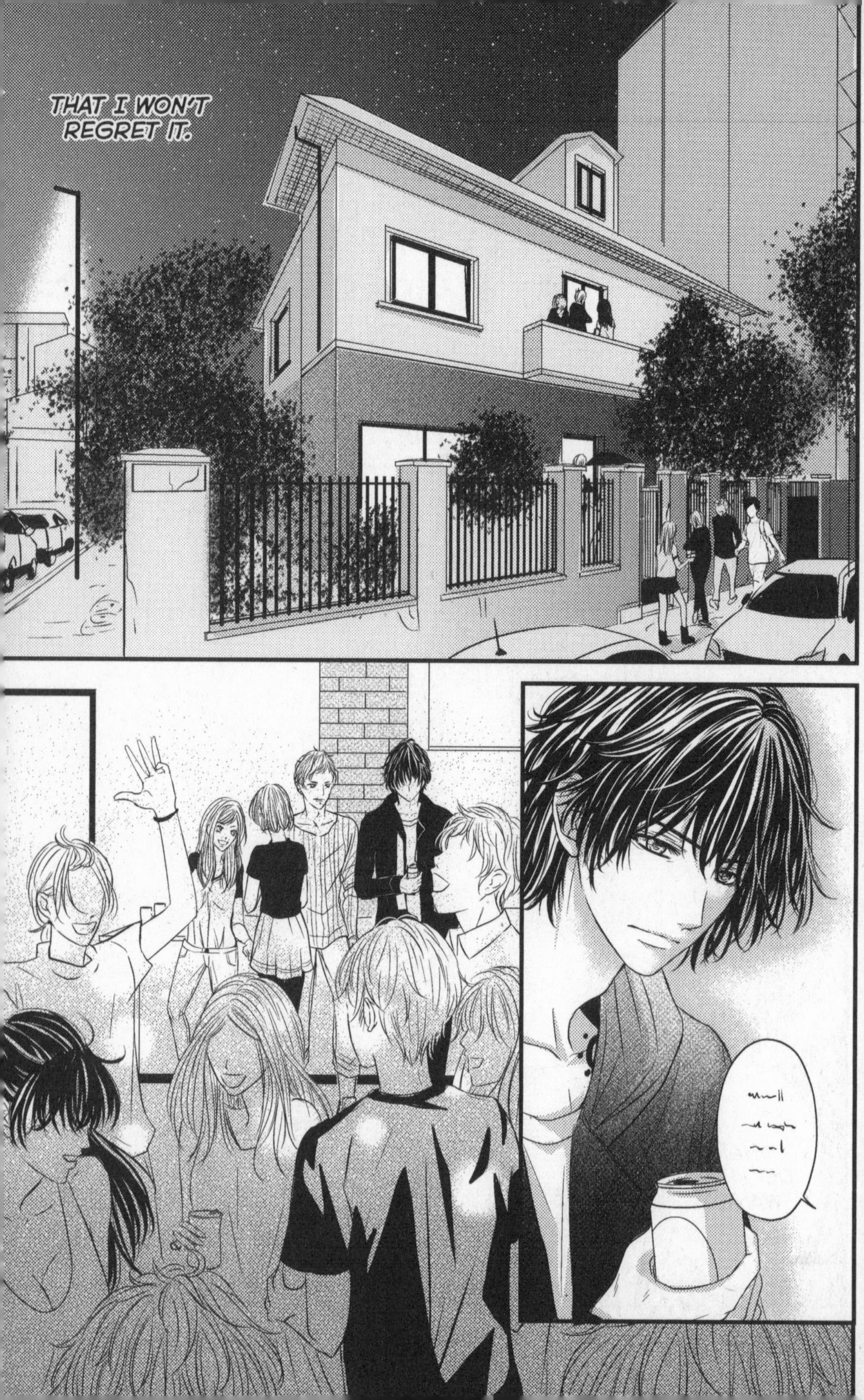
THAT I WON'T REGRET IT.

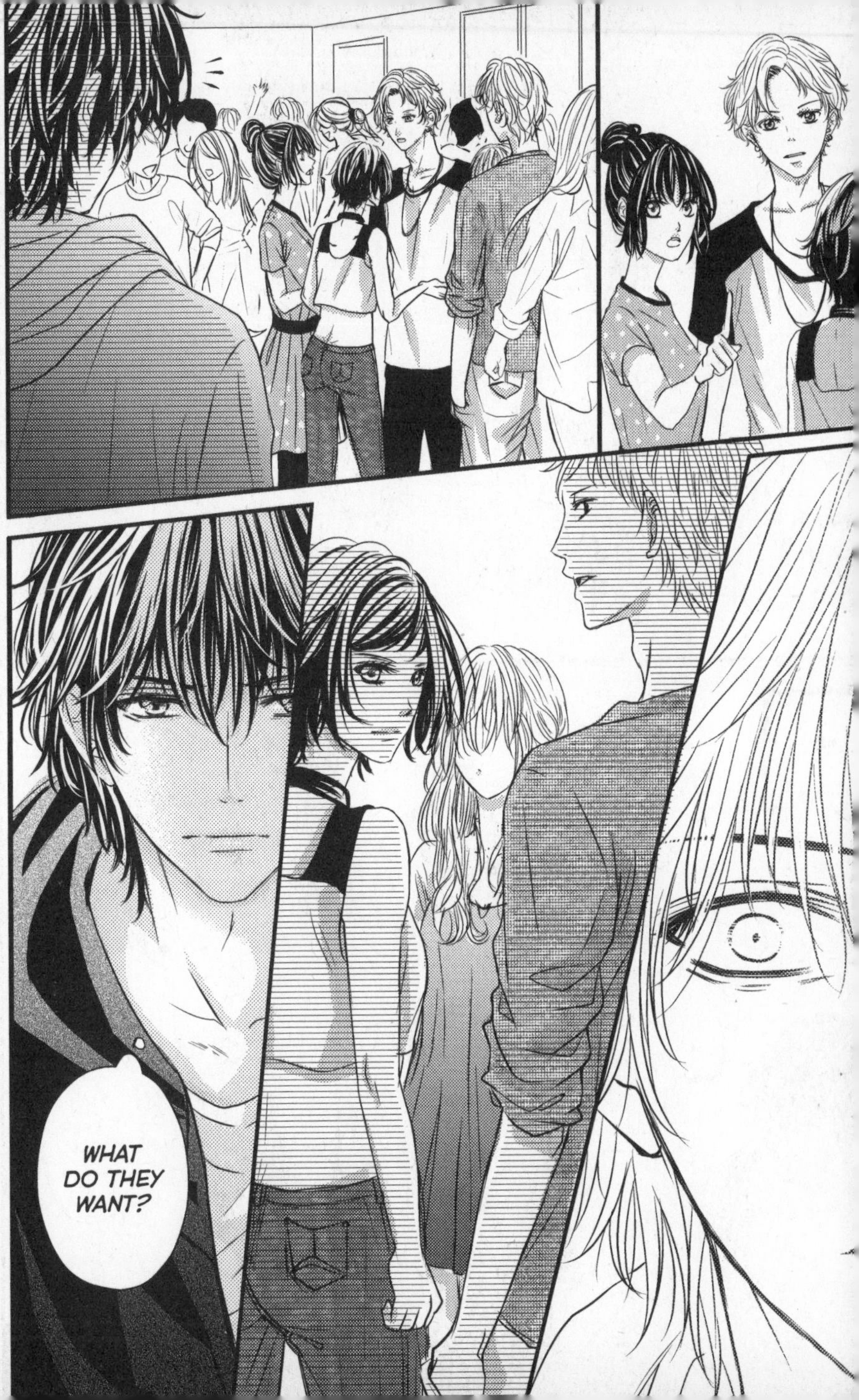
WHAT DO THEY WANT?

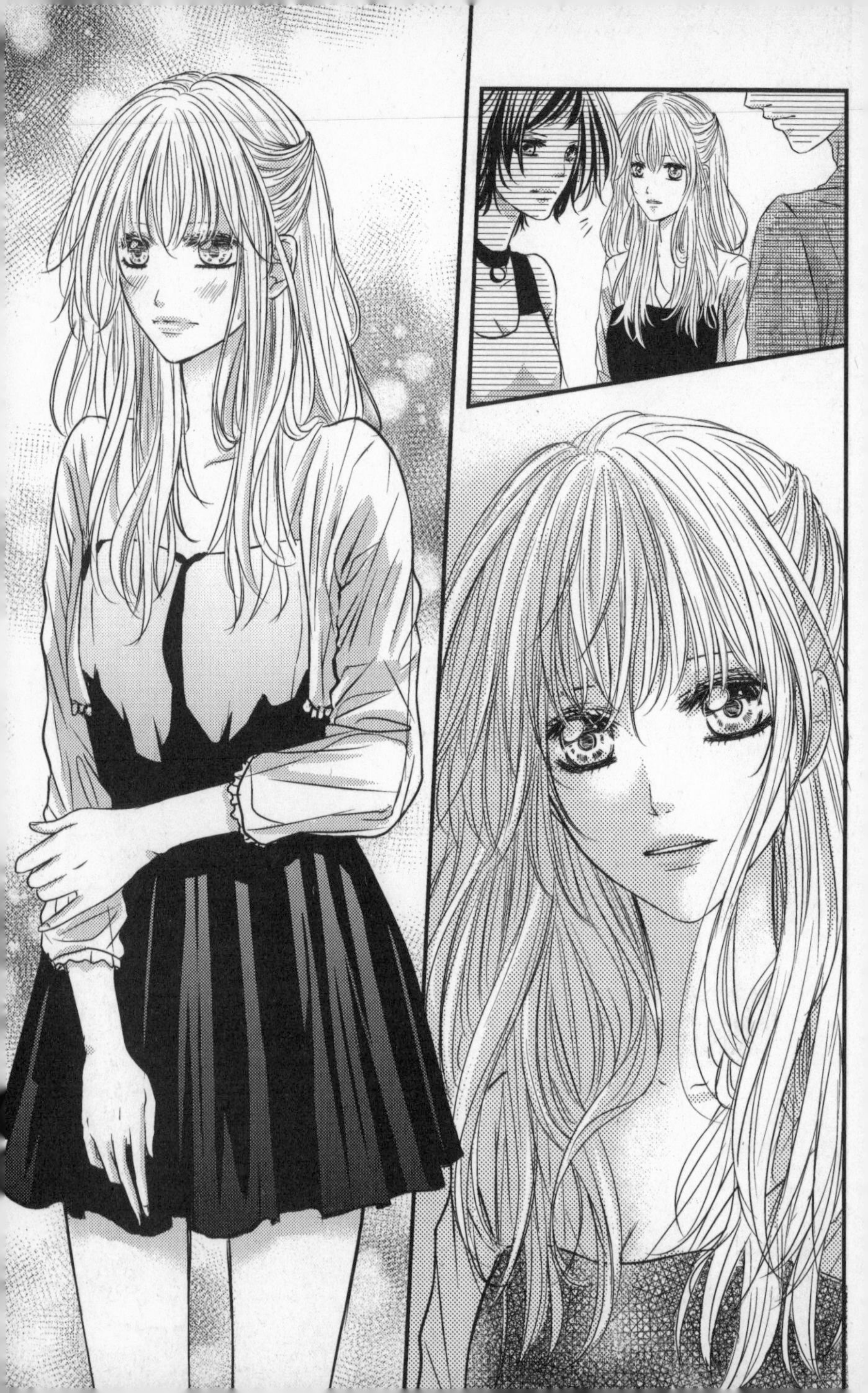

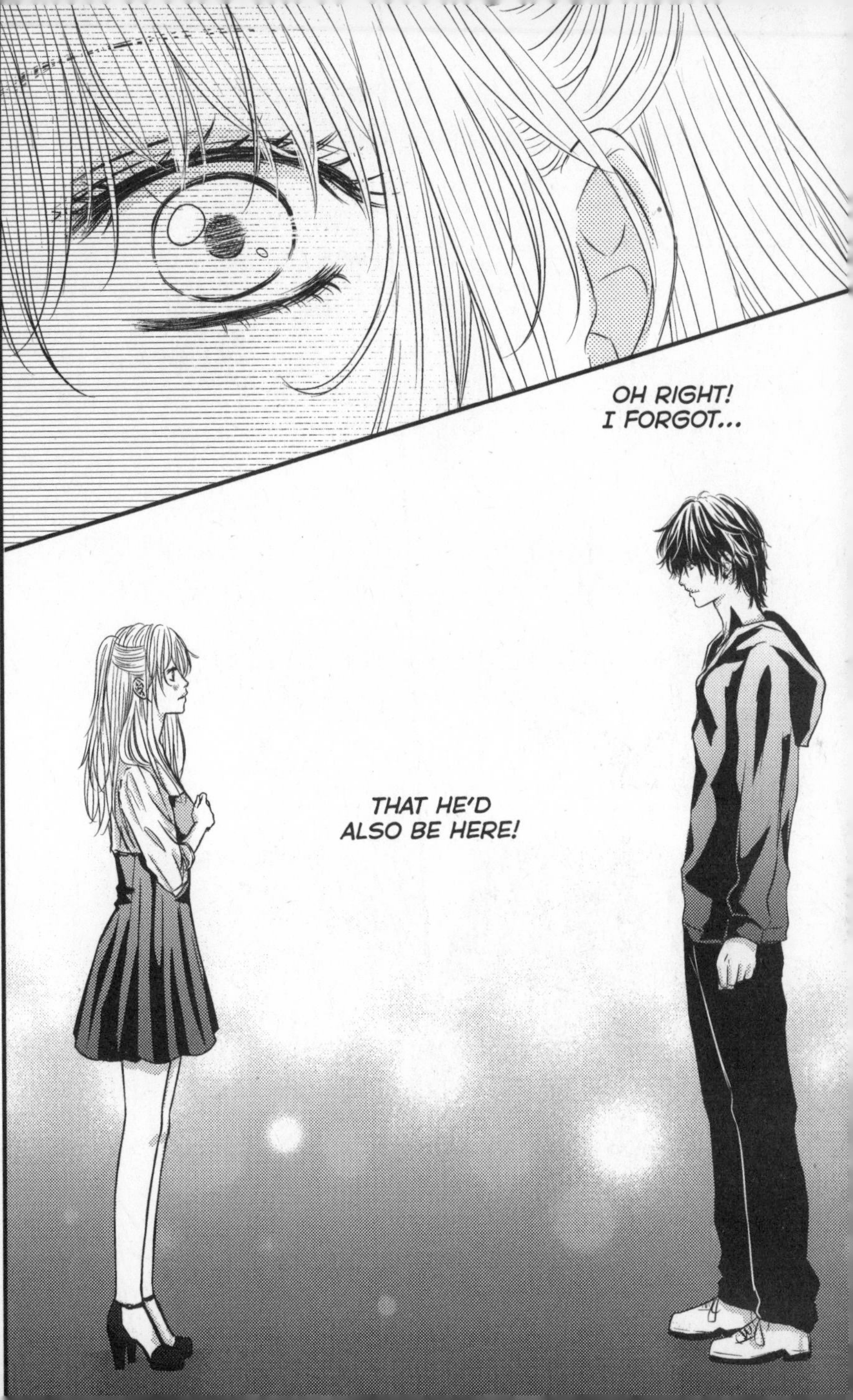
OH RIGHT!
I FORGOT...
THAT HE'D
ALSO BE HERE!

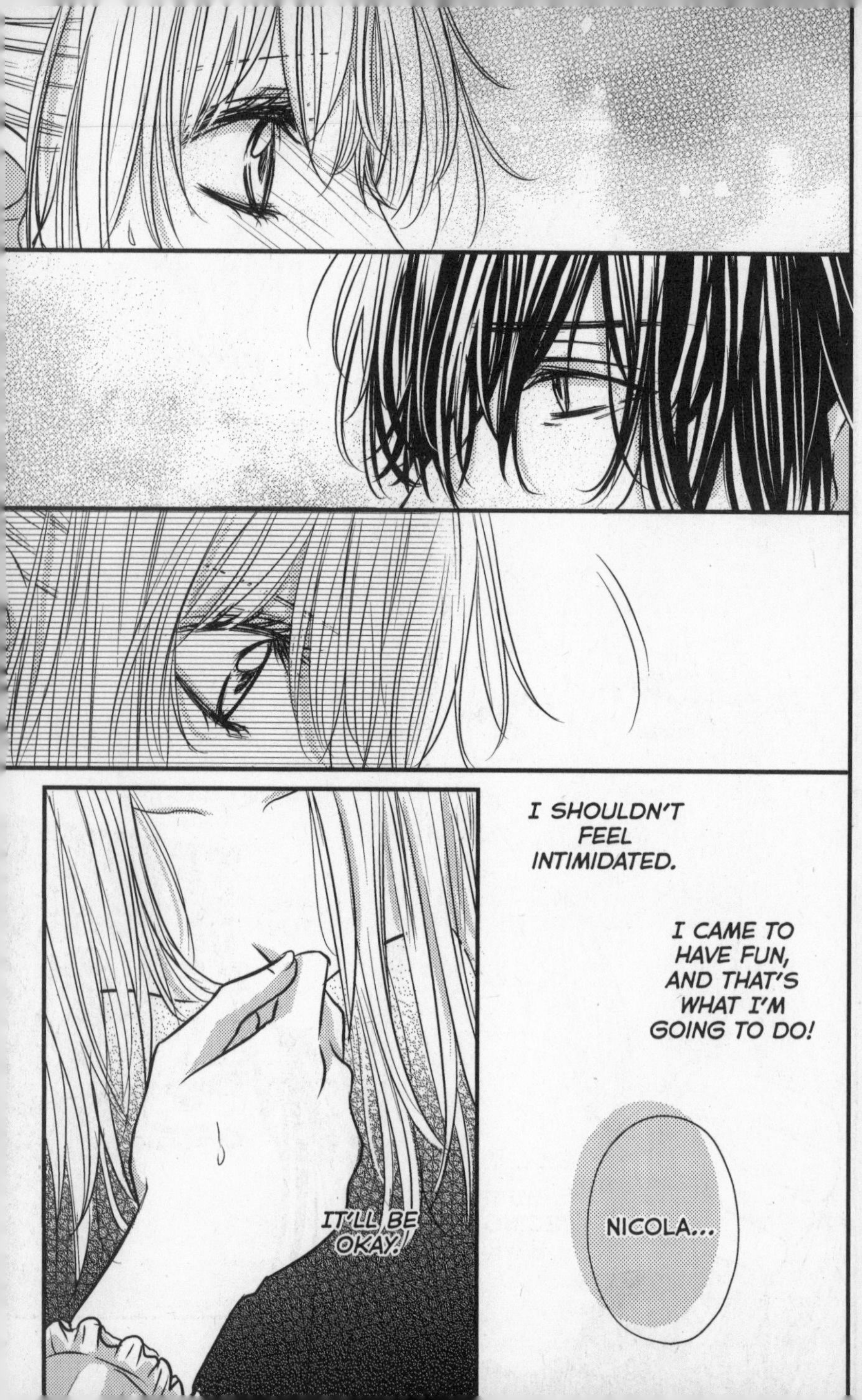
I SHOULDN'T FEEL INTIMIDATED.
I CAME TO HAVE FUN, AND THAT'S WHAT I'M GOING TO DO!
IT'LL BE OKAY.
NICOLA...

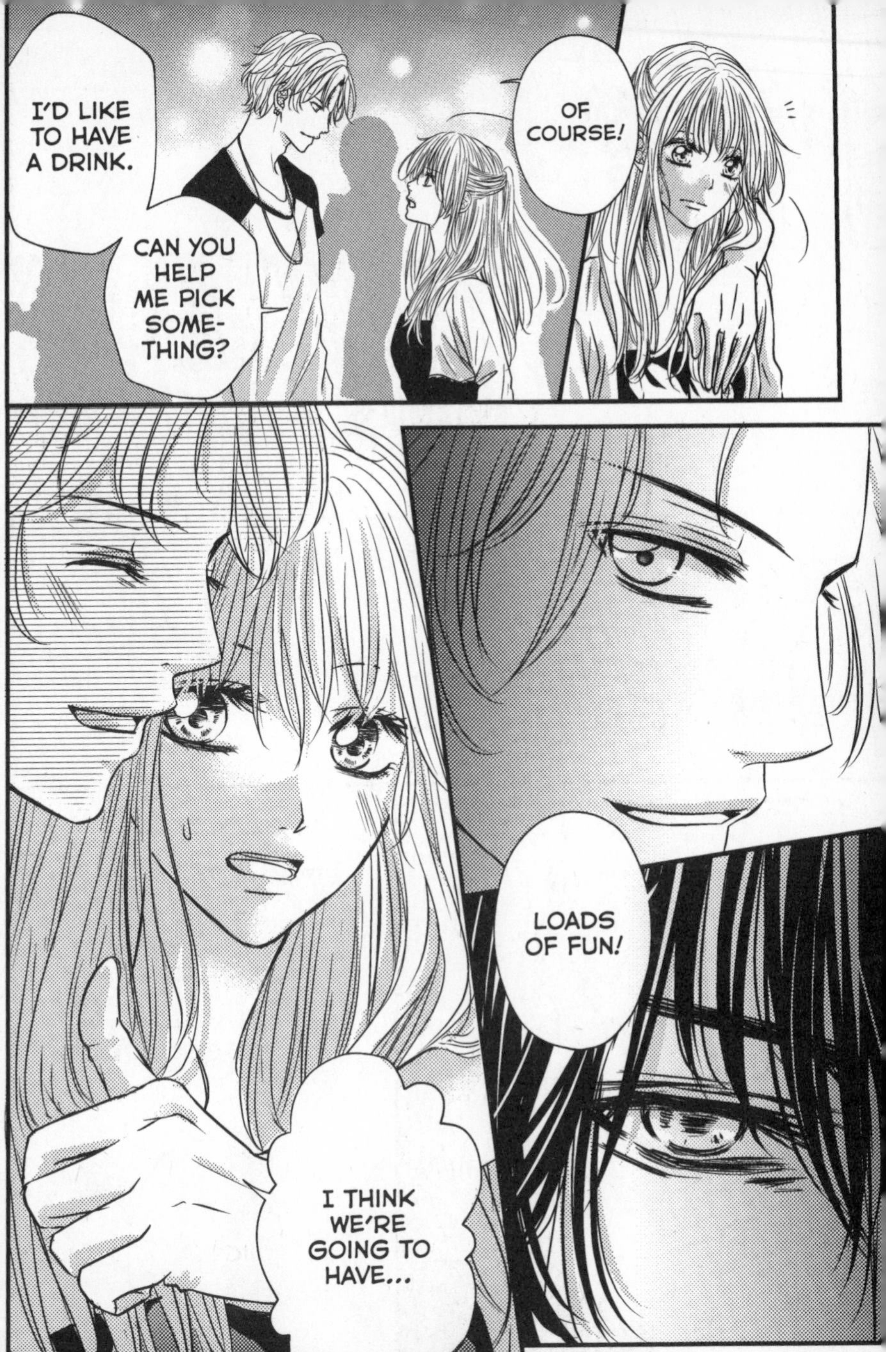
I'D LIKE TO HAVE A DRINK.
CAN YOU HELP ME PICK SOME-THING?
OF COURSE!
I THINK WE'RE GOING TO HAVE...
LOADS OF FUN!

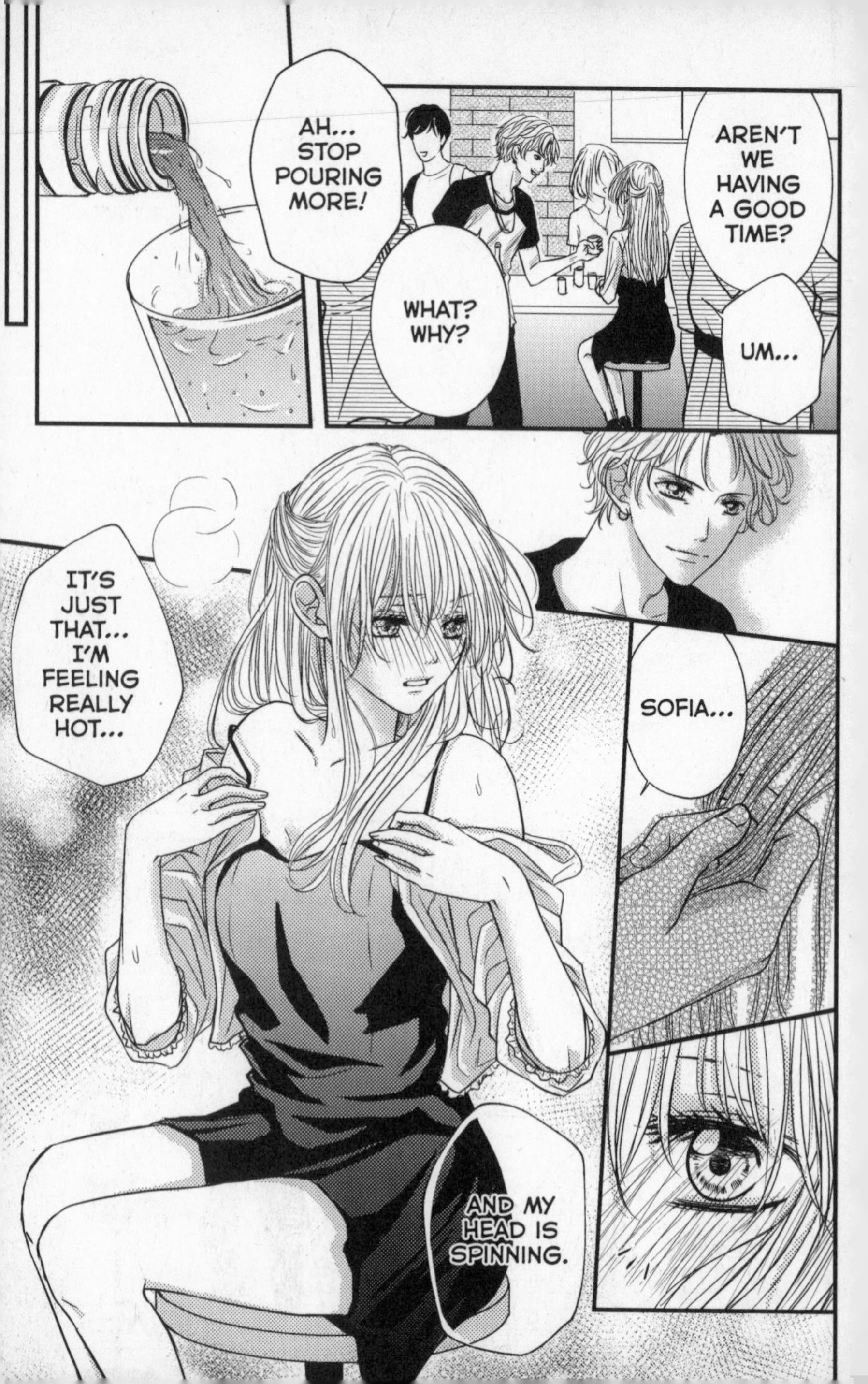
AREN'T WE HAVING A GOOD TIME?
UM...
AH... STOP POURING MORE!
WHAT? WHY?
IT'S JUST THAT... I'M FEELING REALLY HOT...
AND MY HEAD IS SPINNING.
SOFIA...

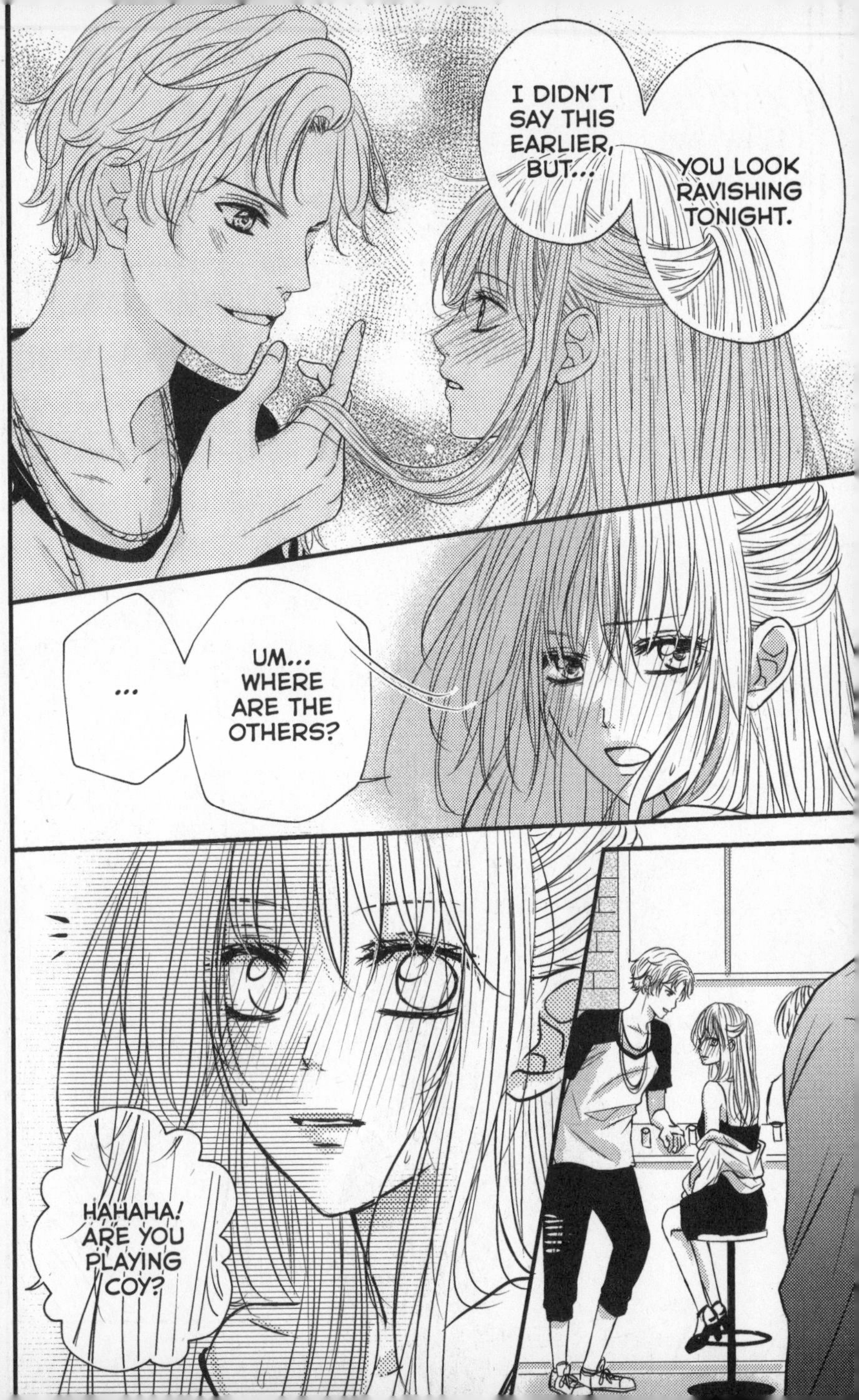
I DIDN'T SAY THIS EARLIER, BUT...
YOU LOOK RAVISHING TONIGHT.
UM... WHERE ARE THE OTHERS?
...
HAHAHA! ARE YOU PLAYING COY?

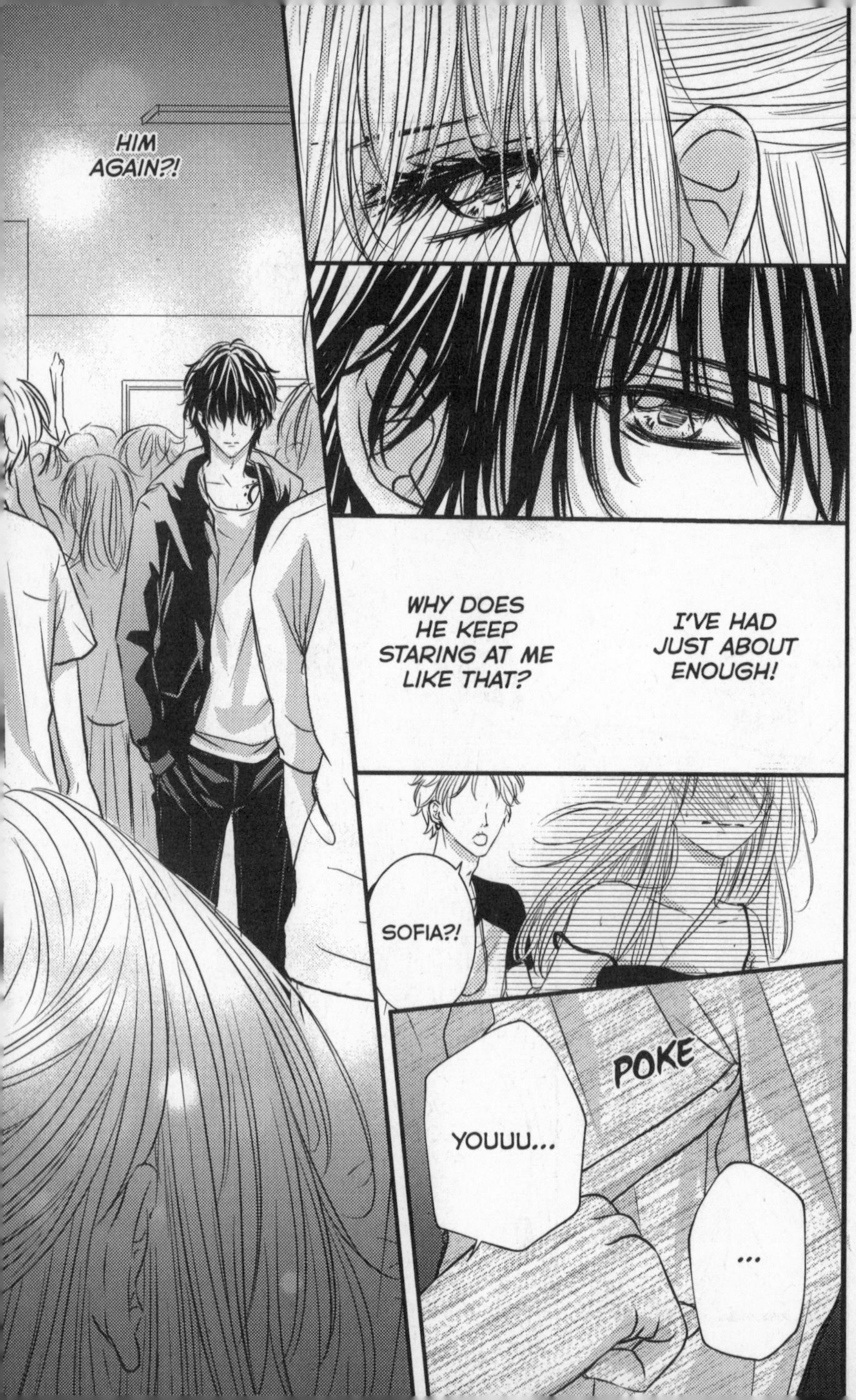
I'VE HAD JUST ABOUT ENOUGH!
WHY DOES HE KEEP STARING AT ME LIKE THAT?
SOFIA?!
POKE
...
YOUUU...
HIM AGAIN?!

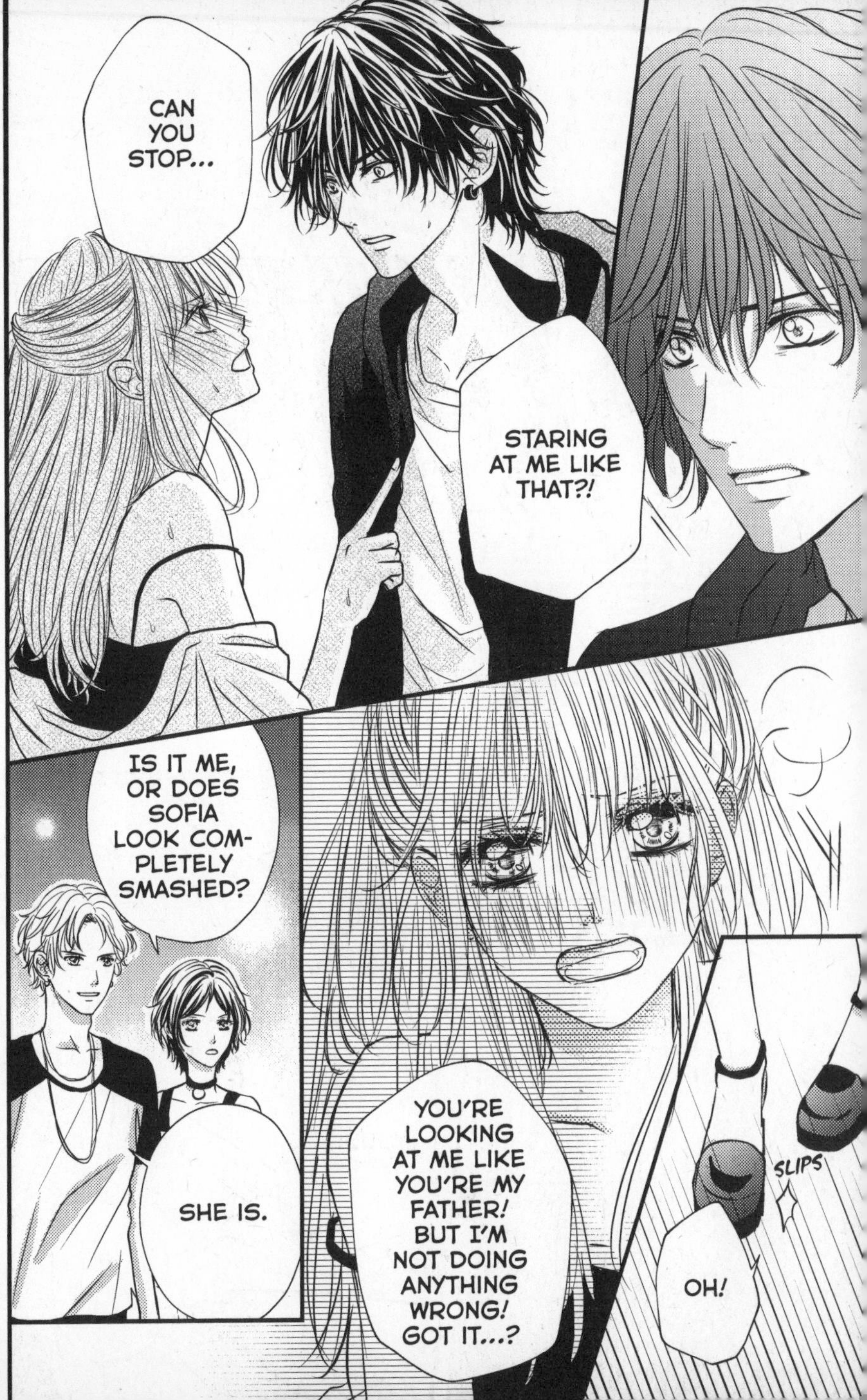
CAN YOU STOP...
STARING AT ME LIKE THAT?!
YOU'RE LOOKING AT ME LIKE YOU'RE MY FATHER! BUT I'M NOT DOING ANYTHING WRONG! GOT IT...?
SLIPS
OH!
IS IT ME, OR DOES SOFIA LOOK COM-PLETELY SMASHED?
SHE IS.

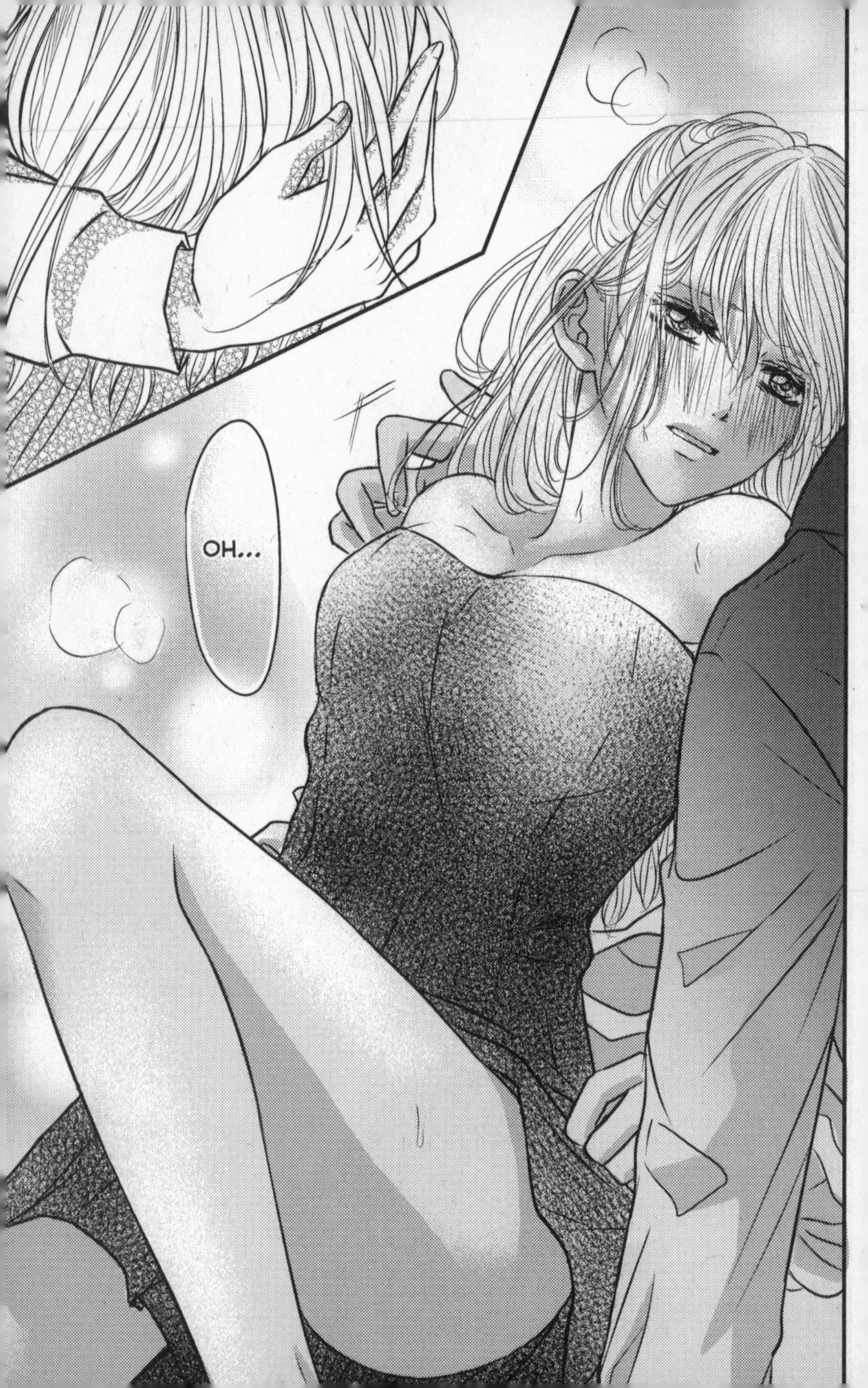
OH...

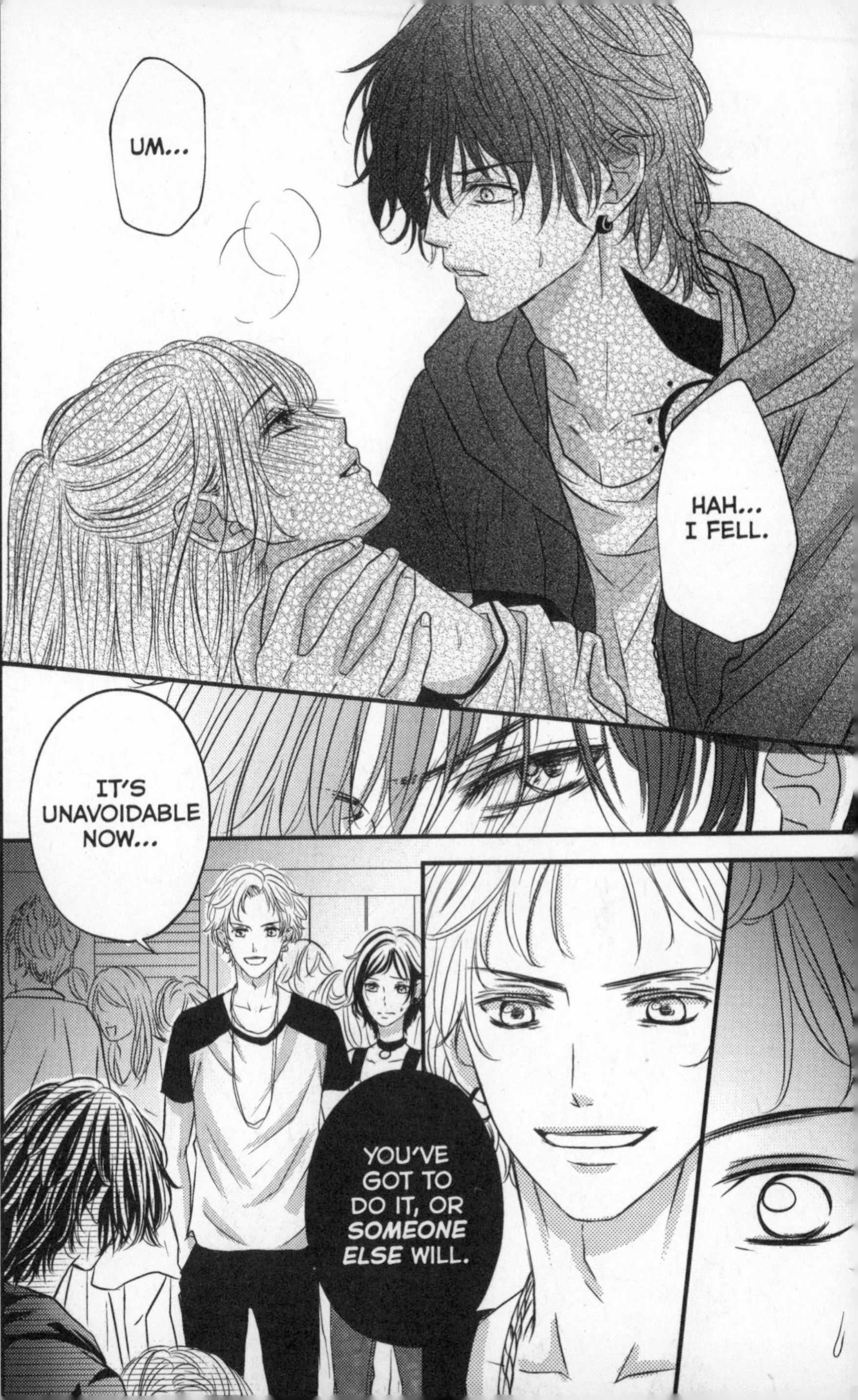
HAH... I FELL.
UM...
IT'S UNAVOIDABLE NOW...
YOU'VE GOT TO DO IT, OR *SOMEONE ELSE* WILL.

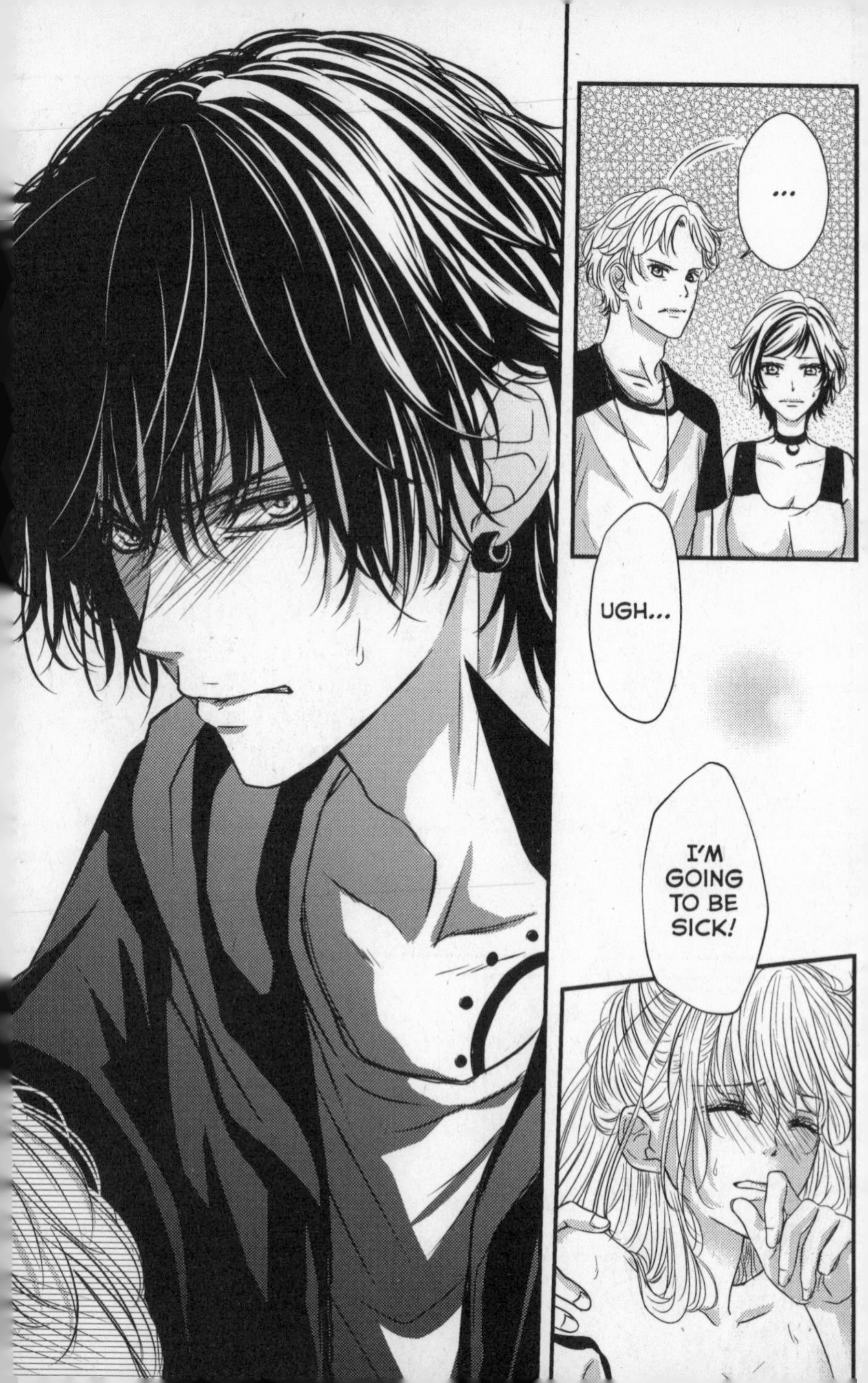
...
UGH...
I'M GOING TO BE SICK!

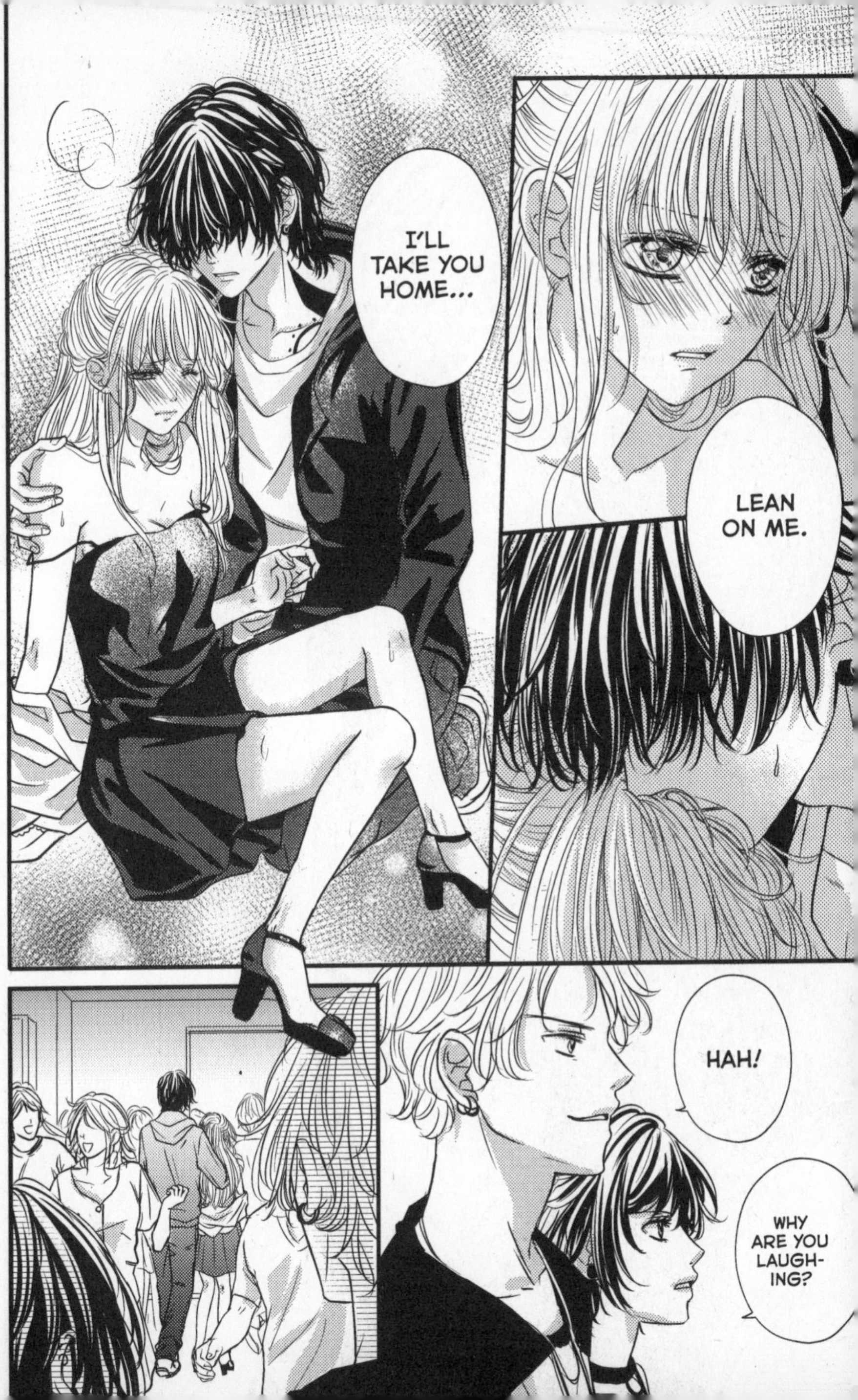
LEAN ON ME.
I'LL TAKE YOU HOME...
HAH!
WHY ARE YOU LAUGH-ING?

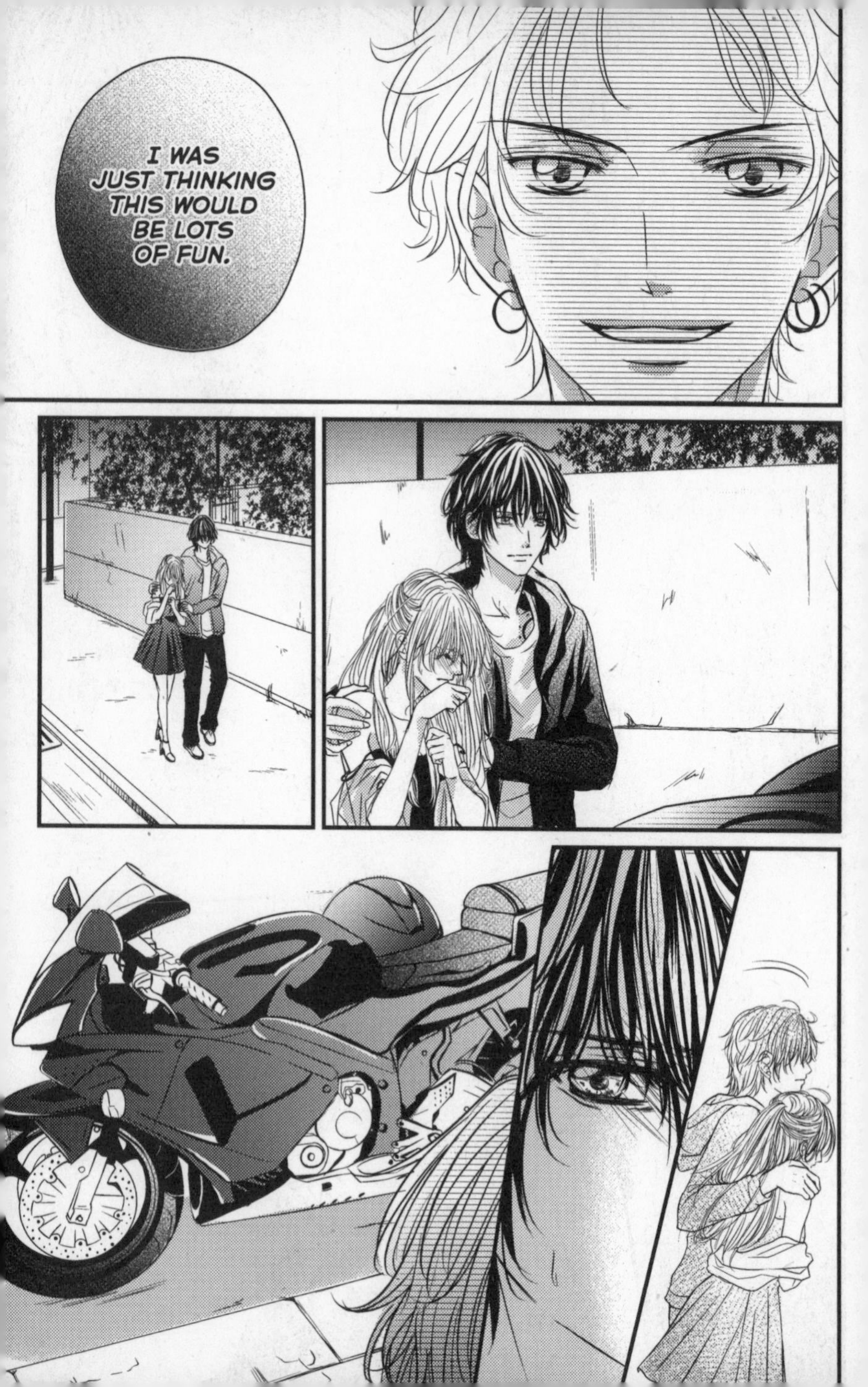
I WAS JUST THINKING THIS WOULD BE LOTS OF FUN.

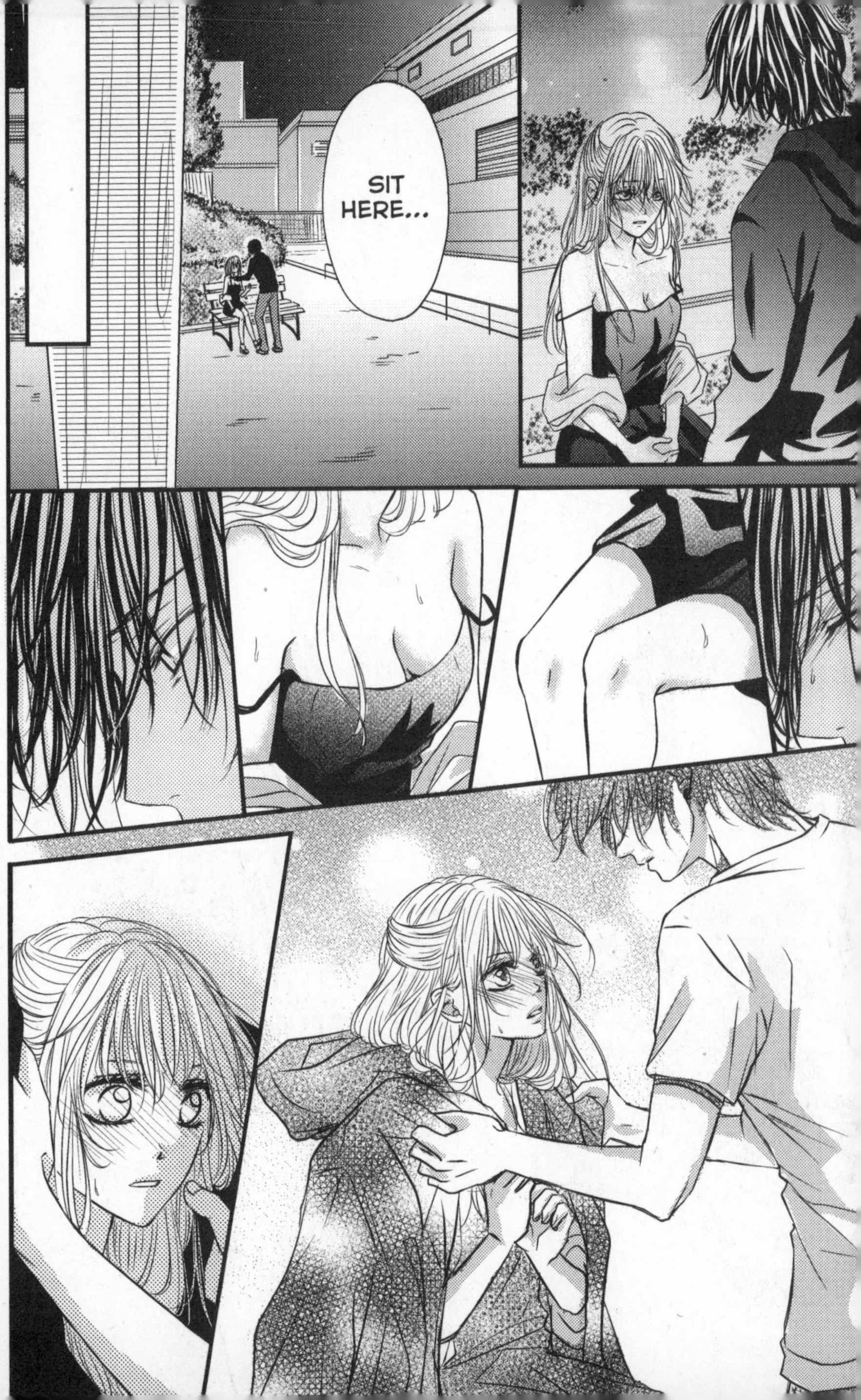
SIT HERE...

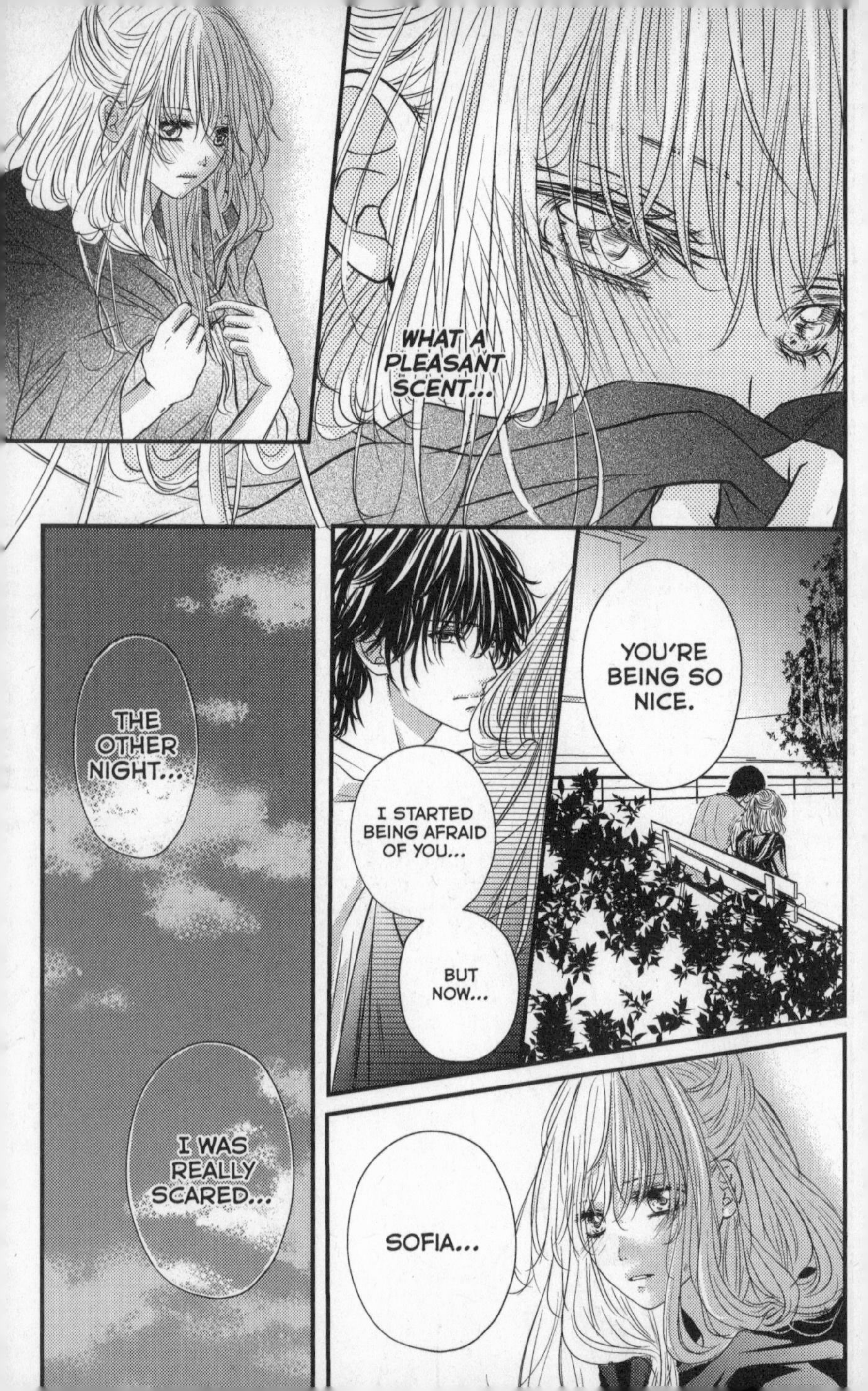
WHAT A PLEASANT SCENT...
YOU'RE BEING SO NICE.
I STARTED BEING AFRAID OF YOU...
BUT NOW...
SOFIA...
THE OTHER NIGHT...
I WAS REALLY SCARED...

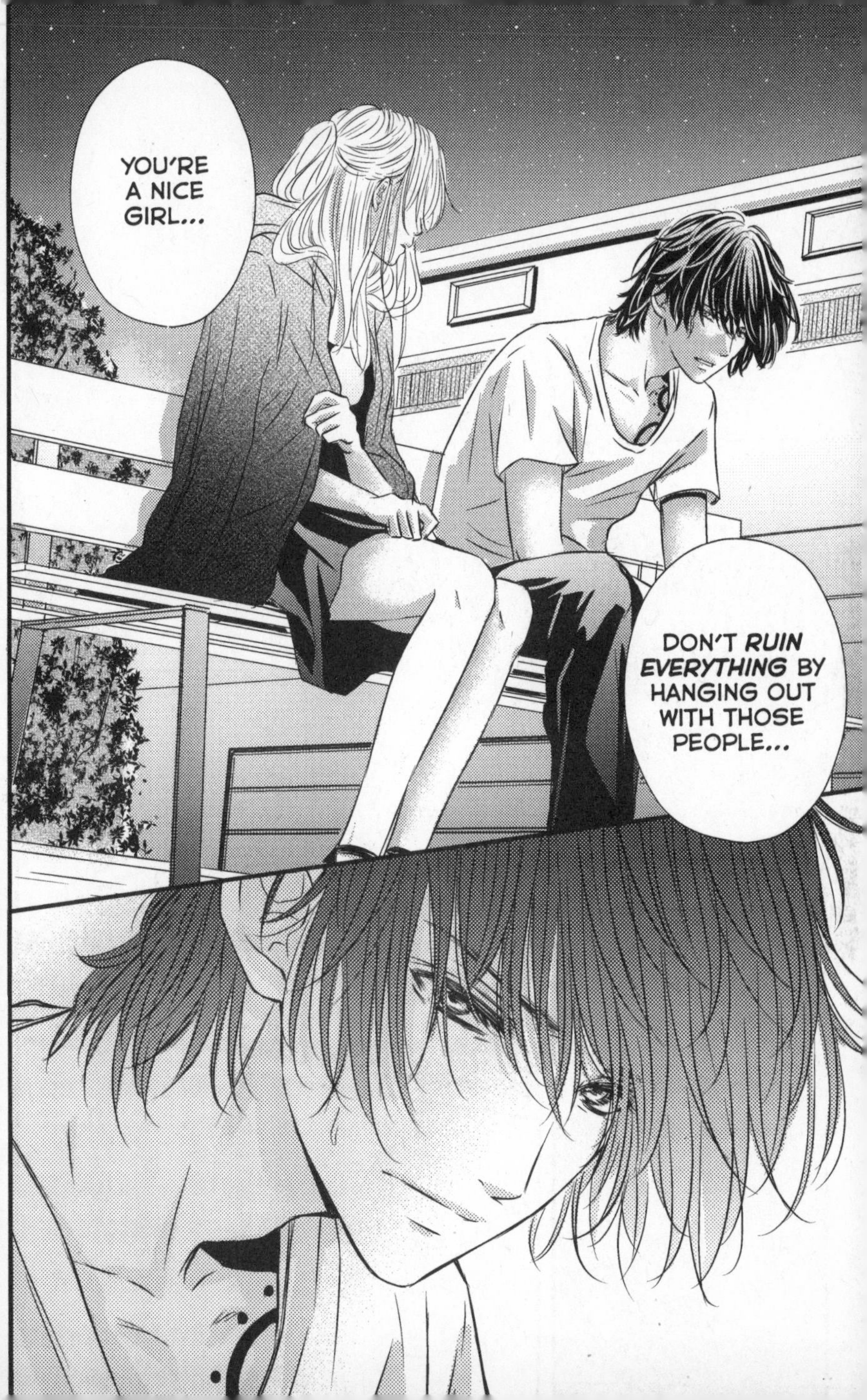
YOU'RE A NICE GIRL...
DON'T *RUIN EVERYTHING* BY HANGING OUT WITH THOSE PEOPLE...

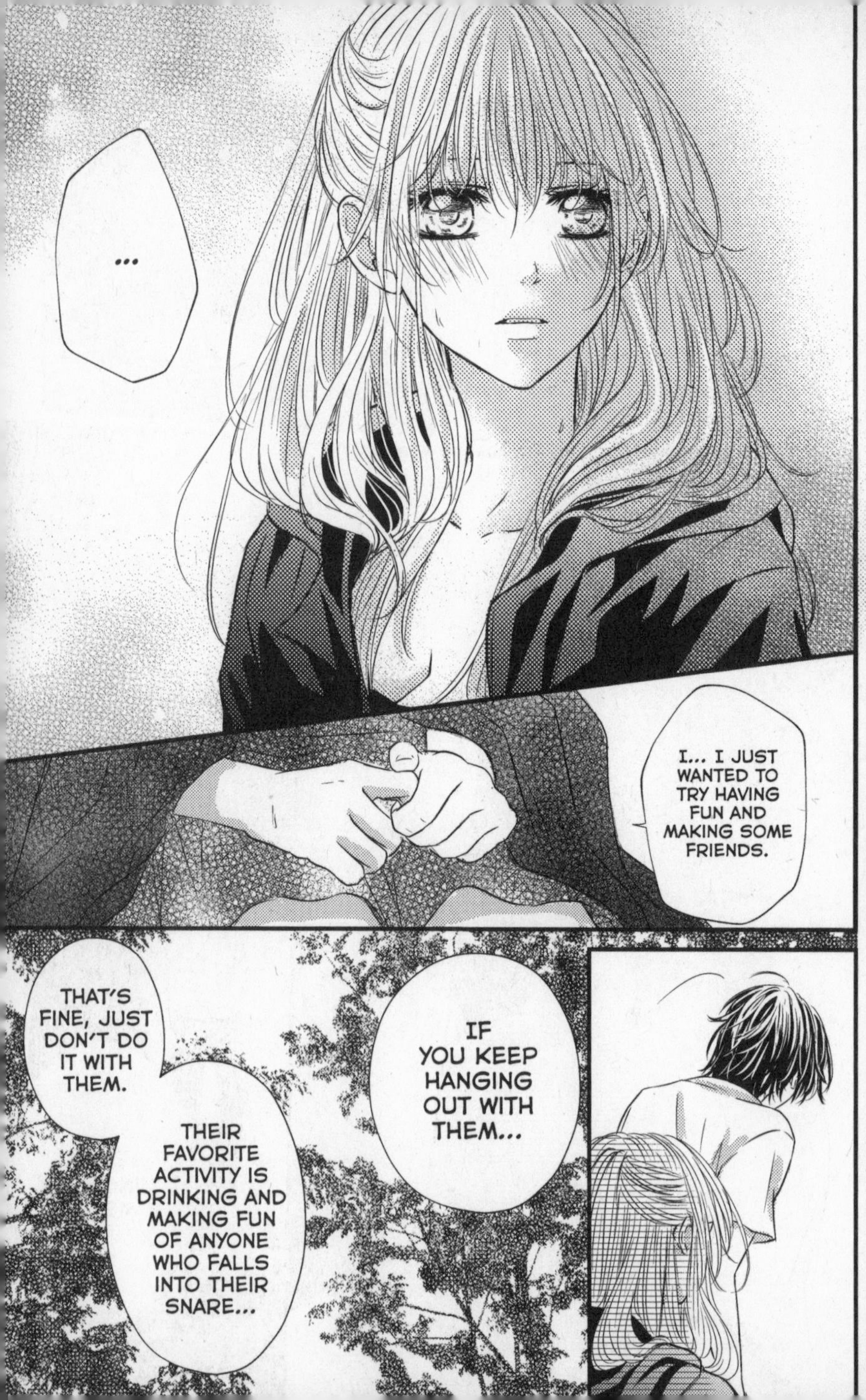
...
I... I JUST WANTED TO TRY HAVING FUN AND MAKING SOME FRIENDS.
IF YOU KEEP HANGING OUT WITH THEM...
THAT'S FINE, JUST DON'T DO IT WITH THEM.
THEIR FAVORITE ACTIVITY IS DRINKING AND MAKING FUN OF ANYONE WHO FALLS INTO THEIR SNARE...

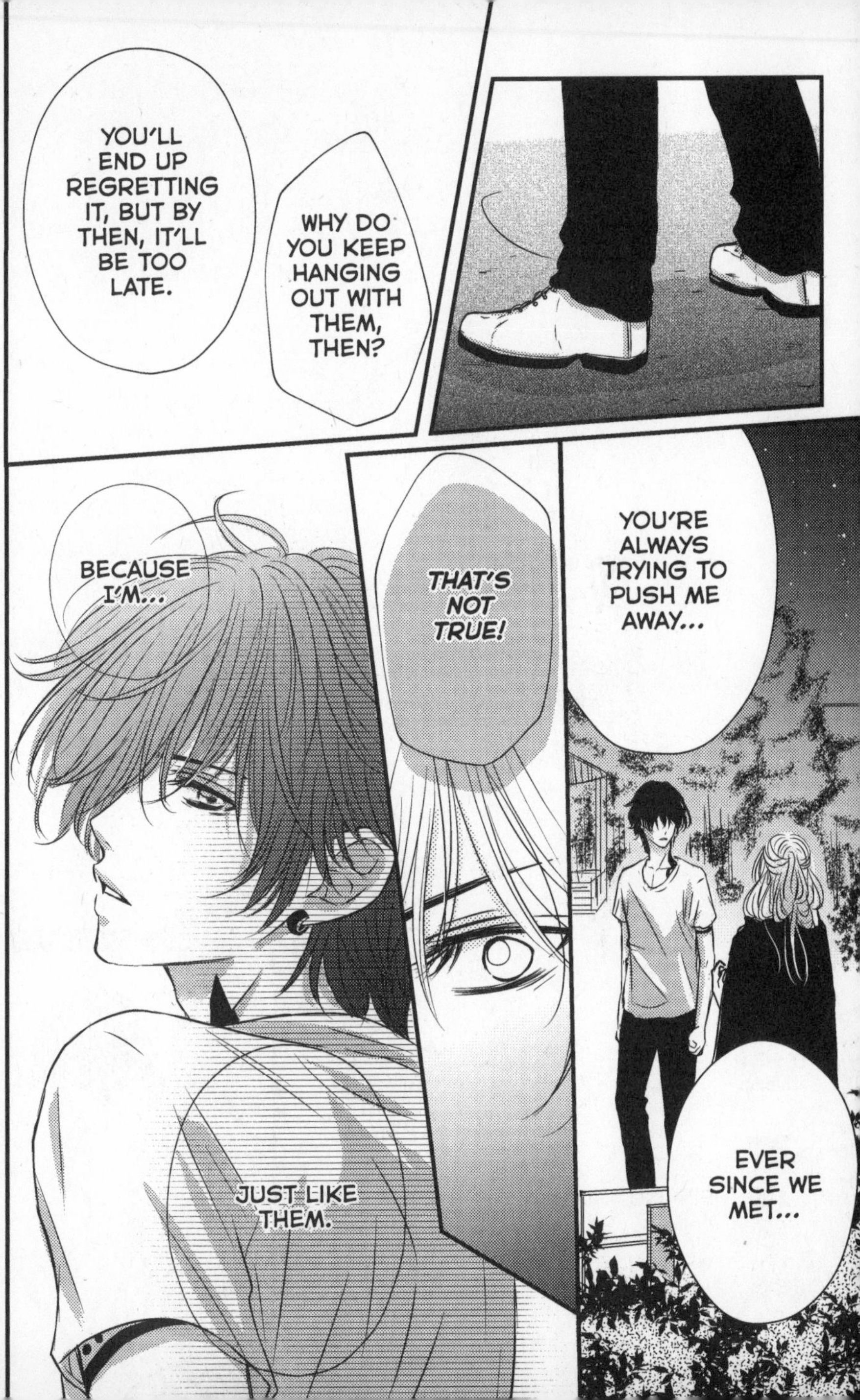
YOU'LL END UP REGRETTING IT, BUT BY THEN, IT'LL BE TOO LATE.
WHY DO YOU KEEP HANGING OUT WITH THEM, THEN?
YOU'RE ALWAYS TRYING TO PUSH ME AWAY...
EVER SINCE WE MET...
THAT'S NOT TRUE!
BECAUSE I'M...
JUST LIKE THEM.

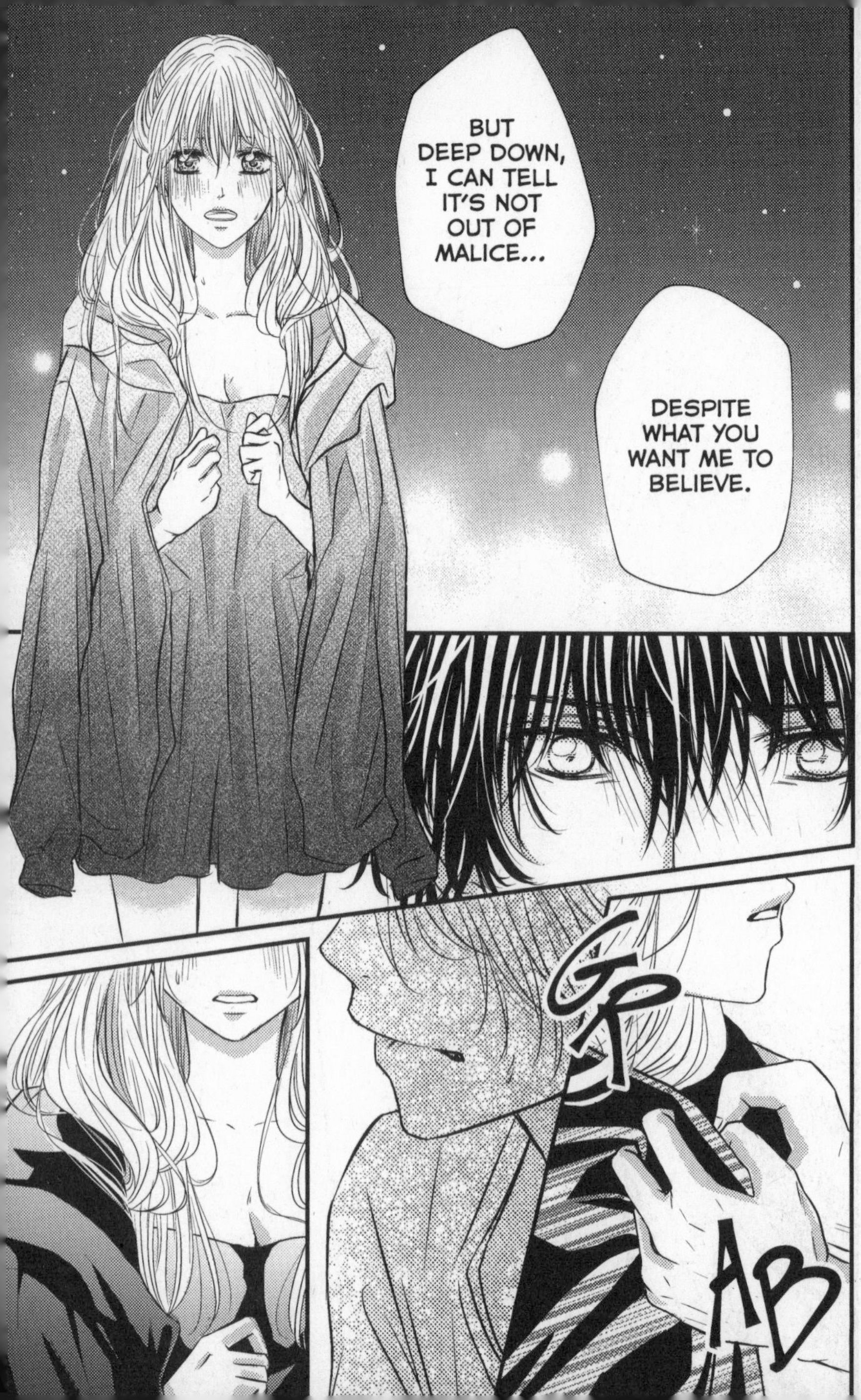
BUT DEEP DOWN, I CAN TELL IT'S NOT OUT OF MALICE...
DESPITE WHAT YOU WANT ME TO BELIEVE.
GRAB

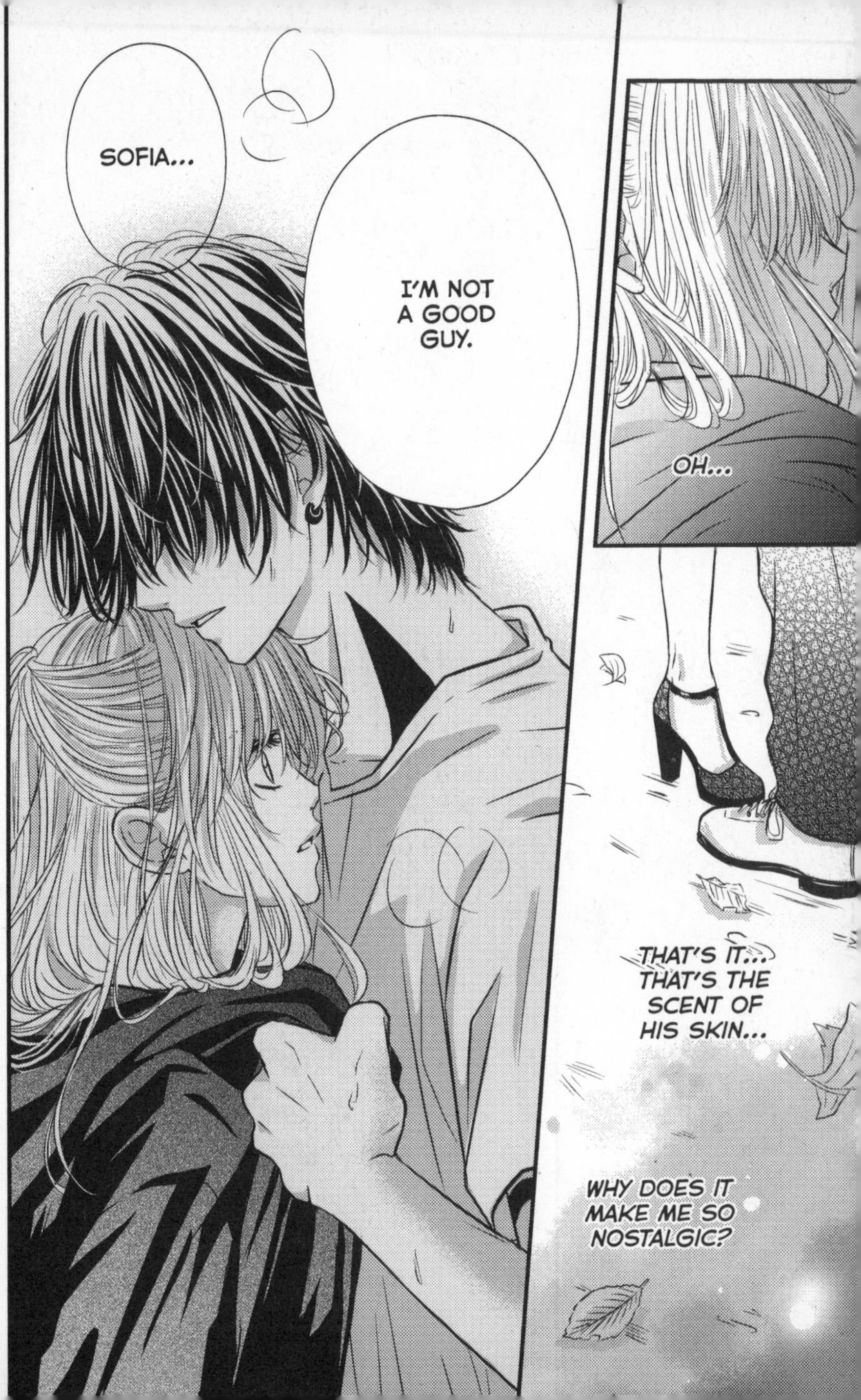
OH...
THAT'S IT... THAT'S THE SCENT OF HIS SKIN...
WHY DOES IT MAKE ME SO NOSTALGIC?
SOFIA...
I'M NOT A GOOD GUY.

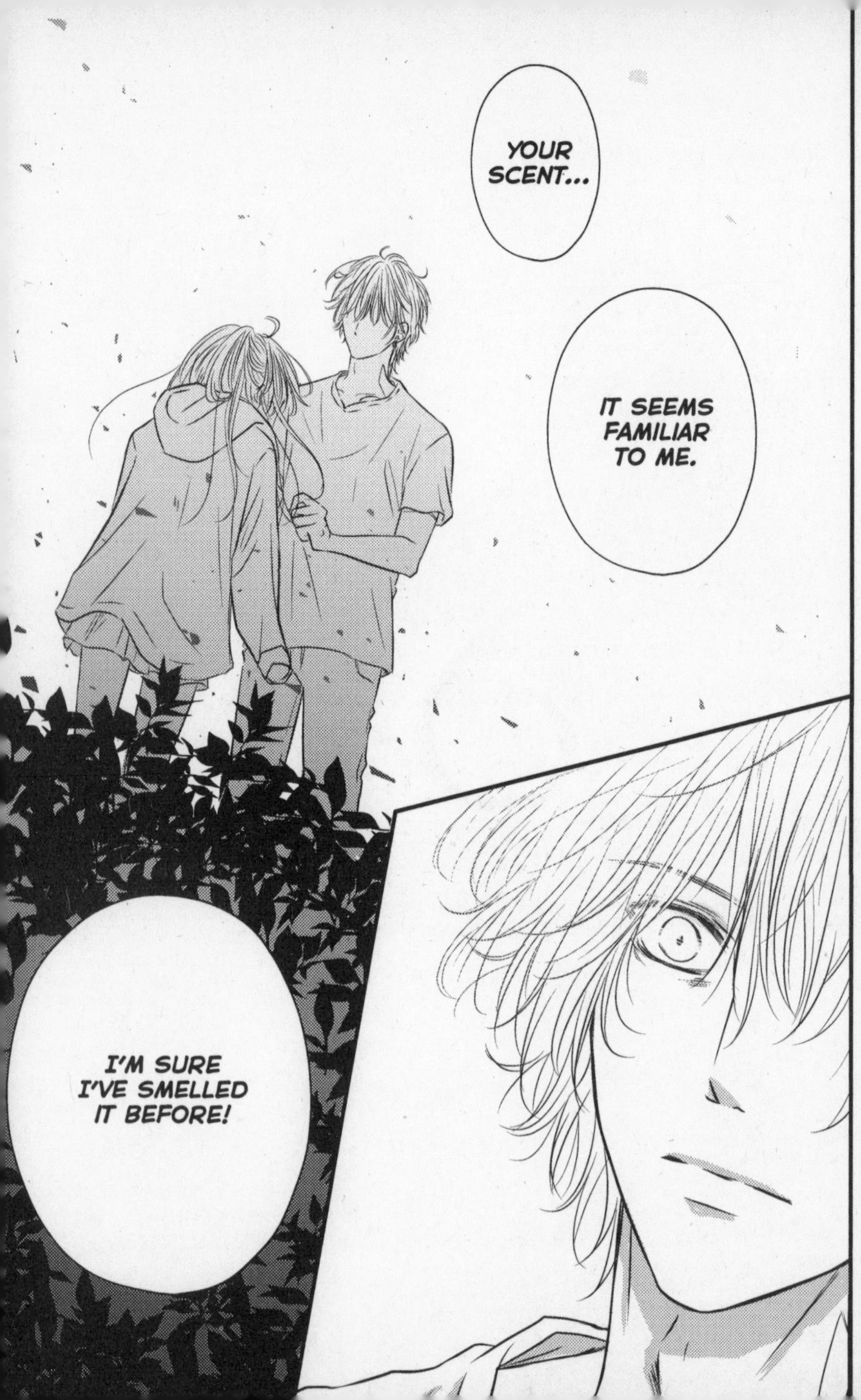
YOUR SCENT...
IT SEEMS FAMILIAR TO ME.
I'M SURE I'VE SMELLED IT BEFORE!

DEEP Scar

To be continued in Volume 2

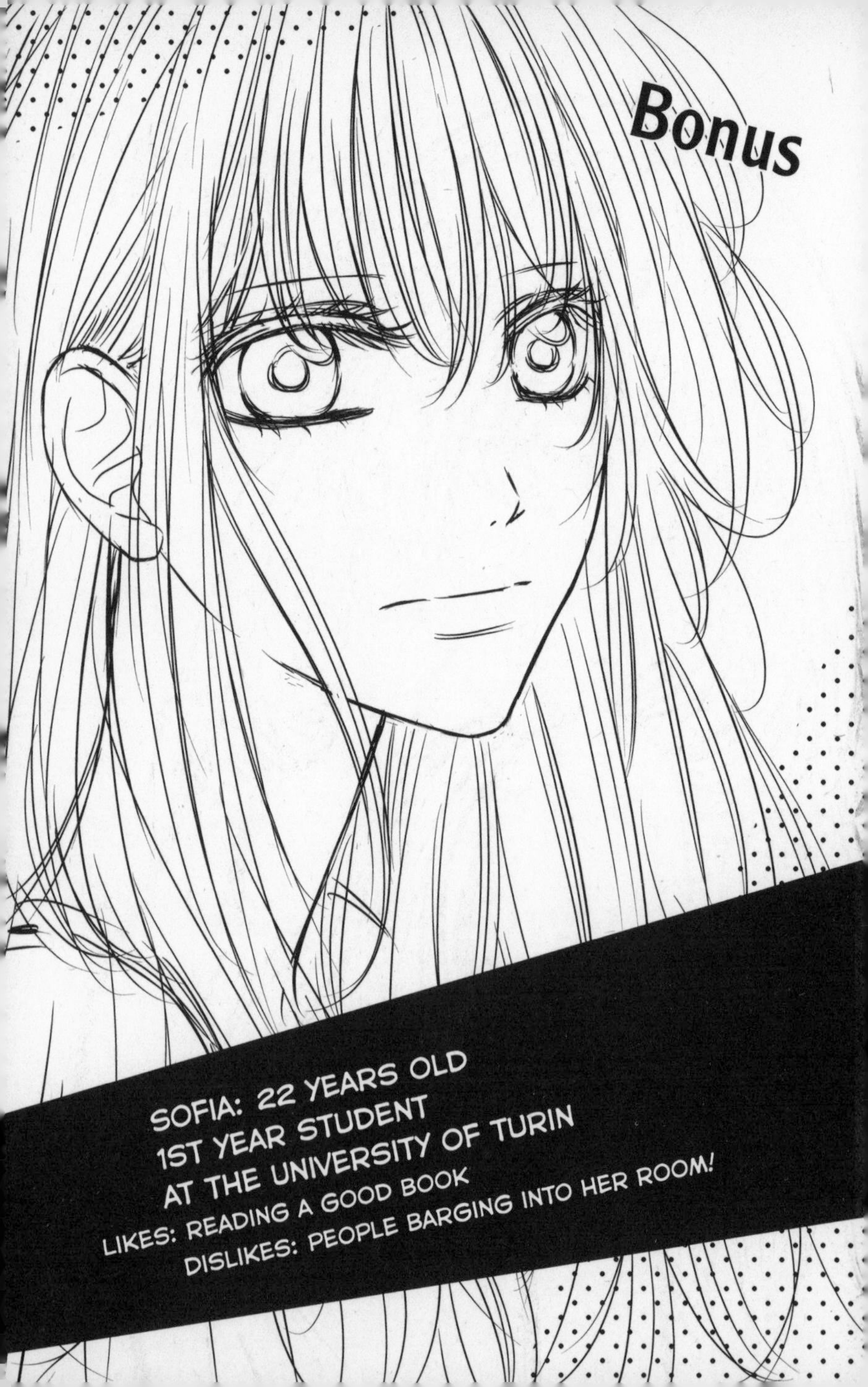
Bonus
SOFIA: 22 YEARS OLD
1ST YEAR STUDENT
AT THE UNIVERSITY OF TURIN
LIKES: READING A GOOD BOOK
DISLIKES: PEOPLE BARGING INTO HER ROOM!

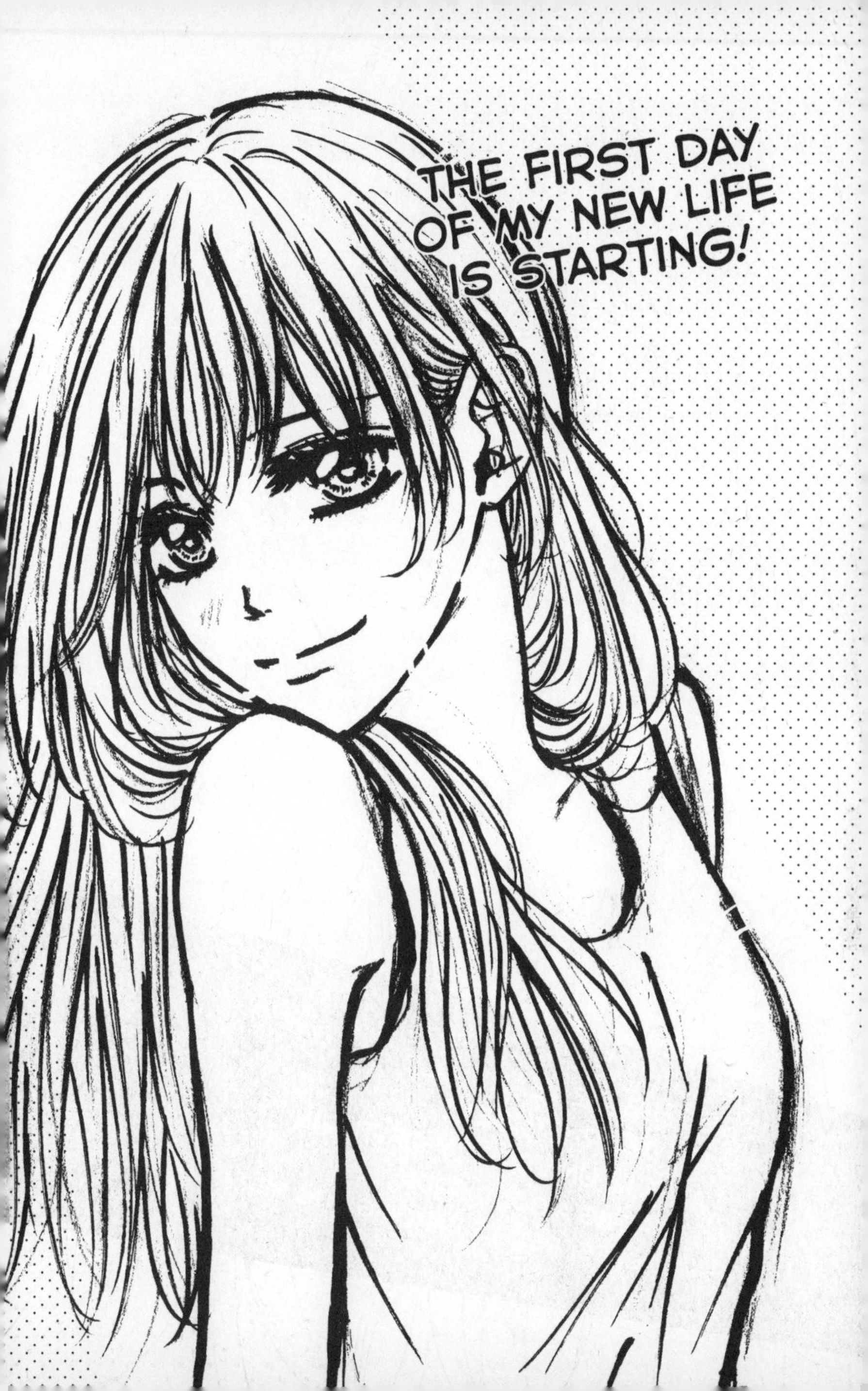
THE FIRST DAY OF MY NEW LIFE IS STARTING!

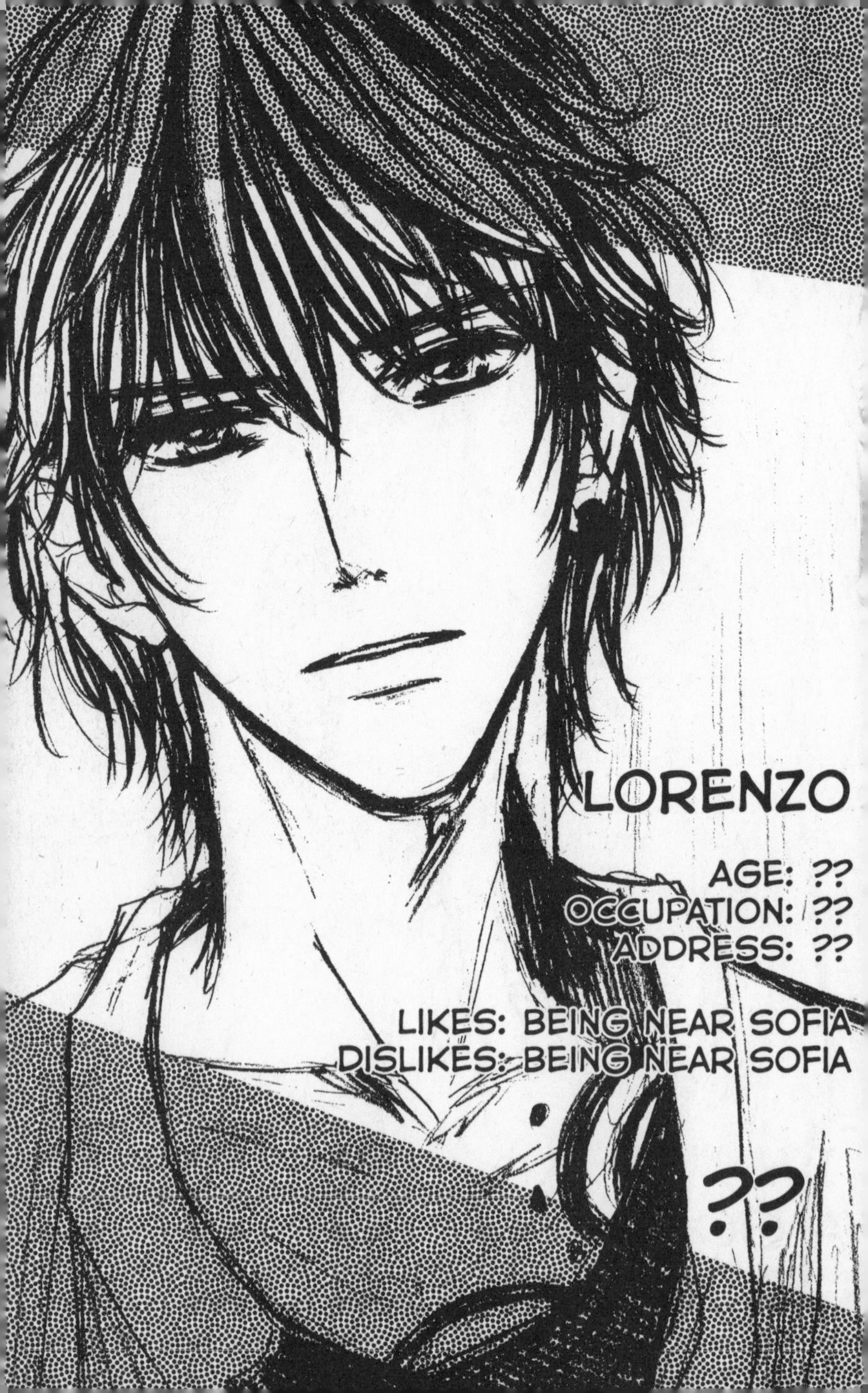
LORENZO
AGE: ??
OCCUPATION: ??
ADDRESS: ??
LIKES: BEING NEAR SOFIA
DISLIKES: BEING NEAR SOFIA
??

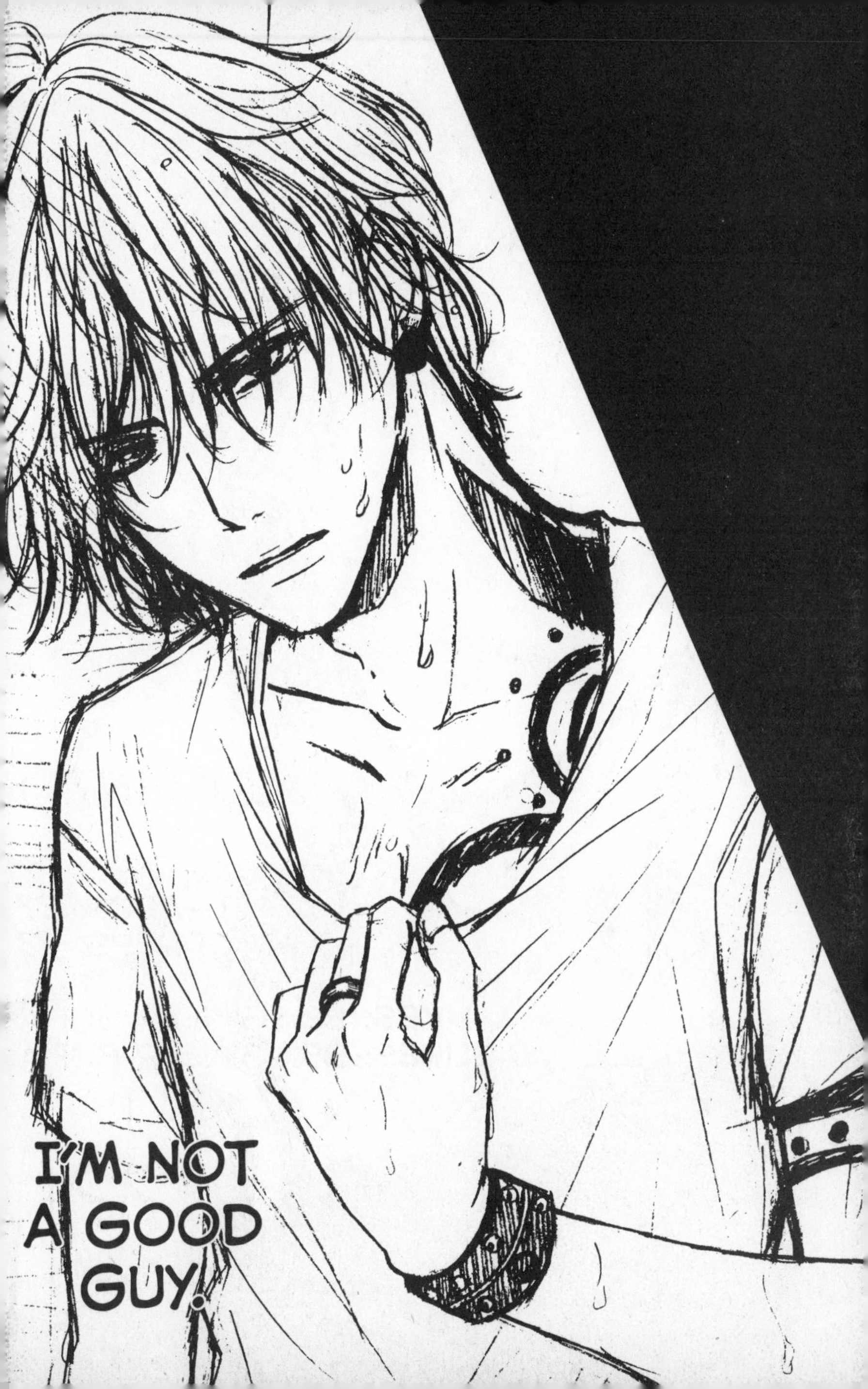
I'M NOT
A GOOD
GUY.

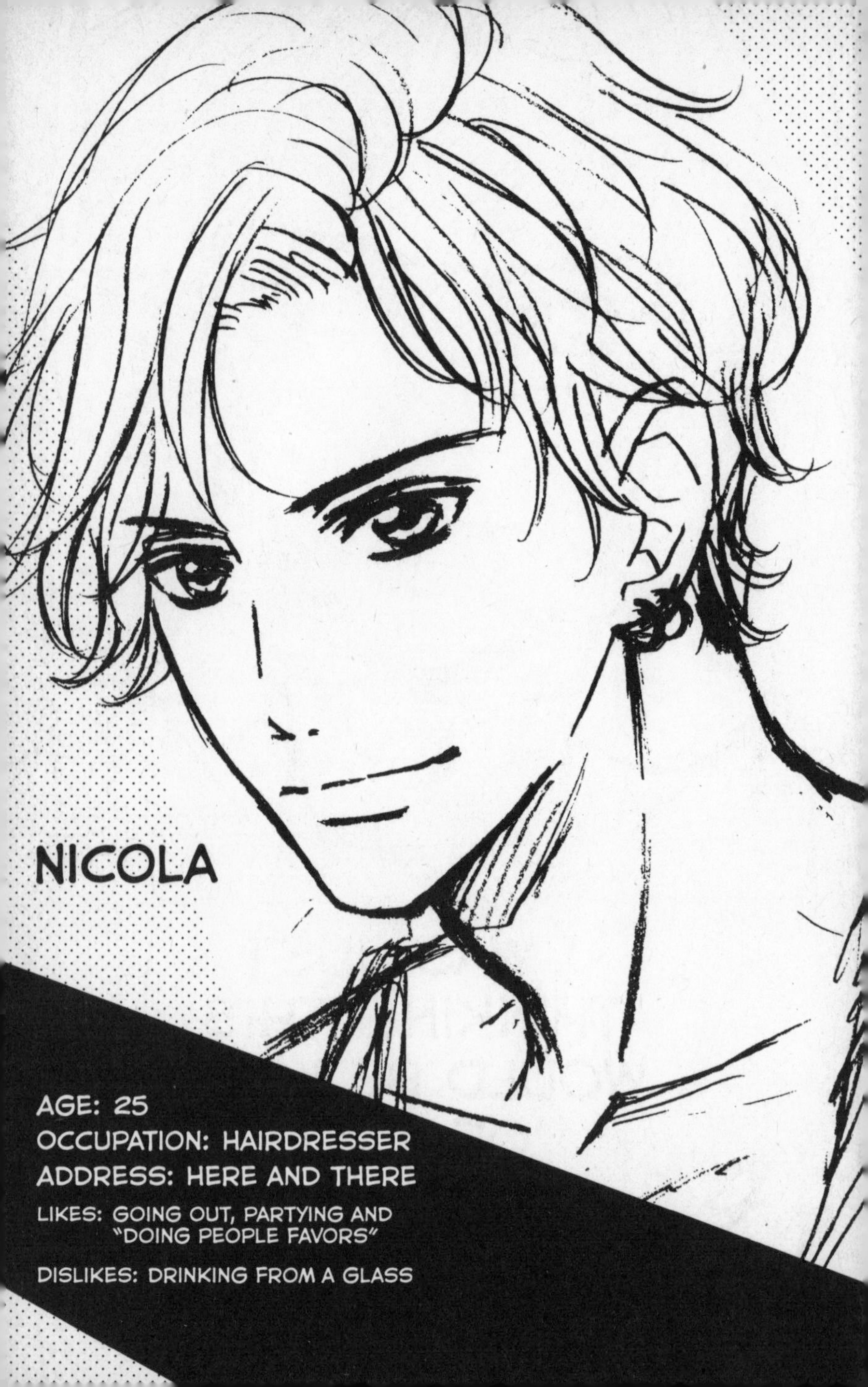
NICOLA
AGE: 25
OCCUPATION: HAIRDRESSER
ADDRESS: HERE AND THERE
LIKES: GOING OUT, PARTYING AND "DOING PEOPLE FAVORS"
DISLIKES: DRINKING FROM A GLASS

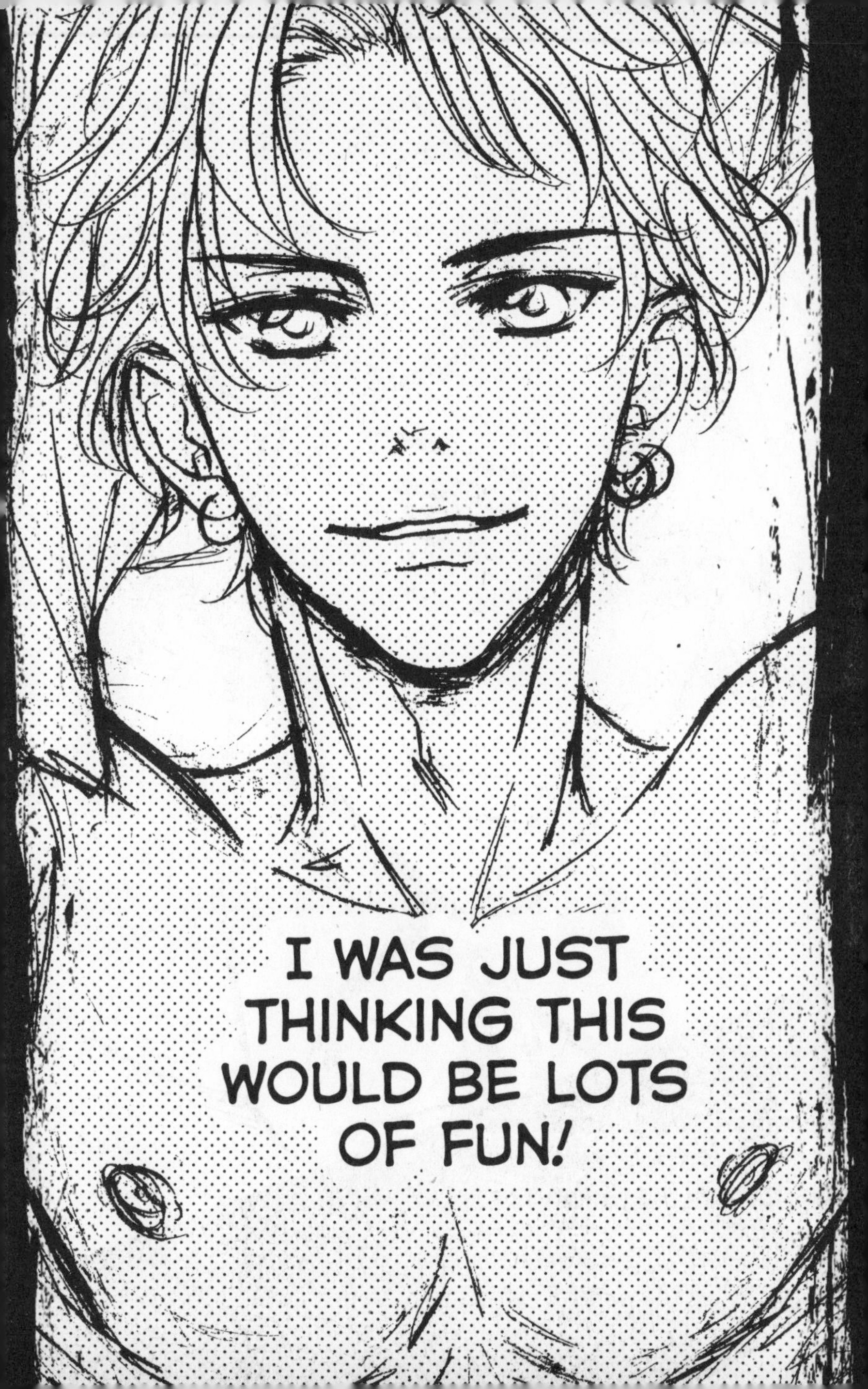
I WAS JUST THINKING THIS WOULD BE LOTS OF FUN!

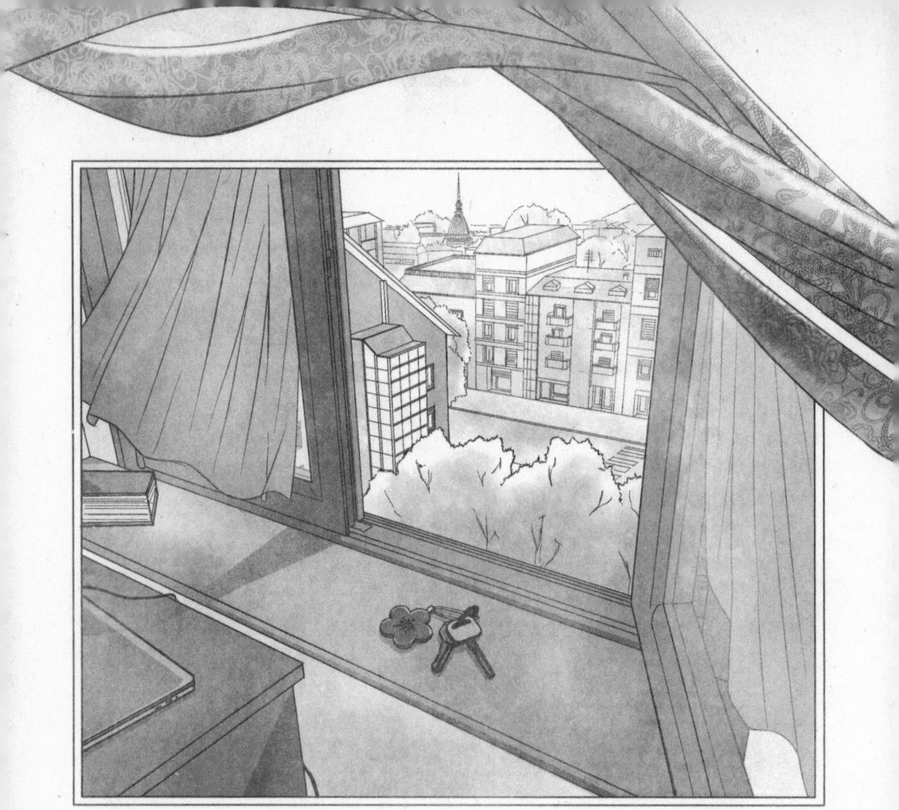


## ACKNOWLEDGEMENTS

THANK YOU TO EVERYONE FOR READING THIS VOLUME! I HOPE YOU'LL KEEP FOLLOWING SOFIA'S STORY AND HOPEFULLY SEE HER INITIAL WORRIES TURN INTO POSITIVE AND OPTIMISTIC FEELINGS! THANKS TO EVERYONE WHO SUPPORTED ME DURING THIS PROCESS. I'M ETERNALLY GRATEFUL! SEE YOU IN VOLUME 2!

DEEP *Scar*

TOKYOPOP
• PRESENTS •

# INTERNATIONAL
# WOMEN *of* MANGA

## NANA YAA

GOLDFISCH

An award-winning German manga artist with a large following for her free webcomic, *CRUSHED!!*

## Sophie-Chan

Ocean of Secrets

A self-taught manga artist from the Middle East, with a huge YouTube following!

## Ban Zarbo

KAMO
PACT WITH THE SPIRIT WORLD

A lifelong manga fan from Switzerland, she and her twin sister take inspiration from their Dominican roots!

## Gin Zarbo

UNDEAD MESSIAH

An aspiring manga artist since she was a child, along with her twin sister she's releasing her debut title!

## Natalia Batista

Sword Princess Amaltea
Natalia Batista

A Swedish creator whose popular manga has already been published in Sweden, Italy and the Czech Republic!

TO LEARN MORE PLEASE VISIT OUR WEBSITE

www.TOKYOPOP.com

TOKYOPOP PRESENTS

© TOKYOPOP GmbH / *Goldfisch* - NANA YAA / *Kamo* - BAN ZARBO / *Undead Messiah* - GIN ZARBO / *Ocean of Secrets* - SOPHIE-CHAN / *Sword Princess Amaltea* - NATALIA BATISTA

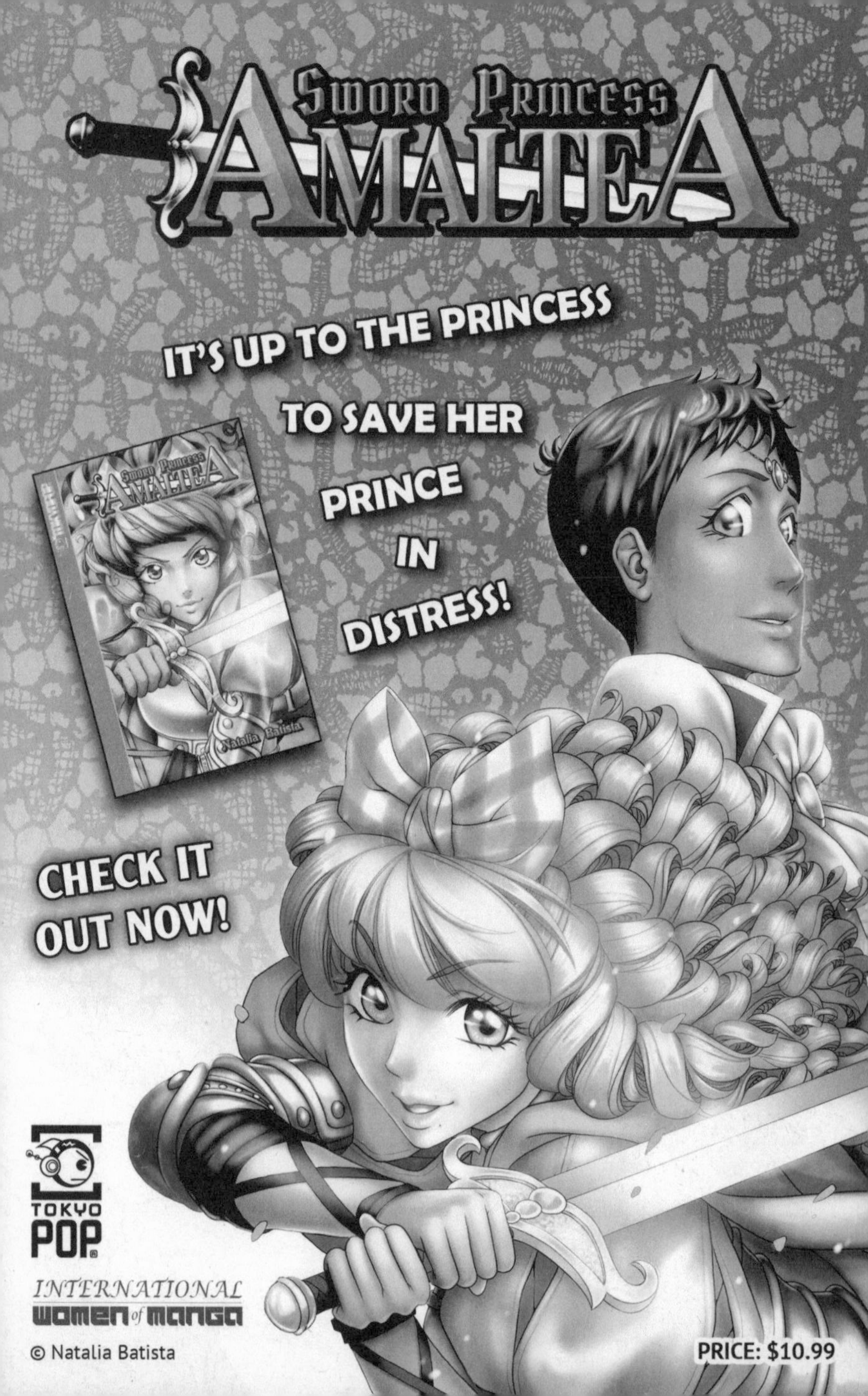
Sword Princess
AMALTEA
IT'S UP TO THE PRINCESS
TO SAVE HER
PRINCE
IN
DISTRESS!
Sword Princess
AMALTEA
Natalia Batista
CHECK IT
OUT NOW!
TOKYO
POP
INTERNATIONAL
women of manga
© Natalia Batista
PRICE: $10.99

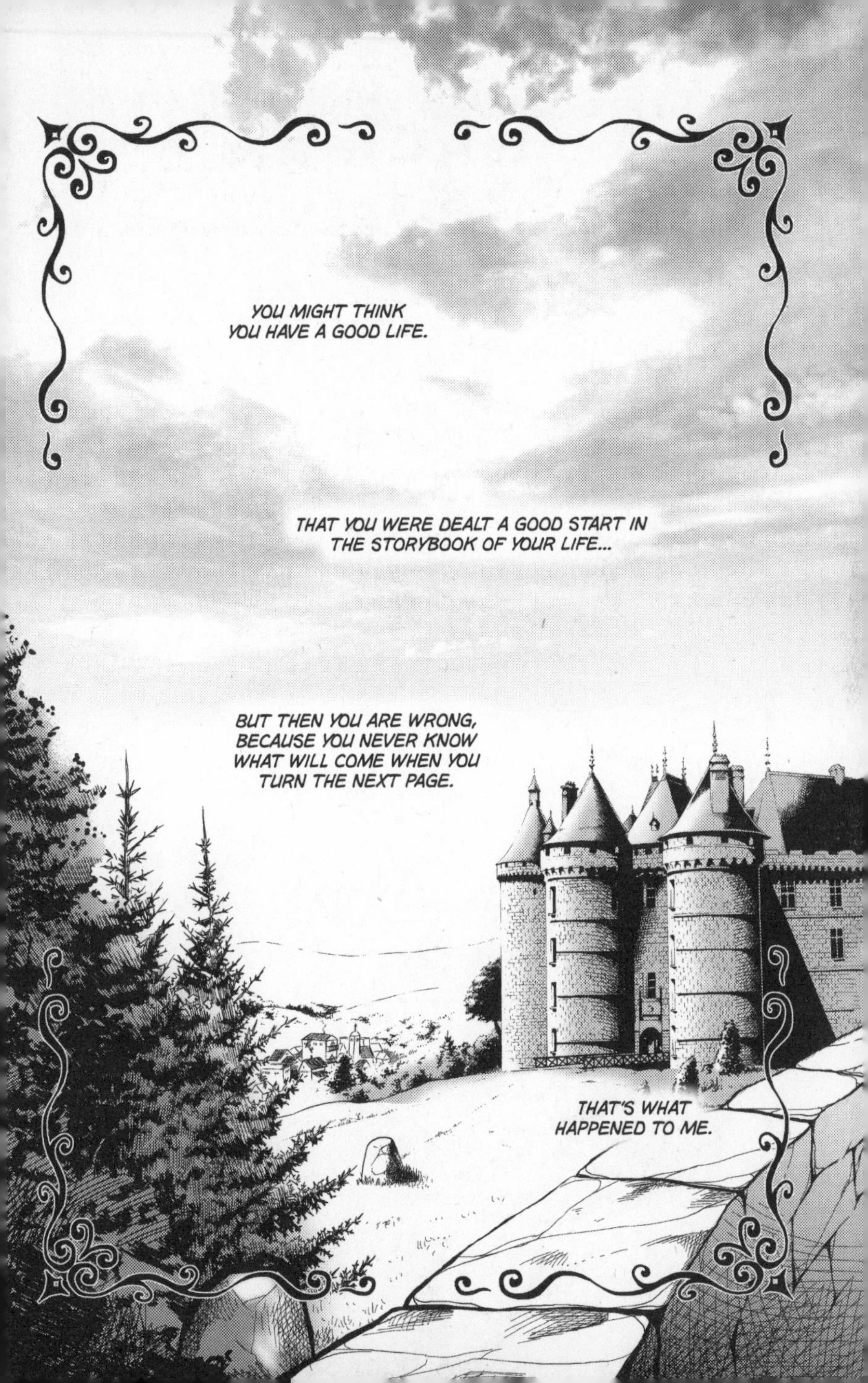
YOU MIGHT THINK YOU HAVE A GOOD LIFE.
THAT YOU WERE DEALT A GOOD START IN THE STORYBOOK OF YOUR LIFE...
BUT THEN YOU ARE WRONG, BECAUSE YOU NEVER KNOW WHAT WILL COME WHEN YOU TURN THE NEXT PAGE.
THAT'S WHAT HAPPENED TO ME.

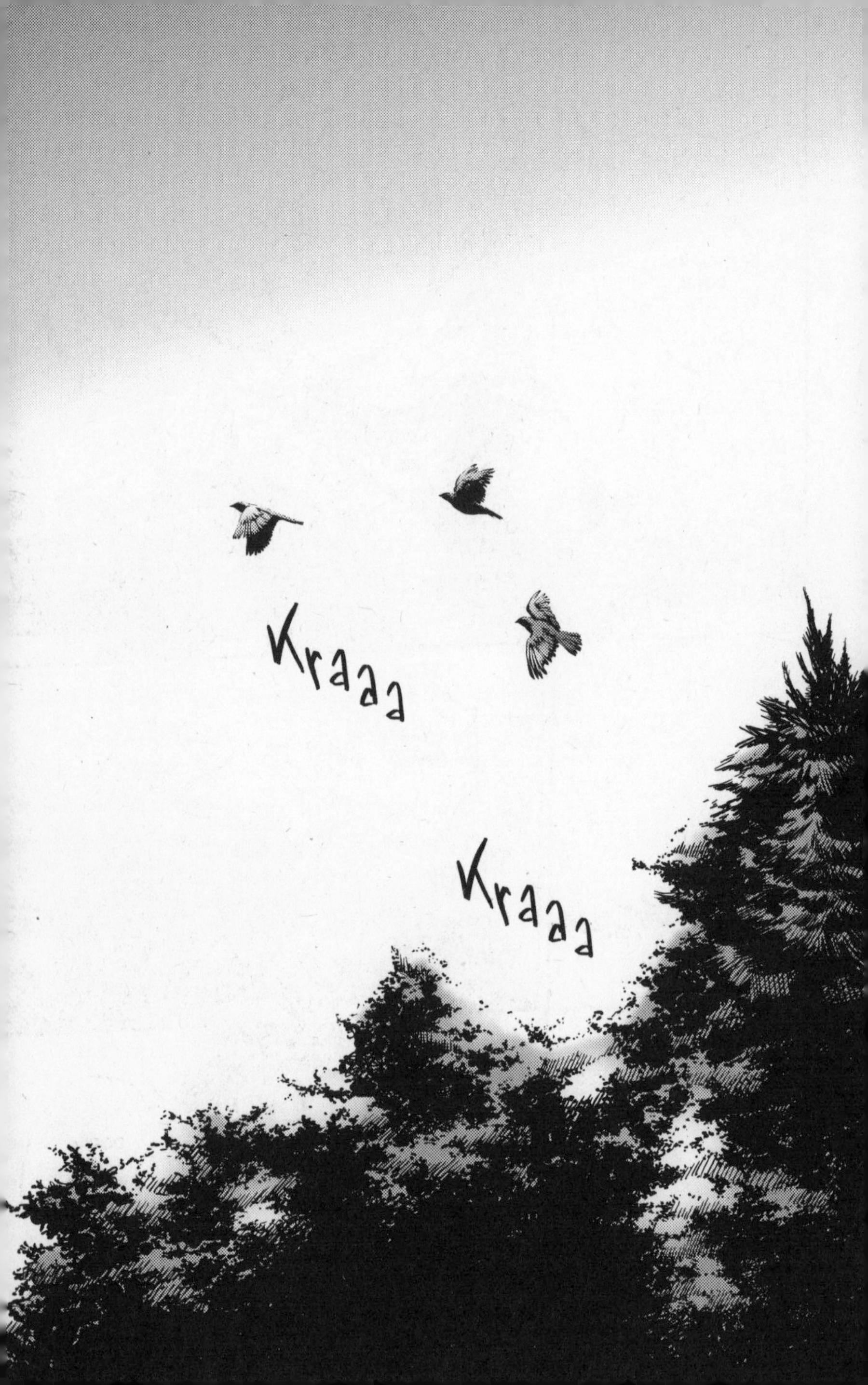
Kraaa
Kraaa

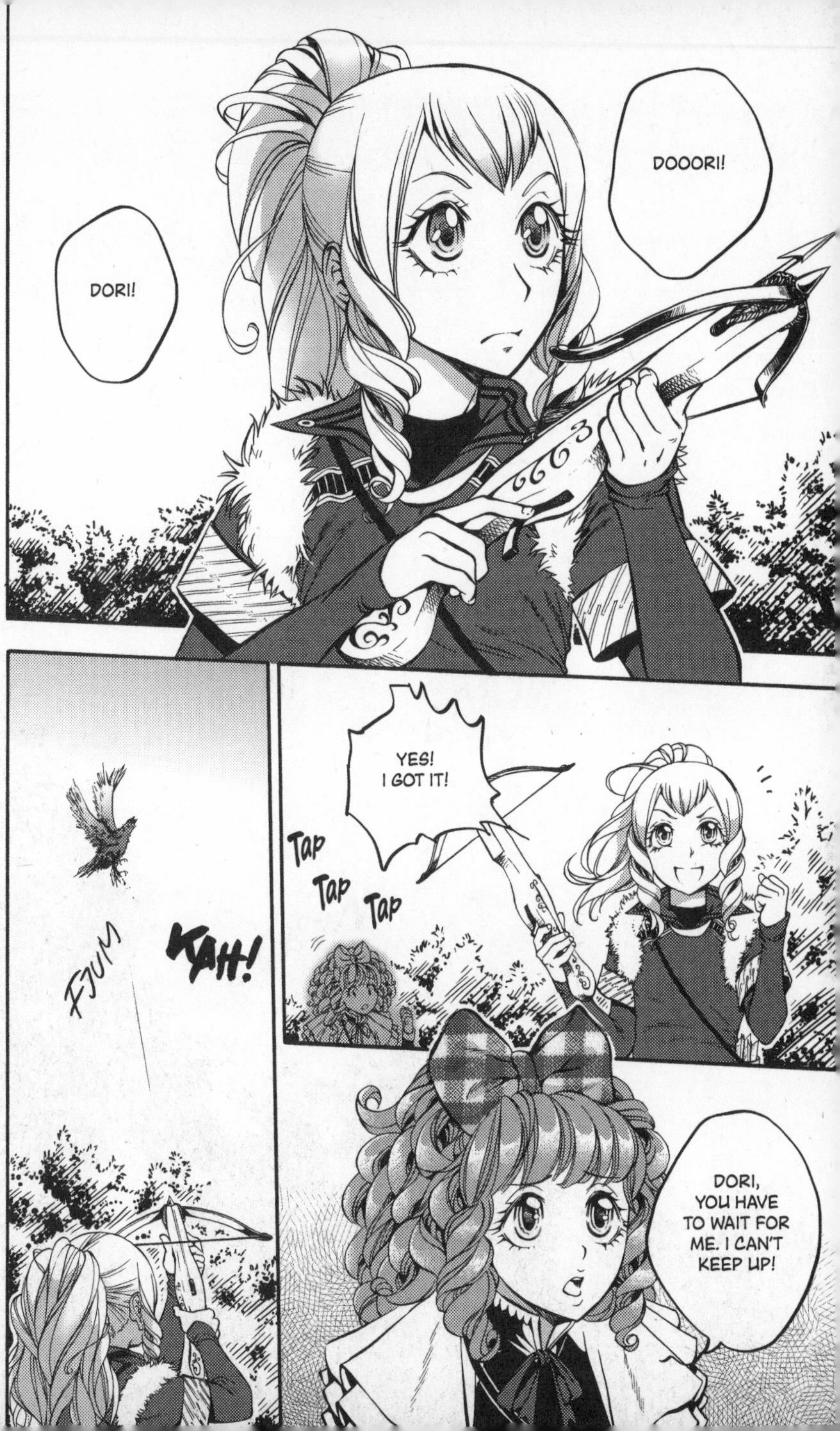
DORI!
DOOORI!
FJUM
KYAH!
Tap
Tap
Tap
YES! I GOT IT!
DORI, YOU HAVE TO WAIT FOR ME. I CAN'T KEEP UP!

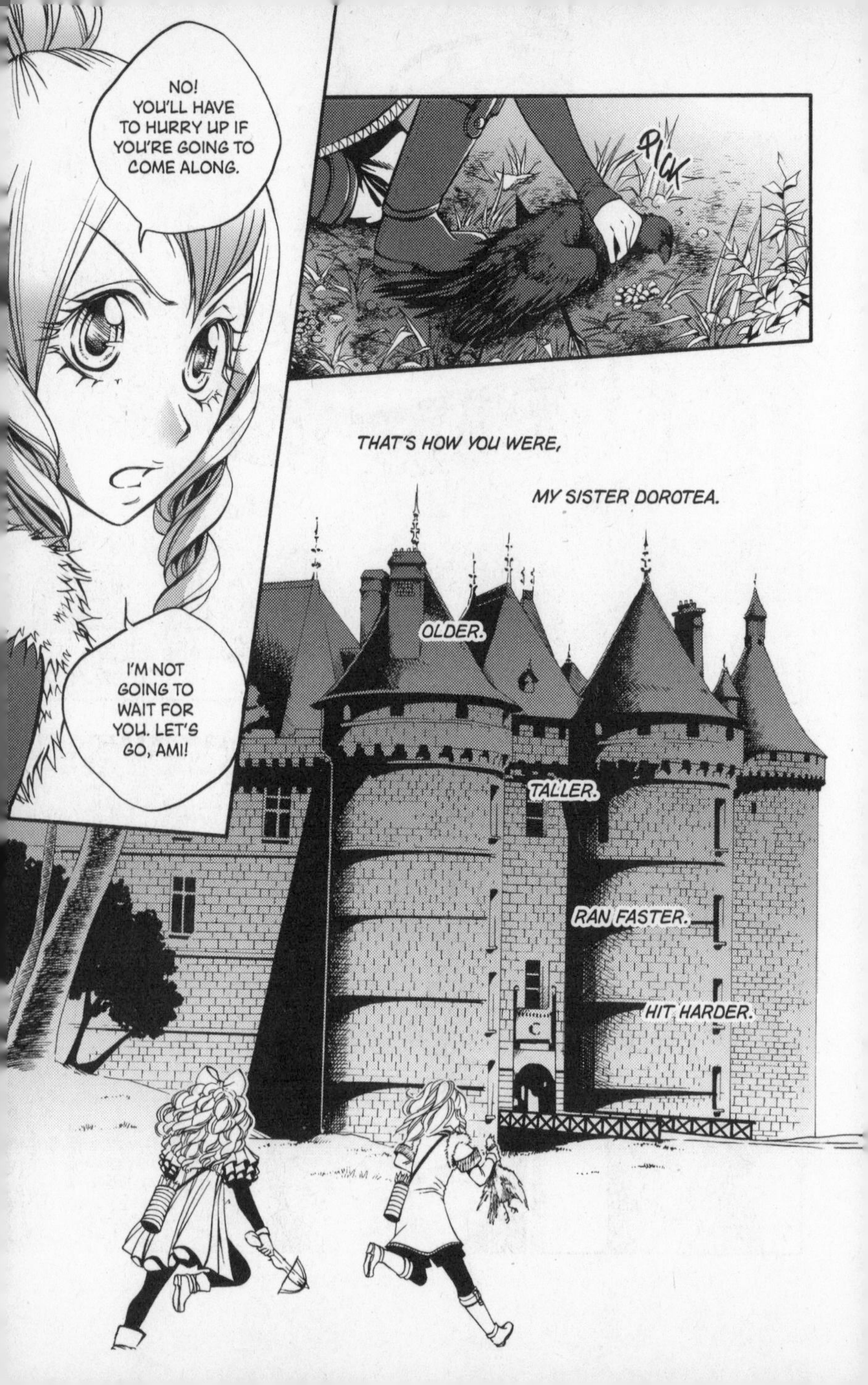
PICK
NO! YOU'LL HAVE TO HURRY UP IF YOU'RE GOING TO COME ALONG.
I'M NOT GOING TO WAIT FOR YOU. LET'S GO, AMI!
THAT'S HOW YOU WERE,
MY SISTER DOROTEA.
OLDER.
TALLER.
RAN FASTER.
HIT HARDER.

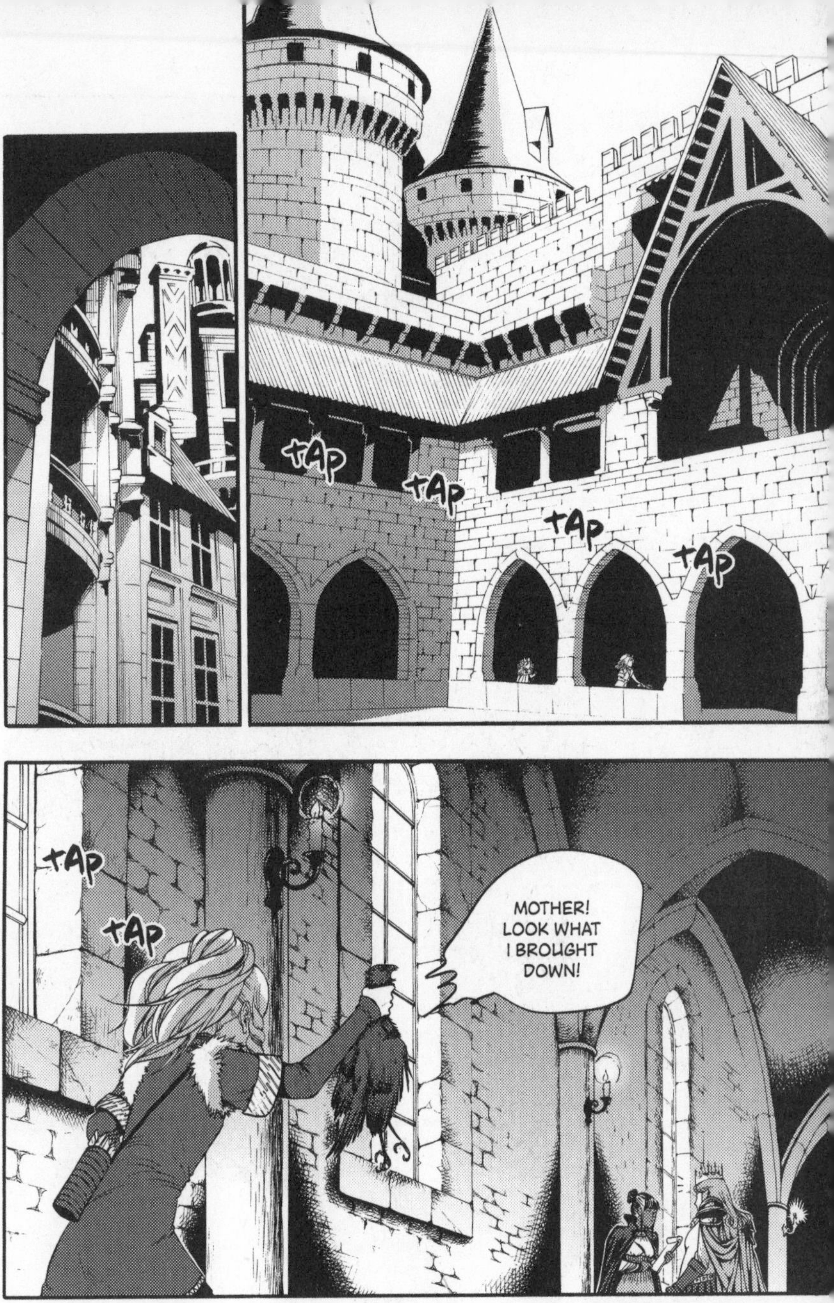
TAP
TAP
TAP
TAP
TAP
TAP
MOTHER! LOOK WHAT I BROUGHT DOWN!

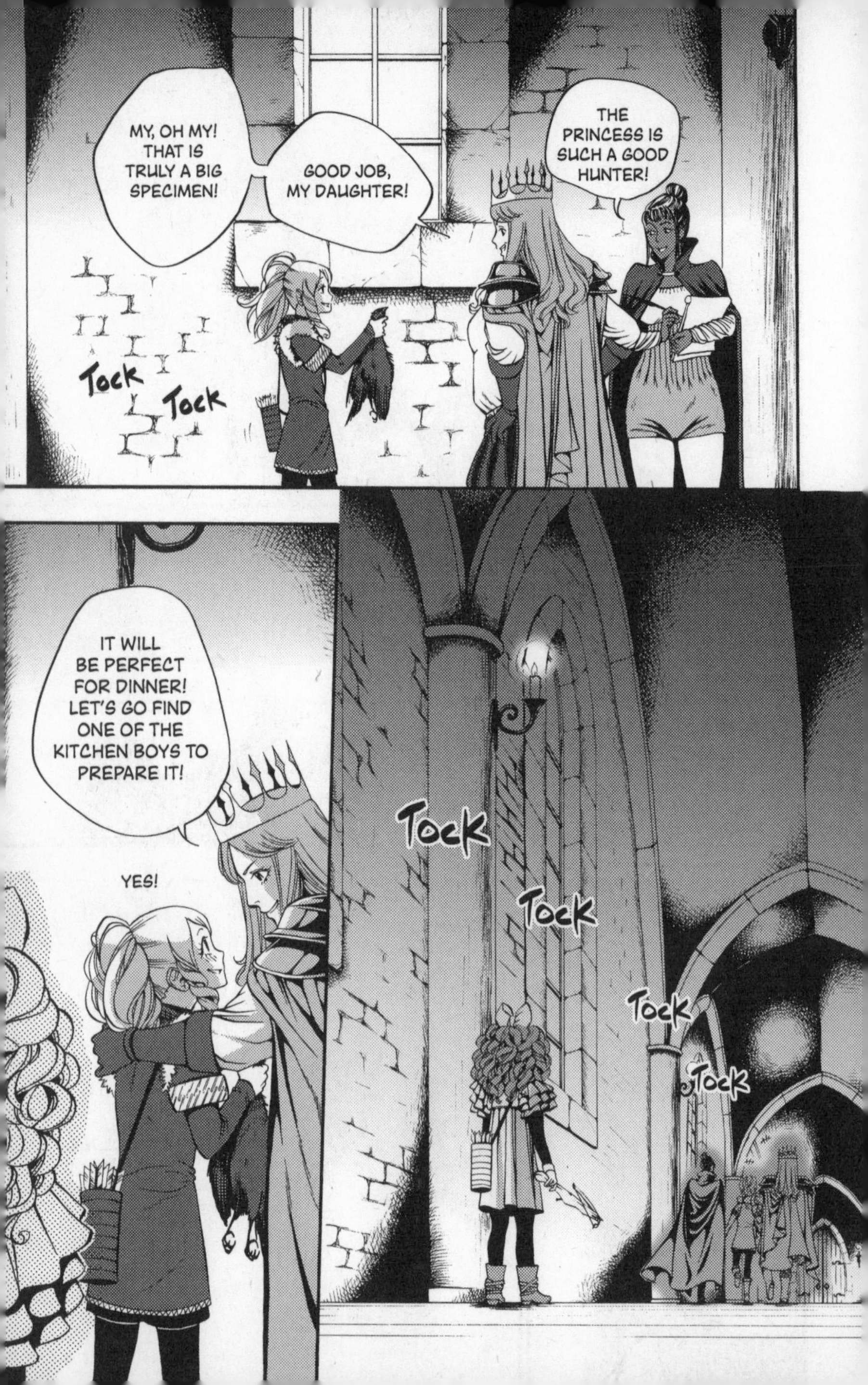
MY, OH MY! THAT IS TRULY A BIG SPECIMEN!
GOOD JOB, MY DAUGHTER!
THE PRINCESS IS SUCH A GOOD HUNTER!
Tock
Tock
IT WILL BE PERFECT FOR DINNER! LET'S GO FIND ONE OF THE KITCHEN BOYS TO PREPARE IT!
YES!
Tock
Tock
Tock
Tock

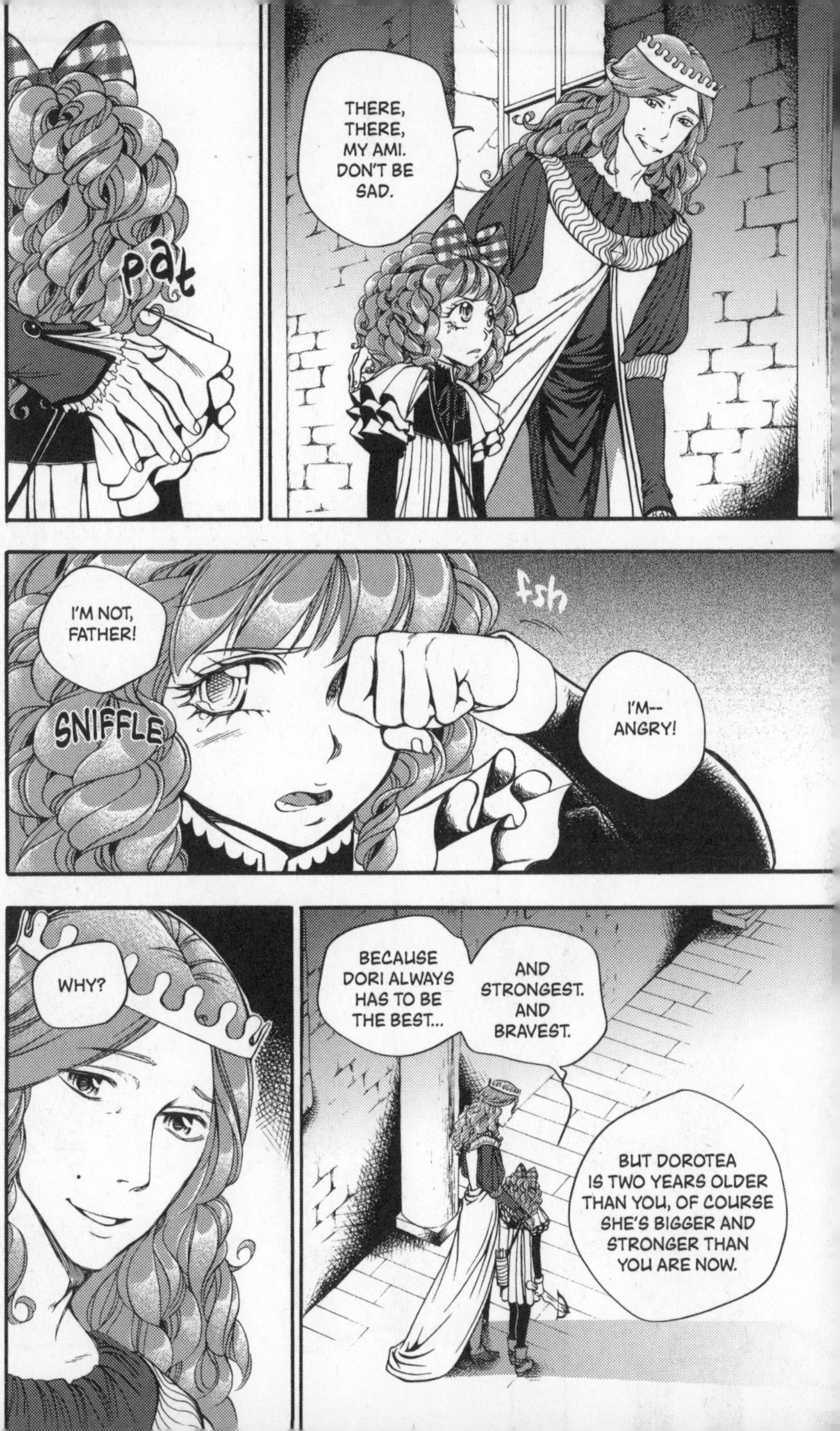
pat
THERE, THERE, MY AMI. DON'T BE SAD.
I'M NOT, FATHER!
SNIFFLE
fsh
I'M-- ANGRY!
WHY?
BECAUSE DORI ALWAYS HAS TO BE THE BEST...
AND STRONGEST. AND BRAVEST.
BUT DOROTEA IS TWO YEARS OLDER THAN YOU, OF COURSE SHE'S BIGGER AND STRONGER THAN YOU ARE NOW.

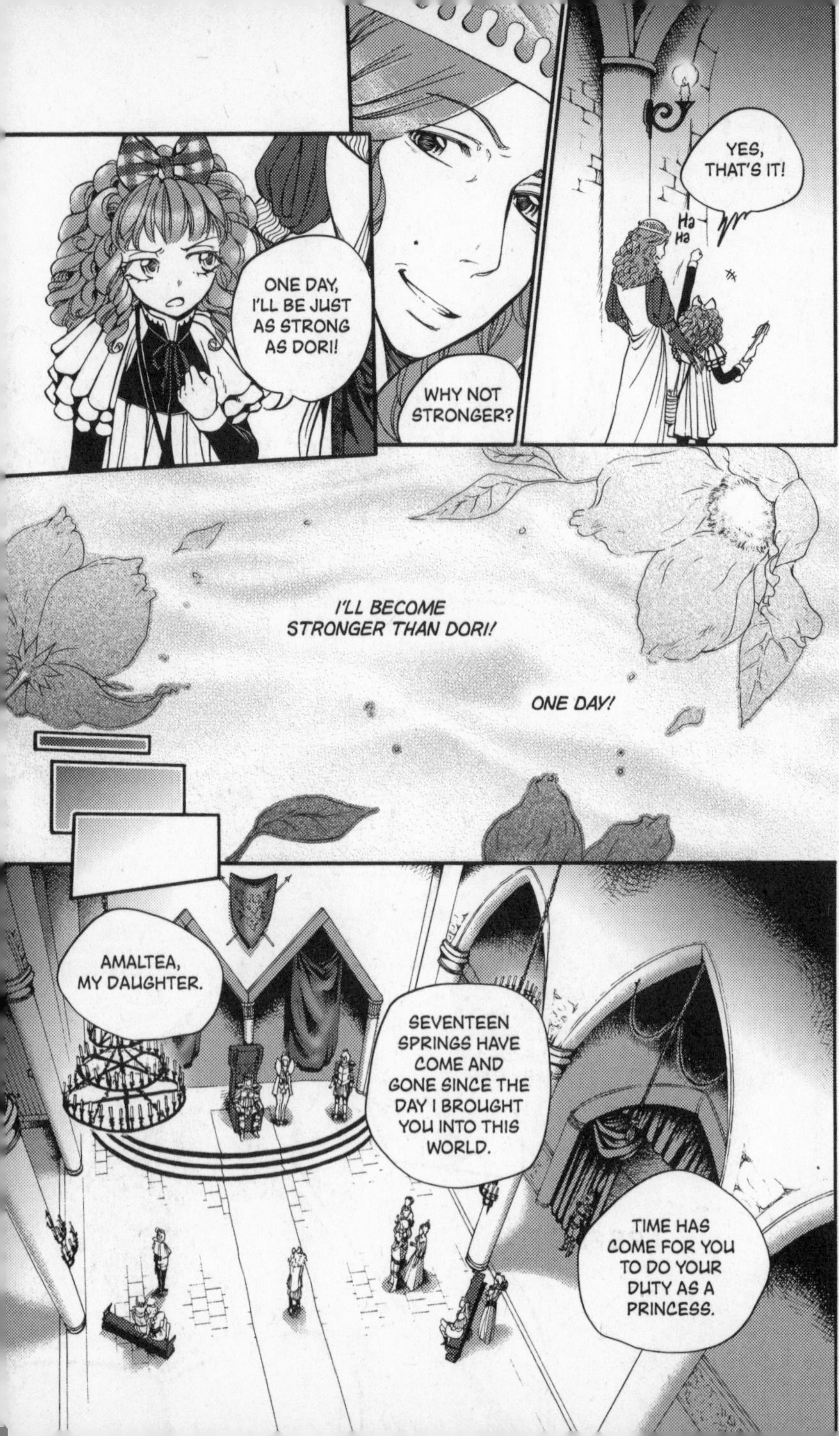
ONE DAY, I'LL BE JUST AS STRONG AS DORI!
WHY NOT STRONGER?
YES, THAT'S IT!
Ha Ha
I'LL BECOME STRONGER THAN DORI!
ONE DAY!
AMALTEA, MY DAUGHTER.
SEVENTEEN SPRINGS HAVE COME AND GONE SINCE THE DAY I BROUGHT YOU INTO THIS WORLD.
TIME HAS COME FOR YOU TO DO YOUR DUTY AS A PRINCESS.

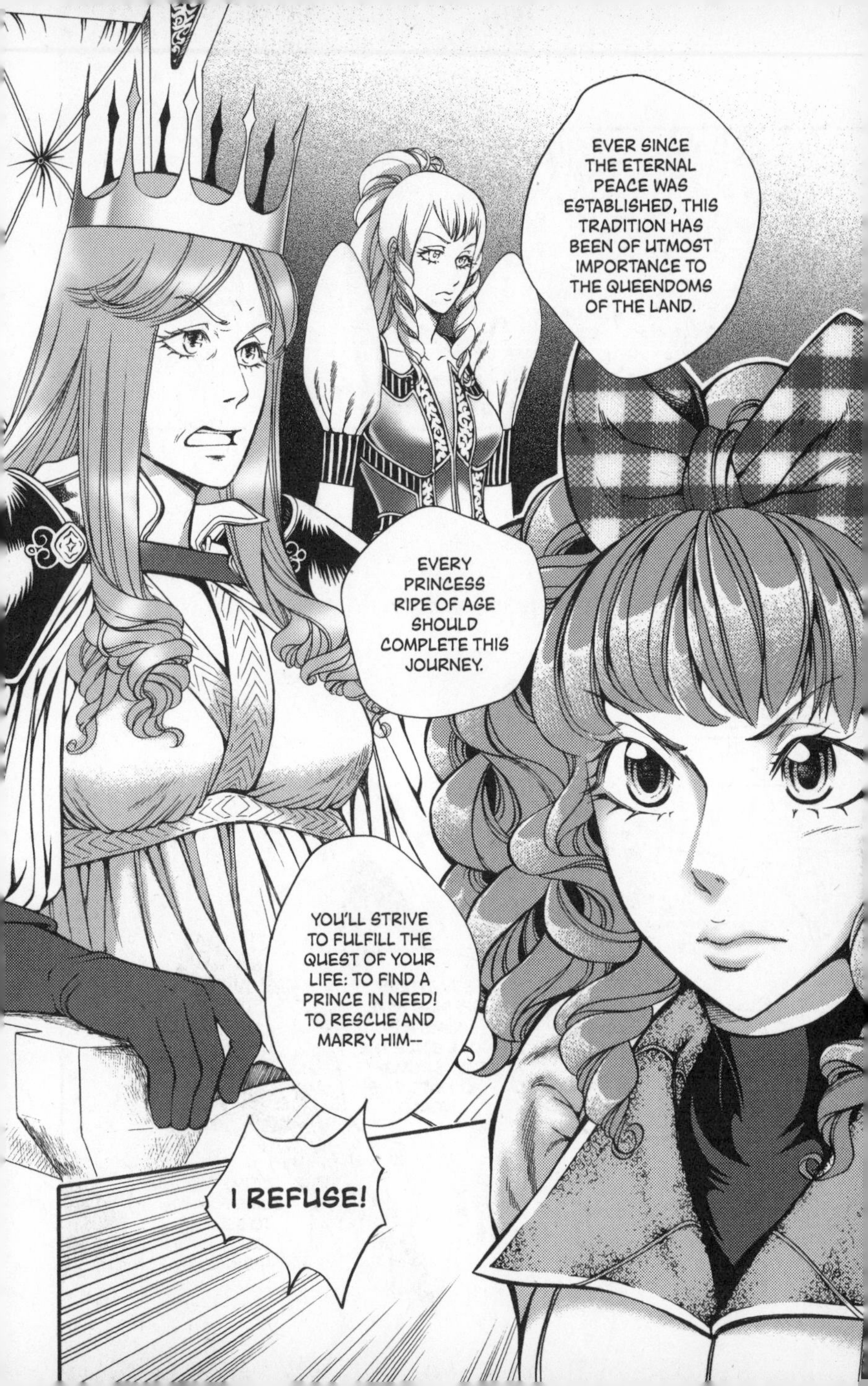
EVER SINCE THE ETERNAL PEACE WAS ESTABLISHED, THIS TRADITION HAS BEEN OF UTMOST IMPORTANCE TO THE QUEENDOMS OF THE LAND.
EVERY PRINCESS RIPE OF AGE SHOULD COMPLETE THIS JOURNEY.
YOU'LL STRIVE TO FULFILL THE QUEST OF YOUR LIFE: TO FIND A PRINCE IN NEED! TO RESCUE AND MARRY HIM--
I REFUSE!

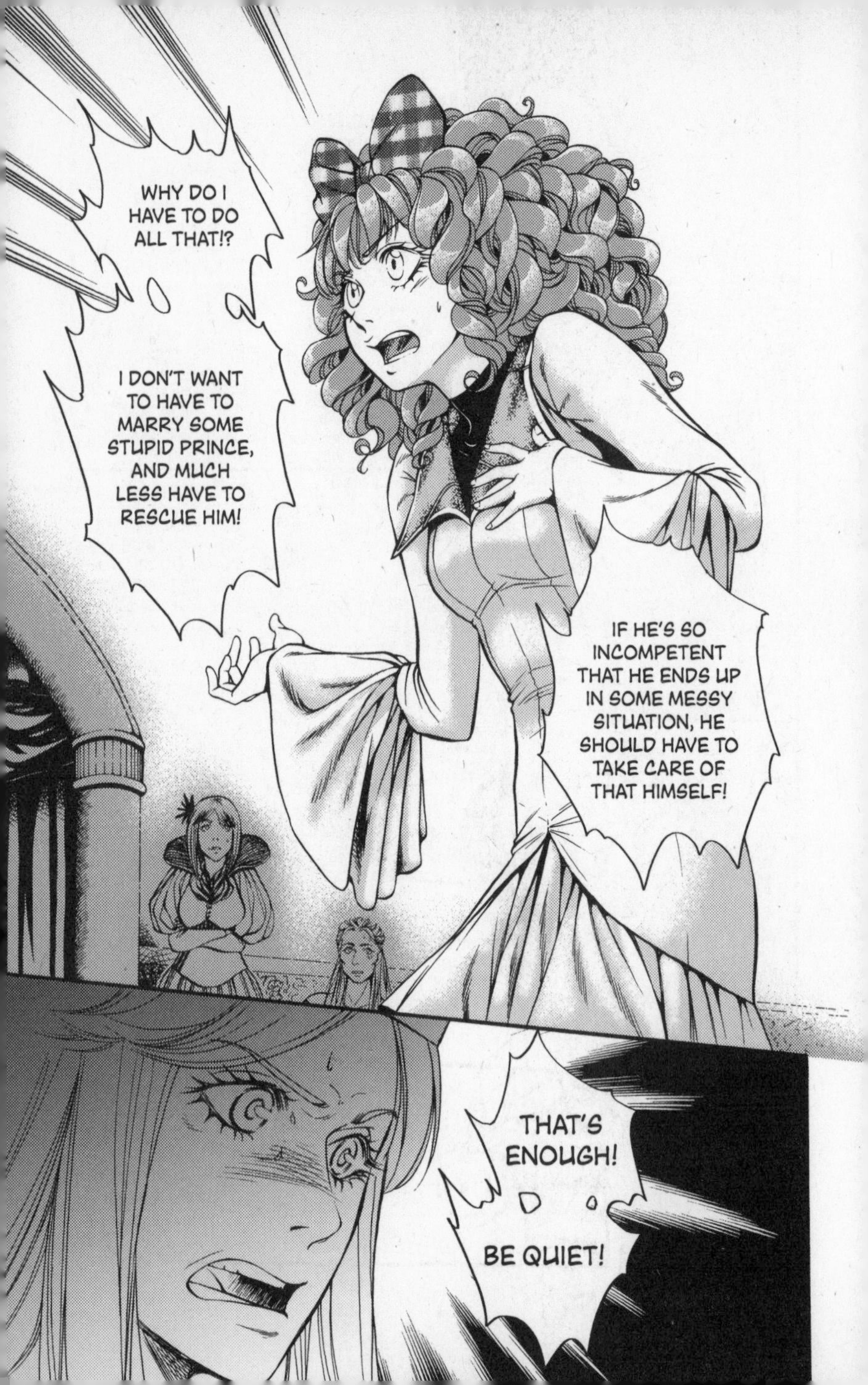
WHY DO I HAVE TO DO ALL THAT!?
I DON'T WANT TO HAVE TO MARRY SOME STUPID PRINCE, AND MUCH LESS HAVE TO RESCUE HIM!
IF HE'S SO INCOMPETENT THAT HE ENDS UP IN SOME MESSY SITUATION, HE SHOULD HAVE TO TAKE CARE OF THAT HIMSELF!
THAT'S ENOUGH!
BE QUIET!

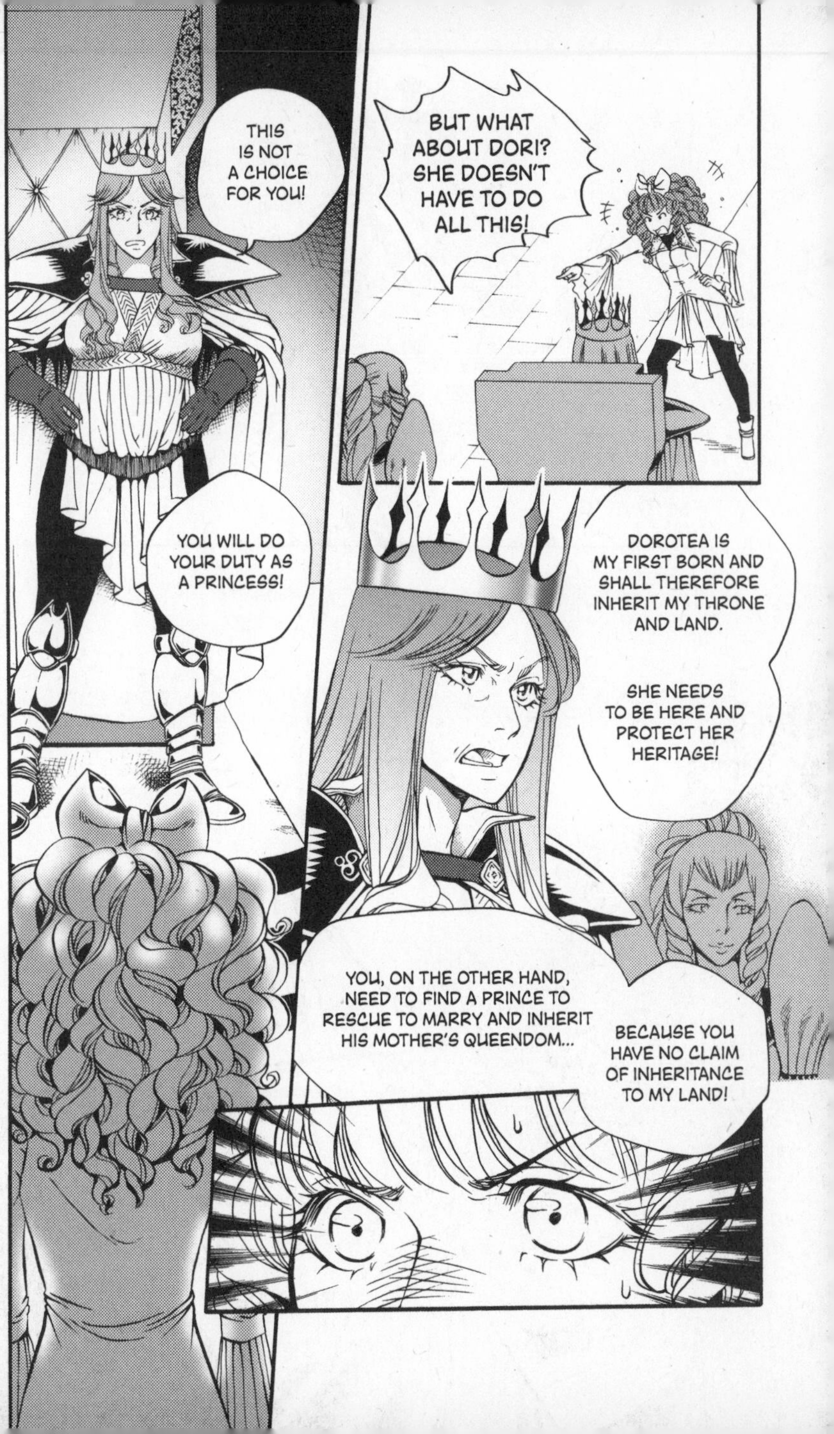
THIS IS NOT A CHOICE FOR YOU!
YOU WILL DO YOUR DUTY AS A PRINCESS!
BUT WHAT ABOUT DORI? SHE DOESN'T HAVE TO DO ALL THIS!
DOROTEA IS MY FIRST BORN AND SHALL THEREFORE INHERIT MY THRONE AND LAND.
SHE NEEDS TO BE HERE AND PROTECT HER HERITAGE!
YOU, ON THE OTHER HAND, NEED TO FIND A PRINCE TO RESCUE TO MARRY AND INHERIT HIS MOTHER'S QUEENDOM...
BECAUSE YOU HAVE NO CLAIM OF INHERITANCE TO MY LAND!

*Deep Scar, Volume 1*
Manga by: Caly

Editor - Lena Atanassova
Marketing Associate - Kae Winters
Technology and Digital Media Assistant - Phillip Hong
Translator - Liz Vandalovsky
Graphic Designer - Phillip Hong
Retouching and Lettering - Vibrraant Publishing Studio
Licensing Specialist - Arika Yanaka
Editor-in-Chief & Publisher - Stu Levy

A  Manga

TOKYOPOP and 🌀 are trademarks or registered trademarks of TOKYOPOP Inc.

TOKYOPOP Inc.
5200 W. Century Blvd. Suite 705
Los Angeles, 90045

E-mail: info@TOKYOPOP.com
Come visit us online at www.TOKYOPOP.com

f www.facebook.com/TOKYOPOP
🐦 www.twitter.com/TOKYOPOP
𝓅 www.pinterest.com/TOKYOPOP
📷 www.instagram.com/TOKYOPOP

©2019 TOKYOPOP
All Rights Reserved

All rights reserved. No portion of this book may be reproduced or transmitted in any form or by any means without written permission from the copyright holders. This manga is a work of fiction. Any resemblance to actual events or locales or persons, living or dead, is entirely coincidental.

TOKYOPOP 2019
DEEP SCAR © 2018, by Rossella Sergi

First published in France in 2018 by Editions H2T – PIKA EDITION
English translation rights arranged by Pika Edition, France.

ISBN: 978-1-4278-6153-5
First TOKYOPOP Printing: August 2019
10 9 8 7 6 5 4 3 2 1
Printed in CANADA